# A KINGDOM
# ON EARTH

## Also by Paul T. Phillips

*Britain's Past in Canada: The Teaching and Writing of British History*

*The Sectarian Spirit: Sectarianism, Society, and Politics in Victorian Cotton Towns*

*The View from the Pulpit: Victorian Ministers and Society* (editor)

Paul T. Phillips

# A KINGDOM ON EARTH

Anglo-American
Social Christianity,
1880–1940

The Pennsylvania State University Press
University Park, Pennsylvania

Library of Congress Cataloging-in-Publication Data

Phillips, Paul T., 1942–
     A kingdom on earth : Anglo-American social Christianity, 1880–1940 /
Paul T. Phillips.

          p.        cm.
     Includes bibliographical references and index.
     ISBN 0-271-01497-0 (cloth)
     ISBN 0-271-01580-2 (paper)
     1. Social gospel—History—19th century.  2. Social gospel—History—20th century.
3. Socialism, Christian—Great Britain—History—19th century.  4. Socialism,
Christian—North America—History—19th century.  5. Socialism, Christian—Great
Britain—History—20th Century.  6. Socialism, Christian—North America—
History—20th Century.  7. Sociology, Christian—History of doctrines—19th century.
8. Sociology, Christian—History of doctrines—20th century.  9. North America—
Church history.  10. Great Britain—Church history.  I. Title.
BT738.P477   1996
261.8′09′034—dc20                                                              95–14590
                                                                                            CIP

Published by The Pennsylvania State University Press,
University Park, PA 16802-1003

*For Christina, Carla, and David*

America and England are in the furnace, and the fires are hotter by seventy times than is their wont. Everywhere everything social is astir.

—John Clifford, *Jesus Christ and Modern Social Life*

# Contents

# List of Illustrations

## Gallery of Social Christians (pages 156–161)

## Americans

Washington Gladden (Ohio Historical Society)

Lyman Abbott (Bowdoin College Library)

Walter Rauschenbusch (American Baptist–Samuel Colgate Historical Library, Rochester, New York)

Henry George (Henry George Papers, Rare Books and Manuscripts Division, New York Public Library, Astor, Lenox, and Tilden Foundations)

Richard T. Ely (Wisconsin State Historical Society)

Frank Mason North (Frank Mason North Papers, Drew University Library)

Charles Stelzle (with Calvin Coolidge) (Charles Stelzle Papers, Rare Book and Manuscript Library, Columbia University)

George D. Herron (Grinnell College Library Archives)

Norman Thomas (Norman Thomas Papers, Rare Books and Manuscripts Division, New York Public Library, Astor, Lenox, and Tilden Foundations)

Sherwood Eddy (Special Collections, Yale Divinity School Library)

George Coe (Special Collections, Yale Divinity School Library)

Vida Scudder (Wellesley College Archives)

Harry F. Ward (Archives of the Burke Library, Union Theological Seminary)

Reinhold Niebuhr (Archives of the Burke Library, Union Theological Seminary)

## Canadians

S. D. Chown (United Church of Canada / Victoria University Archives, Toronto)

Charles Gordon (pseudonym Ralph Connor) (United Church of Canada / Victoria University Archives, Toronto)

J. S. Woodsworth (United Church of Canada / Victoria University Archives, Toronto)

# Acknowledgments

At first glance this study must seem incredibly wide in scale, embracing as it does religious, political, and social affairs of three countries on two Continents. The fact that such a study has been called for by a host of historians through the years is not always comforting when an author is faced with the actual task of carrying out the research and, even more important, drawing comprehensible conclusions after analyzing such a large quantity of material. But the readers in the last resolve must make the final judgment as to the worth of the labor and its results.

My debt to others is enormous. Among historians I found early inspiration in the advice given to me by Robert Kelley of the University of California at Santa Barbara, Peter d'A. Jones of the University of Illinois at Chicago, and the late Stephen Koss of Columbia University. As my study progressed I received invaluable suggestions from William R. Hutchison of the Harvard Divinity School, Arthur Mann of the University of Chicago, Howard Quint of the University of Massachusetts, Ramsay Cook of York University (Canada), John Moir and Kenneth McNaught of the University of Toronto, Robert Handy, Henry Sloane Coffin Professor Emeritus of Church History at Union Theological Seminary, the late E. P. Thompson , Alan D. Gilbert of the University of New South Wales, Bryan R. Wilson of All Souls, Oxford University, and Standish Meacham of the University of Texas at Austin.

From my stay at Cambridge I am particularly grateful for the advice and hospitality shown me by David Thompson of Fitzwilliam College, Owen Chadwick, former Regius Professor of Modern History, Bill Pickering of Wolfson College, and Ian Markham, now of the University of Exeter.

I wish to express my appreciation to Trevor O. Lloyd and Richard J. Helmstadter of the University of Toronto for extraordinary efforts in reading and, in the latter case, rereading this manuscript. Early advice given by the Penn State Press assessors was also most helpful. This manuscript benefited greatly from the guidance provided by Peter J. Potter and the editorial staff.

My debt to archivists and librarians in three countries is substantial. Without their cooperation this book would not have been possible. Rather than risk missing one in my list, I shall thank them all. I must also acknowledge collectively those individuals and officials who granted me access to sources and permission to quote from them. Required acknowledgments are made to the American Baptist–Samuel Colgate Historical Library; Miss Felicity Ashbee; the Master and Fellows of Balliol College, Oxford University; the Bodleian Library, Oxford University; the Borthwick Institute of Historical Research; Bowdoin College Library; Drew University Library; the Dean and Chapter of Durham Cathedral; the University of Hull Brynmor Jones Library; the Journal of Religious History; the Lambeth Palace Library; the Corporation of London, Greater London Record Office; the Master and Fellows, Magdalene College, Cambridge University; the New York Public Library, Astor, Lenox, and Tilden Foundations; the Ohio Historical Society; the Rowntree Archive at the Joseph Rowntree Foundation; the Director and University Librarian, the John Rylands University Library of Manchester; the National Library of Scotland; Christie, Viscountess Simon, and the United Church of Canada/Victoria University Archives. Specific citations of manuscript sources and their locations are found in footnotes to each chapter. Those libraries supplying photographs and portraits are found in the List of Illustrations.

The research for this book was supported by grants from the Social Science and Humanities Research Council of Canada and the St. Francis Xavier University Council for Research. This generous support also enabled me to acquire the services of a very capable research assistant, Monique Lamontagne, in 1988–89.

Last, I thank my family and my secretary, Helen MacRae, for their patience in these matters.

# Introduction

From the closing decades of the nineteenth century until the Second World War a tide of social concern swept through the ranks of Protestant clergy and some laity in Britain and North America. This social concern, which climaxed somewhere in the years just before 1914, was named Social Christianity. Awareness of widespread human suffering had been exhibited in varying degrees by Christian pastors throughout the ages, of course. In that general sense there was nothing particularly new about their compassion, nor was it unexpected that they would exhibit an acute awareness of the human condition for the period under consideration. In the age of population explosion, of new factories and new towns, similar worries were roused among some Continental Protestant leaders and in influential circles within the Roman Catholic Church. However, in Britain and North America the thoughts and actions of influential groups of Protestant Christians,[1] mainly clergy, were so distinctive, extensive, and intense as to evoke this special descriptive label.

1. The Social Christians were not necessarily allied with one specific organization. Associations between them were often informal. However, concrete organizations did exist throughout the period. The earliest British society in the era of the Christian Social Revival was the Guild of St. Matthew, founded in 1877, which was followed by the far more influential Christian Social Union (1889–1919), or CSU. The membership of both was largely confined to Anglicans. The successor to the Christian Social Union in terms of mainstream influence was the Industrial Christian Fellowship, formed in 1920 after the old Navvy Mission society had absorbed the CSU. The fellowship was not by any means confined to Anglicans. In addition, there were a host of lesser organizations, such as the Christian Socialist League (1894–98), which was mainly for Nonconformists (members of the Protestant churches outside the Established Church of England). The most ecumenically minded organization of the nineteenth century was the Christian Socialist Society, which was conceived to serve members of all the churches, but it lasted only from 1886 to 1892. Groups such as the Socialist Quaker Society (f. 1889) had a strong political commitment from their inception.

In the United States the earliest formal Social Christian organization was the Society of Christian Socialists, founded by the Boston Episcopalian minister William Dwight Porter Bliss in 1889. Not

These thoughts and actions were distinctive in that they were based upon a corpus of theological tenets that were generally coherent and focused. They were extensive in that the multifarious forms of expression employed are almost overwhelming to the modern eye, including oratory and printed literature of every description and organizations involving most of the important sectors of human activity. The intensity is evident in the earnestness of belief that Social Christianity could revitalize civilization as a whole and would do it very quickly.

The goals and major ideas of Social Christianity were conceived in the first half of the nineteenth century. They go back to the first and generally unsuccessful Christian Socialist movement in England led by John Frederick Denison Maurice and John Malcolm Forbes Ludlow in the turbulent 1840s and 1850s.[2] Maurice and his Broad Church group of supporters introduced theological concepts that were augmented by the sermons and writings of other figures such as Frederick W. Robertson,[3] until a second wave of writings and speeches appeared in the 1880s, which further elaborated on the earlier themes. This corpus of thought provided a general direction for the activities associated with the movement.

The underlying belief expressed in this book is that, to paraphrase George Kitson Clark, religious thought profoundly affects temporal affairs.[4] By the late nineteenth century Social Christianity was also a truly transatlantic phenomenon, drawing upon traditions of concern already in place in American liberal Protestantism when it crossed the ocean.

The concern with the social environment, which characterized Social Christians, impelled them to interact with secular movements from the very beginning. Indeed, their intersection with educational, political, and economic reform movements reflected the basic belief that there were no barriers to the

---

long thereafter other denominations produced their own equivalents, such as the Baptist Brotherhood of the Kingdom (1893–1915). In 1906 the Christian Socialist Fellowship was founded as an affiliate of the Socialist Party. Within three years the organization established itself in Britain and Canada. The Canadian organizations were usually formed in imitation of British and American societies, beginning with a very early branch of the CSU appearing in Ontario in the 1890s.

2. For a discussion of the early figures of English Christian Socialism, see Edward R. Norman, *The Victorian Christian Socialists* (Cambridge, 1987); P. R. Allen, "F. D. Maurice and J. M. Ludlow," *Victorian Studies* 11, no. 4 (1968): 461–82; and Torben Christensen, *Origin and History of Christian Socialism, 1848–1854* (Aarhus, 1962).

3. "Robertson of Brighton" (1816–53), minister of Trinity Chapel in that town, was a renowned Anglican preacher. His appeal to the laboring masses often raised alarm in those who saw radicalism in his rhetoric. The posthumous publication of his Brighton sermons made him even more famous in death both in Britain and in the United States.

4. George Kitson Clark, *The English Inheritance: An Historical Essay* (London, 1950), 10.

regenerative influence of Christianity. There was a mixing of the sacred and the secular, but the sacred was never forgotten. It was the wellspring of Social Christian thought and activity.

It would be naive to assume that the interaction between the sacred and the secular did not introduce into the thoughts of Social Christians concerns and priorities that lay outside the normal purview of churches. There were also many instances later in the history of Social Christianity in which members of the movement were absorbed by movements whose goals included the relegation of religion to the sidelines of public life. For some in the ranks of Social Christians such movements were undoubtedly a vehicle for the abandonment of formal identification with Christianity. For others such movements certainly involved the marginalization of the role of churches as a by-product of activity. Was Social Christianity then a conduit for secularization? In one way it was exactly the opposite. But in relation to the survival of the churches as institutions of public importance perhaps this was the case, especially in Britain. There was always a latent danger in this respect. However, as Jeffrey Cox has argued, the decline of the churches was not synonymous with secularization, especially in a situation in which many Social Christians pointedly did not identify the unfolding of the Christian message with the health of churches qua churches.[5]

The suspicions harbored by Christians of different persuasion always gave rise to such questions. For many conservative Evangelicals, later to be referred to as fundamentalists in North America,[6] Social Christians came to be identified with a lack of spirituality, as well as an abandonment of serious consideration of the "next life" and of a sense of personal responsibility for sin. Conservative, evangelical hostility toward some forms of Social Christianity was perhaps as much a reflection of differing social and political views as it was a response to the alleged secular tendencies within Social Christianity, especially when the latter was associated with liberal theology.

5. Jeffrey Cox, *The English Churches in a Secular Society: Lambeth, 1870–1930* (Oxford, 1982), chaps. 6 and 8.

6. The term *fundamentalism* first came into use in the United States after World War I. It refers to *The Fundamentals: A Testimony to the Truth,* consisting of twelve volumes published between 1909 to 1912, which rigorously defended, among many points, the infallibility of views expressed in the Bible. *The Fundamentals* were widely distributed among clergy and laity. As fundamentalism spread, the term lost its specificity and was often used in place of *Evangelicalism.* It was associated with a strong rejection of the religious principles and social agenda of the Social Gospel in the interwar period. For a discussion of the complexities of the concept, see George M. Marsden, *Fundamentalism and American Culture: The Shaping of Twentieth-Century Evangelicalism, 1870–1925* (New York, 1980). In relation to Britain, see David W. Bebbington, *Evangelicalism in Modern Britain: A History from the 1730s to the 1980s* (London, 1989). For Canada, see John G. Stackhouse Jr., *Canadian Evangelicalism in the Twentieth Century* (Toronto, 1993).

The decline of the churches, of course, is a far more complex subject. It is not clear that a liberal theology and an accentuated concern for social problems weakened the churches by deflecting them from the straight and narrow path of religiosity. Proponents of the sociological theory of secularization would contend that the decline was rooted in an emerging rational, scientifically based viewpoint that was increasingly embraced by many as an alternative to religion.[7] Religion faded into the background because it no longer worked for most people as a framework of explanation. The "mistaken" move toward Social Christianity in the long run was therefore not all that significant in the decline of religion or the advance of secularization (which seems to be the same thing in this theory). In the long run the result would have been the same. This, however, does not explain the considerable differences in religiosity between countries such as modern Britain and the United States, which have experienced roughly the same degree of modernization.

This book does not attempt to deal with the issue of secularization in the depth it deserves. It does surface as a problem from time to time within the discussion of Social Christianity. Only in that tangential way is there any modest contribution to an area of debate that is at the moment overburdened with theory and at the same time lacking in generally agreed definitions.

Definitions are indeed important, and it is just as well at this point to review the contemporary and later meanings of *Social Christianity* and related terms in greater specificity. In Britain the most consistently used term, aside from *Social Christianity*, was *Christian Socialism*. There was some disagreement with the term when it was employed by the founders themselves in the 1840s. Though Maurice lacked a discerning eye for both current politics and social and economic conditions and, in fact, came to repudiate the term *Christian socialist*, he was the dominant influence upon his followers. Maurice believed that the movement was essentially religious, based upon certain theological precepts, but generally, in practice, an attempt to suffuse the current atmosphere of economic grievances and social confrontation with a positive-directing Christian influence. The object of Maurice's efforts was the creation of social harmony in place of social discord.[8] The means was the application of Christian

---

7. For the history of this viewpoint in Britain, see Alan D. Gilbert, *Religion and Society in Industrial England: Church, Chapel, and Social Change, 1740–1941* (London, 1976), and idem, *The Making of Post-Christian Britain: A History of the Secularization of Modern Society* (London, 1980). A historical work on Canada that would conform to this school of thought is David Marshall's *Secularizing the Faith: Canadian Protestant Clergy and the Crisis of Belief, 1850–1940* (Toronto, 1992).

8. See John Frederick Denison Maurice, *The Kingdom of Christ; or, Hints to a Quaker Respecting the Principles, Constitution, and Ordinances of the Catholic Church*, 2d ed. (London, 1842). For a

principles, on a broad front, to social relationships. Socialism, with all its meanings at that time and since, could only be used in a very general sense with emphasis upon the Christian. No restrictive social philosophy would embrace Maurice's view of the Kingdom of Christ. It implied adherence neither to a political party nor to the concept of collectivism. John Malcolm Ludlow and Edward Vansittart Neale had differing views of what Christian Socialists should do from the start,[9] but as Edward R. Norman and Peter d'A. Jones have stated, it was the legacy of Maurice's religious thought that was to endure to the later, revived, and more significant Christian Socialism of the late nineteenth century.[10] Were it not for this religious legacy, the continuity between the first Christian Socialists and the greater movement of the late Victorian and Edwardian period might have been completely severed in the mid-Victorian period, when it survived largely in minor educational enterprises and submerged within a multiplicity of influences in the cooperative movement. The Fatherhood of God, the Brotherhood of Humanity, Incarnationism, and the concept of the divinely immanent Kingdom shaped much that would follow (see Chapter 1).

The period from 1880 to 1940, the period of this study, which displayed a continuity of unceasing political and social activity by Social Christians, brought some further attempts at definition. The message of some groups was given in greater specificity, which entailed the melding of definitions of socialism, in the more conventional sense, with what they viewed as constituting Christian Socialism. But the mainstream of the movement, represented by figures such as Brooke Foss Westcott,[11] preferred a Maurice-style broad sweep, rooted firmly in religion but open to involvement with actual socialist parties as well as the more numerous variants of political reformism that were not socialist.

In North America the term *Christian Socialist* was also used. Initially it was linked with Mauricean influences, which came into circulation in the mid-

---

sound appraisal of Maurice's social thought in this respect, see Norman, *The Victorian Christian Socialists*, chap. 2.

9. See Philip N. Backstrom, *Christian Socialism and Co-operation in Victorian England: Edward Vansittart Neale and the Co-operative Movement* (London, 1974).

10. Ibid. and Peter d'A. Jones, *The Christian Socialist Revival, 1877–1914: Religion, Class, and Social Conscience in Late-Victorian England* (Princeton, 1968), 10. Jones contrasts the abundance of this religious legacy with the later dearth of references to J.M.F. Ludlow's economic thought. Ludlow was certainly as much as Maurice a founder of the earlier Christian Socialism and outlived him by thirty-nine years (d. 1911).

11. Brooke Foss Westcott (1825–1901) was appointed Regius Professor of Divinity at Cambridge in 1870 and consecrated bishop of Durham in 1890. While a distinguished biblical scholar, he was also very concerned with what Thomas Carlyle termed the Condition-of-England question. He was president of the CSU from its creation in 1889 until his death.

Victorian era largely as a set of religious concepts in Episcopalian, though soon also in non-Episcopalian, circles.[12] Later it had a sharper meaning, often directly political and with a ring of militancy, but was not in wide circulation. As Robert T. Handy has pointed out for the period before 1900 and even after that time, *Social Christianity* was most commonly used to describe an activist promotion of principles of social justice in addressing the acute issues of economic and social distress.[13]

By 1900 the term *Social Gospel* also began to be used on both sides of the Atlantic, though more frequently in North America. It is often assumed to be of American origin. However, David Thompson has recently pointed out that British figures such as Brooke Foss Westcott began using it in the 1880s and that in fact the earliest usage may well have been by Karl Marx in the *Communist Manifesto!*[14] In Britain, by 1900, it again came into wider usage, being identified with liberal theology and assaults upon the old approaches of economic individualism and philanthropy within the Church of England and Nonconformity. For that reason it was treated with much suspicion by both theological and political conservatives.[15] Some American historians have developed more elaborate divisions of terminology. Henry R. May distinguishes between conservative, progressive, and radical Social Christianity in America.[16] May includes in the first category many evangelical, theological conservatives who engaged in areas of organized philanthropy and publication of social evils. The second group, which he links with the term *Social Gospel*, constitutes most of the Social Christian movement in the United States by the early twentieth century. This group adhered to liberal theology and to the idea of an activist state. The third group, the so-called radicals, were socialist Christians for the most part. But May's designations, while useful in some respects, are not always helpful. Certainly the evangelical roots of the Social Gospel must be recognized, as

12. See C. G. Brown, "Frederick Denison Maurice in the United States, 1860–1900," *Journal of Religious History* 10, no. 1 (1978): 50–69.

13. Robert T. Handy, ed., *The Social Gospel in America, 1870–1920* (New York, 1966), 5.

14. David M. Thompson, "The Emergence of the Nonconformist Social Gospel in England," in *Protestant Evangelicalism: Britain, Ireland, Germany, and America: Essays in Honour of W. R. Ward,* ed. Keith Robbins (Oxford, 1990), 258–60. Martin Marty believes that the Iowa Congregationalist minister Charles O. Brown was the first American to use the term, around 1886, in reference to Henry George's *Progress and Poverty.* Martin E. Marty, *Modern American Religion,* vol. 1, *The Irony of It All, 1893–1919* (Chicago, 1986), 286 n. 14:10.

15. David Jeremy, *Capitalists and Christians: Business Leaders and the Churches in Britain, 1900–1960* (Oxford, 1990), 57–58.

16. Henry R. May, *The Protestant Churches and Industrial America* (New York, 1969), 4. May's tripartite analysis of Social Christianity is also described in Robert T. Handy, *Undetermined Establishment: Church-State Relations in America, 1880–1920* (Princeton, 1991), 105–6.

must be the first group's positive contribution to social improvement throughout the period, but a distinction must be drawn between acceptance and
rejection of the individualistic social ethic that pervaded much of the mid-
nineteenth-century evangelical position. Elements of liberal theology and progressive social philosophy were also present. May's category of the conservative, as well as the other categories, is based upon consideration of social action
rather than thought. In some practical contexts this basis for categorization
would make the slotting of the odd theological conservative but socially radical
figure impossible. In Canada, for example, the great Methodist patriarch Albert
Carman could be found in this category.[17]

Kenneth Smith and Leonard Sweet posed a set of categories that included
"romanticists" (Charles M. Sheldon, with his Social Gospel novels), "new evangelists" (mostly Baptist figures such as Leighton Williams), "the scientific
school" (social scientists such as Shailer Mathews, Richard T. Ely), and the
radical Social Gospelers (William Dwight Porter Bliss, George D. Herron, and
all those associated with actual socialist parties).[18] Again this typology seems to
be based largely upon social action.

On the other hand, William R. Hutchison, in reacting against expanded
definitions of *Social Gospel* to embrace virtually all groups who support social
reform, has handled the problem of Evangelicals by suggesting use of the term
*Social Gospel* only in reference to those who adhered to the idea that social
salvation precedes individual salvation.[19] This is perhaps too restrictive, though
it probably would apply to many Social Gospelers in this century. I would be
more comfortable with the concept of parity between the two, if not primacy
given to social salvation. Hutchison notes that even this would be quite distinct
from the evangelical position.[20] Hutchison's classification has also influenced
one Canadian historian, Michael Gauvreau, to move toward his seemingly
greater precision.[21]

As a final complication, Willem Adolph Visser 't Hooft asserted in 1928
that the Social Gospel was both the majority view of American Protestants

17. Albert Carman (1833–1917) was the first general superintendent of the Methodist Church of
Canada from the union of Methodist churches in 1884 until 1915. He was known for his theological
orthodoxy, though he was a constant critic of plutocrats.

18. Kenneth Smith and Leonard I. Sweet, "Shailer Mathews: A Chapter in the Social Gospel
Movement, Part I," *Foundations: A Baptist Journal of History and Theology* 18, no. 3 (1975): 219–21.

19. William R. Hutchison, *The Modernist Impulse in American Protestantism* (Cambridge, Mass.,
1976), 164–74.

20. Ibid., 165 n. 36.

21. Michael Gauvreau, *The Evangelical Century: College and Creed in English Canada from the
Great Revival to the Great Depression* (Montreal, 1991), 154, 334–35 n. 82.

toward their society as well as their unique contribution to world Christi-anity.[22] Predictably this has led to further debates about where to place the American Social Gospel in relation to similar movements in the North Atlantic Triangle.[23]

These debates naturally lead to an explanation, or perhaps defense, of the approach taken in this book. A recent forum discussion in the *American Historical Review* has pointed to the advantages as well as the perils of engaging in transnational history.[24] Naturally what is unique in developments within national borders or indeed regions must be appreciated through detailed studies. My own early works in British religious and social history were very much in that tradition.[25] However, there is also the need for a wider perspective to explore interactions and parallel developments that knew no borders.[26] The value of comparative studies and studies of interaction, if indeed the two can be separated, has already been demonstrated. In the case of political thought, for example, Robert Kelley's *Transatlantic Persuasion: The Liberal-Democratic Mind in the Age of Gladstone* (New York, 1969) has made a valuable contribu-tion.[27] In the religious area Charles D. Cashdollar's *Transformation of Theology, 1830–1890: Positivism and Protestant Thought in Britain and America* (Prince-ton, 1989) is a major contribution, as are a number of works—including W. Reginald Ward's *Protestant Evangelical Awakening* (Cambridge, 1992)—that

22. Willem Adolph Visser 't Hooft, *The Background of the Social Gospel in America* (Haarlem, 1928), 1–2 and elsewhere. It is interesting that Visser 't Hooft was unaware of the origins of the term *Social Gospel* (15).

23. Charles Howard Hopkins adheres to the view that the Social Gospel was a distinctly American phenomenon. See Hopkins, *The Rise of the Social Gospel in American Protestantism, 1865–1915* (New Haven, Conn., 1940), and Ronald C. White Jr. and Hopkins, *The Social Gospel: Religion and Reform in Changing America* (Philadelphia, 1976). Against this view, see Winthrop S. Hudson, "How American Is Religion in America?" in *Reinterpretation in American Church History,* ed. Jerold S. Brewer (Chicago, 1968), 153–167, and esp. William R. Hutchison "The Americanness of the Social Gospel: An Inquiry into Contemporary History," *Church History* 44, no. 3 (1975): 367–81. Richard Allen, in *The Social Passion: Religion and Social Reform in Canada, 1914–28* (Toronto, 1971), 9, would argue that the Social Gospel in Canada was also part of the currents of thought sweeping the Western world.

24. "AHR Forum," *American Historical Review* 96, no. 4 (1991): 1031–72. The essays by Ian Tyrell and Michael McGern focus mainly on the question of American exceptionalism.

25. See, for example, Paul T. Phillips, *The Sectarian Spirit: Sectarianism, Society, and Politics in Victorian Cotton Towns* (Toronto, 1982).

26. An appeal for a comparative approach to British and American historiography can be found in Robin W. Winks, *The Imperial Revolution: Yesterday and Tomorrow* (Oxford, 1994).

27. See also James T. Kloppenberg, *Uncertain Victory: Social Democracy and Progressivism in European and American Thought, 1870–1920* (Oxford, 1986), and, specifically for Anglo-American connections, Arthur Mann, "British Social Thought and American Reformers of the Progressive Era," *Mississippi Valley Historical Review* 13, no. 4 (1956): 672–92.

have dealt with Evangelicalism.[28] This exchange of ideas was no less relevant for Social Christians who treated their world, for much of the period under consideration, as one transatlantic religious entity. By realizing that fact, perhaps one can more fully appreciate what is unique to a particular national or regional development. Differing religious views could also reflect, in part, differing social landscapes as well as divergent lines of intellectual development. Thus the comparative approach must be employed. The need for such an approach has been pointed out by many, including William McGuire King, Brian Fraser, and above all William R. Hutchison.[29] On the other hand, limiting the study to the North Atlantic Triangle reflects the way in which ideas and movements functioned in the English-speaking world at the time.[30] But other, lesser influences, especially German, are also considered.[31]

28. See also Richard Carwardine, *Transatlantic Revivalism: Popular Evangelicalism in Britain and America, 1790–1865* (Westport, Conn., 1978); Keith Robbins, ed., *Protestant Evangelicalism: Britain, Ireland, Germany, and America: Essays in Honour of W. R. Ward* (Oxford, 1990); Mark A. Noll, David W. Bebbington, and George A. Rawlyk, eds., *Evangelicalism: Comparative Studies of Popular Protestantism in North America, the British Isles, and Beyond, 1770–1990* (New York, 1993); and George A. Rawlyk and Mark A. Noll, eds., *Amazing Grace: Evangelicalism in Australia, Britain, Canada, and the United States* (Grand Rapids, Mich., 1993). The edited collections must be considered comparative history primarily in their totalities in that many of the essays in themselves are not comparative studies. Also of note is an early thesis by Peter d'A. Jones, "Christian Socialism in Britain and the U.S.A., 1880–1914," (Ph.D. thesis, London, 1964), though it is mainly concerned with England.

29. See William McGuire King, "Hugh Price Hughes and the British 'Social Gospel,' " *Journal of Religious History* 13, no. 1 (1984): 67 n. 8; Brian J. Fraser, *The Social Uplifters: Presbyterian Progressives and the Social Gospel in Canada, 1875–1915*, SR Supplements, vol. 20 (Waterloo, Ont., 1988), xiv–xv n. 9; and Hutchison "The Americanness of the Social Gospel."

30. Historical studies have begun to deal in part or whole with Social Christianity in Australia. See, for example, J. D. Bollen, *Protestantism and Social Reform in New South Wales, 1890–1910* (Melbourne, 1972); Walter Phillips, *Defending "A Christian Country": Churchmen and Society in New South Wales in the 1880s and After* (St. Lucia, 1982); Renate Howe, "Protestantism, Social Christianity, and the Ecology of Melbourne, 1890–1900," *Historical Studies* 19, no. 74 (1980): 59–73; and Joan Mansfield, "The Social Gospel and the Church of England in New South Wales in the 1930s," *Journal of Religious History* 13, no. 4 (1985): 411–33. As yet no major work has been produced on Australian developments in comparison with the North Atlantic, though British influences have been analyzed.

31. German influences in the theological field are the most obvious and have received the most treatment (see Chapter 1). Less clear are the lines of transmission through particular denominations, such as the Baptists. The field of social science is rife with broader studies that include discussions of German influences. Particularly useful is Jürgen Herbst, *The German Historical School in American Scholarship: A Study in the Transfer of Culture* (Ithaca, N.Y., 1965). Other non-British influences can be gleaned from studies scattered through periodicals and collections, such as Robert T. Handy, "The Influence of Mazzini on the American Social Gospel," *Journal of Religion* 29, no. 2 (1949): 114–23.

Some selected work on Social Christianity on the Continent provides the basis of fruitful comparisons. Of note are W. Reginald Ward, *Theology, Sociology, and Politics: The German*

There was another limitation to this study. Britain (with the exception of central and southern Ireland), the United States, and English Canada were predominantly Protestant (for much of the period), and in any case, the term Social Christianity was used in reference to Protestantism.

Social Catholicism has not been considered as an integral part of this study. While the language and the broadest theological concepts of some Roman Catholic groups bore a superficial resemblance to those of the Social Christians examined here, the inception of and support for Social Catholicism was quite different. Drawing from a wealth of Continental figures such as Bishop Ketteler of Mainz, it proceeded at a rather different pace and to a different tune. The late but considerable impact of "Rerum Novarum" points to the uniquely important position of the papacy in accelerating the advance of both Catholic social teaching and action.

This book focuses mainly upon movements bound up with the concerns of the socially dominant groups within the English-speaking countries in this period. Both British and North American Social Christians were very conscious of their Protestant heritage. Until the early twentieth century, Roman Catholicism in Britain, the United States, and Canada was, in large measure, a religion of the dispossessed.[32] Social Catholicism deserves a separate book. Social

---

*Protestant Social Conscience, 1890–1933* (Berne, 1979); Ronald L. Massanari, "True or False Socialism: Adolf Stoecker's Critique of Marxism from a Christian Socialist Perspective," *Church History* 41, no. 4 (1972): 487–96; and Jean Baubérot, "Le christianisme social français de 1882 à 1940: Évolution et problémes," *Revue d'Histoire et de Philosophie Religieuses* 67, no. 1 (1987): 37–61.

For a specific work of comparative history covering the later period, see Kenneth C. Barnes, *Nazism, Liberalism, and Christianity: Protestant Social Thought in Germany and Great Britain, 1925–1937* (Lexington, Ky., 1991).

32. There is no major work that treats the exchange of views by Europeans and North Americans or makes systematic transatlantic comparisons of Social Catholic groups. On Britain, see Edward R. Norman, *The English Catholic Church in the Nineteenth Century* (London, 1984), and two biographies of Edward Manning—Vincent A. McClelland, *Cardinal Manning: His Public Life and Influence, 1865–1892* (London, 1962), and Robert Gray, *Cardinal Manning: A Biography* (London, 1985). While Manning's influence over the crafting of "Rerum Novarum" is now somewhat in doubt, it is often instructive to reread his own celebrated works: *The Dignity and Rights of Labour* (London, 1874); "A Pleading for the Worthless," *Nineteenth Century* 23 (January–June 1888): 321–30; and "Leo XIII on 'The Condition of Labour,'" *Dublin Review* 109 (July–October 1891): 153–67. For North America the best recent work has been by David J. O'Brien in his books *American Catholics and Social Reform* (New York, 1968) and *Public Catholicism* (New York, 1989), esp. chap. 7. Specialized studies focus on a number of subjects, from Cardinal James Gibbons's career to the Catholic bishops' program of social reconstruction of 1919 to Catholicism and the New Deal. In Canada more studies have recently appeared on English-speaking Catholicism, but the interest in Social Catholicism has not been impressive. Gregory Baum's *Catholics and Canadian Socialism: Political Thought in the Thirties and Forties* (Toronto, 1980) is of use for the late period.

Christians, of course, were conscious of Social Catholicism and made both positive and negative assessments of its accomplishments from time to time.

Roman Catholicism was also seen as one of the insidious influences at work among the dispossessed. Something equally disconcerting in the eyes of Social Christians was the danger of alternative secular ideologies of liberation. The Social Christian responses in this area were complicated. Hardly defenders of the prevailing economic system and its attendant, dominant social milieu, the Social Christians, in contrast with the majority of Protestants speaking on such issues in earlier generations, were also fearful of the infection of insurrectionary thought. Before World War I a host of British, American, and Canadian Social Christians pointed to the folly of Marxism (though they could not help being influenced by it) and its variants.[33] A minority, of course, embraced it, particularly in the twentieth century. Fears concerning the social attitudes of immigrants were of acute importance to North American Social Gospelers.

The advancement of women's rights was, as Martin Marty has indicated, not an area of primary concern to Social Christians, though related groups, such as the Women's Christian Temperance Union (WCTU), did assist indirectly in that cause.[34] Historians such as Ronald White and Ralph Luker have suggested, in contrast with the views of more senior historians in the field, that furtherance of racial reform must be considered more than a marginal concern of Social Gospelers in the United States.[35] In the case of Luker, however, the attempt to place racial reform at the center of Social Gospel concerns elicits further debates about defining the movement itself, for his scope widens to include much of the general reformist sentiment in American life. White retains a concept of the Social Gospel, largely in agreement with more traditional definitions, seeing it as a religious movement with a more clear-cut perimeter. His extensive revelation of some Social Gospelers' concerns about racial issues is most welcome, as are Luker's revelations. But in keeping with a reasonably cohesive view of Social Christianity, one must say that racial reform was not the

33. However, W. Reginald Ward makes the point that English Social Christianity was not "distorted by the political challenge of an organized Marxism," in "The Way of the World: The Rise and Decline of Protestant Social Christianity in Britain," *Kirchliche Zeitgeschichte* 1, no. 2 (1988): 293.

34. Marty, *The Irony of It All, 1893–1919*, 291–94.

35. Ronald C. White Jr., *Liberty and Justice for All: Racial Reform and the Social Gospel (1877–1925)* (New York, 1990), and Ralph E. Luker, *The Social Gospel in Black and White: American Racial Reform, 1885–1912* (Chapel Hill, N.C., 1991). Among the historians and their works Luker criticizes, Arthur M. Schlesinger Sr.'s "A Critical Period in American Religion, 1875–1900," *Massachusetts Historical Society Proceedings* 64 (1932): 523–47, receives special attention because of its possible influence upon a host of early treatments of the Social Gospel. See Luker, *The Social Gospel in Black and White*, 2 and 327 n. 7.

central concern. This may well have been a function of the transatlantic exchange of ideas in which the early respect accorded to the British experience by American writers focused early American Social Christianity to an excessive degree upon social issues stemming from the common experience of urbanization, population increase, and industrialization. Beyond these issues of social tension, British writers had virtually nothing to say about racial questions, save in a very minor way, often as a result of trips to the United States (usually in reference to the South). The publication, for example, of Joseph H. Oldham's condemnation of colonial racism, *Christianity and the Race Problem* (London, 1924), or other utterances at the same time or even slightly earlier,[36] came far too late to influence the course of the American Social Gospel. However, American Social Christians did not always follow the lead of their British counterparts to the letter, and racial reform was clearly an important issue for them well before 1918. The degree of racial concern among American Social Christians as well as its relationship to the general reformism of the age in the United States remains an area for further discussion among historians of the Social Gospel.

The focus of this book is the interaction of a primarily religious movement with the wider social environment. Given the fact that Social Christianity was a response to concerns generated by modernization, its ongoing relationship with the social environment is obviously a major concern. Though essentially religious, Social Christianity involved a multiplicity of interactions with issues of social and political philosophy and policy, blurring distinctions between religious and social and political history. Indeed, the catalyst bringing forth Social Christianity was a deteriorating social fabric, in turn the product of economic transformations and social dislocations.

During the decade of the 1880s, Social Christianity emerged as a major force in the public life of Britain and North America. The mixture of secular social conscience and Social Christianity was present both in Britain and America at this time. The spark that initiated so much concern and activity on behalf of the distressed, laboring masses is still not clear. But the impulse unleashed both Social Christianity and general political and social reformism for decades to come. The altruism of members of the middle and upper classes cannot be discounted. This is clear from an examination of the background of Social Christians and other social reformist leaders of the period as well as many of their supporters.[37] But Social Christianity in Britain and North America was not

36. Edward R. Norman, *Church and Society in England, 1770–1970: A Historical Study* (Oxford, 1976), 270–71.

37. For example, see Clyde C. Griffen, "Rich Laymen and Early Social Christianity," *Church History* 36, no. 1 (1967): 45–65.

merely a reflection of the generally more enlightened outlook of a portion of the propertied classes on the question of the social misery of others. I would disagree with views such as that of José Harris, that the revived Christian Socialism of Britain in the 1880s was nothing but a subspecies of a wider revival of public spirit.[38] Those engaged in this Christian Socialist revival declared their indebtedness to the religious thought of the late F. D. Maurice, in particular. It was this religious legacy, rather than any socioeconomic ideas gleaned from the original Christian Socialists, that animated their interest in reforms during the 1880s.[39] Though its approach was to engage in dialogue with the community of the unfortunate, Social Christianity did not merely reflect current middle-class tastes in that regard.

What is argued in this book is that Social Christians were not moved primarily by secular fashions of social thought. They were not insulated from such influences, of course. There is no doubt that secular humanitarianism in those years stirred the imagination of political reformers. Social Christians, engaging by nature, did not shun such company as compassion of the broader sort pervaded the age, forging bonds of common cause. Some religious historians would be in agreement with José Harris concerning the primacy of the social reformism of the times. Edward Norman believes that secular social and political thought set the agenda for theological, or religious, thinking, especially in relation to Christian Socialism in Britain.[40] However, as A.M.C. Waterman and Boyd Hilton have demonstrated, there was a mesh of subtle interconnections between social and religious thought through much of the nineteenth century.[41] Social Christians, born and bred in such a milieu, indeed most Christians of those generations, would not have adhered to the more twentieth-century view of the separate worlds of religion and social thought. This was no less the case for North America than for Britain.[42]

The religious beliefs on which Social Christianity was based remained important throughout its history. Belief in the Incarnation entailed the concomitant views of the Fatherhood of God and the Brotherhood of Humanity. These were closely linked to belief in the doctrine of the Divine Immanence, of God's

38. José Harris, *Private Lives, Public Spirit: A Social History of Britain, 1870–1914* (Oxford, 1993), 249.

39. See Peter d'A. Jones, *Christian Socialist Revival*, 10.

40. Norman, *Church and Society in England, 1770–1970*, 11.

41. See A.M.C. Waterman, *Revolution, Economics, and Religion: Christian Political Economy, 1798–1833* (Cambridge, 1991), and Boyd Hilton, *The Age of Atonement: The Influence of Evangelicalism on Social and Economic Thought, 1795–1865* (Oxford, 1988).

42. See, for example, Kloppenberg, *Uncertain Victory*, 264, where he notes that the "strong identification of reform with religion" was traditional in American life.

presence in humanity and nature, sanctifying the world and expanding the sacred to all things. These ideas were as alive in the twentieth century as they were at the time of the early English Christian Socialists. Such beliefs led immediately to concerns transcending the barrier between the sacred and the secular. Other theological concepts were not always universal or constant among all Social Christians, especially by the 1920s, but these principles endured.

Social Christianity became a formidable movement in the public life of three nations, each with its own set of social, economic, and political circumstances. Religious thought in this situation transcended the particular conditions of each country, motivating individuals and organizations toward a set of goals common to the English-speaking peoples of the North Atlantic. Though obstacles on the road to the New Jerusalem were similar on both sides of the Atlantic, the movement was not merely the result of a coincidental, common reaction to like problems. The religious element brought coherence to the vision of the Kingdom and encouraged a bridging of the Atlantic in the exchange of ideas at least until the First World War.

It is not the purpose of this study to deal in depth with either the earliest roots of Social Christianity or its lasting consequences for the present day. There are excellent studies on aspects of the early precursors of Social Christianity from evangelical missions in early English industrial centers and the American frontier to the birth of American liberal Protestant thought.[43] Relevant causal factors, such as the ideas of F. D. Maurice, from earlier decades are included, of course. At the other end, the survival of Social Christianity into the hostile political environment of Margaret Thatcher, Ronald Reagan, and Brian Mulroney as well as the religious Right does not form part of this study. That story is not finished.

The period of this study has been selected with some care. As many historians have noted, the continuous period of Social Christianity begins in the late 1870s and 1880s. The terminal date of approximately 1940 is less conventional; many older studies ended with the First World War. I strongly believe that the story of Social Christianity did not reach its dénouement until the interwar period.[44] New trends, albeit many of short duration, appeared at this

43. See, for example, Timothy L. Smith, *Revivalism and Social Reform: American Protestantism on the Eve of the Civil War* (New York, 1957), chap. 10, for the evangelical origins of Social Christianity. Mark A. Noll believes that evangelical traditions were more closely associated with the early Social Gospel movement in Canada. Noll, *A History of Christianity in the United States and Canada* (Grand Rapids, Mich., 1992), 279.

44. I would agree with those historians who argue that even a proper understanding of the question of secularization requires the inclusion of the twentieth along with the late nineteenth

time. Though many leading figures died before or during the First World War, the same could be said of the Second.[45] More significantly, it was only with the Second World War that the present framework of the modern welfare state was firmly laid. This fact, together with the enmeshed politics that went with it, was of great importance in the final disposition of Social Christianity.

The organization of this book flows from its focus and theme. Chapter 1 provides an analysis of the interplay between theology and social thought in Social Christianity. Though by the twentieth century its theology was more diverse than its original, predominantly liberal theology, a constant body of basic concepts suffused the thoughts and actions of the practitioners of Social Christianity from beginning to end. Chapter 2 examines the uniquely significant impact of urban life and its attendant social ills upon the thinking of Social Christians, shaping most of their important, specified social concerns as well as institutional adaptations. Chapter 3 is a discussion of the efforts put forth by Social Christians as a function of their social thought and in response to the exposure of massive societal problems. This chapter reveals not only a willingness to employ new techniques of social investigation but also a degree of organization and innovation hitherto unseen from churches in service of a better society, as well as complications involved in working within the new fields of social science progressively more secular in orientation. The path from the rejection of almsgiving through the systematic organization of philanthropy to the acceptance of aspects of the modern welfare state is an important theme in this chapter. Chapter 4 reveals the ways in which Social Christians sought to enlist public support for their causes through the use of advanced forms of communication. Chapter 5 analyzes the desire of many Social Christians to establish a Christian commonwealth through the elimination of the division between church and state, as well as the attainment of unity among the churches. Chapters 6 and 7 explore the attempts of Social Christians to realize their goals through the agency of politics.

These chapters are therefore topical, taking the reader through the whole time frame in each case (with the partial exception of Chapters 6 and 7, which, though topical, follow one another chronologically). It is hoped that the reader will find that the effect is to display with greater clarity the richness of the various interactive components within this complex and often perplexing movement.

---

century. See John Kent, *The Unacceptable Face: The Modern Church in the Eyes of the Historian* (London, 1987), 98–99.

45. William Temple, archbishop of Canterbury, Charles Stelzle, the great New York Social Gospel leader and Christian publicist, and James Shaver Woodsworth, founding leader of the Canadian Cooperative Commonwealth Federation, all died in the early 1940s.

# 1

# THE WAY OF THE KINGDOM: THEOLOGY AND SOCIAL THOUGHT

Notions of a Kingdom of God on earth can be traced to the New Testament. Whether the Kingdom involves an internal reign of Christ over the hearts of individuals or an external order accompanying the Second Coming has been discussed at length by theologians. For many Social Christians, however, its earliest use as a metaphor was probably in Englishman F. D. Maurice's *The Kingdom of Christ* (1838). Originally prepared as a series of Anglican tracts for purposes of dialogue with Quakers, the book revealed Maurice's vision of a contemporary society based upon the spirit of Christian compassion rather than the spirit of Mammon. For Maurice the New Jerusalem was realizable, linking together all baptized citizens from vicars to street hawkers and sanctifying their multifarious tasks within an organic, harmonious whole.

The metaphor of the Kingdom repeatedly surfaced in the writings of Social Christians long after Maurice's death in 1872. Regardless of the country or the region or the denomination, the message was always clear. The Kingdom was the community of righteousness about to be established upon earth. It was not an idealized target never fully to be attained in this life but rather a real, living, and fully functioning community that would be realized through the social application of Christ's teachings. According to Social Christians, the historical completion of the Christianizing of communities was imminent. It was the expression of God's mission to humanity, the fulfillment of the Incarnation.

For most Social Christians, therefore, the dividing line between the sacred and the profane was never clear. All life was touched by the Divine. Their desire to promote social righteousness brought them into realms of social thought also inhabited by secular thinkers. The demarcation between theology and social thought was therefore not readily discernible for Social Christians, nor should it have been, in their view. Broadly speaking, of course, the notion of an interplay between religious ideas and social thought was generally accepted, even by those social reformers who challenged Social Christians in their reverence for the primacy of religious beliefs.

By the 1880s Maurice had become in death an inspiring saint for the next generation of Christian Socialists. This came about in many ways, from his quotable comments upon the ethical imperative of dealing compassionately with the social problems of the less fortunate as much as from a reverence for his theology, which even his most dedicated disciples found somewhat difficult to follow. Indeed, it is still not always easy to capture exactly what it was in his religious convictions that was most significant for future generations. Yet there can be no doubt of the centrality of religious thought within the Mauricean legacy.

Maurice seemed to oppose both Evangelicalism and Ritualism, while upholding the Church of England. Since Maurice was born a Unitarian and only converted to Anglicanism as a mature university student, elements of Nonconformity may well have remained in his theology to the end.[1] Rigorous systems of thought from utilitarianism to German metaphysics also concerned him deeply, leading him to defend the use of reason in discovering essential religious truths. J. M. Ludlow, cofounder of early Christian Socialism, who frequently referred to Maurice as "the prophet," admitted that it was impossible to separate philosophy from theology in the great man's writings.[2] And it was in fact this seemingly pronounced rationalism that led to much trouble for Maurice personally.[3] Later it probably contributed to the vehement and continuous opposition of conservative evangelical Protestants, or fundamentalists, as they would someday be called, to the religious thought of most Social Christians.

This came principally as a result of Maurice's *Theological Essays*, which questioned the idea of eternal punishment, among other things, and whose publication in 1853 led to a forced resignation from his professorship in theol-

1. See David Young, *F. D. Maurice and Unitarianism* (Oxford, 1992).
2. "Memoirs of J. M. Ludlow," chap. 18, add. 7450/5, f. 11, Malcolm Forbes Ludlow Papers, Cambridge University Library.
3. For a discussion of the complexities of this issue, see David M. Thompson, "F. D. Maurice: Rebel Conservative," in *Modern Religious Rebels*, ed. Stuart Mews (London, 1993), 123–43.

ogy at King's College, London. But both before and after this Maurice's ideas were under suspicion by many Anglicans, especially the Evangelicals. His example did much to move others, both inside and outside the Established Church, toward a more questioning, liberal Protestantism. Maurice's 1853 ordeal made followers like Thomas Hughes "lose all Christian patience thinking of the Pharisaism of the attackers."[4] Maurice's *Religions of the World and their Relations to Christianity* (1847) was one of the earliest examples of comparative religion, albeit in service of understanding Christianity, as well as what Edward Norman has called "a precursor of the sociology of religion."[5] Maurice's flirtation with Comte and his "religion of humanity" could be understood in this context. But there was a more profound notion at work in Maurice's mind. Maurice believed that Christianity could once again become a great force in improving the human condition in the modern world. Without the advance of these religious principles, Maurice feared that other systems of thought might prevail, believing that "Mill, Fourier and Humbolt are more in danger of making a system which shall absolutely exclude" God not just when they are at their worst "but even when they are best."[6]

What was most significant and clear was the emphasis upon the Incarnation, though Maurice was not by any means original in this emphasis. The Incarnation infused all of Maurice's sometimes disparate thoughts with a unity of purpose. He criticized the Old Hebrew concept of God for its detachment from humanity. Many of the Old Testament patriarchs had not experienced God directly. So, too, arid systems of thought designed for the betterment of humankind were uninformed by the Incarnate God. A familiar phrase used by Maurice's disciples was that the Incarnation infused "Christ in every man."

But it was the Incarnation that also placed God in fatherhood over society and would ultimately be the informing principle of the Kingdom of Christ. The Fatherhood of God was linked to the Brotherhood of Humanity, themes later to be stressed by other, more articulate apologists of Social Christianity. The implications of such thought as a basis for redemption of society were inescapable no matter how imperfectly they were developed by Maurice himself. Maurice sought not only social compassion through increased charitable work by the church, but also social unity, especially evident in *The Kingdom of Christ*, which argued both against the "sect spirit" among rival religious groups and against parallel secular movements such as the Owenites, which seemed to be the result of fads for new systems of thought. Maurice urged unity in church and

---

4. Hughes to Ludlow, 4 September 1853, add. 7348/6, f. 27, Ludlow Papers.
5. Edward R. Norman, *The Victorian Christian Socialists* (Cambridge, 1987), 34.
6. Maurice to Ludlow, 24 September 1852, Add. 7348/8, Ludlow Papers.

nation, believing the Divine worked through both. Thus a belief in the Divine Immanence was also present in his thoughts. Breaking the barrier between the sacred and secular rested on the notion of the ever-present infusion of Christ's spirit in all aspects of daily life.

Beyond these basic beliefs much of Maurice's thinking remains elusive. Historians debate the magnitude of impact Maurice's ideas had upon contemporary theologians.[7] While it has been suggested that his influence on the subsequent theology of Christian Socialism can be exaggerated, Maurice's religious ideas were better remembered by the later generation of Christian Socialists than were, for example, the economic notions of J. M. Ludlow.[8] That Maurice's theology does not comfortably fit within the traditions of Anglicanism may also help to explain why his ideas were so widely received. It is instructive that over sixty years later the British Methodist leader Scott Lidgett could lecture upon Maurice's gospel of the Incarnation, which ended distinctions between sacred and secular, emphasizing the kinship between God and humankind, a truth that "lies at the heart of the doctrine of the Fatherhood of God."[9] His appeal transcended denominational lines, especially with the passage of time.

Frederick W. Robertson (1816–53) the Brighton vicar who was well versed in the new approaches of German theology, seems to have had almost as great an influence as Maurice upon the very next generation of Social Christians on both sides of the Atlantic. Robertson did much to move religious thinking in the second half of the nineteenth century away from emphasis upon the Atonement, thereby assisting the progress of Maurice's ideas. Like Maurice he can be seen as a liberal Anglican, though he was not associated with any party, even the Broad Church circle that surrounded Maurice. Unlike Maurice, Robertson possessed exceptional skills as a preacher and writer. His appeal to the laboring masses made some suspect radicalism in his rhetoric. His open abandonment of Evangelicalism for liberal theology gave an indirect but enormous boost to the fortunes of the Mauriceans. Throughout the English-speaking world the audience for his printed sermons, as well as for Stopford Brooke's *Life and Letters of F. W. Robertson*, was even greater in death than it had been in life.[10] He

7. For example, Torben Christensen has argued that Maurice's ideas were not well received after the publication of his *Theological Essays* (1853). See Christensen, "F. D. Maurice and the Contemporary Religious World," *Studies in Church History* 3, ed. Geoffrey J. Cuming (1966).

8. Peter d'A. Jones, The *Christian Socialist Revival, 1877–1914: Religion, Class, and Social Conscience in Late-Victorian England* (Princeton, 1968), 85 and 10.

9. Scott Lidgett, *The Victorian Transformation of Theology* (London, 1934), 29 and 76.

10. In spite of his enormous popularity, the publication of Stopford Brooke's *Life and Letters of F. W. Robertson* in 1865 stirred minor debate about his liberal views in the aftermath of the much greater controversy concerning *Essays and Reviews*.

remained a figure of reverence for decades to come. Robertson preached that one must appreciate the human nature of Christ before proceeding to a proper understanding of his divine nature. Thus the news of the Incarnation was in fact Christ's central message, and all teachings would flow from this.

In the United States the influence of Maurice and Robertson served to reinforce indigenous liberal theological tendencies already building in the Republic. Foremost in leading American Protestantism in new directions was the New England Congregationalist Horace Bushnell. Parallels may readily be drawn between Bushnell and Maurice. Both men reacted against rigid dogmatism, thereby incurring the displeasure of theological conservatives. Indeed, Bushnell, in Maurice-like fashion, was almost tried for heresy following the publication of *God in Christ* (1849). Bushnell's attempts to restate Trinitarianism and to downplay revivalism and the Atonement were met with deep suspicion. His overview of morality as a product of social evolution was bold. But the greatest legacy of Bushnell was the opening of Protestantism to the new learning. In *Christian Nurture* (1847), his most famous work, Bushnell argued against the emphasis upon original sin and moved toward the characteristically liberal position of humankind's perfectibility through education. Like Maurice he was optimistic about humankind. Throughout his writings Bushnell blurred the demarcation lines between the "supernatural" and "natural" worlds, much as Maurice had done for the line between the sacred and secular in emphasizing the presence of Christ in the world.

Bushnell, like Maurice, was called a prophet by a later generation of liberal theologians and social Christians. W. R. Hutchison has noted that in their relation with science both men exhibited "a benign religious imperialism in their efforts to envelop it."[11]

Such close parallels made it easy for the later Social Christians of America to accept Maurice and Robertson almost as their own. In time their ideas blended in well with the predominant Postmillennialism of Protestant thinking in America.[12] Theodore Munger, the leading disciple of Bushnell, believed that

11. William R. Hutchison, *The Modernist Impulse in American Protestantism* (Cambridge, Mass., 1976), 44.

12. *Postmillennialism* referred to the belief that a period (literally one thousand years) of unequaled righteousness, peace, and prosperity would precede the Second Coming of Christ. It was held that the present age would be transformed into this Kingdom through the triumph of Christianity. American Protestantism was deeply influenced by this belief. In the early nineteenth century many believed that religious revivals would hasten this development. After a period of difficulty for those holding such an optimistic view (the period around the middle decades of the century, especially during the Civil War), it reemerged in the late nineteenth century, reinforcing the efforts of Social Gospelers in their quest for social reform—now seen as the most direct avenue

Robertson was the first preacher to "show the place [in] which the divine-humanity of Christ falls in the development of society."[13] Concerning Maurice, Munger summarized these parallels and blends of influences by recounting a meeting with a leading Mauricean disciple, Thomas Hughes, shortly before the latter's death: "I heard him [Hughes] say in his own library at Chester, before an exquisite portrait of Maurice, his voice tremulous with an emotion that almost bowed that strong man, 'Oh he was the prophet, he was the prophet!' You felt the same about Bushnell."[14]

The advocates of Social Christianity did not regard their religious thought as revolutionary in doctrine. In America, disciples of Bushnell were quick to pounce on conservative distortions of their mentor's thought, emphasizing his evangelical roots. Indeed, both Bushnell and Maurice were sufficiently vague in many areas of their thought to allow their apologists ample latitude for defense. Their appeal, aided by their own disdain for rigid theological dogmatism, also transcended denominational lines. In time their vagueness encouraged their enshrinement as oracles of a new age. In spite of a realistic attitude in their treatment of scriptural accuracy, they also had reverence for the Bible in the great and general Protestant tradition. This may have encouraged popular reappraisals of Scripture, often of the Old Testament as well as the New, that lent themselves to the cause of Social Christianity. It was not uncommon to find emphasis placed upon the Prophetic Revolution of the seventh and eighth centuries B.C., with its familiar focus upon social justice, in sermons of the last decades of the century.

Perhaps the best example of the Prophetic Revolution's invocation in the service of Social Christianity is the Lyman Beecher Lecture series delivered at Yale by Sir George Adam Smith in 1898–99. In the lectures Smith argued that the Hebrew prophets were contemporary in their concerns with progressive Christians in the late nineteenth century. For Smith the Hebrew prophets were unconcerned with miracles and otherworldliness in general but confined themselves "to the political and ethical facts."[15] The prophets were in fact leaders of

---

to the Kingdom. This anticipation of the Kingdom merged well with Immanentism and liberal theology.

*Premillennialism* was the belief that at some point in the future the one-thousand-year reign of Christ would be preceded by a period of intense conflict between good and evil, accompanied by the virtual destruction of contemporary society. It tended to be taken up by literalist interpreters of scripture in smaller sects and some Evangelicals and fundamentalists. Dispensationists, a subgroup, specialized in the prophecy of these future events.

13. "Frederick W. Robertson: The Preacher of Insight," 1866, box 13, folder 166, Theodore Munger Papers, Sterling Library, Yale University.

14. Theodore T. Munger, *Horace Bushnell: Preacher and Theologian* (Boston, 1899), 292.

15. Sir George Adam Smith, *Modern Criticism and the Preaching of the Old Testament: Eight*

what he called a "national religion" that included "the recognition of God's hand in the nation's history; the acceptance of great ethical institutions and personalities as from His hand; the instinct and effort of moral process; the sense of a mission to the world; the acknowledgment of the Divine calling of other nations, and sympathy in particular with such as are weak and oppressed."[16]

According to Smith, the duty of prophets, as leaders of the national religion, was not to defer to the power of ecclesiastical, political, or financial interests, as would fashionable preachers, but to be the "strong conscience of their people's sins and civic duties."[17] Smith at one point described very clearly his view of the prophets' teachings, and this description might easily serve as a summary statement of Anglo-American Social Christian concerns at the end of the nineteenth century:

> To go into detail upon the subjects of the civic preaching of the Prophets would amount to an exposition of the larger part of the Books of Amos, Hosea, Isaiah, Micah and Jeremiah. Let these four statements suffice. *First*, the careers of the Prophets were contemporaneous with the development of Hebrew society from an agricultural to a commercial condition, and with the rise of the City. The social evils, therefore, with which the Prophets deal, are those still urgent among ourselves. *Second*, the Prophets, while inculcating, from God's treatment of the nation, tenderness and pity in the nation's treatment of their poor and enslaved, dwell with still greater emphasis upon the need of justice and equity. We enjoy a legal freedom and justice far beyond those of the Oriental Society which the prophets addressed; but no man can deny the frequent want of honour and equity among us in social relations as are outside the laws. *Third*, the Prophets, when enforcing religious observances and institutions, do so most frequently for social ends, or with regard to the interests of the poorer classes of the community. And *fourth*, there is the emancipation of the individual from a *merely* national religion: the soul awakening to feel its solitary relation to God and its independence of the community only to discover a new duty and loyalty to the latter, that extends to the sharing of their sorrows and bearing of their sins—all the higher sense of individuality resulting in a truer altruism as we have

---

*Lectures for the Lyman Beecher Foundation, Yale University* (London, 1901), 266.

16. Ibid., 269.
17. Ibid., 270.

already seen instanced in Jeremiah. There could not be preaching more relevant to the conditions and temptations of our own life.[18]

The emphasis upon the social justice teachings of the prophets can be found in the writings of many Social Christians thereafter. As late as the 1940s the Reverend Robert B. Y. Scott of Princeton, for example, in his well-known textbook *The Relevance of the Prophets* (1944), based upon a series of summer school lectures given at MacDonald College, Quebec, in 1937, argued not only for the social teaching of the prophets but for "the remarkable contemporaneousness of these ancient spokesmen of religion and the perennial freshness of their message."[19]

The fundamentals of the theology of modern Social Christianity were probably laid by the 1880s. The Divine Immanence, the belief that God was at hand in a type of Second Coming emphasizing the blurring of the sacred and secular through his omnipresence, was evident in Maurice and Bushnell. Incarnationism, with the focus upon God's intimate relationship with humankind, upon this Fatherhood and the Brotherhood of Humanity, in which civilization and the purposes of God are fused, was since Maurice emerging in Social Christian thought on both sides of the Atlantic. Variations on these themes would be endlessly repeated in the writings of Social Christians for the next sixty years.

In the years that followed, much would be added to Social Christianity from the realm of social thought to give the theology more of a punch for social and political activism. Occasionally such additions raised questions about the thoroughness and rigor of such theology. This could explain the eventual belief of a number of Social Christian practitioners, that there was no need for a formal theology at all.

A sharp distinction between philosophy and theology is difficult to maintain when looking at the late nineteenth century. Even the earliest pioneers of Christian Socialism did not observe the borders carefully. J. M. Ludlow found it impossible to separate philosophy from theology in Maurice's writings. Certainly for a movement that emphasized concern for the society beyond the churchyard, moral and social philosophy understandably suffused much of theology.

---

18. Ibid., 272–73. The argument that one awakens to a new sense of individuality through social service is not unlike the view, found in interwar literature, that one discovers one's true personality in similar endeavors.

19. See also George Elliott, "The Social Message of Prophets," in *Social Ministry: An Introduction to the Study and Practice of Social Service,* ed. Harry F. Ward (London, 1910), 1–26.

The giant figures who influenced all branches of thinking in the nineteenth century were secular. John Kent, in his important article "The Victorian Resistance," has identified the dominant currents of thought as secular, with some religious figures fighting good rearguard action, so to speak, while most Christians fell into retreat.[20] David Friedrich Strauss's *Life of Jesus* (1835) and Charles Darwin's *Origin of Species* (1859) and *Descent of Man* (1871) introduced a new view of natural and human history. These authors' more strident disciples developed philosophical concepts from their research discoveries that had profound implications for moral and social philosophy. Placing the human mind and free will into the realm of nature undermined belief in the spiritual side of humanity.[21] The advocates of these new views did not want to see the destruction of morality, however. Rather, many argued for a new superior system of ethics based upon progressive, scientifically based views of humankind.

Herbert Spencer, the father of social Darwinism, certainly did not see his role as that of the destroyer of morality. Indeed, he believed that a new, progressive, ethical foundation could result from an understanding of human behavior within nature. But this was ethics with a materialist approach to the study of humankind. This, of course, ultimately led Spencer to an attempt at establishing a science of ethics.

In some instances Spencer's ideas could be made useful to the Christian cause. Spencer's view of progress in societal development and of general evolutionary philosophy inspired the American John Fiske to reinstate a natural theology with humanity's progress at the center of nature. Henry Drummond in Scotland had pressed much the same point. The American William Graham Sumner, former Episcopal rector, had further added fuel to the fire with his variations upon the ideas found in Spencer's *Study of Sociology*. But Sumner's ideas seemed to vindicate the older Protestant individualistic ethic, which would be of no comfort to socially progressive-minded Christians.

Openness to the new scientific ideas was particularly characteristic of university-educated Anglican clergy in Britain, and many of them tried to bridge the chasm between science and religion.[22] Among them members of the Broad Church circle, associated with Maurice, embraced the new philosophical

20. John Kent, "The Victorian Resistance: Comments on Religious Life and Culture," *Victorian Studies* 12 (1968): 145–54.
21. See Robert M. Young, "The Impact of Darwin on Conventional Thought," in *The Victorian Crisis of Faith*, ed. Anthony Symondson (London, 1970), 13–35.
22. See Frank M. Turner, *Between Science and Religion: The Reaction to Scientific Naturalism in Late Victorian England* (New Haven, Conn., 1974), and James R. Moore, *The Post-Darwinian Controversies: A Study of the Protestant Struggle to Come to Terms with Darwin in Great Britain and America, 1870–1900* (Cambridge, 1979).

movements in Germany, combining them with an appreciation of British empiricism. *Essays and Reviews* (1860) was their most famous production. Many, using Maurice as a guide, also were open to the new attitude toward the church's responsibilities to society. Like Maurice they were also skeptical of many old theological dogmas, such as the natural depravity of humankind and eternal damnation, so cherished by old Evangelicals.

For these men Auguste Comte, with his emphasis upon a progressive application of scientific principles to the improvement of the whole society (sociology),[23] provided greater inspiration than Herbert Spencer. Though Comte's religion of humanity was a severe threat to Christianity, the impulse behind his position was greatly appreciated. F. D. Maurice had been influenced by Positivism, as were William Henry Fremantle and Brook Foss Westcott—the leading theorists of modern Christian Socialism.[24]

Hegel's notions of history were also modified to accommodate the notion that Christianity was the culmination of the religious impulse through the saga of civilization. British Hegelianism, or idealism, was a powerful influence upon liberal Protestantism in Britain, though one can demonstrate the differences between the two in relation to the historical Jesus.[25] The proponents of idealism were the Scottish Presbyterians, John and Edward Caird, and the mentor to many English Broad Churchman, T. H. Green. It was not surprising that Green, being himself influenced by F. D. Maurice, had many Broad Church disciples. Green's influence was extraordinarily wide,[26] engulfing the spheres of theology, social science, and politics. Though not as careful a writer as the Caird brothers, Green was able to inspire a generation of young Oxford undergraduates in the 1870s and early 1880s, as well as the generation to follow, with the idea of a newer, rational approach to Christianity. So wide was his influence that Green is remembered as much for inspiring *Lux Mundi: A Series of Studies*

23. Auguste Comte (1798–1857), originally a follower of Saint-Simon, produced important philosophic works, such as the six-volume *Cours de la philosophie positive* (1830–42), which formed the basis of what would be known as Positivism. In his last years he founded the Positive Society and attempted to apply his ethical ideas to social questions.

24. See Charles D. Cashdollar, *The Transformation of Theology, 1830–1890: Positivism and Protestant Thought in Britain and America* (Princeton, 1989), esp. part 1.

25. See Peter Hinchliff, *God and History: Aspects of British Theology, 1875–1914* (Oxford, 1992). Incarnationism obviously produced an intense interest in the earthly life of Jesus as a historical reality.

26. For example, Theodore Munger in America noted that he learned of T. H. Green both from his works edited by R. L. Nettleship and from the fictionalized version of the man depicted in *Robert Elsemere* by Mrs. Mary [Humphry] Ward. See Munger's review of Green's work, *The Literary World*, 16 March 1889, box 9, folder 27, no. 68, Theodore Munger Papers, Sterling Library, Yale University.

*in the Religion of the Incarnation* (1889),[27] a work by High Churchmen published seven years after his death, as for his work among Broad Churchmen. As the subtitle suggests, *Lux Mundi* stressed the Incarnation, directing High Churchmen toward this world and away from an aesthetic, detached view of affairs. It is beside the point whether Green himself would have approved of the other theological ideas of these High Churchmen. Indeed, there is considerable debate about Green's "theology." Melvin Richter emphasizes his religious philosophy, and I. M. Greengarten sees his theological terminology as more of a cloak for his political ideas (see Chapter 6). Certainly Green's version of Immanentism was the subject of some debate in his own time and after his death.

Oxford remained a center of influence, reinforced by Edward Caird's migration from Glasgow to assume the mastership of Balliol College in 1893. From there he increased his circle of supporters, including the American Lyman Abbott. After Caird's appointment, W. H. Fremantle wrote to him, concerning Caird's own writings: "They express the view of things which I have been trying all my life to enforce—I fear with little success: and if you can make it prevail at Oxford you will in my opinion do the work which is most needed at the present moment."[28]

A more minor influence on English thought came from the disciples of another German, Albrecht Ritschl.[29] The Ritschlians rejected the extremes of Hegelian rationalism, exhibiting a more pragmatic approach to Christianity rooted in the spiritual and ethical facts of religious experience. Their stress upon the need for a practical, moral Christianity produced attitudes toward society not unlike those of the idealists (whom Ritschlians did not renounce) and blended in with the general push toward Social Christianity.

The fusion of Incarnationism and Immanentism produced a call for social action influencing all churches from the Anglican High Church to the New Church.[30] Though some of the individuals could hardly be termed "liberal" in

27. *Lux Mundi: A Series of Studies in the Religion of the Incarnation,* ed. Charles Gore (London, 1889).

28. Fremantle to Caird, 14 November, box 7, "Letters to Caird," Edward Caird Papers, Balliol College Library, Oxford University.

29. Albrecht Ritschl (1822–89) was professor of theology at Göttingen for most of his career. His reputation was even greater among American liberal Protestants, who regarded him as the prime mover of the considerable German influence on theology in the United States from about 1890 onward (see William R. Hutchison, *The Modernist Impulse in American Protestantism,* 122–32). Among those associated with Ritschl were the philosopher Rudolf Hermann Lotze and the historian Adolf Harnack, who, like Ritschl, also taught a comparatively large number of Americans who came to Germany to pursue graduate studies.

30. The term *Immanentalism* is used by Peter d'A. Jones to describe the sanctification of the material life, which concept also supported the socialist call for the Divine Kingdom on earth (*Christian Socialist Revival,* 86–87).

relation to issues of rubric and doctrine, most shared a desire to address themselves in a more forceful way to the social and philosophical problems of the age. Evangelicals, who stressed individual self-reform in this life as the best route to the next, were to share progressively less with those in the new movement.[31]

It has been argued that Anglican "sacramental" socialists (mainly High Church) had, in their doctrines and rituals that emphasized organic wholeness within society, an even more recognizable foundation for their Christian Socialism. Stanley Pierson claims that Anglican and Nonconformist views of the Christian commonwealth differed.[32] But David Thompson and Richard J. Helmstadter believe that the cardinal belief in Incarnationism profoundly influenced many Nonconformist Social Christians just as it did Anglicans.[33] While not specifically associated with Nonconformity, Incarnationism was not difficult to assimilate. In Westcott's discussion of the subject in 1892 it would have been hard for most Christians to take issue with its sense of mission: "When we ponder the Incarnation not only in its essence but in its circumstances we come to realize that the Incarnation of the Son of God adds to authority the grace of sacrifice, to obedience the joy of Divine fellowship, to the energy of service the endurance of love, while it offers the sense of the presence of God as the present pledge of unity."[34]

Virtually every denomination had its spokesman for the cause by the end of the 1880s. R. W. Dale's New Evangelicalism had a few years earlier started to push Nonconformity toward more involvement with the societal issues in

31. Again, as indicated in the Introduction, there are always complications of terminology in such contexts. Like many North American historians, David W. Bebbington makes the arguable point that the "Social Gospel" in Britain was "grounded in Evangelicalism" (*Evangelicalism in Modern Britain: A History from the 1730s to the 1980s,* [London, 1989], 211–12). However, the liberal theology of Maurice and Robertson, as that of Bushnell in America, contributed to a shift in religious principles that had widespread and enduring influence over the next generations of Social Christians. For Nonconformists in particular, as for many American churches, terms such as *New Evangelicalism* and liberal Evangelicalism were often employed in discussing the transition to a new religious vision. However, for Peter d'A. Jones, the "Social Gospel" established in Britain by 1908 owed much to R. J. Campbell as well as to *Lux Mundi (Christian Socialist Revival,* 7, 224, 422).

32. Stanley Pierson, *Marxism and the Origins of British Socialism: The Struggle for a New Consciousness* (Ithaca, N.Y., 1973), chap. 1, "Anglican and Nonconformist Visions of a Christian Commonwealth," 3–21.

33. David M. Thompson, "The Emergence of the Nonconformist Social Gospel in England," in *Protestant Evangelicalism: Britain, Ireland, Germany, and America,* 255–56, and Richard J. Helmstadter, "The Nonconformist Conscience," in *The Conscience of the Victorian State,* ed. Peter T. Marsh (Syracuse, N.Y., 1979), 167.

34. Brooke Foss Westcott, *The Incarnation Visitation: A Revelation of Human Duties: A Charge delivered at his Primary Visitation, November 1892* (Cambridge, 1892), 61–62.

national life.[35] Hugh Price Hughes spoke for Wesleyan Methodists in hoping that Christians would strive for the salvation of society as a whole as well as that of individuals. A. M. Fairbairn (Congregationalist), John Clifford (Baptist), Philip H. Wicksteed (Unitarian), and many in other churches could be found expressing similar thoughts. Theosophy, the New Church, and spiritualism contributed their own particular theologies of social salvation.[36] Liberal theology pushed relentlessly onward in the service of humanity, discarding or modifying any beliefs that seemed in the secular sphere to lend themselves to economic individualism or the untruth of competition, as Maurice would have phrased it. However, it did not follow that the religious concept of individual salvation had to be abandoned in the process.

The Congregationalist R. J. Campbell took the train of thought concerning Incarnationism and Immanentism to the ultimate in almost fusing God and humanity in his so-called New Theology. As he stated in *Christianity and the Social Order*, "We cannot too strongly insist that the work of Christianity is to realise the Kingdom of God on earth and nothing else. Christianity has not, and never has had, any other Divine commission."[37] Campbell was motivated by the need for social action, which he saw as better developed in Anglicanism, especially by High Church clergy, than in Nonconformity.[38] He was also strongly allied to secular reformism, stating of his New Theology: "The great social movement which is now taking place in every country of the civilized world towards universal peace and brotherhood, and a better and fairer distribution of wealth, is really the same movement as that which, in the more distinctively religious sphere, is coming to be called the New Theology."[39]

35. See John Kenyon, "R. W. Dale and Christian Worldliness," in *The View from the Pulpit: Victorian Ministers and Society,* ed. Paul T. Phillips (Toronto, 1978), 187–209.

36. See Chapter 6 below, including note 62. For New Church, or Swedenborgian, religious arguments for social activism, see Peter d'A. Jones, *Christian Socialist Revival,* 353–67. For the Theosophist view, see Anne Taylor, *Annie Besant: A Biography* (Oxford, 1992), and Janet Oppenheim, "The Odyssey of Annie Besant," *History Today* 39 (September 1989): 12–18. A peculiar blending of the views of Robert F. Horton and Annie Besant can be found in E. R. McNeile, *Theosophy and the Coming Christ* (London, 1913). For accounts of these views in the United States, see Sylvia L. Cranston, *H.P.B: The Extraordinary Life and Influence of Helena Blanatsky* (New York, 1993), and Marguerite Beck Block, *The New Church in the New World: A Study of Swedenborgianism in America* (New York, 1932), esp. chap. 12, "The New Church and the Social Gospel." For an important insight into the links between the Social Gospel and spiritualism, in this case in Canada, see Ramsay Cook, "Spiritualism, Science of the Earthly Paradise," in *Canadian Historical Review* 65, no. 1 (1984): 4–27.

37. R. J. Campbell, *Christianity and the Social Order* (London, 1907), 149.

38. Ibid., 17–18.

39. R. J. Campbell, *New Theology* (London, 1907), 14.

Campbell may have strayed from the acceptable line of argument in this area of his discourse. His New Theology, then, was viewed by some as not theology at all. It was vigorously attacked by the more orthodox and beyond Social Christianity gave many Evangelicals cause for concern in its threat to legitimate social reformism. Upon reflection it may ultimately have worked upon Campbell himself, leading to his conversion to the more theologically structured Church of England in 1915, which had earlier impressed him in any case with its social concern.

The more acceptable part of Campbell's argument was that the New Theology in fact was not new but went back to the fundamentals of early Christianity. This was a line of assertion quite common among British Social Christians of the 1890s.[40] But this assertion also enabled Campbell to make what seemed to some outrageous statements about socialism more closely approximating pure Christianity in this life than were the churches. As he stated: "Socialism is actually a swing back to that gospel of the Kingdom of God which was the only gospel the first Christians had to preach; the traditional theology of the churches is a departure from it."[41] Campbell went on to point out that he did not make "the foolish statement that primitive Christianity was identical with the Socialism of today."[42] However, his lumping together of believers and nonbelievers, the "avowed agnostics" and the "convinced sacerdotalists," as "both Christian" in that they preached socialism,[43] left many with precisely that impression.

The controversy over Campbell's New Theology, which lasted until the First World War, did not deter the advance of liberal theology among British Nonconformists. The Christian perfectionism of the Methodist Robert Newton Flew[44] and the acceptance of new intellectual and social challenges by the Baptist Charles Aked continued to move many Nonconformists toward acceptance of liberalization and relaxation of older, more rigid theological ideas. Westcott, in his leadership of the Christian Social Union (CSU), cleverly distanced even the Christian Socialist wing of the Church of England from direct identification of socialism with Christianity. His famous 1890 address to the Church Congress entitled "Socialism" was a masterpiece of vagueness wherein he reviewed the existing meanings of socialism from Bismarck to the Fabians and then asserted

---

40. Peter d'A. Jones, *Christian Socialist Revival*, 86–87.
41. Campbell, *Christianity and the Social Order*, 19.
42. Ibid., 20.
43. Ibid., 150.
44. See Robert Newton Flew, *The Idea of Perfection in Christian Theology: An Historical Study of the Christian Ideal for the Present Life* (London, 1934). Flew placed heavy emphasis upon Ritschl; perfection was to be found in the common life of the community (ibid., 379).

that his definition of socialism was not "committed to any one line of action."[45] Yet in the haze Bishop Westcott perhaps understood the danger of subordinating the church to a secular system of social thought, preferring to see the church select and advance those ideas that might "hasten a Kingdom of God on earth." Westcott was also quite protective of individuality in any vision of a socialist future.

In another equally famous set of sermons published about the same time, "Social Christianity," Hugh Price Hughes, leader of the Methodist Forward Movement, made it clear that his efforts to move his coreligionists toward social reformism at all levels of government was inspired by basic Christian teachings. Hughes began one sermon by admitting his awareness of the criticism by an "excellent Christian gentleman" that a past sermon dwelt on the duties of citizens rather than preaching the gospel."[46] At the same time, however, Hughes argued vehemently that it was necessary at times to preach "about the public application of the Gospel" in order to avoid the "menacing advance of atheistic socialism, communism, and Nihilism in Europe."[47] Clearly no subordination to secular ideology was in his mind, though he could admire sincerity in the efforts of a Mazzini.

What was in his mind was suspect to some, however. Beginning with Methodism and then spreading through Nonconformity and Low Church circles was a growing fear of socialism enveloping Protestantism through the Social Gospel, and this fear led in 1910 to the formation of the Anti-Socialist Union of Churches. To some degree this obsession made the religious works of John Clifford among Baptists and of Hughes among Methodists suspect.[48]

The broader issue was the relation between the sacred and secular in the pursuit of socially desirable goals. How far could the two be mingled? Certainly flowing from the idea of the Divine Immanence, ultimately from Incarnationism, and augmented by the necessity of cooperation with compatible secular forces was the progressive reduction of the barrier between the two in the minds of many Social Christians. Broadly speaking, this was perhaps the most important religious development on both sides of the Atlantic for its implications in the area of social thought. For example, in the United States the new thoughts along this line found expression in Theodore Munger's *Freedom of*

45. See Brooke Foss Westcott, "Socialism," from "The Official Report of the Church Congress" (1890), reprinted in *Religion in Victorian Society: A Sourcebook of Documents,* ed. Richard J. Helmstadter and Paul T. Phillips (Lanham, Md., 1985), 461.

46. Hugh Price Hughes, "Jesus Christ and Social Distress," in *Social Christianity: Sermons Delivered in St. James's Hall, London* (London, 1890), 19.

47. Ibid., 20.

48. Bebbington, *Evangelicalism in Modern Britain,* 215–16.

*Faith* (1883), which argued a "New Theology" that disregarded the line between sacred and secular in its enthusiasm for a divine design manifest in the progress of the age. According to W. R. Hutchison, there was a considerable relationship between the Immanentism of these American New Theology advocates, such as Munger and American liberalism.[49]

Somewhat earlier in Britain a similar development can be traced through the works of B. F. Westcott and W. H. Fremantle, lineal theological descendants in the tradition of Maurice and Robertson. Bishop Westcott, formerly Regius Professor of Divinity at Cambridge, was a noted Biblical authority who became interested as a young scholar and priest in connecting church life with the concerns of the wider world. This interest can be seen throughout his writings, from his earliest works, such as the *Gospel of the Resurrection* (1866), to quite late writings, such as the *Gospel of Life* (1892), where the influence of Comte became progressively more important in its emphasis upon the interaction of an ethical system with everyday life. As Westcott stated in a charge to the clergy of Durham in 1896: "The Christian society is neither secluded nor lost in the world."[50] Indeed, in one of his last letters to F. D. Maurice, he urged that theology professors teach candidates for Holy Orders "to feel that 'Social Morality' is one side of the doctrine of the church."[51] Twenty years later, he again made the point that "[a] National Church witnesses that the corporate life of the society is a divine life."[52]

Perhaps Westcott's call was heeded. The young Conrad Noel about this time decided to take Holy Orders but was refused ordination by the bishop of Exeter, mainly on the grounds of his Romish tendencies and his view of "God immanent in Nature and Man."[53] His father, Roden Noel, subsequently wrote to the bishop of Chester (who also refused Conrad), indicating that "the doctrine moreover in which my son understood that your lordship thought him heretical is as he believes the very doctrine urged upon him by Bishop Westcott as a most important one to be believed—the Immanence of God." Regarding his son's

49. Hutchison, "The Americanness of the Social Gospel," 373–74.

50. Brooke Foss Westcott, *Some Conditions of Religious Life: A Charge delivered to the Clergy of the Diocese of Durham as his Visitation, October 1896* (Cambridge, 1896), 51.

51. Westcott to Maurice, 13 September 1871, box 7, Brooke Foss Westcott Papers, Westcott House Library, Cambridge.

52. Brooke Foss Westcott, *"The National Church and the Nation": A Speech by the Right Reverend The Lord Bishop of Durham in Westminster Town Hall, 14 May 1891 at annual meeting of Church Defence Institution* (London, 1891), 2.

53. Copies of correspondence relating to refusal by the bishop of Exeter to ordain Conrad Noel, 1893–94, p. 1, 7 miscellaneous 3/1, Papers of Conrad Noel, Brynmor Jones Library, University of Hull.

views on Holy Communion and other matters, Roden Noel thought his son might modify his views but added, "[W]hether he would ever be led to exchange them for the evangelical opinions to which your Lordship probably refers when you speak of the 'simplicity of the faith as it is in Jesus' is of course quite problematical."[54] Within two years Conrad Noel was ordained and was fortunate a few years later, in 1910, to be offered the living at Thaxted, Essex, by Lady Warwick of Easton, who supported both his Anglo-Catholicism and his efforts on behalf of socialism.

W. H. Fremantle, the influential East London vicar and fellow of Balliol College, Oxford, took Comte's criticism of Christianity's overemphasis on the supernatural even more to heart. While his 1882 book *The Gospel of the Secular Life* argued for the unity of the ordinary with spiritual life in the spirit of God's creative unity over the universe, some contemporary critics thought he was more of a tool in the hands of forces wishing to dissolve the formal church.[55] His more lasting influence was to come a year later, when he delivered the Bampton lectures at Oxford. Eventually published under the title *The World as the Subject of Redemption* (1885), it was the clearest expression of the need to remove the barriers between the church and the world. The essence of *The World as the Subject of Redemption* was that the church consists primarily of the community of believers—not in the doctrines, rubric, or priesthood of any particular Christ persuasion. Fremantle opposed the artificial separation of the sacred from the secular, seeing all worthwhile activities as "religious." The commonly used term *church*, according to Fremantle, was misused in its reference only to the organizations of Christians for worship, for "the Christian Nation is in the fullest sense a church."[56] That worship was but part of the redeeming process. Redemption meant saving society in all sorts of ways.

Most of Fremantle's ideas were not new. The tradition of Maurice, Coleridge, and Thomas Arnold shone through. But it was presented in a clear and compelling form. Within a few years the book was a great success in the United States and eventually stimulated renewed interest in the subject back in England itself, proof of the mutually supportive nature of Anglo-American Social Christianity. W. R. Hutchison believes that Fremantle's enthusiastic reception in the United States followed from his enthusiastic Immanentism, which was

54. Roden Noel to Bishop Bickersteth of Chester, 23 December 1893, Papers of Conrad Noel.
55. Cashdollar, *The Transformation of Theology,* 388.
56. William Henry Fremantle, *The World as the Subject of Redemption: Being an Attempt to set forth the Functions of the Church as designed to embrace the Whole Race of Mankind: Eight Lectures delivered before the University of Oxford in the Year 1883,* 2d ed., with an introduction by Richard T. Ely (New York, 1895), 307.

uncharacteristic of many English writers but very similar to the ideas espoused by American Social Christian leaders of the period.[57]

While the Anglican background of Maurice, Fremantle, and Westcott may have especially encouraged Episcopalian Social Christians in the United States and perhaps induced some, such as Richard Ely, W.D.P. Bliss, F. D. Huntington, and Elisha Mulford to become Episcopalians, their influence was not confined to the Episcopal Church. As Washington Gladden, a Congregationalist, and for many the father of the American Social Gospel, said of Maurice: "Thy gentleness hath made me great."[58] Interdenominational exchange of ideas was also quite common, as revealed in the correspondence between the Boston Episcopalian Phillips Brooks and Washington Gladden.[59] The Nonconformist Christian Socialists were equally well received in the United States. Given the dearth of good American theologians, writings by figures such as A. M. Fairbairn and R. J. Campbell were most welcome, often reinforcing indigenous liberal theology in the process.

Paralleling the establishment of national denominational organizations such as church congresses to discuss social policy, which often derived from the writings of these eminent British figures, was the development of international church gatherings. In reality, of course, they were primarily meetings of British and American church leaders. Anglicans met at the Lambeth Conferences after 1888, and at such events as the Pan-Anglican Congress of 1908; Methodists gathered at their ecumenical conferences every ten years beginning in 1881; Congregationalists established an International Council; and the Baptists gathered at meetings of the their World Congress. Such gatherings brought together major religious figures in the English-speaking world on a more regular basis than speaking tours or extraordinary events such as the Chicago World's Parliament of Religions in 1893. Invariably Social Christians had much to say to each other at these meetings or in affiliated international conferences such as those of the Methodist Epworth Leagues. At the Baptist Congress meeting in Philadelphia in 1911, for example, Shailer Mathews and Walter Rauschenbusch presented papers on the salvation of society and the social crisis, and Britain's John Clifford delivered the keynote presidential address on the Social Gospel

57. Hutchison, "The Americanness of the Social Gospel," 375, 377–78.

58. Quoting Ps. 18:35 in "Frederick Denison Maurice," 15 January 1888, sermon no. 3231, introduction, "Sermons and Lectures, 1887–October 1888," boxes 34–36 (microfilm roll 20), Washington Gladden Papers, Ohio Historical Society.

59. Brooks's papers include letter exchanges not only with Washington Gladden but also with Francis Greenwood Peabody, Lyman Abbott, and others. Phillips Brooks Papers, Houghton Library, Harvard University.

**Civic Reception to Delegates to Ecumenical Conference**

The Methodist Ecumenical Conference, Toronto, 1911. This gathering was very similar to others sponsored by the major churches at regular intervals. Held at different locations on both sides of the Atlantic, the conferences were convenient occasions on which British, American, and Canadian church leaders, including Social Christians, could exchange ideas face to face.

and the necessity of "brotherhood" in dealing with the enormous social problems of the age.[60]

With regard to the general direction of social thought, the New York pastor Frank Mason North said of Britain's Hugh Price Hughes and the Forward Movement: "Mr. Hughes believes with all his soul, as did Oliver Cromwell—and as did our Pilgrim Fathers that the principles of Christianity must be applied to society as to the individual and that Jesus Christ came into the world not merely to 'save men' and get them to heaven but to reconstruct society on a Christian basis."[61] Beyond those basic notions so readily received from their British mentors, the early American Social Gospelers such as Washington Gladden and Josiah Strong added little but the advice that applied Christianity de-emphasize but not abandon the finer points of theological argumentation. That was an approach echoed by a host of younger Social Gospelers in the United States and Canada for decades to come.

60. Record of proceedings, Baptist World Alliance, 2d Congress, Philadelphia, 19–25 June 1911, Baptist Union Library, London, and *Baptist Times and Freeman,* 23 June 1911.

61. "Forward Movement: Its Spirit, Method and Scope," November 1893, 8, box "The City," Frank Mason North Papers, Archives and History Center of the United Methodist Church, Drew University.

Aside from the unusually strong influence of Mazzini, as well as Comte,[62] the only other Continental Europeans to exert significant influence upon American liberal Protestants were the German philosophers and theologians. Hegel had a great influence directly and indirectly over American Christian thought, as he had over British idealism. But in addition to Hegel and his interpreters and disciples, a number of other figures assisted in the general liberal and Social Christian trends of the time. Isaac Dorner appears to have had an important midwife role in the adjustment to Darwinism at a crucial stage in the late nineteenth century.[63] It is interesting that Theodore Munger could embrace Darwin, in spite of Bushnell's reservation, through Dorner's mediating influence. Dorner also countered the disciples of David Friedrich Strauss by insisting that it was possible to verify the historical accuracy of the Bible and indeed to validate scientifically Christ's life. Dorner's main effect, however, was to reinforce the emphasis—found in Maurice, Robertson, and Bushnell—upon the Person of Christ.

As in Britain, Ritschl's thought also tended to reinforce many of the existing liberal patterns of thought correcting errors in Hegelianism in the cause of Christianity. Ritschl's pragmatism also had a special appeal for Americans. However, some have viewed this "course correction," as Hutchison has called it, as an actual revolt against prevailing liberal theological trends in the 1890s.[64] A central figure in this development was the Ritschl disciple Rudolf Lotze.[65] This philosopher rejected the determinism and rationality found in the prevailing historicism of most liberals. True history, not metaphysics, was the area in which one could seek out God's purpose. The historical Christianizing process of communities was, in fact, a part of God's being (a reminder of the pantheistic quality of much Immanentism)—the fulfillment of the Kingdom. For William

62. See Gillis J. Harp, *The Positivist Republic: Auguste Comte and the Reconstruction of American Liberalism, 1865–1920* (University Park, Pa., 1994).

63. Isaac August Dorner (1809–84) was a renowned Lutheran theologian who taught at a number of German universities, but especially at the University of Berlin after 1862. His stress upon the person of Jesus in his lectures and writings blended in well with the teachings of F. D. Maurice and F. W. Robertson, which "merely supplemented," according to William R. Hutchison, the eschatology of Bushnell and the English churchmen (*The Modernist Impulse in American Protestantism*, 87).

64. Ibid., 123.

65. Rudolf Hermann Lotze (1817–81) was professor of philosophy at the University of Göttingen and a colleague of the theologian Albrecht Ritschl. Lotze argued for the importance of an ethical approach to philosophy based upon personality; through the reality of one's own personality and ethical relationships with others, one could come to know God. According to William R. Hutchison, this personalism, especially as developed by disciples such as philosopher Borden Parker Bowne (1847–1910), led to a "social line of application" strongly supportive of the Social Gospel (*The Modernist Impulse in American Protestantism*, 126).

McGuire King such views formed part of the nascent theology of the American Social Gospel, later developed by Walter Rauschenbusch and others, that represented a fundamental break with earlier liberals.[66]

Whatever position one takes on this question, it is obvious that important developments were taking place in the first decade of the twentieth century. The Social Gospel had been established in Britain with R. J. Campbell as a major influence (see note 34). This was approximately the same time that Walter Rauschenbusch published *Christianity and the Social Crisis* (1907), urging a new ethical base of behavior for American society along collectivist lines. What is striking about both authors is that neither was really an accomplished theologian in the accepted sense of the word. Walter Rauschenbusch was by this time professor of church history at Rochester Theological Seminary. Though he had had suddenly to accept the relevance of social conditions in a sort of baptism of fire as pastor of the Second German Baptist Church in the "Hell's Kitchen" district of New York in 1886, perhaps a more significant turning point in his intellectual development was a sabbatical spent in England and Germany in 1891. In the latter country in particular he became thoroughly acquainted with the work of Ritschl and others, developing his own liberal theological views in the process. His indebtedness to the Germany of his ancestors occasionally moved him to a state of adulation that smacked of outright racism. On one occasion, addressing alumni at Rochester, he pointed to the "alien strains of blood" in American life, the French, Spanish, Slav, and Italian, as opposed to "the English blood and the German blood," which is "one blood and mixes like twin raindrops."[67] For Rauschenbusch there was no question of the special contribution of Germans to American life in general. Needless to say, this was said and written before World War I.

In *A Theology for the Social Gospel* (1917) Rauschenbusch wrote that Social Gospelers had essentially responded to societal pressures for new ethical directions in national life and that now there was an imperative to establish a doctrinal base to the ethical movement already in progress. Though the book appeared to place the cart before the horse, what it actually attempted was a clearer statement of somewhat obscured religious principles that had motivated a previous generation of American Social Christians and their allies. He went on to argue that the doctrine of the Kingdom of God entailed "the establishment

66. William McGuire King, " 'History as Revelation' in the Theology of the Social Gospel," *Harvard Theological Review* 76, no. 1 (1983): 109–29.

67. "The Contributions of Germany to the National Life of America," Alumni Oration, 1902, 9, "Biographic Family" box, Walter Rauschenbusch Papers, American Baptist Historical Society, Colgate-Rochester Divinity School.

of a community of righteousness in mankind," which was "just as much a saving act of God as the salvation of an individual." This doctrine for Rauschenbusch was "not merely ethical, but [had] a rightful place in theology."[68] According to this view, the concept moved through history and was "always both present and future,"[69] demanding a constant reconsideration of the purposes of Christ's redemptive work. Like the views of Fremantle and others, it broke down the barrier between sacred and secular for the sake of the "Christian transfiguration of the social order."[70]

In Canada theology was on the whole derivative of trends in the wider world of religious thought. But while there were no theologians of international stature, all of the churches were aware early on of transatlantic trends. Methodists were acquainted with the Forward Movement of Hugh Price Hughes, in spite of the theological conservatism of Superintendent Albert Carman.[71] Presbyterianism was affected by the Caird brothers and other Scottish sources. Some struggle did exist between the Established Church and the Free Church traditions following the Great Disruption.[72] However, the theology of the Free Church, as opposed to the idealism supported by the teachers at Queen's University, tended to dominate Canadian circles.[73] Sir George Adam Smith of Glasgow seems to have had some influence with his blend of the Higher Criticism with an almost paradoxical, renewed reverence for scripture itself.[74] British and American Social Christian writings were circulated throughout English Canada. London became a pilgrimage point for many Social Gospelers, and books written by Americans, especially Rauschenbusch, became increasingly popular. Theological schools reflected the new trends in thinking, some with increased emphasis on simply the application of the Social Gospel.[75] Wesley College (United College), Winnipeg, by the 1920s stood out as a training

68. Walter Rauschenbusch, *A Theology for the Social Gospel* (New York, 1917), 139.
69. Ibid., 140–41.
70. Ibid., 145.
71. Albert Carman last displayed his conservative, evangelical views in public by intervening in a debate titled "The Permanent Results of Biblical Criticism" at the Ecumenical Methodist Conference of 1911 in Toronto. In the eyes of the British *Methodist Recorder* (2 November 1911), "Very pathetic it was to see this veteran stand up to plead against conclusions which he deemed harmful, in the presence of an assembly which in the main accepted them." As the editor noted, in the failure of his "extreme conservatism," he was "unwillingly singing the swan song of his views."
72. See Richard Vaudry, *The Free Church in Victorian Canada, 1844–1861* (Waterloo, Ont., 1989).
73. Brian J. Fraser, *The Social Uplifters: Presbyterian Progressives and the Social Gospel in Canada, 1875–1915*, SR Supplements, vol. 20 (Waterloo, Ont., 1988), chap. 2, 23–48.
74. Ibid., 9.
75. See Michael Gauvreau, *The Evangelical Century: College and Creed in English Canada from the Great Revival to the Great Depression* (Montreal, 1991), and David Marshall, *Secularizing the Faith: Canadian Protestant Clergy and the Crisis of Belief, 1850–1940* (Toronto, 1992), 184, 187, and elsewhere.

center for Social Gospelers such as J. S. Woodsworth, Stanley Knowles, and Tommy Douglas.[76] Canada seemed quite advanced in this respect. J. Bruce Wallace of the Brotherhood Movement, on meeting a group of Queen's alumni in 1909, stated, "I fancy the Canadian colleges must be at present, in matters theological, very far ahead of the average. I thought in Canadian churches the students were being saturated with progressive teaching."[77]

Union Theological Seminary in New York had the same distinction, especially under the guidance of Henry Sloane Coffin, when it became the leading school in the cause of Social Christianity.[78] Earlier, from 1886 to 1907, Harvard had been the trendsetter; during this period, through the influence of Professor Frances Greenwood Peabody, courses in Christian social ethics were offered at both the Divinity School and Harvard College. Courses in applied Christianity, however, originated with Professor George Herron at Iowa College. Though having a strongly political aspect to them, Herron's departure from the college in 1900 did not occasion their disappearance from other schools that followed his example.[79]

In Britain the theological education of many Anglicans was influenced heavily by the disciples of Maurice and Westcott. But growing factionalism entered the picture by the end of the century. Evangelicals resisted the Social Gospel, adhering in large measure to their traditional Premillennial convictions.[80] Modernism began to emerge from the Broad Church circle with figures such as W. H. Fremantle as great transitional leaders.[81] The antipathy between

76. Ramsay Cook, "Ambiguous Heritage: Wesley College and the Social Gospel," *Manitoba History* 19 (spring 1990): 2–11.

77. J. Bruce Wallace, "Letters from Canada, II," *Brotherhood,* no. 20 (December 1909): 504.

78. See Morgan Phelps Noyes, *Henry Sloane Coffin: The Man and His Ministry* (New York, 1964), and Robert T. Handy, *A History of Union Theological Seminary in New York* (New York, 1987), esp. chap. 7.

79. Robert Michaelsen, "Religion in the Undergraduate Curriculum," in *The Making of Ministers,* ed. Keith R. Bridston and Dwight W. Culver (Minneapolis, 1964), 53–54.

80. See Kenneth Hylson-Smith, *Evangelicals in the Church of England, 1734–1984* (Edinburgh, 1989).

81. *Modernism* was a movement within both the Roman Catholic and Protestant Churches to reconcile the interpretation of traditional teachings with the new perceptions of the world emanating from the intellectual and scientific developments of the late nineteenth century. In British Protestantism the term *Modernist* was applied in particular to those associated with the Modern Churchmen's Union. With the decline of the Broad Church circle in the late Victorian period, some theological liberals found a new home in the movement. W. H. Fremantle, for example, was considered to be an early exponent of Modernism. In the interwar period Modernism was also somewhat of a reaction against Anglo-Catholicism in the Church of England. On the other hand, the social political views of many prominent Modernists, such as the Reverend William Ralph Inge (1860–1954), tended to be quite conservative. In the United States and Canada the term was used

Evangelicals, Modernists, and Anglo-Catholics began to emerge well before the war.[82] There was also the beginning of the professionalization of disciplines[83] and the marginalization of resident clergy. As F. C. Burkitt of Cambridge could write to Hastings Rashdall, Oxford's leading Modernist, on 16 December 1909: "I don't know about Oxford, but Cambridge is becoming less and less a Church 'preserve' and the Theological Faculty seem to me to have less and less weight as a body. They are simply so many individual scholars, with individual influence (or want of influence) that attaches to an individual."[84]

For British Nonconformists there were even more significant changes. The newly found, post–R. W. Dale embrace of liberal theology and social activism represented an abandonment of the old cultural separatism that had been inextricably linked to older Evangelicalism. Mark Johnson has demonstrated how the Evangelicals' most ambitious attempt to embrace the wider culture and yet preserve the Nonconformist (Congregationalist in this case) heritage in the establishment of Mansfield College, Oxford, ended in failure.[85] Yet figures at the college made important intellectual contributions in advancing theology to perhaps its outward limits.

A. M. Fairbairn's comment concerning the impact of social change on belief—"the old theology came to history through doctrine, but the new comes to doctrine through history"[86]—was extremely insightful. Mansfield College along with Manchester College (Unitarian), Oxford, had been among the first

broadly with reference to those opposed to excessively conservative evangelical or fundamentalist theological views. Although in the 1920s the term was applied widely in the United States to extreme positions held on issues of science and traditional interpretations of the Bible, it could also apply to more moderate liberal Protestant views.

82. *Anglo-Catholicism* was the conventional term used to describe the twentieth-century Anglican descendants of the Oxford Movement. The terms *Ritualism, Tractarianism,* and, of course, *High Church,* were often used imprecisely and interchangeably to identify the views of those wishing to uphold the Catholic tradition within the Church of England. Although these adherents initially chafed at the term, they tended to find it more acceptable especially after the inception of Anglo-Catholic congresses in the 1920s. Their most outstanding figure was Charles Gore (1853–1932), noted theologian, founder of the Community of the Resurrection, and variously bishop of Worcester, first bishop of Birmingham, and bishop of Oxford. On the question of terminology and other matters pertaining to Anglo-Catholicism, see William S. F. Pickering, *Anglo-Catholicism: A Study in Religious Ambiguity* (London, 1989). For an assessment of Anglo-Catholics' role at the time of their greatest influence in British Social Christianity, see Willem Adolph Visser 't Hooft, *Anglo-Catholicism and Orthodoxy: A Protestant View* (London, 1933).

83. See Thomas W. Heyck, *The Transformation of Intellectual Life in Victorian England* (London, 1982), esp. chap. 6.

84. Burkitt to Rashdall, 16 December 1909, MSS English letters, d. 371, f. 203, Hastings Rashdall Letters and Papers, Bodleian Library, Oxford University.

85. See Mark D. Johnson, *The Dissolution of Dissent, 1850–1918* (New York, 1987).

86. A. M. Fairbairn, *The Place of Christ in Modern Theology* (London, 1893), 3.

colleges to introduce the study of comparative religion into the curriculum.[87] Fairbairn was a personal friend of Max Müller, who earlier, in 1873, had published *Introduction to the Science of Religion*, perhaps the single most important text in the early history of the new discipline. Maurice, of course, had made his contribution much earlier, in 1847. With this new approach not only were other religions to be studied (which had been done before), but non-Christian movements held value on a graduated scale ending, of course, with the greatest and purest in Christianity. This historical, evolutionary study, for liberal Christians, always led to a climax in the message of Jesus. This was somewhat more advanced than the viewpoint, for example, of the Canadian George Grant, who in *The Religions of the World* (1895) argued that in the study of other religions much could be learned, though the end of this learning was ultimately to fortify the work of missionaries.[88] Far closer to Fairbairn's notion of comparative religion was the popular anthropological work *The Golden Bough*, by Sir James Frazer, which revealed a common set of myths relied upon by most world religions. It was for that reason that Frazer found it impossible to accept in 1904 Britain's first professorship of comparative religion at Manchester, since it was offered by the theology faculty.[89] The recipient, Thomas Davids, undoubtedly found it easier to accept the underlying assumption that Christianity was superior to all other religions. In time, however, in Manchester and elsewhere, the view that other religions were as good as Christianity would emerge. Liberal Protestants, of course, had believed that Christianity would always withstand the test of scientific scrutiny. For Social Christians, Christianity could also fit into the vision of a Divine Immanence at work in the world. But nonbelievers could study religion, even Christianity, as they would any academic subject. By the interwar years departments of religious studies would appear in many universities, religious and secular, on both sides of the Atlantic. Unfortunately, comparative religion had by then experienced problems as a discipline both in itself and in the esteem of some Social Christians.

Around the time of the First World War many Social Christians had come to desire the reattachment of social activism to well-articulated theological principles. In Britain such a reattachment was conceivable given the strong association

87. See Arthur J. Long, "The Life and Work of J. Estlin Carpenter," in *Truth, Liberty, Religion: Essays Celebrating Two Hundred Years of Manchester College*, ed. Barbara Smith (Oxford, 1986), 265–89.

88. Marshall, *Secularizing the Faith*, 104–5.

89. See Eric J. Sharpe, *Comparative Religion at the University of Manchester, 1904–1979* (Manchester, 1980), 50–52.

of Anglo-Catholicism with Christian Socialism. But it was not clear that any theology would be acceptable to all Social Christians. It had always been possible to advocate some radical proposals while even being a theological conservative, as in the case of Canada's Albert Carman. In Canada, historian Phyllis D. Airhart, using W. R. Hutchison's rather strict definition of a Social Gospeler, raises the question whether only a handful of prewar Canadian Methodists could be so designated because so few would exchange individual salvation for salvation of the social order.[90] Canada could certainly initiate social reform movements along quite radical lines. Ways of categorizing people abounded then and now. Gladden and even Rauschenbusch have been termed liberal Evangelicals in their belief that individual salvation still had its place in the scheme of things. "Progressive Orthodoxy" was used by Andover intellectuals to justify their new theological positions.[91] In Britain the New Theology or the more mainstream Social Gospel of Westcott and Hughes increasingly held sway in most church leadership circles, but their unity of ideas had yet to be thoroughly tested by the hostility of other Christians or by growing indifference to religion itself. As Hastings Rashdall reflected in an 1899 essay, "theological reconstruction seems to me the most important intellectual task of our day."[92]

There is no question that the theological ideas associated with Social Christianity became increasingly diverse by the early twentieth century. Yet continuities persisted. Social policy remained wedded to the idea that it was ethically necessary to realize the ideals of the Brotherhood of Humanity. Immanentism—and, for many, Incarnationism—constantly resurfaced in this concept of God's earthly Kingdom of social righteousness. Such ideas remained at the core of the religious thought of Social Christians regardless of their other theological persuasions.

The absence of a detailed, officially accepted theology of Social Christianity or of the Social Gospel, despite the efforts of figures like Rauschenbusch, explains why the 1928 publication of *The Background of the Social Gospel in America*, by Visser 't Hooft, created so much more confusion than it should have. Visser 't Hooft was a respected Dutch Protestant theologian and future general secretary of the World Council of Churches who developed long-lasting friendships with such prominent Social Christian figures as William Temple and

90. Phyllis D. Airhart, *Serving the Present Age: Revivalism, Progressivism, and the Methodist Tradition in Canada* (Montreal, 1992), 104–5. Airhart seems to move in the direction of Michael Gauvreau on this question. See note 21 to the Introduction.

91. Editors of *The Andover Review, Progressive Orthodoxy: A Contribution to the Christian Interpretation of Christian Doctrines* (Boston, 1885; reprint, Hicksville, N.Y., 1975).

92. "The Oxford Movement," p. 18, Lectures box, Hastings Rashdall Papers, Pusey House, Oxford University.

Reinhold Niebuhr. His depiction of the Social Gospel as a uniquely American phenomenon, and indeed as virtually synonymous with Protestantism in the United States, was certainly a disservice to history. While acknowledging that some European thinkers had had influence, Visser 't Hooft argued before his fellow Europeans that the American Social Gospel arose primarily out of indigenous roots from the Pilgrim Fathers onward. As he stated: "The process of moralization which we have already seen at work in [Jonathan] Edwards and later in revivalism takes the form of a subordination or complete suppression of the notion of God's Sovereignty in the interests of his love and benevolence for humanity. This tendency is by no means the monopoly of social gospel theology. It is a general characteristic of all modern theology in America."[93]

Visser 't Hooft was correct in perceiving an American emphasis upon "the moral power which is potentially given in every individual" to build a Kingdom of God in existing circumstances.[94] A fusion of positive attitudes toward Liberalism with a strong belief in the Divine Immanence was undoubtedly an encouragement to both British and German theological liberals so disheartened by the Great War and the decline of their political counterparts. In his discussion Visser 't Hooft also found certain Positivistic tendencies in the American Social Gospel, indicated in the writings of figures such as Rauschenbusch, who, in blending religion and ethics, also blended God with humanity.[95] Often there was also the fusion of religious and cultural values in the American passion for democracy.[96] Visser 't Hooft saw some of these tendencies as a drawback to the American message, though he felt that the majority would adhere to an "objective existence of God" along with a "humanizing theology."[97]

Perhaps Visser 't Hooft's most valuable insight concerned the concept of God held by American Social Gospelers and the distorted European view thereof. As he stated:

> Some would say that it is impossible to define this relationship because of the largely untheological and often anti-theological character of the movement. In fact a number of advocates of the Social Gospel have written as if they were proud of having no theology at all. But there are others who have seen the need for constructive theological work. There is however no really fundamental difference between these two

93. Willem Adolph Visser 't Hooft, *The Background of the Social Gospel in America* (Haarlem, 1928), 174.
94. Ibid., 182.
95. Ibid., 177.
96. Ibid., 186, 177.
97. Ibid., 186.

groups for both possess a theology. In the first case one must read it between the lines. In the second it is clearly formulated.[98]

While noting some vagaries of Social Gospel theology, those within the movement who professed to have no interest in theology, and the creeping inroads of Comtean Positivism and American Progressivism, Visser 't Hooft still viewed the movement as an essentially religious one, and therefore as bearing a relationship to theological principles. The issue of resisting secularization was present but was not new, having been addressed as early as the 1880s by Theodore Munger.[99]

Certainly by the 1920s, Social Gospelers in North America tended to veer away from the discipline of theology in its formal sense. Formal theology presented an "image problem" for the Social Gospelers, who wanted to avoid any semblance of separating the movement from the general public. Charles Stelzle, long before the 1920s, had made a point of not using formal theological argumentation, especially when addressing the public. S. D. Chown, the Canadian Methodist, did much the same and at about the same time. Henry Carter in Britain also worried about the effects of the New Theology controversy on churchgoers.[100]

Yet the interwar period brought to Social Gospel circles new problems along many lines, some related to theology or the lack of it. In Britain, perhaps inspired by Rashdall's late promptings that work in theology was of the greatest necessity, new formulations began to emerge, but from very different directions. Evangelicalism within the Established Church, on the defensive against the inroads of Anglo-Catholicism as well as liberal theology, fell to a low point in the interwar period.[101] In any case Anglo-Catholics were considered the main supporters of Christian Socialism.

Through this period, many Modernists also engaged in conflict with Anglo-Catholics but, unlike Evangelicals, had a history of involvement, albeit through its Broad Church roots, with Christian Socialism. The progress of Modernism was to have a largely complicating, disruptive impact on Social Christianity by the interwar period.

Modernism can be traced to a variety of sources. In a sense any religious thinker who linked God to modern culture, who stressed God's immanence through new, positive intellectual and social developments, was a Modernist. But the movement did more than simply emphasize the use of particular language; it embraced the desire to alter thinking on social and ethical issues

98. Ibid., 172.

99. See Hutchison, "The Americanness of the Social Gospel," 373.

100. Henry Carter, *The Church and the New Age* (London, 1911), pt. 2, chap. 3, 102.

101. See Randle Manwaring, *From Controversy to Co-existence: Evangelicals in the Church of England, 1914–1980* (Cambridge, 1984).

based upon the latest intellectual currents. Such thinking characterized Non-conformists such as R. J. Campbell and A. M. Fairbairn as well as Broad Church Anglicans or Americans such as Horace Bushnell and Theodore Munger, not to mention the Roman Catholic Modernists. Though the official beginnings of the non-Roman Catholic Modernist movement in Britain can be dated from the foundation of the Modern Churchmen's Union in 1898, the movement came to full bloom in the 1920s. Its leading figures, both Anglicans, were Hastings Rashdall and William Ralph Inge.

Hastings Rashdall, fellow of New College, Oxford, and later dean of Carlisle, was an accomplished writer on subjects such as the Incarnation, winning considerable support for his views especially among "liberal" Anglicans. Cecil Torr of Devon, writing in the 1920s, could recall how his youthful days had been dominated by the "Harrow generation" of Rashdall and Charles Gore—"our most learned and original theologians."[102] In spite of agreements over areas of social policy within the CSU, however, Gore, the patriarch of Anglo-Catholicism, and Rashdall were obviously miles apart theologically.[103]

Rashdall's writings embraced a variety of subjects, for he was principally an ethical philosopher, with an interest in history. His theological Liberalism, however, was clear in *Doctrine and Development* (1917) and especially in his paper "Christ as Logos and Son of God," presented at the Modern Churchmen's conference held at Girton College, Cambridge, in August 1921. The Girton Conference was important because it led to the formation of the Church of England Commission on Doctrine as well as an open rift between liberal Protestants and Anglo-Catholics with Modernist tendencies.[104] Rashdall, former president of the Modern Churchmen's Union, was accused of denying the divinity of Christ. A 1921 press cutting from Rashdall's papers summed up the situation:

> The scandal said to have been given by the Cambridge Conference is not, and never was, a genuine scandal; it was engineered by sectarian agitators, and has been kept alive, with difficulty, for sectarian ends. The lay mind is frankly not interested in the questions raised, judging rightly that they have little connection either with religion or reason; theologians raise a dust and then complain that they cannot see. If the

102. Torr to Rashdall, Easterday 1923, MSS English Letters, d. 362, f. 89, Rashdall Papers, Bodleian.

103. Gore, of course, did not believe that a social conscience preceded religious conviction. See Boyd Hilton, *The Age of Atonement: The Influence of Evangelicalism on Social and Economic Thought, 1795–1865* (Oxford, 1988), 278.

104. See Alan M. G. Stephenson, *The Rise and Decline of English Modernism: The Hulsean Lectures, 1979–80* (London, 1984), chaps. 6 and 7.

average churchgoer is startled by some of the Dean's statements, it is because popular piety has fallen out of touch with its formal standards. Nothing, in fact, is as unorthodox as orthodoxy; a popular religion, says Cardinal Newman, is always corrupt.[105]

W. R. Inge succeeded Rashdall as the leading Modernist, following the latter's death in 1924. In departing from the CSU many years earlier, Inge had also ceased to support the concepts of Social Christianity. He was an Eton and Cambridge man who had been influenced by the Tractarians in his youth. As he moved toward Modernism, his career advanced; he became Lady Margaret Professor of Divinity at Cambridge in 1907 and dean of St. Paul's in 1911. His 1899 Bampton lectures on Christian mysticism established him as a leading religious thinker and Cambridge Platonist. Paul Crook has suggested that Inge emphasized "a supra-temporal" idea of spiritual progress, injecting a more complicated variant into old-style liberal notions.[106] Writing to Rashdall from Cambridge in 1909, Inge made it clear he viewed himself as engaged in the struggle with the Anglo-Catholics, a struggle that could produce odd alliances: "I am working mainly with the Evangelicals here. If they can tolerate my Liberalism I am well content with their company. The ECU [English Church Union] party are laying siege to Cambridge with extreme vigor, and our good folk are so simple that they are easily captured."[107]

In fact, a mingling of Modernists and Evangelicals could be found in the Oxford Group Movement. Its conspicuous abandonment of pure theological utterances and its popular enthusiasm appealed to both groups. But it was ultimately rejected by Evangelicals who were conservative theologically.[108] Politically and socially the Oxford Group Movement tended to be conservative by default, which was similar to the orientation of Modernists such as Inge and even more so Percy Gardner, Disney Professor of Archaeology at Cambridge and president of the Churchmen's Union (1915–22), who started out under the influence of Comte and Maurice but eventually ended in staunch conservatism. According to Alan M. G. Stephenson, the Modernists, unlike the Social Gospelers, did not believe in a "this-worldly Utopia."[109]

105. *Spectator,* 27 August 1921.

106. Paul Crook, "W. R. Inge and Cultural Crisis, 1899–1920," *Journal of Religious History* 16, no. 4 (1991): 410–32.

107. Inge to Rashdall, 19 November 1909, MSS English Letters, d. 361, f. 163, Rashdall Papers, Bodleian.

108. See David W. Bebbington, "Oxford Group Movement Between the Wars," *Studies in Church History* 23 (1986): 495–507.

109. Stephenson, *The Rise and Decline of English Modernism,* 8–9.

Not all prominent Modernists took this path, however. One Anglo-Catholic who continued to be called a Modernist, Canon Alfred L. Lilley, contributed regularly to *The Pilgrim* and *Christendom* into the 1930s. For Lilley the fusion of modern idiom, Anglo-Catholicism, and Social Christianity worked. As he stated in a 1935 manuscript for *Christendom*: "It is called, Divinely called, to study the forces which operate in the life of the world and the laws under which they operate. But if it is to translate the results of its study into really beneficent and redemptive action, it must first have learned from ascetic theology, from a study of the method and laws of Christian perfection, how also to set loose to the world which it would influence and subdue."[110] Some liberal Protestants within the Modernist camp also continued the old alliance with Christian Socialism, as did Charles Raven, Regius Professor of Divinity at Cambridge.[111]

Nonconformist circles in Britain tended not to be as deeply divided over issues of Modernism; and compared with denominations in the United States, those in Britain argued less stridently over these issues. Fundamentalism did appear in the interwar period but did not take substantially from older conservative Evangelicalism.[112] Modernist issues had arisen, of course, as when in 1913 charges were laid against George Jackson in the Methodist Church. But the momentum for liberal theology linked with Social Christianity continued with such organizations as the Fellowship of the Kingdom (founded 1917) and leaders such as Scott Lidgett, who continued to write supportive Social Gospel theological works. The Baptist Church leadership and journals also took an increasingly liberal line of thinking. Among Congregationalists, Mansfield College provided general theological guidance to the Social Gospel through such organizations as the Minor Prophets Society.[113] The Oxford Group Movement may have held conservative Evangelicals and liberals together for a brief period.

Modernism in the United States was more disruptive. Hastings Rashdall had his American followers,[114] but it was Shailer Mathews who made the most

110. "The Catholic Doctrine of the World," 25, 5, 1935, 27, MS 30888, Papers of the Reverend Alfred L. Lilley, St. Andrews University Library.

111. Raven disliked some of the close ancestors of Anglo-Catholicism for not giving support to the original Broad Church Christian Socialists. See Charles E. Raven, *Christian Socialism, 1848–1854* (London, 1920).

112. Bebbington, *Evangelicalism in Modern Britain,* 217–28.

113. In 1899 W. B. Selbie, Silvester Horne, T. H. Darlow, and W. H. Bennett founded the Minor Prophets Society at Mansfield to revitalize Congregationalism, especially for the benefit of youth. Its membership at various points included W. J. Dawson (see Chapter 4), A. E. Garvie, P. T. Forsyth, and R. J. Campbell. Theology, social questions and politics were regularly discussed. Minute books until 1911 survive. Later, in the 1930s, the Fairbairn Society did much the same things.

114. Edward S. Parsons in a letter to Rashdall, 21 March 1923, reported on a Modern Churchmen's Union being founded in the United States. MSS English Letters, d. 362, f. 87, Rashdall Papers, Bodleian.

important contributions to Modernism in the service of the Social Gospel. Upon publication of Mathews's *Church and the Changing Order* (1907), in the same year that Rauschenbusch produced *Christianity and the Social Crisis*, those committed to the social sciences hailed Mathews as placing the Social Gospel on a firm scientific footing, a characteristic Visser 't Hooft later ascribed to the American Social Gospel as a whole.[115] As dean of the University of Chicago Divinity School, Mathews had important connections with progressive Christians who were accomplished social scientists, such as Graham Taylor. Kenneth Smith and Leonard Sweet place Shailer Mathews at the head of the Corpus Christi Club in Chicago, which devoted itself to the scientific study of religion and was "more liberal in terms of its theology and more conservative in terms of its politico-economic program" than Richard T. Ely or the Baptist Brotherhood of the Kingdom led by figures such as Rauschenbusch.[116]

Other individuals, such as A. C. McGiffert at Union Theological Seminary, had undoubtedly, under the influence of German mentors, including Adolph Harnack, made a commitment to "scientific" history and with it some deemphasis of the divinity of Christ and reemphasis of service to humanity.[117] But Mathews held the greatest attention, especially after the publication of *The Faith of Modernism* (1924). His desire to recast Christianity in more modern metaphors incurred the harshest reactions from fundamentalists. However, his desire for social harmony through the message of the Social Gospel was quite an old line, very reminiscent of the social thought of F. D. Maurice.

Others who strongly advanced the inclusion of Modernism in education found that the defense of theology was at stake. Under the influence of John Dewey's instrumentalism, a strong antitheological bias prevailed in the education field. Stressing a secular experimentalism, courses were to be focused on societal issues, and in that context values would emerge. This influence was noticeable in the area of religious education training, which expanded from the 1920s onward, and was enhanced when schools of religion were established in state universities at the urging of Professor Charles Foster Kent of Yale.

The importance of George Coe in the field of religious education in many ways paralleled that of Dewey in the field of public education. Of Methodist background, trained in theology and then philosophy in Germany, Coe began his teaching career as a philosopher of religion at the University of Southern

---

115. Visser 't Hooft, *Background of the Social Gospel*, 149–51.

116. Kenneth Smith and Leonard I. Sweet, "Shailer Mathews: A Chapter in the Social Gospel Movement, Part II," *Foundations: A Baptist Journal of History and Theology* 19, no. 1 (1976): 220.

117. For Harnack's influence on American liberals, see Hutchison, *The Modernist Impulse*, 129–32. For McGiffert, see Handy, *History of Union Theological Seminary*, 144–57.

California and then moved on to Northwestern University. In *Religion of a Mature Mind* (1902) he argued that the study of religion should be rooted in the social sciences, very much a Modernist line. He moved rapidly toward the application of psychology to religious education, helped to found the Religious Education Association in 1903, and assumed the professorship of religious education and the psychology of religion at Union Theological Seminary. His books *Education in Religion and Morals* (1904), *The Psychology of Religion* (1916), *A Social Theology of Religious Education* (1917), and *What Is Christian Education?* (1929) not only made him a leading authority in the field but also powerfully advanced the notion that religion is something that emerges when all values and modern ideas have been empirically explored. His advocacy of the Social Gospel within and beyond traditional church structure was vigorous.

Yet even at this stage in his career theology did not become totally irrelevant. In a response to an interesting letter from the Reverend George Gibson of Hyde Park, Illinois, Coe made the following observation: "Your remark about the lack of systematic theology on the part of religious educators and 'social gospellers' (Why the epithet?) I could readily assent to if I could suppose that the term 'theology' means to you what I wish it meant to all of us. Here is another term that needs to be used with extreme caution. I should like to think of theology as any reflection and discourse with respect to God."[118]

Perhaps understandably, given the vagueness of such "theology," enthusiasm among Americans for the Social Gospel approach had begun to wane by the late 1930s. Neoorthodoxy emerged on both sides of the Atlantic in the 1920s and 1930s, led by the German Karl Barth and the American Reinhold Niebuhr. Both theologians' work represented reactions against Liberalism and Modernism, seeking a return to more traditional Protestant theology as a way of giving renewed direction to enterprises for social justice. Barth, according to Joseph Betts, was perhaps more profound than Niebuhr in attacking the empirical theories of human nature that were at the base of the extreme liberal viewpoint.[119]

Niebuhr, who had much more impact on the North American and British reading public, concentrated on the visible tip of the iceberg with his famous *Moral Man and Immoral Society* (1932), attacking extreme liberals and using such terms as *Marxist Christian* to describe his galvanized social activism based upon a more traditional Christian need for justice. Richard Wrightman Fox, however, has demonstrated that Reinhold Niebuhr remained essentially a

---

118. Coe to Gibson, 24 June 1939, box 2, folder 12, George Coe Papers, MS Group 36, Yale Divinity School Library.

119. Joseph Betts, "Theology and Politics: Karl Barth and Reinhold Niebuhr on Social Ethics After Liberalism," *Religion in Life* 48, no. 1 (1979): 53–62.

liberal in such works as *The Nature and Destiny of Man* (1941).[120] Rejecting his earlier, naïve, utopian quest for the Kingdom on earth, Niebuhr embraced more traditional theology in an imperfectible world. His thought was still part of the liberal tradition and included some acceptance of Dewey's social science approaches in spite of his sharp criticisms of them.[121] But a letter to Britain's Joseph H. Oldham revealed great reservations about social scientists' fundamental approach: "The Church must certainly use the most adequate social techniques, and it can also learn social wisdom from the social scientists on particular issues. But are not the social scientists wrong in their approach to existential issues?" For Niebuhr, in seeking the Social Gospel's objective of ending the power of special interests "we must not merely plead that the redeemed soul must avail itself of the best social wisdom, but that a genuine conversion of heart is necessary to break the relationship with past privilege and prestige."[122] Niebuhr, ironically, became a prophet primarily to the intellectual and politically influential in American society. In general, the core religious concepts of the Fatherhood of God and the Brotherhood of Humanity remained intact through all the anguish over theology in the period, continuing to inform the general direction of social thought.

In Canada the struggles over Modernism were not as conspicuous. Though charges of heresy were hurled against liberals, the brisk advance of church union among Methodists and eventually among Methodists, Congregationalists, and some Presbyterians to form the United Church of Canada in the 1920s required doctrinal accommodation. For all his rantings against the Higher Criticism, evolutionists, and the like, Albert Carman, first general superintendent of the unified Methodist Church, Canada's largest Protestant denomination, did not stand in the way of these developments. Therefore the transition early in the twentieth century to a new chief superintendent, S. D. Chown, who was overtly in the Social Gospel mold, did not bring an abrupt change in the direction of church policy. While holding out hope, at least to the end of the First World War, for the radical wing of the Social Gospel, S. D. Chown managed to steer the mainstream of the clergy and laity to a reconciliation between the old articles of evangelical faith with newer intellectual ideas that had emerged in the late nineteenth century.

120. Richard Wrightman Fox, "The Niebuhr Brothers and the Liberal Protestant Heritage," in *Religion and Twentieth-Century American Intellectual Life,* ed. Michael J. Lacey (Cambridge, 1989), 94–115.

121. See Bruce Kuklick, "John Dewey, American Theology, and Scientific Politics," in *Religion and Twentieth-Century American Intellectual Life,* 92–93.

122. Niebuhr to Oldham, 29 September 1947, container 10, general correspondence, Reinhold Niebuhr Papers, Library of Congress.

Ironically Chown had been helped by the social policies of his predecessor, Albert Carman. Carman's attacks upon plutocratic influence in the church, coupled with his own theological conservatism, dispelled any automatic identification in the public mind, and in particular in the minds of the affluent, between liberal theology and social radicalism, at least insofar as church leadership was concerned.[123] Upper-middle-class opinion had been divided on issues of theology, especially in Carman's era, with many supporting Modernist heretics. The discomfort expressed in British and American literature (see Chapter 4) concerning the hostility of wealthy members of congregations to the Social Gospel was not so clear.

There was an ever-present danger of Social Christianity's progress being halted in its tracks, of course. This is more or less what happened in Scotland by 1930, when a conservative, middle-class element triumphed after Presbyterian Church union had been achieved.[124] Nevertheless, it could also be argued in that case that a weak theological base to Christian Socialism had contributed to a recapture of the church by a stronger, traditional group of Evangelicals.[125]

Chown in fact spoke out against strict theological conservatism, or "judge-made law," in the church.[126] At the same time, he muddied the waters by moving somewhat away from theology itself, likening theology in religion to what "grammar is to speech," adding that "though we may not know much about grammar we may yet make ourselves fairly well understood in connection with the ordinary things of life."[127] This was certainly the style of an administrator interested in internal cohesion at a time when the potential for all-out war between older Evangelicals and Modernists was possible. In relation to the latter group Chown once stated: "The opposition to modernism within the Church of Rome is not directed against scientific investigation in itself. It operates only when investigation trenches upon the proclaimed dogmas of the Church. If true to itself, Protestantism will not erect such compartments in the human mind, and it would be fatal for Methodism to attempt. Protestantism is a

123. Ramsay Cook, *The Regenerators: Social Criticism in Late Victorian Canada* (Toronto, 1985), 192.

124. See Stewart J. Brown, "The Social Vision of Scottish Presbyterianism and the Union of 1929," *Records of the Scottish Church History Society* 24 (1990): 76–96.

125. See Donald C. Smith, *Obedience and Prophetic Protest: Social Criticism in the Scottish Church, 1830–1945* (New York, 1987). This is not to say that a Social Christian conscience had not been developed by 1900. See Donald J. Withrington, "The Churches in Scotland, c. 1870-c. 1900: Towards a New Social Conscience?" *Records of the Scottish Church History Society* 19 (1977): 155–68.

126. Sermon, "Holiness. Series IV. The Very God of Peace sanctify you wholly," n.d., p. 4, box 5, S. D. Chown Papers, United Church Archives.

127. Sermon, "That they all may be one," January 1912, 6, box 7, Chown Papers.

movement for intellectual freedom and general progress."[128] By appealing in the name of Protestant freedom for understanding, Chown was able to contain the wrath of old Evangelicals.

In fact, no strong fundamentalist movement appeared within the mainline churches in the American style, and smaller churches led by charismatic individuals and caught up in new fads proliferated less in Canada. In the post–World War I years the danger of secessionist, ideologically charged church movements came more from the radical wing of the Social Gospelers and took the form of such developments as the People's Churches led by William Ivens and James Shaver Woodsworth. Salem Bland, the venerable Social Gospeler, published a book entitled *The New Christianity* in 1920, in which he announced his belief that a new religion must emerge from the ashes of capitalism and the old-style churches. A fusion of what he called American Christianity (out of the additional ashes of Protestantism) and Labour Christianity, Great Christianity would be the ultimate expression of social solidarity. The accompanying new social order would choose its own "saints" (suggested figures included Francis of Assisi, John Wesley, and General William Booth) in the pursuit of its ecumenical, democratic ideals. One can only imagine what theology would mean under these circumstances.

Moderate Social Gospelers prevailed in the leadership circles of the Methodist and Presbyterian churches, and their liberal theology continued into the United Church after 1925. Social service continued to occupy the attention of former Methodist and Presbyterian leaders in the new church, and this, together with the ongoing ecumenical quest for unity without and within, made ambitious classifications of theology inappropriate. Michael Gauvreau has argued that beneath the surface a more serious wave of uncertainty gripped Canadian Protestant theology in the ten years or so before World War I, an uncertainty that was "less noisy" than the old divisions between liberal and conservative, but more deadly. A crisis of confidence arose similar to situations in Britain and the United States, linked with the impact of Modernism. Gauvreau, like George Marsden for the United States, emphasizes the internal intellectual tensions creating the core of the difficulty. Historical relativism, among other things, then formed a wedge between the pulpit and the lectern.[129] Gauvreau sees much of this as the basis of the uncertain 1920s. Later, in an attempt to deal with the dilemmas of the earlier period, the Reverend Richard Roberts created a dualistic theology of transcendence and Immanence,

---

128. "Adaptation of Church to Modern Life," 1911, p. 6, box 1, Chown Papers.
129. Gauvreau, *Evangelical Century,* 220–22.

a theology of dynamic tension, for the United Church of the 1930s.[130] A more understandable reaction was that of the aged Social Gospeler S. D. Chown in his *Some Causes of the Decline of the Earlier Typical Evangelism* (1930), which lamented the abandonment of older theological tenets, an abandonment Chown had aided and abetted.

In spite of an initially favorable reception, the Oxford Group Movement proved to be unhelpful in bringing factions together.[131] It was divisive in the eyes of some Social Gospelers, "giving up secular concerns entirely for new forms of evangelism," according to historian Donald Creighton in a recollection of his own father's opposition to it.[132]

In Britain, perhaps because of the relatively greater physical and psychological impact of the Great War than in Canada, the disillusionment that bred the demise of political liberalism also made the country open to the ideas of neoorthodoxy. Karl Barth was popular but went too far in emphasizing the dark side of human nature. Niebuhr was very popular. But developments peculiar to the country, already in progress before the war, now took center stage.

Though many of Anglo-Catholicism's leading lights, such as Stewart Headlam and Scott Holland, had died by the end of the war, Charles Gore emerged a theologian of eminent stature who was attached to the cause of Christian Socialism based solidly upon Incarnationism. Since *Lux Mundi* Gore had acted as a beacon to High Churchmen coming to terms with the realities of modernity. As the unsympathetic Hensley Henson described it, "Gore's subtle and courageous intellect had imagined the possibility of saving Tractarianism by a process analogous to inoculation. A mild installment of Modernism would avert the fatal malady."[133] Yet in the period after 1914 Gore would cautiously remind High Churchmen of their traditional beliefs (including miracles), especially in his final great work, *The Reconstruction of Belief* (1921–22). Anglo-Catholics such as J. N. Figgis, as well as supporting socialism, also pointed Christians once again toward the view that God's church is a supernatural institution.[134] The Community of the Resurrection, founded by Gore in Mirfield, Yorkshire, became the center of a revived sacramental, organic view of society.

130. Ibid., 266–67.

131. See Marshall, *Secularizing the Faith,* 213–27.

132. Donald Creighton, "My Father and the United Church," in *The Passionate Observer: Selected Writings* (Toronto, 1980), 98.

133. Hensley Henson, *Retrospect of an Unimportant Life* (London, 1942), 156.

134. "In Returning and Rest Shall Ye Be Saved," bundle no. 27, p. 3, Papers and Sermons 2, J. N. Figgis Papers, Papers of the Community of the Resurrection, Mirfield, deposit 9, Borthwick Institute, York.

Though Mirfield residents in the 1920s devoted considerable theological energies toward dialogue with the Roman Catholic Church in the Malines conversations, the Prayer Book controversy, and opposition to birth control and ordination of women, attention was also given to the continuing religious basis of social action. Lionel S. Thornton believed "the gospel includes the proclamation of a new ethical revelation which determines the character of the Christian social order."[135] The Gospel, properly interpreted, brought direction to society with the sacraments as "prophetic symbols of a transformed creation." Speaking of the overall need to blend earthly needs with the spiritual, Thornton stated:

> The secular character of our present civilization impoverishes the life of the Church by withholding the great mass of human material which underlies civilization from the intensive process of redemption. Thus the Church is called upon to bear witness to supernatural resources which remain largely intangible, vague and obscure, because they are never seen in their due concrete embodiment. It follows that the intensive process of redemption within the Church can obtain its full depth, clarity and power only in cooperation with the extensive process which seeks to leaven, and *if* need be to bring about the reconstruction of, the whole of human society. When the Convergence of these two processes reaches the point of complete mutual reinforcement, then, and not before,—Christendom will have arrived.[136]

Adrian Hastings believes that by 1900 Anglo-Catholicism was the essential inspiration behind "almost all Christian socialism" and helped to unify the somewhat disparate efforts of socialist bishops such as Gore and Frere, slum priests such as Basil Jellicoe, professional Christian social scientists such as Tawney, radical Catholic political crusader and Thaxted movement leader Conrad Noel, the members of the Industrial Christian Fellowship, and the Christian sociologists of the Christendom Movement.[137] As Lionel Thornton outlined in the quotation above, Christendom was to be achieved by a Christian sociology representing a Catholic stress upon an organic, corporate life more collectivist than Protestant individualist. Informed by belief in the Incarnation and guided by the sacraments, the church would once again spearhead the

135. "The Meaning of Christian Sociology," 20 July 1930, p. 12, MS Papers, L. S. Thornton Papers, Papers of Community of Resurrection, deposit 8.

136. Ibid., 37–38.

137. Adrian Hastings, *A History of English Christianity, 1920–1985* (London, 1986), 174–75.

quest for justice and a new order modeled somewhat upon the old order that predated the Reformation and the rise of capitalism. For members of the Christendom Movement this Christian or Catholic sociology was therefore a form of moral theology used to guide a host of activities. It drew inspiration from Gore, but its Catholicism also linked it to old Catholic theological traditions such as Thomism as well as contemporary British and Continental Roman Catholic writers. As the Christendom Movement continued into the 1930s, this Continental and Roman aspect alienated some older Anglo-Catholics such as T. S. Eliot. On the other hand, the movement also spread to American Episcopalian circles. In 1933 W. G. Peck, on tour in the United States, wrote to Maurice Reckitt, another major figure in the British movement: "I have found everywhere that the American church is waiting to drink up what we have to say."[138]

The Christendom group regarded themselves in many ways as a collection of prophets not always to be understood or followed in the short term. In writing a tribute to the Tractarian William Edmund Moll (1856–1932), the Reverend P.E.T. Widdrington recalled:

> The Church of England has never known what to do with priests who have the equipment and the call to command the principles of Catholic philosophy to those outside her borders. She mistakes the Via Media for the Via Sacra. To her all prophets, until they have been safely buried, are either cranks or fanatics. She branded Maurice as a heretic and turned him out of his chair, Headlam was banned for years, Charles Marson was left to live out his life in a remote country parish, Thomas Hancock, one of the most learned men of his time and a prophet, was never given an opportunity of putting his remarkable gifts at the service of the Church. ("What a lecturer," as Headlam said, "he would have made in a theological college!")[139]

Members of the movement vigorously explored links to Roman Catholic moral teaching, and the new stress upon the old doctrine of natural law represented a breakthrough in their thinking. The *Signposts* series of twelve paperbacks published by Dacre Press on the Anglo-Catholic design for society, launched in 1940, was one of the most ambitious undertakings of any church group in recent history. Designed to reach a general readership interested in the moral discussion of current problems, they were essentially theological works.

---

138. Peck to Reckitt, 8 November 1933, 10/17, Maurice Reckitt Papers, University of Sussex Library.
139. P.E.T. Widdrington, "A Priest in Politics: A Tribute to William Edmund Moll, 1856–1932," *Christendom* 2, no. 7 (1932): 220.

Predictably, much stress was placed on the return to traditional practices or beliefs helpful to Social Christianity, such as the Incarnation, as well as specifically Catholic theology. In number 12, *The Faith in England* (1941), A. Herbert Rees pointed to the fact that the classical Protestant concept of God could not support the "Social Gospel" (181). But he equally attacked the liberal account that reduced God to "the position of senior partner in the firm of Cosmos and Co. It is only in the Catholic doctrine of God the Blessed Trinity which receives classic expression in the first article of Religion that Christian social action can find adequate sanction" (182).

J. V. Langmead Casserley, in number 11, *Providence and History* (1940), specifically said of Modernists, "In every society there are always those who seek to recommend their faith to the world by compromising it with contemporary moral and intellectual standards" (104). For Casserley Nazism was but another form of Modernism (105).

All their works suggested that a return to the ancient articles of faith would revitalize Social Christianity. W. G. Peck, in number 10, *The Catholic Design for Society* (1940), stressed that the Catholic doctrine of original sin was a social concept, not just an individual tendency to commit sin, and was a call for social remedies (23). For the Signpost writers what was out-of-date was the attempt to bring theology up-to-date. Traditional Catholic theology had always had the answers in the first place, to their minds.

Though W. G. Peck wrote that the reception to Christendom's ideas in the United States was enthusiastic earlier in the 1930s and that with supporters such as Bishop Rhinelander the "American Church [was] ready . . . for a great and intelligent move toward a real Social Gospel," the movement had not achieved a great impact by the time *Signposts* was launched. Perhaps "Aunt" Vida Scudder perceived the problem; she surprised Peck "by saying that she thought [the Anglo-Catholic] group was becoming narrow and arrogant."[140]

In chapter 6 of *Faith and Society*, a fuller assessment of the American situation, Maurice Reckitt came to accept the assessment of Vida Scudder (herself a "Catholic" Episcopalian and socialist), that the Anglo-Catholics were "absorbed, at best in spiritual disciplines, at worst in the self-conscious display of Catholic traditions," while the "socially progressive forces" in churches were led by those who were "straight Protestants or Modernists."[141] Reckitt believed the Protestant side, "in many ways seen at its best in the Social Gospel school," was "tending to throw overboard much of its old Calvinist dogmatism" but still

---

140. Peck to Reckitt, 8 December 1932, 10/17, Reckitt Papers.
141. Maurice Reckitt, *Faith and Society* (London, 1932), 210.

retained "the tendency to identify somewhat too rashly one's own social ideals
with the ultimate purposes of God." This, Reckitt termed, was the "New
Puritanism," and it tended to be associated with a new and negative spirit of
nativist intolerance, rules, and prohibition.[142]

The Social Gospel, as a whole, whether led by Protestant Puritans or
Modernists, seemed to be concerned "not with the thought of man as a citizen
of the Kingdom of God, but with the notion of God as the inspirer of the
Kingdom of Man. It [had] evolved a doctrine of God almost purely instrumental
to human ideals, or, to quote the title of one of its most authoritative sources
[Rauschenbusch], 'a theology *for* the social gospel.' " Reckitt indeed believed
that the American Social Gospel, "however great the value of its social challenge, [was] nullifying the authenticity of its religious claims by preparing what
amounts to a secularization of religion from within."[143]

Reckitt's book was published the same year as Niebuhr's *Moral Man and
Immoral Society* (1932) and so would probably have had a slightly different
assessment to make of the American theological wasteland in a few years.
According to at least one historian, a theology of the Social Gospel survived
into the 1930s, but this was a self-critical decade that validated the importance
of the personality in society somewhat more clearly.[144] Such a tendency was
present at the same time in Britain in speeches and writings from Seebohm
Rowntree to William Temple. Of course, the most radical Social Christians in
America, such as George Coe, could make the question of personality seem
almost areligious: "I conclude that the rule of God take place in and through the
performance of the functions of personality wherein we are members of one
another, and that love is the revelation of God. The reasoning that culminated in
the aphorism that 'God is love' is the greatest piece of theology that I know
anything about."[145] Harry Ward and others who advocated altering religious
beliefs and behavior in the service of causes such as the Marxist *New America*
seemed to confirm R. H. Tawney's point that political arithmetic in place of
theology is the root heresy of the modern world.[146]

Back in Britain, among the ranks of the Christendom group, perhaps the
most creative, youthful figure was V. A. Demant. Like F. D. Maurice, Demant
was converted from Unitarianism to Anglicanism, also earning in the process

142. Ibid., 188–89.
143. Ibid., 187.
144. William McGuire King, "An Enthusiasm for Humanity: The Social Emphasis in Religion and
Its Accommodation in Protestant Theology," in *Religion and Twentieth-Century American Intellectual Life,* 49–77.
145. Coe to the Reverend George M. Gibson, 24 June 1939, box 2, folder 12, George Coe Papers.
146. W. G. Peck, referring to R. H. Tawney, in *Christians, Politics, and Parties* (London, 1944), 10.

the unusual distinction of having been trained first for the Unitarian ministry (Manchester College, Oxford) and then the Anglican priesthood (Ely Theological College). In the early 1920s, following ordination, he studied anthropology at Oxford; from there he went on to a series of distinguished appointments in the church and toward the end of his career became Regius Professor of Moral and Pastoral Theology at Oxford (retiring in 1971). His most vital period of creativity, in the 1930s and 1940s, was connected with the Christendom movement. Some of the impetus for his writing at this time was clearly his fear of the advance of fascism and the threat of war. This explains in part the good response to what was a fairly theoretical work, *God, Man, and Society* (1933), in which Demant wrote that the basic problem facing "a Christian's view of the priority of spiritual principles" was the movement toward an all-powerful state devoid of a religious conscience.[147] At the Malvern Conference eight years later he also added his well-known disdain for the domination of the economy by interests only governed by laws of profit, exchange, and sale, urging "the dethronement of trader man."[148] He also linked old natural theology to a new ecological attack upon the present economic system. As he stated: "The earth upon which we live is being drained of its power to support plant, animal and human life, by the breaking of its reproductive life under the spur of capitalist aggressiveness."[149]

Demant became important to a variety of Social Christians by demonstrating the necessity of a Christian sociology that would intervene as a normative and prescriptive influence, rather than one that made observations and drew conclusions with no basis in spiritual values. As the first issue of *Christendom* stated, concerning this extended moral theology: "Yet however technically unsatisfactory may be the term 'Christian Sociology,' it does, we think effectively convey the idea of the creation of a social order responsive to the demands of truth, beauty and moral perfection as revealed to mankind uniquely in Christ, and implicit—though far too little explicit—in the Catholic philosophy of the Church He established."[150]

In the 1930s and early 1940s William Temple emerged as the central ecumenical prophet of Social Christianity in Britain. A scholar trained by Edward Caird in his last period at Oxford, Temple's roots were in the idealist school and

147. V. A. Demant, *God, Man, and Society: An Introduction to Christian Sociology* (London, 1933), 115.

148. *Malvern, 1941: The Life of the Church and the Order of Society: Being the Proceedings of the Archbishop of York's Conference* (London, 1941), 137–42.

149. Ibid., 145.

150. *Christendom: A Journal of Christian Sociology* 1, no. 1 (1931): 6–7.

the Broad Church. During and after World War I he produced credible theological works such as *Mens Creatrix* and *Christus Veritas*. As time passed, his interests broadened to include social philosophy and, in particular, the ways in which the churches could actively improve social and economic conditions in society. In one sense, this change in his interests might suggest that Temple was becoming an activist public statesman for social justice (though he also had withdrawn from active membership in the Labour Party). Certain studies of Temple, especially the biography by John Kent,[151] have dwelt on this public persona, which undoubtedly was reinforced by his clear and steady elevation in the church hierarchy. Many of his actions, however, were rooted in his early identification with Incarnationism and Immanentism, the religious core of Social Christianity. His excellence as a preacher and popular figure, if anything, can distract us from his accomplishments as a theologian.

His work on behalf of ecumenism made him doctrinally cautious, of course, but he did believe it was "quite simply a movement of the Holy Spirit."[152] In his early period he displayed a Broad Church background and would have agreed with an article by Anthony C. Deane that called for a revival of Broad Churchmanship in the tradition of Maurice but avoided its past intolerance of Evangelicals and Catholics.[153] Though sometimes classified as a Modernist in the 1920s, he was much closer to his arch critic, "old latitudinarian," Hensley Henson. Henson, of course, disliked his social activism and his politic handling of different factions inside and outside the church. But this was precisely Temple's strength, which was rooted in a belief that "the great issue for religion in our day is not to be found in our differences about sacramental doctrine; it is not to be found in our disagreements about validity of ministries, it concerns faith in the living God."[154]

Temple's belief in original sin would never allow for true Modernism in his thinking. In time he drifted toward the Anglo-Catholic group, partly out of interaction with them in the service of Christian Socialism. Much to the chagrin of Henson and other critics, his popularity soared through the late 1930s and early 1940s. His *Christianity and Social Order* (1942) was published as a Penguin Special and sold very well. The fact that he was elevated to the Primacy at the same time undoubtedly added to his celebrity status and to suspicions about his

151. John Kent, *William Temple: Church, State, and Society in Britain, 1880–1950* (Cambridge, 1992).

152. William Temple, "Christian Unity: The Theological Background," *The Pilgrim* 1, no. 1 (1920): 106.

153. Anthony C. Deane, "The Need of a Broad Church Movement," *The Pilgrim* 1, no. 3 (1921): 311–18.

154. "The Majesty of God," St. Paul's Cathedral, 1930 Opening Sermon of Lambeth Conference, f. 102, vol. 68, "Sermons and Speeches 1922–41," William Temple Papers, Lambeth Palace Library.

role as a popularizer of Social Christianity. But *Christianity and Social Order* contained much theology that attempted to strike a reasonable balance between the ethical necessity to speak for social justice and the spiritual necessity to recognize the significance of the Incarnation. Temple had direct contact with Niebuhr, Visser 't Hooft, and others who showed reservations about too secular an approach by Social Christians. In concluding the main part of *Christianity and Social Order* he noted: "This book is about Christianity and the Social Order, not about Evangelism. But I should give a false impression of my own convictions if I did not here add that there is no hope of establishing a more Christian social order except through the labour and sacrifice of those in whom the spirit of Christ is active."[155]

Temple's use of the natural law as a guide for social behavior also revealed an indebtedness to Anglo-Catholics, who constituted the bulk of his Christian Socialist colleagues. As he explained, "Thus it is Natural, not a Supernatural, Order with which we are concerned; but as God is the Creator, this Natural Order is His order and its law is His law."[156]

Temple revealed further indebtedness to V. A. Demant in his mother earth arguments, blending emphasis on God the Creator and criticism of the excesses of capitalism. In yielding to criticism of Protestant individualism, Temple unfortunately, on at least one occasion, also used the line of argument from Demant (and Jacques Maritain), that Luther paved the way for Hitler by contributing to a detached and noncommittal attitude toward the state.[157] This was impolitic, given Temple's usual desire to appeal to all non-Roman elements, but it was based upon the conviction that Lutheran Reformers pushed their view of the Fall of Man to the point that they were concerned solely with the work of grace and were incapable of apprehending divine truth in the operations of a state, which was separated and invested with largely coercive power to control human passions.

In January 1941 Temple, then archbishop of York, called a conference at Malvern College to consider from the Anglican point of view "what are the fundamental facts which are directly relevant to the ordering of the new society, and how Christian thought can be shaped to play a leading part in the reconstruction."[158] While admiring the "great medieval synthesis," Temple believed scholasticism, in its narrow form, had alienated many, leading to the

---

155. William Temple, *Christianity and Social Order* (Harmondsworth, Middlesex, 1942; London, 1976), 98.
156. Ibid., 89.
157. *Malvern, 1941,* 13.
158. Malvern Conference, f. 141, vol. 33, Temple Papers.

secular humanism of the Renaissance, where ancient pagan philosophers were pressed into service without coming to terms with Divine Revelation. As he stated in this time of grave crisis during World War II:

> Political science has been worked out on a purely secular basis and has either ignored Christianity or has tried to relate it, as an afterthought, to conclusions reached independent of it. But now we find ourselves fighting for human rights and a conception of life which we have no justification except in the Christian doctrine of God and of Man. All the great political questions of our day are primarily theological; and we have not got ready to our hands the body of accepted theological doctrine vindicating the treasures of our inheritance and of pointing the defenders of these to the source from which they may draw inspiration and steadfastness.[159]

Temple's message was received very favorably in general, in a way that specifically Anglo-Catholic views were not. His theological views were broader than those of Anglo-Catholics, but even in a specific area, such as Incarnation-ism, he held views that were shared by a wide range of figures both inside and outside the Church of England.[160] In America Vida Scudder could at last report that a direction was being given to Social Christianity. As she wrote following the Malvern Conference of 1941:

> Specially welcome here in thoughtful religious circles, both within the Anglican and beyond is the emphasis in the "Malvern" documents on theology: the attempted solution of every concrete issue by principles implicit in the doctrine of "Creation, Incarnation, Redemption and Grace." Such emphasis has often been sadly lacking in the earnest and facile American Social Gospel. Our approach has been too often undifferentiated from the ethical or the humanistic.[161]

159. "Chairman's Opening Address," f. 153, vol. 33, Temple Papers.

160. See, for example, R. J. Campbell (by that time an Anglican), "The Place of the Incarnation in Modern Thought," *Report of the Church Congress, 1928*, ed. H. A. Wilson, 261–69. Campbell was then vicar of Holy Trinity Parish, Brighton. See Keith Robbins, "The Spiritual Pilgrimage of the Reverend R. J. Campbell," *Journal of Ecclesiastical History* 30, no. 2 (1979): 261–76. As an example in Nonconformity, see Dr. W. E. Orchard, minister of King's Weigh House, in "Poverty and Riches— and the Incarnation," *Crusader* 2, no. 14 (1920): 9.

161. Vida Scudder, *Echoes of the Malvern Conference from America*, pamphlet, n.d., found in file 1/7, "Individual Christian Fellowship," Papers of the Reverend Canon Stanley G. Evans, Brynmor Jones Library Archives, University of Hull.

Temple, in a Malvern speech, had actually given credit to Niebuhr's *Christianity and Power Politics* for placing God, rather than man, in the center of public affairs.[162] Niebuhr was well known and well received in Britain, and many of his arguments fused nicely with those of Temple. While in his last days Modernists, Evangelicals, and the socially indifferent in the churches were impressed with Temple's message; the general decline of the churches in public life made his message quite personalized, but when he died, so died the message.

In Britain theological consistency in service of Social Christianity had been achieved by the Anglo-Catholics in the interwar period. However, as even some within their ranks realized, they were self-absorbed in spiritual displays of Catholic traditions consistent and clearheaded but ultimately unappealing to the wider society. Modernism had been a well-thought-out set of opposing ideas and tendencies but was of little service to Social Christianity or perhaps to Christian theology. Temple represented the best attempt to supply society with a theological package which blended the best of Maurice and Oxford idealism with the best of Anglo-Catholicism. He influenced more people than any of the groups previously mentioned had, but it was not clear that his charisma necessarily flowed from the rigors of his theology.

In North America pragmatism was a stronger tradition in religious, as in secular, affairs. Liberal theology and then its various manifestations held sway over Social Christianity from the 1880s to the Second World War, assuming one accepts Niebuhr's thoughts as essentially a variant of Liberalism. It seemed to be part of the revival of Social Gospel influence in the 1930s. But increasingly Social Gospelers were also distracted by their attacks upon Protestant Premillennialism, which grew following the catastrophe of World War I, as a threat to their position within the general culture.[163]

The Social Gospel continued to be proclaimed with routine vigor from many pulpits until the Second World War. Certainly it can be argued that its message was progressively weaker in secular circles, though superficially it appeared stronger in North America than in Britain. It can also be argued that its theology did not bring people to the churches, even though those churches were better filled than in Britain. In Canada the urge to find an appropriate theological version of the Social Gospel that would capture the attention of the

162. "Chairman's Opening Address," f. 157, vol. 33, Temple Papers.

163. Paul Merkley believes that because of the decline of Progressivism the Social Gospel was by that time already part of a religious subculture. See Merkley, "The Vision of the Good Society in the Social Gospel: What, Where, and When Is the Kingdom of God?" *Historical Papers* (Ottawa, Canadian Historical Association, 1987), 138–56.

mainstream of the religious and the less-than-religious public continued. By implication the theology of the United Church of Canada, and more directly the formulations of the Federal Council of Churches to the south, by the 1930s constituted, in the mind of Maurice Reckitt, "the rejection of the eschatological element in the teaching of Christ."[164] In the eyes of the British Anglo-Catholics the North American Social Gospel had departed from the way of the Heavenly Kingdom. In the eyes of North American Social Gospelers their British cousins had concentrated too much on the City of God and had dropped out of sight. What perhaps was not sufficiently noticed was the continuity of belief in the Brotherhood of Humanity, together with the ethical imperative of its social application in the earthly Kingdom of God. Rooted in belief in the immanent, incarnate God, there was still more common ground among Social Christians in both North America and Britain than they may have realized at the time.

The degree of influence Social Christianity exerted upon the progress of social thought is always difficult to measure precisely in the complex web of interactions. Some historians have directly and indirectly raised doubts about the importance of Social Christianity in national life for both Britons and North Americans. The topical chapters that follow should rebut such skepticism.

164. Maurice B. Reckitt, *Faith and Society* (London, 1932), 187.

# 2

## REDEMPTION IN BABYLON: CITIES AND SOCIAL ILLS

Nothing was particularly new in the 1880s in the discovery that social problems were grave or that cities could be wretched places, threatening to one's moral well-being. What was alarming was the scale of these issues by this time. Whatever the historians' debate about the degree of midcentury urbanization, Britain was clearly a predominantly urban society in our terms by the 1880s, and very settled areas of North America were moving in the same direction. Socially concerned clergy and laity thought that with urbanization came the worst and most plentiful of social ills. The city had become Christianity's crisis point, or, as New York's Charles Stelzle would later call it, "Christianity's storm center." This urban fixation would bind British and North American Social Christians together in a common perspective affecting their approach to a wide range of social concerns.

The enormity of urban social problems was undoubtedly one of the factors contributing to the arousal of public angst, especially among the middle classes, at this time. This again raises the question whether the rise of Social Christianity was a reflection or an appendage of secular reformism. Certainly one cannot deny a symbiotic relationship between social conditions and thought. However, as I have shown, the tenets of Social Christian thought were laid out well before this period. Social Christian response contributed to the evolution of policies toward urban problems and complemented secular reformist thinking on the subject, though it also remained distinct from such thinking. In the response to cities and social ills rose a perspective that was to go beyond the scope of conventional Evangelicalism. The inadequacies of older evangelical efforts to improve cities and social ills, and of the outlook behind it, became painfully clear. But the new impulse was also a religious one, redefining the work of the churches based partially upon Social Christian thought and partially on the need drastically to expand the scope of pastoral activity in light of the enormous challenge of the cities.

The origins of what came to be an urban fixation in Social Christianity are quite understandable. They were religious on the whole, albeit with a considerable amount of secular prodding. In Britain, London, since at least the late seventeenth century, had acquired a notoriety for its dangerous concentration of heathenism. A century later, with the influx of unemployed refugees from the massive population increase and agrarian changes of the countryside, the situation had become that much worse. Street hawking and prostitution caught the critical eye of the religious. Such activities provided substance for Methodist and evangelical sermons against social immorality. And the civil disorder that stemmed from lax morality stirred as much concern among resident clergy as among other segments of well-to-do society. The degradation of morality and social order testified to a weakening influence of Christianity in the growing metropolis.

The onset of the Industrial Revolution, while slow in providing jobs in London, had as its principal effect the creation of a host of secondary cities that duplicated many of the social problems of the metropolis, notwithstanding the more promising picture of respectable employment. Both the Infernal Wen, as William Cobbett once called London, and the provinces would become the target of the religious forces of regeneration, even though the chance of success was better in the latter.

Urban optimism fueled some Christian leaders' initial interest in cities. Among Nonconformists the rising provincial cities had for quite some time represented possibilities of social advancement against the national hegemony of Anglicanism. Historically, Nonconformists were disproportionately numerous in trade, as they were later, as early industrialists, in both urban activities and wealth generation. Their material advantages, coupled with their political ineffectuality and concomitant desire to displace entrenched pre-reform Anglican political power in cities, propelled middle-class Nonconformists into reformist politics in the 1820s and 1830s.

The most extreme form of urban optimism could be found in the evangelical Nonconformist writer Rev. Robert Vaughan. In *The Age of Great Cities* (1843) the

Congregationalist minister argued that cities could be the great hope for a better future. Much like Andrew Ure's defense of factories, Vaughan's book portrayed cities as the setting for a general moral renewal. As he saw it, compared with town dwellers, the peasantry of England and Europe had been held down in "ignorance and wretchedness." In cities, however, he believed not only that the wealthy had become more civilized and moral, but that a trickle-down effect was soon to occur among the poor. As he stated, "[A]s men congregate in large numbers, it is inevitable that the strong should act as an impetus upon the weak."[1]

It may be said in support of Vaughan's hypothesis that wealthy city folk did contribute a considerable amount of money and time to religiously connected philanthropy. London alone had about five hundred charitable institutions at midcentury, according to the 1850 edition of Sampson Low's *Charities of London*. Indeed, they undoubtedly were an important component in the whole array of evangelical enterprises that hoped to create the necessary means by which targeted groups could receive special help in achieving individual redemption. It was recognized quite early in the century that moral reform in the city was to be assisted in a proactive way.

Churchmen also shared in this enthusiastic urban work by midcentury. Their initial interest in cities was early but was perhaps more reactive than that of Nonconformists. Given the preoccupation of many Anglicans with defending the established social order as well as the Established Church, neglect of the cities preyed on their minds. As early as the 1790s even William Cleaver, a nonresident bishop of Chester, could admonish the Church of England for its neglect of the growing towns of the Northwest.[2] Following the Napoleonic Wars there was a flurry of church building with much money invested by government and individuals in the belief that if there were more churches, more people would attend them, and better attitudes toward the political order might ensue. Increased church attendance indeed became a cause célèbre for all the churches through the first two-thirds of the nineteenth century. Here too was another form of urban optimism generating much creative thought and action in the service of a cause with unprovable assumptions. Would innovative techniques reach the unchurched? Would they then regularly attend church? Would these attenders develop better attitudes toward life in general? Certainly the emphasis upon growing numbers in urban life seemed to regenerate a

1. Robert Vaughan, *The Age of Great Cities: Or, Modern Civilization Viewed In Relation to Intelligence, Morals, and Religion* (London, 1843), 6.
2. Richard A. Soloway, *Prelates and People: Ecclesiastical Social Thought in England, 1783–1852* (London, 1969), 285.

parallel attitude toward head counting in religious circles as a measure of success. Hence one can understand the great furor over the Religious Census of 1851 and its seemingly disappointing revelations about religion in urban life.[3]

Concern over losing the masses did not necessarily inspire interchurch cooperation. In fact, a frequent response was an increase in religious rivalry, especially between Church of England and Nonconformity, for the hearts and minds of early Victorian townspeople. The Reverend Abraham Hume of Liverpool, for example, argued in a number of pamphlets in the 1860s that rival Nonconformists abandoned their impoverished coreligionists in decaying city chapels to inevitable heathenism, whereas Anglicanism maintained its mission to the poor as the Church of England.[4] As a by-product of his polemical discourses valuable sociology was disseminated on the affluent middle-class migration from city churches to suburban chapels, though admittedly researched primarily in relation to Nonconformity. Hume's immediate impact was simply to add to sectarian rivalry.

Early Christian Socialists thought less in terms of denominational strife and concentrated on the relation between declining religious influence and growing social tensions between the haves and have-nots. They were in essence urban optimists. Bridges could be built between social communities in the interest of ending social injustice. While espousing ideas that had applications to all of the social landscape, their attention was focused upon cities where the danger of social Armageddon seemed most imminent. This is not to say that their imagery was not derived in large measure from the countryside, with an idealized version of the rural parish as a model of social ministry.[5]

This is also not to say that their urban ministry was not effective. The Broad Church circle associated with Maurice included figures, such as the Reverend Harry Jones, who were not only exemplary pastors in places like London but actually developed a distinctive liberal Anglican approach to pastoral care in

3. See David M. Thompson, "The 1851 Religious Census: Problems and Possibilities," *Victorian Studies* 2, no. 1 (1967): 87–97. See also Horace Mann, "On the Statistical Position of Religious Bodies in England and Wales," *Journal of Statistical Society* 18 (1855): 141–59.

4. See Abraham Hume, *The Church of England, The Missionary To The Poor, Especially In Our Large towns* (London, 1862), and William S. F. Pickering, "Abraham Hume (1814–1884): A Forgotten Pioneer in Religious Sociology," *Archives de sociologie des religions* 33 (1972): 33–48. Hume's argument in favor of the Established Church was echoed about thirty years later by John Marshall Lang for the Established Church of Scotland, who also pointed out that though there were vital preachers in places like New York, they kept themselves to those areas least requiring pastoral activity. Lang, *The Church and the People: Address delivered at the close of General Assembly of the Church of Scotland, 29 May 1893* (Edinburgh, 1893), 34.

5. See George Kitson Clark, *Churchmen and the Condition of England, 1832–1885* (London, 1973), 340–41.

such works as *Priest and Parish* (1866). For Jones resident urban clergy were the equivalent of resident gentry in rural parishes in their capacity as community leaders.[6] W. H. Fremantle was likewise a dedicated urban pastor whose highly creative approaches to the city parish community directly inspired the work of Samuel Barnett and Octavia Hill.[7]

F. D. Maurice, of course, was less enthusiastic about specific actions, fearing the vox populi. He did preside over London Working Men's College, which provided many practical training programs for the working classes. E. V. Neale and others who were leaders in the cooperative movement had more direct influence over the urban laboring classes than did Maurice. However, they did not maintain a presence in politics. In fact, it was the Nonconformists, under the inspiration of J. A. James and R. W. Dale, who achieved the most impressive results in urban social reforms before the 1880s. Their Gospel of Civic Improvement was the basis of municipal socialism from Birmingham to the cities of the West Riding of Yorkshire.[8] These Nonconformist Liberals secured a successful merger of social idealism and political action that the early Anglican Christian Socialists could or would not. Their actions, however, were still limited by the constraints of a rock-bottom belief in individualism, which they continued vociferously to defend in the form of economic liberalism at the national parliamentary level.

Evangelicalism indeed reigned supreme in many urban pastoral circles until well into the 1880s, as typified by Charles Spurgeon's pastorate at London's Tabernacle Church. Social ills such as crime were treated as consequences of moral decay.[9] Poverty was represented as essentially a problematic attitude toward work. This did not mean that urban redemption was neglected. As I have shown, church-related philanthropy and waves of church building were massive. Drunkenness came to be the main target of Victorian moral-improvement campaigns. Thrift, better grooming, and other seemingly middle-class virtues were also mixed into the moral mélange, making self-improvement both a secular and a religious goal.

6. See Brian Heeney, "Harry Jones and the Broad Church Pastoral Tradition," in *The View from the Pulpit: Victorian Ministers and Society,* ed. Paul T. Phillips (Toronto, 1978), 73–74.

7. The Very Reverend and Honorable William Henry Fremantle (1831–1916) was rector of St. Mary's Bryanston Square, London, 1866–83, and canon of Canterbury until 1895. He was a noted preacher and writer on theology and social subjects. Some of Fremantle's works were better known in the United States. He was a fellow and theological tutor at Balliol College, Oxford, 1883–94.

8. The earliest advocacy of the municipal gospel was undoubtedly the Birmingham Baptist preacher George Dawson (1821–76) in his address on the subject in 1866—*Opening of the Free Reference Library, October 26, 1866 Inaugural Address* (Birmingham, 1866), partially reprinted in *Religion in Victorian Britain,* vol. 3, *Sources,* ed. James R. Moore (Manchester, 1988), 296–300.

9. See Richard J. Helmstadter, "Spurgeon in Outcast London," in *The View from the Pulpit,* 161–85.

Besides traditional charity, preaching both orally and in pamphlet form was the usual means to arouse personal reformations in the middle decades of the nineteenth century. As the number of the destitute increased, in spite of the overall growth in national wealth, preaching seemed increasingly ineffectual. Special missions to the people had sporadic results, not adding appreciably to the ranks of churchgoers. Dwight L. Moody and Ira Sankey, the American evangelists, launched missions in London and the provinces, beginning at York in the summer of 1873. Their massive rallies in London the next year and on later tours in the 1880s and 1890s resembled their campaigns in the United States. Like Spurgeon they believed that the mission hall could correct society's ills. Educational enterprises such as the YMCA did make a permanent mark on the urban landscape, though not upon the most destitute.

The Salvation Army, though evangelical in inception, made significant inroads into the working classes after its formation in 1878. William Booth's experience as a former renegade Methodist preacher and Chartist led him to choreograph a military-style assault upon the moral degradation of the laboring masses. His emphasis upon temperance did not initially gain the approval of many within the working classes. Later the approach of the Salvation Army would shift to social service in order to coincide with the changing middle-class consensus of the late 1880s and with Social Christianity. From the beginning, however, there was a concerted effort to bring the message to the masses more in their terms and through organizational innovation.

Innovative adaptation to the enormous challenge of places such as East London was not characteristic of the Salvationists alone. In 1867 there was a now long-forgotten London conference entitled "Working Men and Religious Institutions."[10] The attitudes of working men toward the churches were openly solicited, and they were given in abundance. While not immediately evident, the place of the church within the dismal landscape of social despair must have been the subject of pastoral reflection. Both E. P. Hennock and Stephen Yeo have noted important changes in social thinking by London clergy in the late 1860s and 1870s.[11]

Some Christian Socialists, in organizations such as the Broad Church Curates' Clerical Club, were part of this rethinking. Many club members fused ideas of Mauricean theology with practical pastoral techniques. But such innovation was not confined to Social Christians or Broad Churchmen.

10. *Working Men and Religious Institutions. Reports of the Speeches at the Conference, at the London Coffee House, Ludgate Hill, Monday, January 21, 1867* (London, 1867).
11. E. P. Hennock, "Poverty and Social Theory in England: The Experience of the Eighteen-Eighties," *Social History* 1 (January 1976): 90, and Stephen Yeo, "Thomas Hancock," in *For Christ and People,* ed. Maurice B. Reckitt (London, 1968), 10–11, 34–7.

A growing body of pastoral experience, from Congregationalists to Ritualists within the Church of England, suggested a more systematic, less sporadic approach to the social ills that menaced moral rejuvenation among the masses. The Charity Organization Society was a symbol of the newer, systematic approach that suggested reversing the order of personal reformation followed by social rejuvenation.[12] Though belief that the cumulative effort of individuals could cure social maladies continued, most believed that this effort needed to be better organized.

This approach was clearest in the oldest units of pastoral outreach—the parishes. In the 1820s the domestic mission established in Boston by the Unitarian minister Joseph Tuckerman aroused early interest. Similar missions appeared in London in the 1830s, and Inner Missions were organized in Prussia by Johann Wickern in the next decade. Tuckerman inaugurated a system of personal home visitations by volunteer workers to gather evidence on the lives of the impoverished. Later the Elberfeld system in Rhenish Prussia inspired the idea of dividing urban parishes into subdivisions for the more effective administration of these visitations. Tuckerman has been credited by historians as the father of the modern casework method in social work.[13]

In Britain these concepts bore fruit in a variety of parish enterprises; perhaps the earliest and most conspicuous were the Reverend Thomas Chalmers's modifications in the parish organization of the Established Presbyterian Church in St. John's parish, Glasgow.[14] Chalmers's three-volume *Christian and Civic Economy of Large Towns*, published between 1821 and 1826, became a familiar text in all parts of the British Isles. As historians have pointed out, Chalmers was later claimed as an authority by the American Social Gospelers as well as by some British Social Christian figures.[15] A.M.C. Waterman believes this to be somewhat ludicrous given Chalmers's general economic and social philosophy. It is also worth noting that he was an Evangelical, at least by the time of his greatest prominence.

12. The origins of the Charity Organization Society are disputed. It may have been founded by W. H. Fremantle about 1869 or by Edmund Holland, an associate of J. R. Green, vicar of St. Peter's, Stepney, about the same time. In any case, its origins were Broad Church.

13. See R. K. Webb, "John Hamilton Thom: Intellect and Conscience in Liverpool," in *The View From the Pulpit*, 232.

14. Thomas Chalmers (1780–1847) was a noted theologian and Presbyterian Church leader in Scotland. As a professor in the 1820s at St. Andrews and Edinburgh Universities he established his reputation as a religious thinker. But he is very important for his ideas on relief for the poor, developed especially during his ministry in the slum parish of St. John's, Glasgow. In his last days he was mainly concerned with the foundation of the Free Church after the Great Disruption of 1843.

15. See Stewart J. Brown, *Thomas Chalmers and the Godly Commonwealth in Scotland* (Oxford, 1982), 375–77, and A.M.C. Waterman, *Revolution, Economics, and Religion: Christian Political Economy, 1798–1833* (Cambridge, 1991), 220–21.

Clergymen had become willing suppliers of information to parliamentary investigations of social problems well before the 1880s. Social investigation, as I have indicated, was a growing phenomenon within the churches themselves. The churches, in fact, considering the Factory Acts of the 1830s and 1840s and Disraeli's legislation of the late 1870s, probably welcomed government action taken against many social ills. Yet an open espousal of state interventionism was rare.

The 1880s, however, marked a change in the general public and especially the middle-class attitude toward the Condition-of-England question. The reasons for this awakening are not altogether clear, but the churches' concerns for deteriorating urban life had much to do with it. Economic depression, or at least a cessation in the growth of the economy, undermined the mid-Victorian belief in inevitable progress. Depression may well have been most acute for London because of its particular economic circumstances, such as its great number of casual laborers.[16] In any case the quest for social justice became fashionable in many middle-class circles by the end of the decade, inspired by revelations of urban misery.

No single event was more important in this regard than the publication of *The Bitter Cry of Outcast London* in 1883. Not particularly new in its revelations of urban horrors, it nevertheless stirred the public conscience as no other work of the decade. Though written (anonymously) by a clergyman,[17] it was also not particularly original in that regard. But it nevertheless had the effect of displaying to a general readership what was already recognized in Social Christian circles—the inadequacy of older evangelical efforts to help the downtrodden. As the book's author (Andrew William Mearns or William Preston) stated:

> Whilst we have been building our churches and solacing ourselves with our religion and dreaming that the millennium was coming, the poor have been growing poorer, the wretched more miserable, and the immoral more corrupt; the gulf has been daily widening which separates the lowest classes of the community from our churches and

16. See Gareth Stedman Jones, *Outcast London: A Study in the Relationship Between Classes in Victorian Society* (Oxford, 1971).

17. It was published under the auspices of the Congregational Union. Regarding the dispute over its authorship, whether by William Preston or by Andrew Mearns, Anthony S. Wohl claims that the evidence favors the latter's claim. See Wohl, introduction to *The Bitter Cry of Outcast London: An Inquiry into the Condition of the Abject Poor,* ed. Anthony S. Wohl (Leicester, reprint, 1970), 13–15. More recently, Standish Meacham has agreed with Peter d'A. Jones in supporting Preston's claim. See Meacham, *Toynbee Hall and Social Reform, 1880–1914: The Search for Community* (New Haven, Conn., 1987), 191 n. 14, and d'A. Jones, *The Christian Socialist Revival, 1877–1914: Religion, Class, and Social Conscience in Late-Victorian England* (Princeton, 1968), 414–15.

chapels, and from all decency and civilization. It is easy to bring an array of facts which seem to point to the opposite conclusion—to speak of the noble army of men and women who penetrate the vilest haunts, carrying with them the blessings of the gospel; of the encouraging reports published by Missions, Reformatories, Refuges, Temperance Societies; of Theatre Services, Midnight Meetings and Special Missions. But what does it all amount to? We are simply living in a fool's paradise if we suppose that all these agencies combined are doing a thousandth part of what needs to be done, a hundredeth part of what *could* be done by the Church of Christ.[18]

While pointing to nonattendance at church, immoral behavior, drunkenness, and the like, Mearns/Preston was also quick to point out that the majority of outcasts were decent people who sought to improve their lives by honest means. The problem was that they had sunk so low that no amount of improved social attitudes could rescue them. With the exploitation of tenement dwellers it was necessary that "the state must make short work of this iniquitous traffic, and secure for the poorest the rights of citizenship; the right to live in something better than fever dens; the right to live as something better than the uncleanest brute beasts. This must be done before the Christian missionary can have much chance with them."[19] *Outcast London* soon became household words both in the palace of Queen Victoria and in the meaner habitation of the person on the street. The book moved politicians to do more on matters such as housing, given its criticism of the inadequacies of Disraeli's Artisans' Dwellings Act of 1875. For the churches it moved Social Christianity into a new phase of importance, displacing the older Evangelicalism. Its frame of reference was exclusively urban.

Henceforth those who aspired to the ideals or at least some of the notions of Christian Socialists would converse in a language of urban metaphors, as was already done by most, though some would experience a "culture shock" in the transition. Walsham How, who became one of the most activist and socially conscious suffragan bishops of London (1879–88), had been rector of an obscure Shropshire parish for almost thirty years. The religious situation of the East London masses under his new jurisdiction was described as "a sort of ecclesiastical Botany Bay."[20]

18. *The Bitter Cry of Outcast London,* 55–56.
19. Ibid., 69.
20. F. D. How, *Bishop Walsham How: A Memoir* (London, 1901), 170–71.

The United States and Canada were far behind Britain in urbanization. On the eve of the Civil War the United States had only nine cities with more than a hundred thousand inhabitants, whereas Britain had twenty-eight, in spite of the considerably larger American population. Though North America experienced an accelerated pace of city growth from the late nineteenth century onward, it tended to be very much a regional phenomenon. It was only in 1920 that the United States finally reached its great demographic watershed with over half the population in urban areas—a stage reached by Canada eleven years later. James Bryce had noted the small proportion of urban dwellers in Canada.[21]

In spite of the comparatively rural nature of American life through the entire nineteenth century, there was plenty of thinking about cities in church circles. Perhaps acting to present a sort of ecclesiastical counterpart to the Jeffersonian view of towns as "sores upon the body politic," many religious writers looked upon the city with trepidation. Amory D. Mayo's *Symbols of the Capital; or, Civilization in New York* (1859) brought forth the view of a violated human nature consumed by the demands of survival in the city. This view was quite in keeping with those of many secular writers of the antebellum period. However, no one could deny the importance of cities in the steady growth of the nation's economy, and in that sense many accepted urban growth as a necessary expedient in realizing not the Jeffersonian ideal but rather the aspirations of Alexander Hamilton for the nation.

The mood of American religious leaders was complex through much of the nineteenth century. No one emerged with the degree of urban optimism found in Britain's Robert Vaughan. Resignation to the inevitability of the economic processes that produced cities was evident quite early in a spirit of "making the best of it." Paul Boyer, in his *Urban Masses and Moral Order in America* (1978), has done much to correct older impressions that church leaders were concerned only with frontier heathenism and the morality of slavery in the early Republic. As he demonstrates, talented clergy and laity applied themselves vigorously to multifarious activities and organizations engaged in maintaining moral order among urban masses.

The motivations behind this early and vigorous activity included some element of hope that cities might partially perpetuate the alleged high moral standards of the village if great efforts were applied. Joseph Tuckerman rejected the notion that cities were inherently wicked. Both he and his friend William E. Channing believed, in a sense, in Vaughan's idea of the "trickle-down" moral effect of the wealthy, civilized urban elite upon the masses—provided the elite

21. James Bryce, *Canada: An Actual Democracy* (Toronto, 1921), 2.

would staunchly support religious and philanthropic enterprises on a wide scale.[22]

There was a deeper motive at work, however. Robert Vaughan represented only one side of the British urban elite, that of Nonconformity. In the United States, without an established church, Protestant leaders represented collectively the dominant cultural group in the early Republic, both rural and urban. The outlook of this informal establishment was closer to that of leaders of the Church of England in the same period. Unlike English Nonconformists, Protestants viewed the advance of cities as potentially bringing a decline in their social power. *All* Protestant churches stood to lose something in moral control over the masses, and no motivation is as powerful as fear. While the greatest waves of immigration occurred in the last decades of the century, the early influx of Irish Catholics provided a considerable shock to the confidence in Protestant social leadership. Protestants never thought highly of Catholic moral control, and this suspicion fused with their general Nativist reaction to immigrants. Romanism was not much better than godlessness in the masses. Such developments as the spread of Catholicism made Protestant church leaders work that much harder and made them seek examples from their more experienced English-speaking cousins to control social and moral disorder in cities. As already seen, Britain had begun to experience modern city life as a widespread phenomenon much earlier than North America, and by its example and the contact its writers had with the American intelligentsia, that country came to be regarded as the bellwether for future developments on this side of the Atlantic. This Anglo-American link developed quite early in the nineteenth century and remained constant thereafter.

Beginning in the earliest decades of the nineteenth century, Americans duplicated the innovative methods applied by British clergy to urban problems. Thomas Chalmers's work and writings on social action, for example, quickly reinforced the work of Joseph Tuckerman in his attack on urban poverty. Similar contacts with British figures led to the founding of a wide variety of church-related urban organizations, such as the New York City missions of the 1840s. As in mid-Victorian Britain, there was an emphasis upon aid to the "worthy" poor as well as self-help, the latter notion particularly attractive to many affluent Americans. As in the case of Tuckerman, many of the movements and figures became truly transatlantic as time passed. At the opposite end of the theological spectrum from Unitarianism, the YMCA (founded in

22. Charles N. Glaab and A. Theodore Brown, *A History of Urban America,* 3d ed. (New York, 1983), 62–63.

England in 1844), for example, when it spread to America, did much to inspire a number of American revivalists to become concerned with the plight of the cities. The great urban revival campaigns led by Dwight L. Moody and Ira Sankey from 1875 to 1885 sprang from these influences, and of course, these men repaid their mentors with tours of British cities. One of their assistants on their tours was the Scottish theologian and revivalist Henry Drummond.[23] In writings such as *The City Without a Church* (1893), Drummond could not have been more adamant that the redemption of the world depended on the full Christianization of the city.

In Scotland, Chalmers elicited early concern for urban problems and sug- gested solutions. In these early endeavors, however, Evangelicalism was more apparent than Social Christianity and was frequently preoccupied with nonattendance at church. Some momentum was then lost. The Great Disrup- tion and the subsequent ecclesiological and doctrinal disputes running into the 1870s and 1880s tended to focus many Presbyterians on internal "church issues" in spite of some publications on social problems.[24] That a strong social conscience did emerge in the Scottish churches by 1900 cannot be doubted. But John Marshall Lang's comprehensive Baird lectures for 1901, entitled "The Church and Its Social Mission," expressed a special concern that clergy not exaggerate the challenge of socialism, which perhaps seemed more threatening because of the Church of Scotland's inability to identify with the reforming movements of the dispossessed a decade earlier. As he stated: "What needs to be demonstrated is that, on the one hand, the rejection of the spiritual aspect of life is untruth to the conception of life as a whole, and that, on the other hand, Christianity, in emphasizing the spiritual, does not the less, but all the more, seek to promote all that contributes to social betterment."[25]

Socialists, of whatever description, of course, had an explanation for poverty and a solution in their verbal assaults on the wealthy. Social Christians since Maurice also had an explanation in the lack of Christian social compassion. Hensley Henson, in an early and brief period of tutoring in the company of his university friend Edward Watson, curate of the church in Birkenhead (Liver- pool), while noting the social conditions, stated that "surely something must be

23. Henry Drummond (1851–97) was educated both at Edinburgh and Tübingen Universities. His published works ranged from theology to geology to exploration in Africa. He also led missions to British universities.

24. See Donald J. Withrington, "The Churches in Scotland, c. 1870–c. 1900: Towards a New Social Conscience?" *Records of the Scottish Church History Society* 19 (1977): 155–68.

25. John Marshall Lang, *The Church and Its Social Mission* (Edinburgh, 1902), 278–79.

wrong somewhere in the body politic, that this state of things should exist. I am afraid if I stay here for the next six months I shall become a Socialist."[26]

Henson, of course, did not become a socialist and in fact quickly became critical of schemes to reduce the spending power of the wealthy, which generated so many jobs. His transitional interest in Social Christianity must have come from his early friendship with the Anglo-Catholic socialist James Adderley as well as his brief stint as head of Oxford House, Bethnal Green, in 1888. But in the case of Social Christianity, as in the case of socialist politics, Henson's personal religious ideas and social philosophy led him to different conclusions in spite of firsthand urban experience.

Though continuing to hold the view that moral character was an important element in urban reform, Americans were not slow to realize that the adverse social environment could work against the rehabilitation of the masses no matter what their individual attitudes were. Before 1850 it was apparent that the cores of the largest cities were overcrowded with extremely poor housing. One did not have to wait to read Charles Dickens in order to understand how fundamental was decent housing to well-being. Robert M. Hartley, Louis M. Pease, and other charity workers in New York realized that being sober and reading Bibles alone could not raise the people out of their misery.[27] After 1870 not only did industrialization lead to the more rapid expansion of cities, with growing disparities between rich and poor and concomitant social unrest, it also led to the greatest waves of immigration ever seen. This immigration brought overwhelming challenges both to the Protestant churches and to the American system of government and politics. The ready-made solutions offered by British Social Christians were therefore applied early and vigorously on the American scene, again really in anticipation of complete urbanization.

Beginning with Washington Gladden, perhaps the earliest founding father of the Social Gospel, the British influence and through it the special concern for the city are very evident. Gladden, in describing the impact of Octavia Hill's *Houses of the London Poor* (1875) on his social thought in the late 1870s, stated, "I look back to the reading of that pamphlet as a point of transition in all my thoughts about social questions."[28] Gladden became the most outstanding spokesman for progressive clergy during the remainder of the century. From

26. Hensley Henson, entry for 18 May 1885, *Retrospect of an Unimportant Life (London, 1942),* 1:14. See also Owen Chadwick, *Hensley Henson: A Study in Friction Between Church and State* (Oxford, 1983), 26–27, 40–50.

27. Glaab and Brown, *History of Urban America,* 84.

28. "Reform in England," sermon no. 368, 1888, Sermons and Lectures, Washington Gladden Papers, Ohio Historical Society.

his Columbus, Ohio, pulpit he guided a nationwide generation of clergymen and sympathetic laity toward special concern for social problems and new social scientific approaches to these problems. According to Gladden, there was much to be learned from the developments in British cities, for "there is no more of contrast in the social conditions between England and America than one finds in going from Boston to Richmond."[29] His reading of works by British authors from Dickens to Charles Booth, clearly indicated in his sermons, demonstrates the influence of the British urban factor. As he once wrote concerning the future of America: "For it seems very clear to me that all the deepest interests of the Kingdom of God are focused in our cities, that the critical point of our civilization is the city."[30]

A little later the Reverend Josiah Strong was to write a series of books and articles focusing on the importance of the city in the social redemption of America. His most famous work, *Our Country* (1886), sometimes ranked with *Uncle Tom's Cabin* in its impact on the American Christian conscience, was indebted to *The Bitter Cry of Outcast London* in its stress upon the perils of city life. Strong was convinced that the urban Protestant churches were growing weaker, as they were in England—the "London of today is a prophecy of more than one twentieth century city in the United States."[31] Like other Social Christians at this time, he believed that the churches must do much more than react to urban conditions; they must in fact take initiatives. Urban problems, he believed, were compounded by the influx of immigrants. Anglo-Saxons must exert their influence in cities for the very survival of the old Republic. As he stated, "The city is to control the nation: Christianity must control the city; *and it will.*"[32]

The religions of those other than the Protestant Northern Europeans were frequently discounted in this scenario, even by such an otherwise advanced social thinker as Walter Rauschenbusch. As the recipients of the vast majority of immigrants, cities now had added importance as the setting for efforts to preserve institutions thought to be essential to the survival of the nation as it had been known.

Small wonder that little was said of rural problems in the late nineteenth century by Social Christians. In Britain the concerns of Social Christians were overwhelmingly urban, as reflected in the agendas of all the congresses, conferences, synods, and other assemblies of the churches throughout the

29. Gladden to children, London, 16 July 1888, Letters, Gladden Papers.
30. "Columbus' Future," sermon no. 784, 1898, Sermons and Lectures, Gladden Papers.
31. Josiah Strong, *The Twentieth Century City* (New York, 1890), 77.
32. Ibid., 180–81.

period. In the United States, rural poverty came to be an enormous problem but one found primarily in regions such as the Deep South, where the Social Gospel was weakest among clergy. This in part may explain the indifference of some urban Social Christians to the plight of black Americans and the need for racial reform. Given the fact that black populations constituted less than 5 percent of the largest cities of the Northeast and Midwest, racial issues continued to be thought of largely as a Southern problem until the end of World War I.

This was reinforced by the British factor. British Social Christians, though not racist per se, had virtually nothing to say about the problem. American readers of British publications were apt to concern themselves with the same issues as the British—poverty, crime, illiteracy, and so forth. White immigrant ghettos in the United States were analogous to the Irish areas of London, Liverpool, and Glasgow, being largely non-Protestant in both cases; little beyond anti-Catholicism could be gleaned from the writings of British figures on these areas. British visitors to American cities tended merely to stress in their speeches what was already said in their writings. As far as the black situation was concerned, British observers, when it came to their attention, also seemed to view it as a Southern problem. The chief of staff to General Booth, for example, in a report on "U.S.A. Affairs" in 1894, recommended making the "Black States" into a separate territory with headquarters in Richmond or Charleston. The report suggested that "it would be a great hit and would get the North out of all its difficulty in the dealing with the colour."[33]

On the other hand, while ignoring or separating out the problems of rural life, many in both Britain and the United States idealized rural life. David W. Bebbington has indicated some of the reasons for this in the case of British Social Christians.[34] General Booth's *In Darkest England and the Way Out* (1890) advocated solutions to urban problems that included the establishment of "farm colonies" radiating out into the countryside.[35] Many schemes for placing people (especially orphans) on the farm involved exporting individuals to North America as well, which undoubtedly borrowed from ideas of Dr. Thomas Barnardo and other prominent London evangelical preachers. The Boy Scout movement was influenced by a variety of figures, including many Social

33. Chief of staff to general, October 1894, Letters 1894, folder 10, Correspondence, William Booth Collection, Salvation Army Heritage Room, Salvation Army Headquarters, Judd Street, London.

34. See David W. Bebbington, "The City, the Countryside, and the Social Gospel in Late Victorian Nonconformity," *Studies in Church History* 16 , ed. D. Baker (London, 1979): 415–26.

35. Standish Meacham believes that General Booth saw the city itself, not just poverty, as a source of social evils. See Meacham, "The Church in the Victorian City," *Victorian Studies* 2 , no. 3 (1968): 375.

Christians. Here again proper values for youth were to be gleaned in a rural setting, including the frontier within Britain itself.[36]

The Reverend Henry Solly, Unitarian and former Chartist sympathizer, organized the Society for Promoting Industrial Villages in the 1880s, with a view to stemming migration of people to London by persuading them to remain in the countryside. The society promoted market gardens, allotments around homes, handicrafts, and cooperative farms. Solly received support from, among others, Andrew Mearns, William Booth, and Hugh Price Hughes.[37]

Perhaps the most successful endeavors of this type were the model industrial satellite communities established by Quaker chocolate manufacturers. The first of these was Bournville, founded in 1878, outside Birmingham. Cadbury's Bournville factory grew to be one of the largest chocolate producers in the world, and the surrounding community was designed to be a model of good housing for the working classes. People other than Cadbury workers were allowed to lease or buy cottages there. In time the Cadbury family, who had earlier experience as leaders in Quaker philanthropic enterprises as well as in the adult school movement, also became concerned about labor relations and social services.[38]

In 1900 George Cadbury transferred ownership of the estate to the Bournville Village Trust. Four years later Joseph Rowntree established more or less the same for his industrial satellite New Earswick, outside York. As it was to Cadbury, religious influence was important to Rowntree. The Cadburys allowed no pub in Bournville; the Rowntrees allowed only one church building (the Folk Hall) in New Earswick to avoid "the separate interests in village life" created by separate churches.[39] Intense interest in social surveys, social services, and improved class relationships for industrial workers characterized the Rowntrees as much as the Cadburys. Though the goal was to influence relationships in all urban areas, the first step was to remove workers from the existing cities.

These enterprises could be matched by Americans, who earlier had come to similar conclusions. In the 1860s William Augustus Muhlenberg, rector of New

36. See Robert H. MacDonald, *Sons of the Empire: The Frontier and the Boy Scout Movement, 1890–1918* (Toronto, 1993).

37. Correspondence, Society for Promoting Industrial Villages, vol. 4 (b), Papers of the Reverend Henry Solly, British Library of Political and Economic Science, London.

38. See Charles Dellheim, "The Creation of a Company Culture: Cadburys, 1861–1931," *American Historical Review* 92, no. 1 (1987): 13–44. George Cadbury Jr. argued that in the strategic area of housing and in other endeavors in cities the efforts of social reformers were isolated and spasmodic, leading to "very unsatisfactory results" (*Town Planning* [London, 1915], 2).

39. Joseph Rowntree, "An Address on Occasion of Opening the Folk Hall," 5 October 1907, p. 3, Rowntree Trust, York.

York's Church of the Holy Communion, had planned for a cooperative farming community on Long Island, composed of deserving urban exiles. He was inspired by the writings and work of English Broad Churchmen in spite of his own vacillation between Low Church Evangelicalism and Tractarianism.[40]

Charles Loring Brace, in Dr. Barnardo fashion, attempted to export children to upstate New York and points west in roughly the same period. While antiurban in flavor, the result of much of this thought and action was ironically to reinforce the overwhelmingly urban orientation of British and American Social Christianity. It also de-emphasized concern over the problem of rural poverty, so acute in places like the Deep South. Even a journal such as *Social Gospel*, edited in Commonwealth, Georgia, had little to say about rural misery: "[T]he poor in the cities suffer immeasurably more and are placed under far greater stress of temptation than the same class in the country."[41]

The alleged strength of the churches in American rural society proved to be of little interest in the urban crusade. While the Reverend Charles Macfarland lectured to Yale Divinity students that "the rural community is the base of support to the city," he was unclear on how this was to serve the new social order.[42] Both Washington Gladden and Paul Moore Strayer thought most resources should be concentrated in the city, the rural areas being "over churched."[43]

In Britain most of the significant Christian Socialist organizations since the revival of the original movement were established in and around the 1880s. All were urban centered, and the reading materials produced by members or other associated persons were quickly disseminated throughout the country and abroad. Some figures, such as W. T. Stead, editor of the *Pall Mall Gazette*, also became transatlantic, as well known in North America as in Britain. Stead understood the American situation very well, producing his sensational *If Christ Came to Chicago!* at precisely the time of the Columbian Exposition, which accentuated urban life. What Manchester had been to the world of the mid-Victorians, Chicago now became—the great shock city of the future. Stead

40. Glaab and Brown, *History of Urban America*, 233. See also A. W. Skardon, *Church Leader in the Cities: William Augustus Muhlenberg* (New York, 1971), and Anne Ayres, *The Life and Work of William Augustus Muhlenberg* (New York, 1880). Sydney E. Ahlstrom attributes the remarkable growth of Episcopalianism in urban America in the century's middle decades largely to Muhlenberg (*A Religious History of the American People* [New Haven, Conn., 1972], 631.

41. *Social Gospel* 2, no. 3 (1899): 31.

42. Charles S. Macfarland, *The Christian Ministry and the Social Order* (New Haven, Conn., 1909), 212.

43. Washington Gladden, "Empty Pews in the Country Church—Why?" *Everybody's Magazine* 34 (May 1916), 615, and Paul Moore Strayer, *The Reconstruction of the Church* (New York, 1915), 290.

subsequently produced a book on New York, which is less well known (*Satan's Invisible World Displayed*, 1898). One reason the latter book was not celebrated was that it was written for a British audience. However, as Stead explained in the preface to the later American edition: "The English-speaking race is one race, and the English-speaking world the common fatherland of all who speak the English tongue. No Englishman ever regards an American as a 'foreigner,' nor can I ever consent to consider that I am outside the limits of my country in New York or in Chicago any more than if I were in Glasgow or Dublin or Melbourne" (iv).

Many of the city reform writers in America—from Jacob Riis, *How the Other Half Lives* (1890), to Lincoln Steffens, *The Shame of the Cities* (1904)—were in fact laymen of various backgrounds who took a more secular outlook on the urban environment. They nonetheless had a strong moralistic quality in their rhetoric, undoubtedly influenced by religiously flavored publications, and were in turn exploited by Social Gospelers. One also discerns in their writing a revival of some optimism concerning urban life. Frank Mason North, the famous New York Methodist pastor, believed that *The Bitter Cry of Outcast London* had been "the impulse" behind the Forward Movements of Robert F. Horton and Hugh Price Hughes in the Congregationalist and Methodist churches respectively. He also believed that the city must not be regarded as some form of plague but rather as "a part of the Divine plan for the race," being "not an accident, the cruel result of some dislocation of the order of Providence." Urban church work should be appreciated as the highest form of missionary activity, being "the creation of our most advanced civilization." Such activity brought the church "into the open" in order to "apply the Gospel to the evils of the social organism."[44]

British and American writings also flowed freely into English Canada. Though Canada was far less urbanized, church leaders had become aware, before 1880, of the misery of the poor, especially children, in places such as Toronto and were joined by others in their cries for municipal reform. Newspaper editors and book publishers, engaged in commentaries on and reprints of the works of leading British and American writers, helped to locate the country with respect to the urban context of Social Christianity. By the turn of the century pilgrimages to London in particular became part of the finishing

---

44. *The Forward Movement: Its Spirit, Its Methods, Its Scope,* November 1893, 6, box "City," Frank Mason North Papers, Archives and History Center of the United Methodist Church, Drew University; *The Story of NY Methodism,* n.d., 2, box "New York City and Methodism," Frank Mason North Papers; *The New Christian Era in Our Cities,* 12 December 1895, 1, box "City and Federation," Frank Mason North Papers; *The Forward Movement,* November 1893, 6–7.

touches in the education of Social Gospelers.[45] *My Neighbour* (1911), by J. S. Woodsworth, is an excellent example of transatlantic influences' shaping the urban perspective in the writing of a prominent Canadian Social Christian.

But not all British advice, when given directly to North America, was well received. Statements by Englishmen that equality had not been achieved in the American city were greated with extreme sensitivty. The concept of equality, as so many writers have observed,[46] was central to the American *Volksgeist*—a revered myth. While problems of inequality were clearly acknowledged, most American reformers stuck tenaciously to the idea that American cities had not really developed a class system in the European sense. This is why the Salvation Army's recognition of a more or less permanent working class repelled so many American clergy and laity. As Washington Gladden stated with regard to the Salvationists, "[W]e have no such stratification; the poorest people do not willingly admit that they are members of a class."[47] Albert Shaw, editor of the *American Review of Reviews* made a similar observation in answer to those who would apply the writings of Charles Booth to the American scene. He wrote, "[W]e simply [do] not have the submerged class in this country that you have assured us exist[s] in London."[48] Perhaps the best example of American self-consciousness was a church press reaction to a walking tour of New York's East Side by Randall Davidson, archbishop of Canterbury, accompanied by Booker T. Washington and Jacob Riis in 1904: "His Grace probably noticed one point of difference between the poor of the East Side and the poor of London. Poverty here is an accident. The man who is starving today hopes to be feasting tomorrow. He fights to better himself. . . . The poverty-stricken inhabitant of the London slums expects to die there—to die poor—even to die by starvation."[49]

Faith in the egalitarian ideal had in fact been ingrained among most urban clergymen and writers since the days of Tuckerman. Implicit in this attitude was the hope for a better future through widespread upward mobility. For a few, of course, the *danger* of urban America turning into a class-ridden society was very real. The Reverend Samuel Lane Loomis, in his highly interesting book

45. Visits to London by S. D. Chown, J. S. Woodsworth, and a host of other figures seem to have been more common than pilgrimages to American centers.

46. See J. R. Pole, *The Pursuit of Equality in American History* (Berkeley and Los Angeles, 1978), and Edward Pessen, "AHR Forum: Social Structure and Politics in American History," *American Historical Review* 87, no. 5 (1982): 1270–341.

47. "In Darkest England," sermon no. 430 (1891), Sermons and Lectures, Gladden Papers.

48. Shaw to William T. Stead, 12 June 1894, Albert Shaw Papers New York Public Library.

49. "The Archbishop, Washington, and Stokes," newspaper clippings, "Visit to U.S.A.," file, 1904, p. 75, R. T. Davidson Papers, Lambeth Palace Library.

*Modern Cities* (1887), contended that it was "to speak wide of the truth" to deny the existence of classes in American cities. In addition to this, he felt such a denial was downright stupid in the face of great danger to both the Protestant churches and American civilization. Looking to London, where "the whole world is centered," he acknowledged a much more clearly formulated class structure with the gap between rich and poor much wider than in America. Yet he felt the American situation to be potentially more dangerous, for at least "in an English Christian home the servants are present at family prayers and attend the same church as their masters"; in America, in contrast, the "capitalists' church" was for the well-fed native stock, and the Catholic Church for the laboring masses largely of foreign extraction.[50]

Even Loomis, however, could write of his hope for an egalitarian future with a little optimism, anticipating the even more cheerful promises of Progressives. Later, in the heyday of Progressivism, Frederic Howe was to write in *The British City* (1907), "[O]ur open-minded democracy assures us a city far more beautiful, vastly more helpful, and infinitely more generous in its ideals than the British city now is."[51] Americans were always apt to speak of the distant past or glorious future in relation to the ideal of equality. Englishmen such as Lord Bryce were apt to look at the present situation and find in the city the failure of American democracy.

Not all of Bryce's revelations concerned equality. Writing in the last years of the nineteenth century Bryce, in *The American Commonwealth*, felt that the laboring masses of the great cities had become as heathenish as those of London. The only difference between Britain and the United States, he believed, was that in the United States "the proportion of working men who belong to some religious body may be larger in towns under 30,000 than it is in the similar towns of Great Britain."[52] However, a growing number of these Christian churchgoers were non-Protestants. Thus, the 1890 census figures, supplied by the churches to the government, which revealed that only about one-third of the population were communicants, were all the more alarming.[53]

---

50. Samuel Lane Loomis, *Modern Cities and their Religious Problems* (New York, 1887), 66, 108, 77–78.

51. Frederic Howe, *The British City* (New York, 1907), 249–50.

52. James Bryce, *The American Commonwealth*, new ed. (New York, 1911), 2:785.

53. See *Compendium of the Eleventh Census* (Washington, D.C., 1894), pt. 2. Communicants included "all who are permitted to partake of the Lord's Supper in denominations observing the sacrament and those having full privileges in denominations like the Friends, Unitarians, and the Jewish temples" (ibid., 261). No figures for communicants can be found in the censuses of 1870 and 1880. Robert T. Handy argues that the membership numbers for all types of churches taken together rose tenfold in the nation from 1860 to 1920. Handy, *A History of Churches in the United States and Canada* (Oxford, 1976), 265.

In spite of a reported increase in church membership in the last decades of the nineteenth century, the relative position of the Protestant denominations in large cities may not have been so different from that in Britain. Peripheral sects such as Christian Science, though tailored to modern life, did not attract multitudes. Urban revivals probably added few new members and more than likely attracted those who already went to church.

By the 1890s many American church leaders and commentators had learned that low church attendance was symptomatic of problems in the relationship between the masses and religion, not simply something to be cured for its own sake. Some clerical writers blamed sectarian rivalries.[54] However, most discussions of the period tended to be charged with social ideology and politics, which made for further divisions. One early commentary by C. M. Morse blamed the difficulty on the growing disparity between rich and poor—"with social inequality among members outside the church, there cannot be religiosocial equality in it."[55] In a 1898 discussion, however, the Reverend H. Francis Perry, a Chicago Baptist minister, tried systematically to solicit the viewpoints of labor leaders, the churchgoing lower classes, and those laboring people alienated from the church.[56] He summarized his findings under five general "indictments" made against the church, together with his own evaluation of each.

1. The church is subsidized by the rich. The minister is, consequently, tongue-tied. The rich man's influence is so powerful that anything which would arouse his conscience will never unwisely escape the preacher's lips.

   While these charges are doubtless true of a few so-called churches and of a very few preachers, yet we know scores and hundreds of men who would resign a pulpit at once where there was a command, either open or implied, to padlock their lips in the presentation of truth. It is culpable beyond ordinary cowardice for a preacher of righteousness to sell his conviction for gold, and such a man would be frowned out of the fellowship of the ministers of any community.

2. The ministry discusses themes which are stale and flat. They are not living issues.

---

54. C. E. Ordway, "Will the Churches Survive?" *Arena* 29 (1903): 593–600.
55. C. M. Morse, "The Church and the Working-Man," *Forum* 6 (1888): 654.
56. H. Francis Perry, "The Workingman's Alienation From the Church," *American Journal of Sociology* 4 (1898–99): 621–29.

This is thoroughly false to the genuine spirit of the church. The pulpit teaches preparation for this world's conflicts and temptations, as well as safety in a future world. These themes ought not to be stale and flat to the earnest man.

3. The ministry is not well enough informed on economic and social questions.

To this we plead guilty in part. Social science is a new study, and could not be found in the college curriculum ten or fifteen years ago. To have studied economics or ethics years ago is not now to be informed in sociology. To study the labor movement as the ordinary laboring man glances at it would be far from satisfactory.

4. The workingman is not welcome in the churches of the land.

This is a mistake on the part of wage-earners. Some churches may be icy toward him, but these are the isolated exception, not the rule.

5. The church is not aggressive enough in assisting the workingman to secure his rights.

Grant all the necessary exceptions to the rule, and deduct considerable for sluggishness in the performance of duty, and even then the fact remains that most of those who unselfishly are aiding the causes of humanity are Christian men, and a large proportion of these are ministers. In considering the causes dear to the wage-earner which are left unaided by the church, the difficulty often is that the postulates of the workingman are so wide of the truth that the church cannot champion them. It is not true that men are in a prison-house and the church is holding the key. The church may be depended upon to lead in securing justice and truth. It must also warn the workingman that his alienation often results from tendencies within himself rather than within the church. The Jesus who is applauded by the average workingman is a minimized Jesus Christ, a fictitious person, not the Christ of the gospels.[57]

Though some ministers were not prepared to be spokesmen for the cause of labor, dialogue with the working classes was still essential. "Christian neighborliness" began to grow as a concept among American Social Christian pastors at the very end of the nineteenth century. Lord Bryce had already noted

---

57. Ibid., 627–68.

that "the social side of church life" was more fully developed in the United States than in Protestant Europe.[58]

Perhaps the best exemplification of this was the so-called institutional church. A movement and almost a household word by 1900, the concept behind it arose in a number of American cities in the early 1890s. The term may well have originated with President Tucker of Dartmouth College in describing Berkley Congregational Temple, Boston. Essentially the concept was based upon the idea of expanded social services, from soup kitchens to banks to gymnasium classes, operated by churches in an effort to reestablish their central social role in cities. One of its inspirers was William Augustus Muhlenberg, who was deeply concerned about the presence and impact of the Episcopal Church in urban areas. His Church of the Holy Communion in New York operated an employment agency, a day school, and an infirmary in the 1870s.

The Reverend W. S. Rainsford, however, seems to have the strongest claim as father of the idea. Rainsford was born and educated in England, where, as a young Anglican curate, he became critical of the prevalent Evangelicalism of the mid-nineteenth century. In his own words, "The Evangelicals were so absorbed in saving people's souls that they left the masses to look after their own bodies."[59] He departed for North America, where he ministered to various groups in Ontario, eventually becoming rector of St. James Cathedral, Toronto, in the mid-1880s. After tiring of the conservatism of church leadership there, in 1888 he accepted an invitation to become pastor of St. George's Episcopal Church in New York City. As a friend of Phillips Brooks, Episcopal bishop of Massachusetts, he was already a frequent visitor to the United States. St. George's of recent years had experienced a decline in membership, but it had the staunch backing of a group of wealthy patrons led by J. Pierpont Morgan. As a condition of acceptance, Rainsford insisted that pew rents be abolished, along with all existing committees except the vestry, and a fund of $10,000 be placed at his disposal.[60] Thus was the institutional church established.

Already a dynamic preacher and vitally interested in why the poor did not go to church, Rainsford commenced a remarkable twenty-four-year career at St. George's. For Rainsford the parish was all-important. He had noted in his youth

58. Bryce, *American Commonwealth*, 2:787.

59. W. S. Rainsford, *The Story of a Varied Life: An Autobiography* (1922; reprint, Freeport, N.Y., 1970), 63.

60. Ibid., 201. On the question of free pews, Rainsford credited the Roman Catholic Church with being "more apostolic than is the custom of those churches which have broken away from her" (ibid., 212).

in England that evangelical chapels had "no parish boundaries" and through pew rents and the like had built barriers to the poor of the adjacent streets. As Rainsford explained his task: "To put my plans briefly, before all else I wanted to understand my neighbourhood, and did *not* want to draw a curious crowd from all over town, even supposing that I could do it. This was my reason for putting a ban on advertising the services."[61] In time Rainsford and a group of resident young clergy and laity got to know their neighbors, whether they initially attended St. George's or not. Church attendance began to increase, but this was not the only objective in the pursuit of Christian neighborliness. The grounds, music, and recreational activities of the church were vastly improved. So was aid to the poor. Admitting at the beginning of his New York pastorate that "soon or late the state will be obliged to institute great changes" and that private philanthropy cannot eradicate all evils, he nonetheless believed that "the duty of the hour is to bring man nearer to man." Legislation would be "inoperative" without arousing public conscience, a step in drawing all together in "the coming of the Kingdom of the Son of Man."[62]

A similar pattern for other institutional churches emerged a little later with the help of wealthy supporters such as William E. Dodge in New York or organizations such as the Chicago Methodist Society. Millions of dollars were raised for these churches by 1900. Josiah Strong applied the term to at least thirty American city churches in 1908, mainly in New York, noting that they provided "for portions of the community the functions not performed for them by the home and society at large." But he also observed that many more not listed had some institutional program: "[T]here are few churches today in the cities of the U.S. which do not in some way carry on at least one or more activities which might be termed 'institutional.' " But Strong, in spite of his compendium of services, began his lengthy entry on institutional churches for the *Encyclopedia of Social Reform* using a description provided by Dr. A. Dickinson, pastor of Berkeley Temple, Boston (who some claim originated the movement): "The institutional church aims to provide a material environment wherein the spiritual Christ can express Himself."[63]

Too great a commitment to social service in the form of church work could lead to a de-emphasis upon attendance and worship for middle-class supporters of these diverse endeavors. In turn, when social services increasingly came to be directed by secular figures (state or otherwise), superseding church work,

61. Ibid., 63, 209.
62. W. S. Rainsford, "What Can We Do for the Poor?" *Forum* 2 (April 1891): 126, 123.
63. Josiah Strong, "Institutional Churches," in *The New Encyclopedia of Social Reform*, ed. William Dwight Porter Bliss (New York, 1908), 629.

the purpose of church affiliation for the altruistic could be undermined, as hypothesized by Jeffrey Cox for the Lambeth area of London.[64]

Rainsford's line of thinking was oddly similar to that of the London Broad Church circle, a group he professed not to have known while in England, though he was a great admirer of F. W. Robertson.[65] Harry Jones, one of its number, had argued in *East and West London* (1875) for the adaptability of the parish system to changing conditions. L. E. Nettleship believes that Toynbee Hall emerged from an idealized version of the parish held by London Broad Churchmen such as W. H. Fremantle and Samuel Barnett.[66] Certainly the settlement movement that followed from Toynbee Hall and spread to so many cities in Britain and North America was another variant of Christian neighborliness. There was also a quality of eternal urban optimism in all these efforts, as revealed in Barnett's book, *The Ideal City* (London, 1890).

In many ways the institutional church was again an attempt to create the moral economy of the village within the city. But the village was fast becoming a different sort of place, filled with strangers speaking in foreign tongues. Attitudes of Social Christian pastors were often hardened in this respect. In a sermon preached in 1881, Frank Mason North listed these foreign influences as among the greatest difficulties impeding his urban pastorate. As he put it, "The bigotry of Catholic Ireland or Italy. The irrational nationalism of Germany. The artful stupidity of Chinese. The Immoral religiousness of Africans."[67] Successful urban churches and church-related activities were certainly good vehicles for "Americanization." Contemporaries such as Samuel Lane Loomis would probably have agreed with modern sociologist-historians such as Alasdair MacIntyre on that point.[68]

In Canada publications such as J. S. Woodsworth's *Strangers Within Our Gates* (1909) argued much the same point. Following the First World War Social Christian leaders such as S. D. Chown were even wont to use the term "Canadianization" in relation to immigrant groups in cities.[69]

Recent historians have linked the issue of racial reform to Social Christianity and to the Social Gospel in particular. British Social Christians had little or

64. Jeffrey Cox, *The English Churches in a Secular Society: Lambeth, 1870–1930* (Oxford, 1982), esp. chap. 6.

65. Rainsford, *Story of a Varied Life*, 174.

66. L. E. Nettleship, "William Fremantle, Samuel Barnett, and the Broad Church Origins of Toynbee Hall," *Journal of Ecclesiastical History* 33, no. 4 (1982): 564–79.

67. "City Evangelization," 10 July 1881, p. 2, box "City," Frank Mason North Papers.

68. Alasdair MacIntyre, *Secularization and Moral Change* (London, 1967), 32.

69. "Canadian Civics, Lecture 1," n.d., p. 7a, box 2, file no. 49a, S. D. Chown Papers, United Church Archives.

nothing to say on the subject, for British cities possessed few visible minorities until the late 1940s. What comment they made on the American scene, as I have shown, tended to classify race as a rural and Southern problem. By the early 1920s Joseph Oldham did make explicit declarations against racism, but undoubtedly with the Empire in mind.[70] In general, the urban fixation of British Social Christianity, insofar as it influenced Americans, worked against any prolonged consideration of the plight of black Americans by providing such a full agenda on other matters. In the minds of many American Social Christians this urban agenda did not include the black issue as part of the American urban setting before the Great War. This is not to say that Social Christians were unconcerned with the plight of blacks in general.

The Protestant Episcopal Church Congresses raised the issue of relations between the church and "the colored race" as early as one session at the annual meeting of 1882. However, this was the first meeting of the Congress in the South (Richmond, Virginia), and reference was not made to the issue again until the Brooklyn, New York, meeting of 1905, where a session was devoted to "the future of the Negro in America." The agendas of the American church congresses resembled in large measure those of their British parents, and of their Canadian counterparts for that matter.[71] It is no surprise, in spite of the legacy of Phillips Brooks, that a Boston Episcopal priest meeting the visiting Hensley Henson at Wadsworth House in Cambridge, Massachusetts, could state that Episcopalianism in this period had little effect on "coloured people."[72] However, the Episcopal Church should not be singled out in that regard. The Baptist Church, with a far greater number of black adherents, also viewed the race problem as a regional one. One has only to juxtapose the sessions entitled "The Race Problem of the South" and "Enlarged Church Work in Cities" at the Baptist Church Congress of 1890.[73]

Some historians have associated latent or obvious racism with significant liberal Protestant and Social Christian figures from Horace Bushnell onward.[74] Certainly a hierarchy of races in general was present in the thought of Josiah

70. See Joseph H. Oldham, *Christianity and the Race Problem* (London, 1924).

71. See *Authorized Reports of the Proceedings of Congresses of the Protestant Episcopal Church in the United States* for 1882 (Richmond, Va.) and 1905 (Brooklyn, N.Y.). The first church congresses were held in the United States in New York in October 1874 and in Canada in Hamilton, Ontario, in June 1883. They were modeled after those held in England annually since 1861.

72. Hensley Henson, MS Journals, Cambridge, Mass., 14 November 1912, 204, vol. 18, Hensley Henson Papers, Dean and Chapter Library, Durham.

73. *Baptist Congress for the Discussion of Current Questions, 9th Annual Session, New Haven, Connecticut, November 11, 12, 13, 1890* (New York, 1890).

74. For a balanced appraisal of Bushnell, see Ralph E. Luker, "Bushnell in Black and White: Evidences of the 'Racism' of Horace Bushnell," *New England Quarterly* 45, no. 3 (1972): 409–16.

Strong and Walter Rauschenbusch. Washington Gladden raised the possibility of reserving three or four Southern states for black Americans.[75] Most, however, held moderate opinions, according to one study.[76] Pastoral experience, after all, was limited, being for the most part Northern and urban.

Ronald C. White Jr. has demonstrated that some Social Gospel leaders before World War I were quite concerned with the condition of African Americans, including their plight in cities.[77] The issue was certainly raised with greater frequency by both individuals and organizations than had previously been depicted by historians. Ralph Luker, however, in *The Social Gospel in Black and White* (1991) has argued for the centrality of the issue to the Social Gospel and has traced its roots to pre–Civil War movements of evangelical reform. In so doing, however, Luker has stirred debate concerning the centrality of racial reform for the mainstream of Social Christianity and in the very origins and definition of the Social Gospel. At issue are the scope of Social Christianity itself as understood by its practitioners, and the validity of including under the rubric of Social Christianity allied reformers who were in fact not Social Christians. The traditional view of Social Christianity, employed by White, is closer to the view of this study, in which I hope to explain, in part, why American figures before 1914 did not do more on this important question in the cities.

This is not to say that the influence of British writers was totally unhelpful to American Social Gospelers in the cause of racial justice. Lilly Hammond began writing of the racial situation in the early years of this century in journals such as Lyman Abbott's *Outlook* and in book form—*In Black and White* (1914). Ronald White has pointed to her self-acknowledged indebtedness to the early British Christian Socialists as well as to W. T. Stead.[78] Harlan Paul Douglass, an early outstanding Social Gospel advocate of racial reform, produced a ninety-nine-page thesis on English Christian Socialism while a graduate divinity student.[79] In such cases it is clear that the principles and general concerns expressed in British Social Christian writings could be applied to all sorts of settings, including rural ones, very different from those in which they had been produced. These religious and ethical principles had a potential for universality. After 1917, as black migration to the cities continued, the role of black churches

75. Washington Gladden, "The Negro Crisis: Is the Separation of the Two Races to Become Necessary?" *American Magazine* 63 (January 1907): 296–301.

76. Ralph E. Luker, *The Social Gospel in Black and White: American Racial Reform, 1885–1912* (Chapel Hill, N.C., 1991), 230.

77. See Ronald C. White Jr., *Liberty and Justice for All: Racial Reform and the Social Gospel, 1877–1925* (New York, 1990).

78. Ibid., 221.

79. Found at Amstad Research Center, Tulane University.

The Labor Temple, New York. Founded on the East Side by Charles Stelzle in 1910, its avowed purpose was to function as both a spiritual and a social center for working people. Its very appearance exemplifies the traditional urban fixation of Social Christians in North America and Britain over the previous generation.

and settlement houses in urban society would appear more obvious. But, until the 1940s, a time lag always separated these developments from their appreciation by many Social Gospel leaders.

One Social Christian who was conscious of the black presence in urban life quite early on was Charles Stelzle. As he once stated: "Considering the short time that the negro has had any kind of a chance for preparing himself, he has done marvellously. Let us give him a square deal—a man's chance. Neither race hatred nor mawkish sentimentality will settle this very delicate question. The South cannot settle it alone and the North cannot do the work of the South. The North and the South, the city and the country, must attack the situation together, for this is a national problem."[80] Stelzle was vitally concerned with the fate of the church in the city; he was chairman of the Presbyterian Home Missionary Society and was entrusted with a special mission to the working classes after 1903. The son of German immigrants, Stelzle grew up in the Bowery and was apprenticed as a machinist. He trained for the ministry at an older age, attending the Moody Institute in Chicago. On his return to New York, he became involved with the institutional church movement and fell under the spell of Frank Mason North. As a Social Gospeler, however, he was committed to the special mission to the laboring class, rather than to the strictly territorial parish, and opened his Labor Temple in 1910.

For Stelzle the city was "Christianity's storm center," as he entitled one of his books. Combating the standard propertied-class propensity to migrate away from the problem, physically or mentally, he said of the circumstances at the time of the Labor Temple's founding: "The situation confronting the Church downtown should have been the concern of the whole Church and not simply of the downtown churches."[81] Stelzle argued in general that the church or related social institutions be located where people live. But he also recognized that the membership of such an institution would de facto take on the appearance of the dominant class in the institution's neighborhood. In such circumstances he favored other types of organizations, organizations that would pull social classes together, acting as a type of mediator. In the last resolve he argued: "As it is more reasonable to expect the rich and cultured man to attend the enterprise conducted for the benefit of the working man than it is to expect the poor man to attend the rich man's church, such an institution as has been suggested should be located in a community in which working men live."[82]

80. Charles Stelzle, *American Social and Religious Conditions* (New York, 1912), 132.
81. Charles Stelzle, *A Son of the Bowery: The Life Story of an East Side American* (New York, 1926), 117.
82. Stelzle, *American Social and Religious Conditions*, 34–35.

As the twentieth century has progressed, however, it has become more common for one's work site, one's residence, and even one's house of worship to be in quite separate locations. In each case the community of one's associates—workmates, friends, and fellow parishioners—may be even more widely dispersed. "Neighborhood" in the modern city has increasingly lost its meaning.

One solution to this dilemma was again to retreat from the city center and create model satellite communities, as had been attempted since the middle decades of the nineteenth century by Social Christians or by those closely associated with them, with varying degrees of success. One last wave was to take place with the Garden City Movement, whose concept originated with Ebenezer Howard, a London court reporter. Government would own the sites and regulate the building requirements. It was hoped that the sites themselves would be industrially self-sufficient and that their communities would share any profits. The original investors would be paid limited dividends. Green belts were to be present through the cities, and a ceiling of thirty thousand placed upon the population. The basic idea was expanded by Howard in his 1898 book *Garden Cities of Tomorrow*, which was followed by the formation of the Garden City Association a year later in London.

The practical work of the movement was already under way, however, in the early 1890s. Inspired by the model industrial villages of Bourneville and Port Sunlight (though not by the autocratic rule of the Lever family), a Garden City Limited Company was formed in 1893 with £300,000 in capital. A site was purchased thirty-four miles northeast of London on the Great Northern Railway line. Parker Unwin drew up a plan for a town of 1,200 acres with 150 of these reserved for factories—each with its own side track to the Great Northern Railway line. Careful decisions were made in controlling building costs and rental and leasing arrangements. Some of the construction was carried out by cooperative building societies. In 1903 the town was inaugurated with the name Letchworth.[83] A second garden city, Welwyn, was established in 1919. Social Christians—including Quakers Seebohm Rowntree and Edward Grubb, Catholic guild socialist A. J. Plenty, Thomas Child of the New Church, and especially J. Bruce Wallace of the Brotherhood Movement—were quite supportive of the garden cities.[84] Only Letchworth and Welwyn succeeded. Projects around Manchester and Warrington did not result in garden cities. Hampstead Garden suburb, founded in 1908, was the garden city most influenced by Christian

83. See Bliss, *New Encyclopedia of Social Reform*, 532.
84. See d'A. Jones, *Christian Socialist Revival*, 335.

Socialism, having been devised in its earliest stages by Mrs. Henrietta Barnett, complete with a church named after Saint Jude, the patron saint of her husband's church in Whitechapel.[85]

The garden city idea was enthusiastically taken up in the United States, with Boston's well-known Christian Socialist, the Reverend W.D.P. Bliss, as its leader. Josiah Strong gave strong support, arguing that city planning, rather than going back to the land, was the avenue for social reconstruction in the industrial age.[86] The Garden City Association was founded in New York in 1906. Forest Hills Gardens, established on Long Island in 1911, was among the first of the garden cities on the western side of the Atlantic. Very quickly, however, the concept came to be distorted, with developers making large profits. More frequently the garden cities of America simply became prosperous, well-planned suburbs of major cities from New York to California. Some associations also appeared in Germany and France.

In the United States the urban fixation of Social Christianity was maintained throughout the period. The establishment of organizations such as the Federal Council of Churches of Christ (1908) reflected the influence of dedicated Social Christian urban pastors. At the time of the council's inception, Frank Mason North, for example, was giving speeches on "city evangelization" from New York to Butte, Montana.[87]

While perceptive city Social Gospelers such as Charles Stelzle were aware that rural impoverishment was a major social problem, they could also remain adamant that "the country must solve its own problems." For Stelzle, the turn-of-the-century back-to-the-land movement of city dwellers onto farms was a mistake. What rural areas required was a more scientific approach to farming and more cooperative schemes; "this will be one of the most difficult lessons to learn, for the American farmer is a strong individualist."[88] Education and practical improvements, such as better pay for ministers,[89] would also increase the already considerable guidance provided by the churches in rural areas. In the last resolve Stelzle could not see the plight of the farmer as that serious, for the farmer would "never become a peasant as do many of the European farmers. He may be poor, but he has his rights of citizenship."[90] In the minds of

85. Meacham, *Toynbee Hall,* 118–19.

86. Josiah Strong, "The Industrial Revolution: Its Influence on Urban Development," *Garden City: The Official Organ of the Garden City Association* 1, no. 1 (1904): 2–4.

87. "Church and Labour," notes of addresses on city evangelization for sixteen cities 1906–9, Frank Mason North Papers.

88. Stelzle, *American Social and Religious Conditions,* 53, 52.

89. Ibid., 62.

90. Ibid., 59.

urban leaders, the Jeffersonian dream seemed still to be operative in rural areas despite the misery in places such as the Deep South.

Many church groups gave their temporary support to Henry George's single-tax crusade at the end of the century, believing it to be a panacea for *both* rural and urban woes and an exercise in applied Christianity. Richard T. Ely, prominent Social Christian professor at the University of Wisconsin, whose expertise included land economics, opposed George, however. Once offending a large gathering of Methodists in Evanston, Illinois, with his opposition, he explained his position: "Yet it seemed to me that the natural rights doctrine of Henry George was thoroughly unscientific, a belated revival of the social philosophy of the eighteenth century. I believed that the economics underlying Henry George's pleas was unsound. My experience had shown me that his idea of unearned increment worked untold injury."[91] Much later, in 1920, Ely founded the Institute for Research in Land Economics and Public Utilities. But this founding occurred in his so-called conservative period, when to him Social Christianity seemed to apply more to urban than to rural questions.[92]

The growth of populism in the Midwest and migrations from the South did make urban Social Christians more aware of the rural situation. The Dust Bowl of the Great Depression and works such as John Steinbeck's *The Grapes of Wrath*, in book and motion picture form, brought rural conditions high media profile. Social Christians became more prominent among ministers and laity in the Midwest and South, though conservative fundamentalism still predominated. The Fellowship of Southern Churchmen (founded 1934), in conjunction with the Southern Tenant Farmers Union, drew sufficient attention to the plight of sharecroppers to receive the guidance and support of important national Social Christian leaders such as Sherwood Eddy and Reinhold Niebuhr in rural cooperative enterprises in the Deep South in an era when the great cities of the Northeast and Midwest were in dire straits[93] (see Chapter 3). By the 1930s, with the buildup of large black ghettos, the need for racial reform in cities was obvious. However, the comparison of vigorous support for black sharecroppers in Mississippi with unimpressive efforts in the North reveals that racial reform was still viewed as an essentially Southern, rural question rather than a national one. The activities of the clergy of black churches, in conjunction with the Urban League or the NAACP, in advancing

91. Richard T. Ely, *Ground Under Our Feet: An Autobiography* (New York, 1938), 92.
92. Ibid., 238–42.
93. Robert F. Martin, "Critique of Southern Society and Vision of a New Order: The Fellowship of Southern Churchmen, 1934–1957," *Church History* 52, no. 1 (1983): 66–80.

the cause of urban African Americans, would receive more attention in a later generation.

In Canada, political and economic factors, as well as internal church policies, made Social Gospelers sensitive to rural problems. Ironically, a major city, Winnipeg, was crucial to this situation. Wesley College (later United College) was established as a major training center for Social Gospelers before World War I. Most of its graduates assumed positions as rural pastors. Winnipeg, a regional industrial center and funnel for immigrants and agrarian workers, as the "Gateway to the West," was an ideal laboratory in which to test out the Social Gospel in practice, *both* in relation to urban and rural problems. The involvement of prominent Social Gospelers in the Winnipeg General Strike of 1919 gained them national prominence in both church and secular circles (see Chapter 7). Leaders such as J. S. Woodsworth, who had himself written on urban problems, could easily transpose ideas to the rural setting. Farm incomes and federal government policies toward the West oppressed rural populations, which found solace in the support of the Social Gospel. Their discontent found political expression through the leadership of Woodsworth, both in the Progressive Party and ultimately in the Cooperative Commonwealth Federation (CCF). Such regional journals as the *Grain Growers Guide* also revealed the strong bond between rural Western interests and those of the Social Gospel. Nowhere in English-speaking Social Christianity did a concern for rural issues become so prominent as in western Canada in the interwar period.[94]

In Britain rural issues continued to be very much a subordinate concern of Social Christians. Some rural interests had supported Henry Georgism in the belief that landlordism was responsible for the decline of agriculture and the rural way of life. Legislation such as the Small Holdings Act of 1892 elicited support from a minority of Christian Socialists for the small farmer. For example, the Reverend Charles W. Stubbs, dean of Ely, wrote in the 1890s of the urgent need for the "social mission of Christ's Church" to be applied to the village; at stake was the survival of the "national character," since the rural parish was the truest school of "public justice and self-government."[95] Albert Spicer, on behalf of the Congregational Union, wrote a detailed exposition of economic problems in *Christian Economics with Reference to the Land Question* (London, 1890) and

94. See Ben Smillie, *Beyond the Social Gospel: Church Protest on the Prairies* (Saskatoon, 1991), and Richard Allen, "The Social Gospel as the Religion of the Agrarian Revolt," in *The West and the Nation: Essays in Honour of W. L. Morton,* ed. C. Berger and R. Cook (Toronto, 1976), 174–86.

95. Charles W. Stubbs, "The Imperial Christ and His Democratic Creed. Part II. Village Problems," in *Lombard Street in Lent: A Course of Sermons on Social Subjects: Organized by the London Branch of the C.S.U. and preached in the Church of St. Edmund, Lombard Street, During Lent, 1894,* with a preface by the Bishop of Durham (B. F. Westcott) (London, 1894), 80 and 185.

touched on issues of landlordism and rural depopulation, though agrarian problems were ultimately tied into national and hence urban issues.

For the period between the world wars British Social Christianity remained
fixed in its urban attitudes. There was little reason to change. A few years
earlier a small note of urban optimism had even been injected into the thinking
of some Social Christians. The writings of urban planners such as Sir Patrick
Geddes left room for spiritual health as a dimension of their designs for urban
life. In response to Geddes' *City Development* (Edinburgh, 1904) and to the
work of other urban planners, the Reverend Samuel E. Keeble stated, "Chief
amongst those new honorary civic servants will be the clergy and ministers of
the land. They will provide the influential leaders in this work of scientifically
applied Christianity to civic development."[96] With or without the guidance of
clergy, Britain had become the most mature of urbanized societies in the world,
as was made painfully clear by the cursory discussion of rural life during the
Conference on Politics, Economics, and Citizenship (COPEC) meetings of 1924,
a discussion confined to volume 12 of the conference's reports. Ten years later,
the COPEC meetings of the Great Depression produced little more, though
figures such as Bishop George Bell of Chichester urged that distinctions be
made between urban and rural societies in social work.[97] The churches continued discussions at conferences in an effort only to vary their attempts to reach
the urban populations. While membership figures for churches did not indicate
drastic decline, as they did in the post–World War II decades, membership was
nonetheless slowly eroding.

Dealing with social ills and simultaneously reversing the erosion of the
church attendance became too much for the urban British churches well before
the 1940s. On the whole these pressures produced a great deal of gloomy
discussion that disregarded much of the progress that had been made in
lessening social evils, albeit increasingly through state intervention (which
most Social Christians themselves had lobbied for).

In the United States and Canada the churches remained more visible as
institutions in urban life, in part because their facilities were needed to a
greater extent in dealing with the traditional social ills as well as a rising tide of
new ones, such as racism and violence. Church membership in North American
cities appeared to be impressive for the time being. Was this an indication that
the secular city was advancing more rapidly in Britain? Perhaps so, but church

96. Samuel E. Keeble, "The City, or the Service of the Citizens," in *The Citizen of Tomorrow: A
Handbook on Social Questions,* ed. Samuel E. Keeble (London, 1906), 304.

97. Bell to Mrs. Basil Jellicoe, 30 September 1937, vol. 166 "Christian Social Council," f. 305,
George Bell Papers, Lambeth Palace Library.

membership was more a Victorian's way of measuring religious influence. On the other hand, if a Victorian Social Christian had been able to look ahead at the general social conditions in British cities by the 1940s, he or she might have believed that some progress had been achieved. Clearly, by the 1940s, whether the city appeared as Babylon or Jerusalem was very much in the eye of the beholder.

# 3

# SOCIAL SERVICE AND
# SOCIAL SCIENCE

Social Christians faced a formidable challenge, especially in cities, in the realization of the Kingdom. If they were to meet this challenge, they would have to find new and innovative ways of dealing with social ills. In this quest, Social Christian leaders formulated policies that went well beyond the scope of church work as defined by the mid-Victorians. Social service in its various forms emerged early within Christian Social circles. As time passed, these forms of social service became more sophisticated and ambitious, often completely separating from traditional pastoral work. Yet a clear religious underpinning to these efforts remained ever present, at least until the end of the nineteenth century, in both Britain and North America. The emerging branches of social science also gained extreme importance to many Social Christians as a means of improving and giving more refined direction to social service. At the end of the century, as I have shown, liberal theology, especially the New Theology, seemed to mandate both a harmonious relationship between science and religion as well as the urgency of social salvation. While not intentionally replacing theology, the science of humankind and of society came into a new prominence in the thought of those who sought to bring about the New Jerusalem. The hope, as with social service, was that social science could be harnessed in the service of Social Christianity.

F. D. Maurice, J. M. Ludlow, and E. V. Neale engaged in activities that went beyond the bounds of traditional pastoral work in an effort to alter the lives of the dispossessed. Maurice's long period as head of Working Men's College constituted a serious and sustained effort in the field of adult education. It is true that much of the activity at Working Men's College was aimed at self-improvement, a cherished mid-Victorian approach to the Condition-of-England question, but it was multifarious. The courses given were a mixture of the esoteric and practical,[1] designed directly to improve the daily lives of those motivated to avail themselves of their opportunities. The courses enabled individual working people to attain new social awareness. J.F.C. Harrison sees in this endeavor the influence of associationism,[2] the belief that many operations could be run by working people, possibly owned by the state, but not directed by it. Peter d'A. Jones believes that this influence emanated from P. J. Buchez and H.F.R. Lamennais through Charles Kingsley and especially Ludlow, eventually to Maurice. For Jones, associationism led to cooperatives and away from a too powerful state.[3] For Social Christians such as Hugh Price Hughes, the vulnerability of the dispossessed to the evils of a continuing capitalist economy in the last decades of the century left no alternative but the pursuit of policy in the opposite direction from laissez-faire.[4]

The cooperatives started by Christian Socialists, in alliance with Owenites and others, were perhaps of more immediate benefit to the working classes, but were even less connected with the church. They were a practical demonstration of an organized effort to raise the lot of working people. However, the cooperative movement was infused with Christian principles and otherwise might have been directed by those hostile to religion. The effectiveness of this conduit for Social Christianity was evident as late as the 1920s, when Catholic clergy in Maritime Canada reinvented it in the form of the Antigonish Movement.[5]

What was lacking in many of these early attempts at innovative applications of Social Christianity was a conceptual foundation in the new developments in

1. See John Frederick Denison Maurice, *Learning and Working* (Oxford, reprint, 1968).

2. J.F.C. Harrison, *Learning and Living: A Study in the History of the English Adult Education Movement* (London, 1961), 92–93.

3. Peter d'A. Jones, *The Christian Socialist Revival, 1877–1914: Religion, Class, and Social Conscience in Late-Victorian England* (Princeton, 1968), 14–23, 441, 435.

4. See Hugh Price Hughes, *Social Christianity Sermons Delivered at St. James Hall, London* (London, 1889), esp. no. 2, "Jesus Christ And The Social Distress," 3–16, and no. 10, "The National Charter Determined By The National Laws," 135–48. These sermons, together with a collection entitled *The Philanthropy of God: Described and Illustrated in a Series of Sermons* (London, 1890), make it clear that old-style evangelical philanthropy was gone, leaving open the door to an intervening state.

5. See Moses Coady, *Masters of Their Own Destiny* (New York, 1939), and Gregory Baum, *Catholics and Canadian Socialism* (Toronto, 1980).

social philosophy and in other scientific thinking on the world of human affairs. Since publication of *Origins of Species,* if not before, agnostics on both sides of the Atlantic tended to be prominent in the ranks of those scientists interested in placing humankind in the wider materialistic scheme of the universe. Their views were a powerful contributor to the so-called Victorian Crisis of Faith. The need to limit their influence, together with the persistent desire to find orderly ways to cope with social conflict, was a powerful negative inducement compelling Social Christians to wed the intellectual world with applied Christianity. By the 1880s circumstances at leading universities provided Social Christians with opportunities to take initiatives in these matters. In Britain, as Reba Soffer has pointed out, there were wide variations in thought concerning the purposes and content of early social science.[6] What most did agree upon, however, was that the mind of the scientist-collector deeply influenced the empirical collection of data. An accompanying belief was that natural law did not directly predetermine human behavior. Achieving the best results in the work of the new social science became the object of open competition between secular humanists and Christians. It was not unreasonable to hope at this stage that Christians might prevail in the competition.

Into this situation, and at a very opportune time in the British case, came the Oxford idealists. I have already discussed the impact of the so-called Oxford Movement of the 1880s upon theology and social thought. Though not specifically Christian Socialist, the principles enunciated by Thomas H. Green were taken up immediately by many in the Broad Church circle who were also vitally concerned with issues of social salvation, science in its application to human relations, and were at this stage predominant in British Social Christianity. Unlike the general trend of widening the gap between an increasingly specialized academe and the general public, as described by Thomas Heyck,[7] Social Christians, among the ranks of dons at Oxford or elsewhere in Britain, were conspicuous in not doing so. Among Green's intimate disciples was Arnold Toynbee, who exemplified a comprehensive approach and inspired both professional academics and practical social service workers in the cause of Social Christianity.

Toynbee's death at the age of thirty precluded any great quantitative contribution to the field of economic history. However, as a don and early resident of London's first settlement house, he became somewhat of a cult figure among

6. See Reba N. Soffer, *Ethics and Society in England: The Revolution in the Social Sciences, 1870–1914* (Berkeley and Los Angeles, 1978).

7. Thomas W. Heyck, *The Transformation of Intellectual Life in Victorian England* (London, 1982).

undergraduates. His posthumously published book on the Industrial Revolution, reconstructed from student notes of his lectures on the subject, was of
considerable importance to the field.[8] It reveals his belief that economic
developments were the result of intellectual decisions, not of impersonal Spenc-
erian determinism. Likewise, in his other lectures, he argued that positive
actions to improve the distribution of wealth could lead directly to an improvement of conditions for the masses. He also urged a nonviolent, constitutional
approach to problem solving by the educated for the benefit of the people. As a
teacher his message was very clear to a generation of Oxford undergraduates.
Toynbee was one of the leading lights in the so-called historical school of
economics, as exemplified in his work on the Industrial Revolution. The stress
upon the importance of historical development meant that no economic theories, including those of Adam Smith and David Ricardo, could speak to all ages.
According to Mark Blaug, this English historicism was an indigenous movement
tracing its roots to Thomas Carlyle and John Ruskin's critiques of the narrow-
ness of political economy.[9] But among Toynbee's students was Sir William J.
Ashley, who was also aware of the German historical school through the
writings of William Roscher and Gustav Schmoller. Schmoller, Lujo Brentano,
and others were also part of the group known as the *Kathedersozialisten,* or
Socialists of the Chair, who were behind Social Christian activity in Prussia
through organizations such as the Verein für Sozialpolitik (Social Policy Association).[10] They believed firmly in a moral base to social science. Ashley later
attempted to promote the concepts of Schmoller and Brentano in the English-
speaking world, becoming close friends with the Germans, while never actually studying under them.[11]

Many associated with this group would also become members of the Oxford
branch of the Christian Social Union (CSU), which launched the *Economic*

8. Arnold Toynbee, *Lectures on the Industrial Revolution of the Eighteenth Century in England*
(London, 1884), 2–3, stressed the destruction of human relationships by the cash nexus resulting
from the Industrial Revolution. His ideas influenced the writings of later historians such as the
Hammonds.

9. Mark Blaug, *Economic Theory in Retrospect* (Cambridge, 1985), 300.

10. W. Reginald Ward, *Theology, Sociology, and Politics: The German Protestant Social Conscience, 1890–1933* (Berne, 1979), 46.

11. See Bernard Semmel, *Imperialism and Social Reform: English Social-Imperial Thought,
1895–1914* (London, 1960), chap. 11. From 1888 to 1892 Ashley was professor of political economy at
the University of Toronto and then was appointed to the chair of economic history at Harvard. In
1900 he returned to England as the first professor of commerce at Birmingham University. For a
good description of his early career and of the Oxford economists in general, see Alon Kadish, *The
Oxford Economists in the Late Nineteenth Century* (Oxford, 1982), esp. chap. 1, which begins with
Ashley.

*Review*. The Reverend John Carter, a Canadian Social Christian resident at Pusey House, Oxford, was an important figure behind the scenes at the journal, which included regular contributions by Sir William Ashley, his young American associate, Richard T. Ely,[12] as well as a wide range of other figures, including Sidney Webb. Its publication life was from 1891 to 1924.

The Oxford Branch of the CSU met regularly after 1889 to discuss a variety of subjects, with a view to promoting its three basic objectives:

1. To claim for the Christian Law the ultimate authority to rule social practice
2. To study in common how to apply the moral truths and principles of Christianity to the social and economic difficulties of the present time
3. To present Christ in practical life as the Living Master and King, the enemy of wrong and selfishness, the power of righteousness and love.[13]

Its membership included some of the best-known Christian Socialist clergy in Britain, such as Scott Holland, as well as affiliated reading circles as far away as Canada. Members met regularly to discuss topics such as temperance, state protection of children, municipal government powers, the aged poor, the various forms of socialism, the labor movement in the United States, unemployment, and Seebohm Rowntree's study of poverty in York. One meeting, held in the Reverend S. A. Cooke's rooms at St. John's College on 12 November 1890, heard an address by J. T. Dodd of Lincoln's Inn entitled "Housing of the Poor." The result was a set of resolutions, all of which urged state intervention to deal with this problem. The resolutions included the following:

1. Seeing that the State is the largest landlord, and the largest employer of the poor; and seeing also that overcrowding is in great

12. Richard Theodore Ely (1854–1943) was born in Ripley, New York, and educated at Dartmouth, Columbia, the University of Halle, and the University of Heidelberg, where he obtained his Ph.D. under Karl Knies's supervision. Like Ashley, Ely's origins were humble and he was a convert to Episcopalianism. He was a popular speaker and his books sold well on both sides of the Atlantic. As a leading economist he taught at the Johns Hopkins University (1881–92) before his long tenure at the University of Wisconsin and was the main founder of the American Economic Association. Ely was a leader of the German historical school in America, arguing for the importance of cultural and political factors against the prevailing classical economics. After the Red Scare of the 1890s, when his politics was questioned at Wisconsin, he became somewhat more conservative in the social policies he advocated. However, his adherence to Social Christianity remained unshaken.

13. Minutes, 16 November 1889, minute books, Christian Social Union, Oxford Branch, Pusey House, Oxford.

part due to demolitions for schools, streets and the like and is resulting in the deterioration of the race, there is a necessity for the State to interfere and see that suitable dwellings are provided for the poor.

2. The cost of such interference may justly be borne by a tax upon the unearned increment of the holders of land.

3. This meeting approves of compulsory sale of land in a more simple and less costly manner than under the London County Council, so that a fair and just price be given to the landowner.

4. The improvement of the means of locomotion should be recognized as a necessary part of the improvement of the dwellings of the London poor.

5. Any scheme for the housing of the poor should provide for the existence of open spaces where suitable.[14]

The reference to the tax upon the unearned increment of holders of land raised issues that were certainly connected with the influence of the American writer Henry George.

Henry George's single-tax proposal on the unearned increment from landlords' revenues was a moderate approach to redistribution of wealth. His *Progress and Poverty* (1879), which was distributed widely, well before the English translation of *Das Kapital*, seemed to interest Social Christians who sought an orderly path to mild forms of collectivism. In fact, Henry George, in his religious consciousness, which he pursued through social questions, has often been classified as a Christian Socialist. His influence on the British Christian Socialists,[15] reading public, and labor movement was considerable. He also had a following among those well versed in economic theory.

Arnold Toynbee, Richard Ely, and others in the historical school did not approve of George's ideas, however;[16] and as a result of their disapproval a wider range of figures, including Samuel Barnett, became openly anti-Georgist than otherwise would have. The so-called marginalist economists made a generally more receptive audience. The marginalists had developed about the same time as the English historical school. John Stuart Mill, who had abandoned the labor theory of value in the 1860s, was followed by other writers who raised further questions about the demand and supply functions of the market.

14. Ibid., 12 November 1890.

15. See Peter d'A. Jones, *Henry George and British Socialism* (New York, 1991), esp. 201–20.

16. W.H.G. Armytage, *Heavens Below: Utopian Experiments in England, 1560–1960* (London, 1961), 317.

The result was the genesis of marginal utility theory, which was enunciated in more complete form by W. S. Jevons in *The Theory of Political Economy* (1871). Jevons's work was part of a revived interest in Bentham that was also influenced by the so-called Austrian school of marginalists, led by Karl Menger and Eugen Böhm-Bawerk. Jevons had direct experience conducting social investigations of the London slums at midcentury. Though initially poorly received, Jevons's ideas gradually gained acceptance through the 1870s. His last book, *The State in Relation to Labour* (1882), published the year of his death, viewed state intervention as already a fact in the actual workings of the economy.

The full development of marginalist theory found expression in the writings of the Reverend Philip H. Wicksteed, especially his textbook *Common Sense of Political Economy* (1910). A Unitarian minister, Wicksteed had a wide range of intellectual interests; his work shows the influence of Comte and Ruskin. He began to correspond with Henry George in the early 1880s, and the two eventually cofounded the Land Reform Union. About the same time, he read George's works and became his great disciple. Though a man of more profound scholarly accomplishments than George, Wicksteed was also a popularizer of marginalism within the ranks of economists, as well as a proponent of reformism and of mild state interventionism. Among his friends were Fabians such as G. B. Shaw. His close collaboration with fellow Christian Socialists, such as Stewart Headlam, increased Georgist influence, dividing some from the views of Christian Socialists who agreed with the criticism of George propounded by the historical school. Wicksteed's support of the Labour Church (see Chapter 4) in the 1890s brought his influence into the ranks of yet another group.[17] Wicksteed was therefore equally respected in the eyes of Christian Socialists and of the more secular-minded social reformers anxious to assault what was left of orthodox economics.

The new repository of ideas on the economy and society was useful to those middle-class university-educated youths who, heeding the advice of T. H. Green, plunged themselves into working with the underprivileged in both the Oxford extension department and university settlement movement in the practice of good citizenship. Settlements were experimental educational enterprises designed and staffed by resident academics and clergymen to help solve social distress in urban working-class districts. Inspired by Arnold Toynbee's personal example, the first London settlement was renamed Toynbee Hall by its founder, the Reverend Samuel Barnett. Toynbee Hall was in many ways the

17. See Ian Steedman, "Rationality, Economic Man, and Altruism in Philip H. Wicksteed's Common Sense of Political Economy," in *Truth, Liberty, Religion,* ed. Barbara Smith (Manchester College, Oxford, 1986), 291–311.

product of innovative pastoral work in East London led by W. H. Fremantle, Barnett, and others. But it was also designed to present to the masses a new form of teaching through direct instruction, advice, and example. John Ruskin, professor of fine arts at Oxford, who also taught at Working Men's College and wanted to bring culture and beauty to the industrial workers, was an inspirer of some of the activities. In 1885, a year after the founding of Toynbee Hall, Oxford House was established at Bethnal Green with a stronger clerical contingent, led by Tractarians. Within a few years Nonconformist settlements also appeared, with even more pronounced religious affiliations.[18] Settlements now proliferated, influencing religious and nonreligious alike in their quest to uplift the life of the toiling masses. But in its success, in the short run, the settlement movement may also have inhibited the emergence of modern sociology and social work that was *not* based upon an understanding of "social ends as the expression of a moral ideal."[19] This indeed was the basis of a wide variety of activity touching social science. Oscar Browning, for example, an important figure in progressive educational movements and in the National Association for the Promotion of Social Science, could write as late as 1908: "I believe that Jesus came into the world to show the way to a new and higher conception of life to release men from the burden of sin."[20]

This is not to say that in the last decades of the nineteenth century in Britain there was not considerable effort to collect data in an empirical way that might make social service more effective. The investigations of street folk began in a big way with the eighty-two letters published in the *Morning Chronicle* by Henry Mayhew between October 1849 and Christmas of 1850. Mayhew's detailed descriptions of the various classes of London toilers, partially republished in his *London Labour and the London Poor* (1861), revealed a world of street poverty and crime that begged for more information gathering. The most impressive contribution to this trend before the century's end, in sheer volume of output at least, was the massive project directed by Charles Booth that resulted in the publication of the series entitled *Life and Labour of the People in London* (1889–1903).[21] A third series focused upon religious influences in the

18. Among the more celebrated were the Wesleyan Methodists' Bermondsey Settlement, founded in 1890 with Scott Lidgett as first warden, and the Congregationalist settlements Browning Hall in Walworth and Mansfield House in Canning Town.

19. Standish Meacham, *Toynbee Hall and Social Reform, 1880–1914: The Search for Community* (New Haven, Conn., 1987), 104.

20. Browning to *Christian Commonwealth*, 3 December 1908, Oscar Browning Papers, King's College Library, Cambridge University.

21. Charles Booth (1840–1916), who wrote on social questions, was active as partner in a steamship firm. He was already a supporter of trade unions before gathering statistics on the

metropolis. This reflected in part the interests of the many collectors of data who were Social Christians or their close associates.

In the last decades of the century Social Christians in the United States were more conspicuous in numbers and influence among the official ranks of social scientists. Of the fifty members attending the opening meeting of the American Economic Association in 1885, for example, at least twenty were former or practicing ministers.[22] The impetus for such interest was undoubtedly the impact of social Darwinism on American society—an impact more considerable than in Darwin's own country, as witnessed in the enthusiastic reception of Herbert Spencer's *Study of Sociology* (1872). While William Graham Sumner saw ways in which Christian ethics could be combined with social Darwinism,[23] others simply developed the latter into a tooth-and-claw version of natural selection upholding free enterprise. For the next twenty years there was a tremendous outpouring of books and articles on the effect of Darwinism in theology, politics, public affairs, and so forth. Inevitably, negative reactions began to predominate in church circles.[24]

Lester Ward, a preeminent figure in social science circles, developed a dualistic approach, accepting biological evolution but arguing that purposeful action by humans need not restrict them in their efforts to improve the lot of individuals living in society.[25] His corpus of thought became useful in the counterattack by Social Christians and progressives against popular social Darwinism. But his naturalism and agnostic tendencies also shocked the religious.

---

condition of the working classes in the 1880s. His first research findings appeared in *Tower Hamlets Magazine* in 1887. Much more systematic than earlier investigators, such as Henry Mayhew, he prepared the various volumes of *The Life and Labour of the People in London* over a sixteen-year period. Four volumes were on poverty, five on industry, seven on religious influences, and one was devoted to a conclusion. See Harold W. Pfantz, ed., *Charles Booth on the City: Physical Pattern and Social Structure: Selected Writings* (Chicago, 1967).

22. Mary O. Furner, *Advocacy and Objectivity: A Crisis in the Professionalization of American Social Science* (Lexington, Ky., 1975), 75.

23. William Graham Sumner (1840–1910) was the first professor of political and economic science at Yale. Apart from actively espousing the ideas of Herbert Spencer, he argued in lectures and writings for a sound and rigorous basis for the new social sciences. He had been an Episcopal priest in New York before his Yale appointment.

24. See James R. Moore, *The Post-Darwinian Controversies: A Study of the Protestant Struggle to Come to Terms with Darwin in Great Britain and America, 1870–1900* (Cambridge, 1979).

25. Lester Ward (1841–1913) was regarded as a leader in the new field of sociology, influencing generations of students through his writings, from *Dynamic Sociology* (1883) to *The Textbook of Sociology* (1905). For Social Christians, his belief that people could plan a future democratic, more compassionate society was encouraging. He strongly supported government efforts in general education and the reduction of poverty. However, he alarmed many American Christians through *The Iconoclast* and other publications advocating unorthodox freethinking.

By the 1880s it was almost inevitable that Social Christians would have to take the initiative in such circumstances lest the extreme social Darwinians or the followers of Ward triumph. A very powerful assist to this development was the inspiration of Josiah Strong. A dynamic Social Gospel leader and famous writer, Strong moved quickly to enlist scientific evolutionary theory in the crusade to realize a perfectible human society in the 1880s. After meeting with frustration with the Evangelical Alliance,[26] he established the Institute for Social Service in 1898. Dorothea Muller has argued that his social philosophy (closely allied to his theology) powerfully backed the new science of society.[27] Strong inspired Social Christians in North America to delve into statistics gathering and sociological investigations of all sorts.

Graham Taylor, professor of theology at Hartford Seminary and later at the University of Chicago, was greatly influenced by Strong to move toward a more active analysis of and cure for social ills, becoming as much a sociologist as minister. Taylor was impressed by Charles Booth's *Life and Labour of the People of London,* which he stated was not only "the greatest Christian enterprise at the close of the nineteenth century, but is already producing results commensurate with its cost."[28] Albion Small, who rose to be professor and head of the Sociology Department at the University of Chicago, was the foremost leader in the struggle to vanquish the enemies of Christian social science. His letter exchanges with Lester Ward reveal his commitment to a high degree of professionalism as well as to Social Christianity.[29] Small, however, had to contend with challenges from both extremes within the ranks of his fellow Social Christians.

One challenge came from those who claimed to be "Christian sociologists" and "Christian economists" but who in reality were not professional in their approach. Professor J.H.W. Stuckenberg of Wittenberg College perhaps best summed up their position: "Why not make the ethics of the New Testament the test of all social theories?"[30] Unfortunately for Small, the large number of

26. The Evangelical Alliance was established in London in 1846 to foster cooperation among Evangelicals of different denominations. The American branch was not established until 1867, though Americans had participated in the 1846 meeting. American clergy involved with the Evangelical Alliance were consistently interested in closer interdenominational ties. By 1900 it was in decline.

27. Dorothea R. Muller, "The Social Philosophy of Josiah Strong," *Church History* 28 , no. 2 (1959): 183–201.

28. "Christian Faith in an Industrial Age," Chautauqua, 4 July 1908, 4, Graham Taylor Papers, Newberry Library.

29. Bernhard J. Stern, ed., "The Letters of Albion Small to Lester F. Ward," pt. 1, *Social Forces* 13, no. 2 (1933): 163–73; pt. 2, *Social Forces* 13, no. 3 (1935): 323–41; pt. 3, *Social Forces* 15, no. 1 (1936): 174–86; pt. 4, *Social Forces* 15, no. 3 (1937): 305–27.

30. J.H.W. Stuckenberg, *Christian Sociology* (New York, 1880), 16.

Christian social scientists of this type in denominational colleges and seminaries across the United States made it very difficult to convince neutral observers that Social Christians could argue in the field of social science with much authority. By the end of the century, however, Small's position was increasingly supported by the better-educated professors and ministers. As the Baptist theologian Shailer Mathews argued on behalf of the Small position: "The champions of some so-called Christian sociology are dangerously open to criticism similar to that which Voltaire passed upon the Holy Roman Empire—it is neither scientific nor Christian."[31] Above all, those "Christian" social scientists exuded an air of confidence in leading their scientific investigations of society. This confidence was clearly unwarranted.

At the other end of the spectrum, radical Social Christians, who used the name "Christian sociology" largely for political purposes, were also in disagreement with Small. The most conspicuous radical was George D. Herron (see Chapter 6). Originally a Congregationalist minister, with no formal higher education, Herron was an active organizer of the American Institute of Sociology founded at Chautauqua in 1893. The American Institute included respected social scientists such as R. T. Ely and John R. Commons. Later, as professor of applied Christianity at Iowa (Grinnell) College, with the backing of President George A. Gates and Mrs. E. D. Rand, he launched the so-called Kingdom Movement (1893–96). The Rand and YMCA lectureships brought an amazing assortment of social prophet speakers to Iowa, from W. T. Stead to Charles M. Sheldon, including Graham Taylor, professor of Christian sociology at the University of Chicago.[32] Herron's eclectic mixture of theological and philosophic elements, as seen in works such as *Social Meanings of Religious Experiences* (1896), hardly qualified him as a social scientist.[33] His attacks upon capitalists seemed dangerously radical. The controversies around his continued appointment at Iowa, however, may have obscured his influence upon students, including Harlan Paul Douglass, the racial reformer.[34] Herron's call for a Christian reconstruction of the economic order was a powerful one.

31. Shailer Mathews, *The Social Teaching of Jesus: An Essay in Christian Sociology* (New York, 1897), 2.

32. See Robert T. Handy, "George D. Herron and the Kingdom Movement," *Church History* 19 , no. 2 (1950): 97–115.

33. For Albion Small's attack on Herron's professionalism, see note 112 to Chapter 6. Shailer Mathews made the further point, in arguing for a professional Christian sociology, that "Jesus was committed to no political teaching" Mathews, *The Social Teaching of Jesus: An Essay in Christian Sociology* (New York, 1897), 128.

34. Ralph E. Luker, *The Social Gospel in Black and White: American Racial Reform, 1885–1912* (Chapel Hill, N.C., 1991), 302.

This desire by Small and other Social Christians to embrace a degree of professionalism in social scientific endeavors was prudent given that the early desire of most Americans to model their social sciences on natural science was strong. As Dorothy Ross has argued, the reasons for this were complex, the result of circumstances peculiar to the United States in the latter part of the nineteenth century, rather than merely an inevitable course of development in the triumph of reason.[35] Such an approach served the demands of a predominantly liberal, Protestant culture of the republic. But American social science also seemed to insist on a link with national identity and in so doing resembled social science in Germany and France in the same period.[36] Certainly the sense of American exceptionalism, described by Ross, permeated much American social scientific thinking, though the fear of class conflict and rising socialism was not unique to the great Republic. The drive to advance a professional social science in American culture was very apparent, and those who would resist it in academic circles risked being pushed to the fringes.

Undoubtedly one of the most ambitious groups of Social Christians within the field of social science was the so-called Wisconsin Ideal. This included two German-trained academics—sociologist E. A. Ross and, in particular, Richard Ely. Like their mentors, they wanted a firm ethical direction to their research. But ultimately their background may well have limited their influence. As Ross has pointed out, most American social scientists did not embrace the German historical approach.[37]

Ely was trained in the German historical school and together with Ashley and others led the major assault on classical economics as represented by figures such as C. F. Dunbar at Harvard. While he thought English economists lacked the "realism" found in the bulky German treatises, Ely also was influenced by a number of English figures in this area, as in religion. He had very close links with the Oxford CSU's *Economic Review.* As with British Christian Socialists in the field of social science, he also had the magic identification with popular writers, once stating that Walter Besant's fiction and nonfiction works were better than "nine-tenths of economic treatises."[38]

Canada was influenced by the United States in particular in the development of social science. In the 1890s Sir William J. Ashley, of course, had nurtured a small school of Social Christians interested in the English-German historical approach to economics. Queen's University became an important center for the

35. Dorothy Ross, *The Origins of American Social Science* (Cambridge, 1991), xiii.
36. Ibid., xvii–xviii.
37. Ibid., xiv and elsewhere.
38. Richard T. Ely, *Social Aspects of Christianity, and Other Essays,* rev. ed. (New York, 1889), 110.

new thinking based, in part, on the traditions of moral philosophy and theology from Scotland,[39] though eventually here, as in other universities, allegiance shifted to American models. However, early on, Canadian churches came to emphasize social service and made demands upon universities to supply instruction in social sciences whether linked to Social Christianity or not. The University of Chicago became an important center for training academics, including among its pupils W. L. MacKenzie King and Carl Dawson, the founder of serious social research at McGill. Although the Canadian ministry was not as attracted to professional sociology as its counterpart in the United States, Dawson was a conspicuous example of a minister turned sociologist.[40] Though Canadians as a whole did not gain wide reputations in the field, the introduction of social science courses into the curricula of universities and especially theological schools was comparatively rapid. Social service, however, remained the driving force.

In both Britain and North America it was in the area of social service where Social Christians really hoped to distinguish themselves. Bishop B. F. Westcott had repeatedly exhorted ministers and laity to reflect upon the need for social service. On the practical side, Broad Churchmen were conspicuous in founding the Charity Organization Society (COS) in 1869 (the North American equivalents were founded in New York ten years later and in Montreal in 1900). The circle surrounding W. H. Fremantle, at his rectory at St. Mary's, Bryanston Square, also experimented not only with greater efficiency in charity through the proper investigation of needs, but also with provision of job training, rather than relief, through the Walmer Street Industrial Experiment in the Marylebone district of the parish. Octavia Hill, an instructor at Working Men's College, was placed in charge of a number of these projects.

Hill had already taken over the management of three tenement houses known as Paradise Place, with the financial backing of Ruskin. Here she introduced her system of female "visitors" who attempted to inculcate proper social attitudes in tenants as well as collect their rents. Hill wrote to Fremantle of her unpopularity among those who practiced the old charity, but added, "[L]ife has taught me a different way of helping, what seems to be a better way, and I cannot but follow where the Master calls me."[41]

---

39. See A. B. McKillop, *A Disciplined Intelligence: Critical Inquiry and Canadian Thought in the Victorian Era* (Montreal, 1980), 172, 208, 218–19, 230.

40. See Marlene Shore, *The Science of Social Redemption: McGill, the Chicago School, and the Origins of Social Research in Canada* (Toronto, 1987), 78.

41. Hill to Fremantle, 1 November 1874, box 1, Letters to Canon and Mrs. Barnett, Octavia Hill Letters, Collection Mis. 512, British Library of Political and Economic Science, London.

After 1884 the London dwellings held by the Ecclesiastical Commissioners came under her control, all managed according to the same principles as Paradise Place. Indeed, by 1900 Hill had assembled an army of female visitors managing some five thousand London tenement buildings and houses, easily the most comprehensive private enterprise to improve working-class housing in late-Victorian Britain. Hill has been accused of never reaching the most wretched among the working class, and many held a view of her as "the landlady sternly exacting her rents."[42] Her approach seems to have been first to engage in successful dialogue with those individuals who were already linked to Christianity and then to work outward from that base. As she wrote to Mrs. Henrietta [Samuel A.] Barnett concerning her housing projects in their period of greatest growth:

> If too the vast body of working men, now alienated from the Church and Christian world, are to be led back, it must be, it seems to me, by someone who, while entering with hearty sympathy into all the social questions they care for, tells them distinctly that he does so for Christ's sake, and in the faith our Lord taught. Just when, and how, and how directly, to say so will be better learnt face to face with separate people, and among an intelligent body of independent workmen, than it can be among a low class whose only notion of the Church has been as an almsgiver and by whom silence must often seem the coming of preaching.[43]

Octavia Hill's objections to indiscriminate almsgiving, according to Nancy Boyd, did not spring from a view of poverty as the result of moral failure in individuals.[44] Rather she feared its detrimental effects on society as a whole. Indeed, the inspiration for Hill's housing projects, as for the COS, or indeed the settlement movement, came from progressive figures such as T. H. Green. Similarly, the desire to reorganize charity, rather than replace it altogether with state aid, has come to look curious or odd only with the passage of time and through the lens of later historical interpretation, according to Gertrude Himmelfarb.[45] Regardless of the pros and cons of Himmelfarb's rehabilitation of the COS, one can see in retrospect that the new philanthropy of

42. C. E. Maurice, ed., preface to *Life of Octavia Hill As Told in Her Letters* (London, 1913), vi. See Nancy Boyd, *Three Victorian Women Who Changed Their World: Josephine Butler, Octavia Hill, Florence Nightingale* (Oxford, 1982).

43. Hill to Barnett, 1 August 1880, box 1, Octavia Hill Letters.

44. Boyd, *Three Victorian Women*, 138.

45. Gertrude Himmelfarb, *Poverty and Compassion: The Moral Imagination of the Late Victorians* (New York, 1991), 203–6.

this period represented a transitional phase from Christian almsgiving to state intervention.

One of the particular trendsetters in the field of new philanthropy on both sides of the Atlantic was the Salvation Army. Originally an evangelistic crusade to deliver the masses from personal sin and drunkenness, albeit in innovative ways, the Salvation Army, with the publication of William Booth's *In Darkest England* (1890), ushered in a burst of social service on a par with the most successful Social Christian enterprises of the late 1800s. The book advocated the transformation of city refuges into city colonies where the received desti- tute would work in industrial workshops that would expand their line of products and, as a by-product, destroy sweatshops. Some workers would be exported to farm colonies engaged mainly in agricultural pursuits. "Colonies over the Sea" would constitute a third and final alternative, after workers had received agricultural training.[46]

The scheme was designed to provide, "not charity, but work," to deter indolence but also provide basic necessities for those from "darkest England." Appeals to the public would be made to fund this great philanthropic enterprise, for state involvement was not encouraged. In the process the grand scheme would undoubtedly replace existing, competing philanthropic services.

In spite of fraternal kindness extended from figures such as B. F. Westcott and R. W. Dale, *In Darkest England* (1890), written in part by W. T. Stead, received harsh criticism from some sympathetic to Christian social service. Sir William Ashley warned that the all-embracing scheme was but another of "Morrison's Pills . . . cure-alls which promise to relieve . . . at once . . . almost every mal- ady."[47] Trade unionists and many socialists were antagonistic toward it. One staunch critic, in *In Brightest England* (1891), thought that the great scheme really amounted to encouraging all laborers to be capitalists, while Booth in practice controlled all capital.[48] The Reverend Robert Eyton, rector of Upper Chelsea, thought that *In Darkest England* was an immodest proposal, with unreasoned features such as the establishment of industrial villages (whose people would return to London in any case). Eyton also queried

46. See General William Booth, *In Darkest England* and *The Way Out* (Hapeville, Ga., reprint, 1942), chaps. 2, 3, and 4.

47. William J. Ashley, "General Booth's Panacea," *Political Science Quarterly* 4, no. 3 (1891): 537.

48. *In Brightest England (Looking Forward); or, "General" Booth's Scheme Eclipsed by A Plan for the Prevention of Poverty, Misery, Crime, and for Promoting Human Happiness* (London, 1891), 19. The anonymous author suggested that "some Christian ministers (Church and Nonconformist) with Socialist or benevolent sympathies, and a few philanthropists, should be appointed as a Council of Recommendation, Inspection and Supervision," subject to reelection annually by the whole community (ibid., 60).

whether there were large numbers of Londoners who actually wanted work but could not find it. According to Eyton, the book revealed "no appreciation of the experience of other workers, no recognition of what they have achieved, no trace of deep study of a perplexing problem."[49] However, Eyton did concede that because the book painted things in a big way, it should appeal to Americans.[50] Indeed, some suggestions in the book, blended with the general appeal of the Salvationists' evangelism, did appeal to North Americans, as they had to Britons.[51]

On a few occasions General Booth himself expressed a certain ambivalence on the question of excessive social service at the expense of religious missionary activity. As he wrote in 1903 to his chief of staff from Cincinnati, Ohio:

> You are puzzled, you say, with respect to our relations with the poor. I am not surprised that you should be, but I think we have made it pretty plain to ourselves and to the public, there can be no question that the "Darkest England" Scheme lifted us up to a position in public esteem, the world over, which we should never have gained in all human probability for perhaps a Century without it, even if then.
>
> Moreover, it is right. It is in harmony with the teachings of Jesus Christ and the very essence of a great deal of the Bible. It matches the promptings of the heart everywhere. If a man had a brother who was hungry and homeless and naked, his first sense of duty would be to feed and house and clothe him, doing it in the spirit of love and talking to him about his soul all the time. The same practice is called for by Jesus Christ when He says "Thou shalt love thy neighbour as thyself." We are trying to do it. The World can understand that sort of religion and the world believes in those who practice it, and belief in you has to be produced in the world before it will get much benefit out of what you say on other things.
>
> The danger lies in extremes. "Let your moderation be known unto all men" is a text which grows more and more important in my estimation every day. As to whether we get as much real benefit out of

49. The Reverend Robert Eyton, *A Rash Investment: A Sermon on the Salvation Army Scheme of Social Reform* (London, 1890), 20.

50. Ibid., 13–14.

51. See, for the United States, Edward H. McKinley, *Marching to Glory: The History of the Salvation Army in the United States, 1880–1980* (San Francisco, 1980), and Norris Magnuson, *Salvation in the Slums: Evangelical Social Work, 1865–1920* (Grand Rapids, Mich., 1990). For Canada, see R. G. Moyles, *The Blood and Fire in Canada: A History of the Salvation Army in the Dominion, 1882–1976* (Toronto, 1977).

the time and labor and ability bestowed upon feeding the poor as we should do if spent in purely spiritual work is a very difficult question to answer. We have a number of people, and shall have an increasing number of them, who can do this work and who cannot do the other. Let us employ them and make the world pay for it. What I object to is using the time and ability of men and women for Social Work who are required for the Spiritual and using money after the same fashion. This is not very plain but you will know what I mean.[52]

About a year later, however, Booth proposed a "World University for the Cultivation of Science of Humanity in connection with the Salvation Army." The university was to have its "main wings" in England and the United States and would provide training for social operations among the destitute, including labor bureaus and industrial homes for the unemployed.[53]

While General Booth had some reservations about his church of social service, the traditional churches were nonetheless moving fast in this direction. Maurice had envisaged the Church of England as an institution out of which relief could be administered to the impoverished of the nation. Some talked in the early 1880s about incorporating the Salvation Army into the Established Church.[54] But in the last resolve it was the Broad Church circle that again took the initiative by moving from the work of Fremantle and Barnett, fusing it to the idealism of Oxford intellectuals, and emerging with Toynbee Hall, the model for settlement work across the world.

As I have shown, the notion of university-educated people working and living among the dispossessed emerged from the disciples of T. H. Green, especially from Arnold Toynbee, the great hero of the movement. The earliest regular residency among the working class, in 1867, was that of the Reverend Edward Denison, who was also somewhat of a hero. The Reverend Samuel Barnett, however, was the actual founder of the first settlement house, Toynbee Hall. Barnett has been depicted in various ways. His determination to make Toynbee Hall a successful enterprise in reaching the working classes of Whitechapel, East London, cannot be doubted. However, like many of the great figures associated with these efforts, Barnett was necessarily thrown back upon his individual ability to inspire followers in the cause. Charles R. Ashbee,

52. William Booth to Bramwell Booth, Cincinnati, 16 January 1903, folder 24, Correspondence 1903–7, William Booth Collection, Salvation Army Heritage Room, Salvation Army Headquarters, Judd Street, London.

53. Folder "World University of Humanity," c. 1904, William Booth Collection.

54. Norman H. Murdoch, "The Salvation Army and the Church of England 1882–1883," *Historical Magazine of the Protestant Episcopal Church* 55, no. 1 (1986): 31–55.

the noted architect and "romantic" socialist, saw the complexities of this personal-leadership question in the case of Barnett, who was, in his view,

> a man very great—but very evil. Great in that he can meet the nineteenth century, the Devil with his own weapon in that he can organize marvellously, in that he has a magnificent tolerance, in that he knows his own weakness and can assimilate into himself men of corresponding thoughts, in that he is large and earnest and in the Blake sense an "Energy." But his evil is greater than his greatness. He is primarily a eunuch—in spirit and heart—that is the reason for his cold-blooded saintliness. He plays fast and loose with the moral enthusiasm of young men, and has not the strength either to lead on or to be led by them. Being without moral courage he hides himself behind other peoples' ideas and repays their confidences with a moral teaching which no true man who has once felt it can forgive.[55]

In an environment where interpersonal dialogue and direct contact were the modi operandi of the organization, could one ever escape the personality question? Whatever Barnett's weaknesses, the model provided by Toynbee Hall stimulated a transatlantic settlement house movement in short order. By 1900 there were fifty-six settlement houses in Britain and over two hundred in the United States. In Canada ones were formed in connection with the University of Toronto and Montreal's McGill University.

In the United States settlements were both nondenominational and church affiliated. In time there were also women's settlements and black settlement houses as well. In New York, Stanton Coit came close to claiming leadership of the movement under the banner of his own ethical-humanist movement. Impressed with Toynbee Hall, he had developed his own Neighbourhood Guild idea, a secular version of the settlement house. Coit could claim, with some justification, that some figures originally associated with outreach programs conceived by T. H. Green's circle at Oxford were not orthodox Christians. And he was critical not only of Christian dominance of the settlements but of the whole Social Christian approach to work in the field, including Octavia Hill's activities and even those of the long-deceased Evangelical Thomas Chalmers (who was widely and mistakenly regarded as an early Social Christian by Americans). As Coit stated:

55. 28 June 1886, f. 144–45, C. R. Ashbee Journals, King's College Library, Cambridge University.

This special function of gaining insight into the real needs of any family is, of course, fully met by Miss Octavia Hill's system of rent collectors. But in this matter the Guild does not set itself up as a competing system, but rather as a larger plan, comprehending the special methods which Miss Hill has developed. Already the Guild in Kentish Town has applied to the landlord of the worst street in the district to be the rent collector from all he tenants. Miss Hill's method becomes infinitely more powerful for good when joined to the hundred other forces of the Guild, which make for social regeneration. There is also the same objection to be brought against her plan, as against Dr. Chalmers'—that it is aristocratic, that the regenerative work, instead of planting itself among the people themselves, and taking root there, is fed only from the upper classes of society. If for no other reason than this, it must collapse before many years, just as Chalmers' scheme did. Surely the history of the working classes proves that any thorough reform of their social life must rest in a movement from within their own ranks, however much it may need the time and attention of a few men and women of leisure at its inception.[56]

The condescension of settlement leaders was perhaps the Achilles' heel of the movement. Designed to create a sense of shared community between young middle-class residents and working-class neighbors, the settlements may well have accentuated the gulf between the two. Charles Ashbee, one such Toynbee resident, noted during the construction of the nearby People's Palace: "Fearful the sense of class distinction down here. I got into the workman's hair today and my neighbours actually found it necessary to apologise to me for my mistake. This is very painful."[57] Ashbee had doubts about "top hatty" philanthropy. Standish Meacham believes that Toynbee Hall, with this paternalistic, high-minded approach, which evinced failure by 1900 in East London, then became the training ground for William Beveridge, R. H. Tawney, Clement Attlee, and others, who became the elite of the emerging army of welfare-state bureaucracy builders.[58]

Charles Masterman believed that "the wave of enthusiasm which created the modern settlement" ceased to advance after 1900. The hundred or so male resident workers in London at the turn of the century he could not believe would be "the machinery destined to bridge the ever-widening gulf between

56. Stanton Coit, *Neighbourhood Guilds: An Instrument of Social Reform* (London, 1891), 24–25.
57. 28 June 1886, folder 128, Ashbee Journals.
58. See Meacham, *Toynbee Hall.*

class and class."[59] There were lengthy programs and reports but little sign of much beyond these "centres of organisation."[60] His real hope was that the effect on the churches themselves would be a "widening" of the Christian ideal through multifarious activity. For Masterman it was essential to touch the working-class intellect. What he observed was that "[t]he old bitter spirit against the Church and Christianity has largely died away. But this has been replaced by a general indifference perhaps still more difficult to overcome; a quiet putting aside of the claims and calls of the Church which is the despair of all those intimately acquainted with the life of the masses."[61]

Chicago's Hull House, founded in 1889, was one of the earliest and most successful of American settlement houses. Though the model of Hull House took into account the experiences of Toynbee Hall and Working Men's College, some questioned at the outset how successfully the efforts of the British well-to-do had redounded "back to the people" and whether their methods were adaptable to the American scene. Jane Addams noted in her autobiography:

> Nevertheless the processes by which so simple a conclusion as residence among the poor in East London was reached, seemed to me very involved and roundabout. However inevitable these processes might be for class-conscious Englishmen, they could not but seem artificial to a western American who had been born in a rural community where the early pioneer life had made social distinctions impossible. Always on the alert lest American Settlements should become mere echoes and imitations of the English movement, I found myself assenting to what was shown me only with that part of my consciousness which had been formed by reading of English social movements, while at the same time the rustic American inside looked on in detached comment.[62]

Though Addams had reservations concerning Toynbee Hall's elitist approach and greater faith in the egalitarian, democratic spirit of Americans, her approach was essentially the same as that taken in England. As she stated in a more positive way, "Hull-House was soberly opened on the theory that the dependence of classes on each other is reciprocal."[63] This was also the essence

59. Charles Masterman, "Realities at Home," in *The Heart of the Empire: Discussions of Problems of Modern City Life* (London, 1901), 35.

60. Ibid., 36.

61. Ibid., 43.

62. Jane Addams, *Twenty Years at Hull-House: With Autobiographical Notes* (New York, 1910), 38.

63. Ibid., 91.

of the social harmony message of the earliest Christian Socialists. Recent studies have also suggested that Hull House and other settlements were mechanisms by which American values were transmitted to large clusters of immigrants in major cities. In that sense perhaps the bridge between classes was truly conceived less in terms of social classes, in the English sense, and more in terms of communities. Jane Addams once described this underlying belief that "[t]he mere foothold of a house, easily accessible, ample in space, hospitable and tolerant in spirit, situated in the midst of the large foreign colonies which so easily isolate themselves in American cities, would be in itself a serviceable thing for Chicago. Hull House endeavours to make social intercourse express the growing sense of the economic unity of society, and may be described as an effort to add the social function to democracy."[64]

In spite of the distinctive features of American settlements, the British origins of the movement were never forgotten. When much of Toynbee Hall was destroyed in World War II bombing, Sherwood Eddy, the great YMCA leader, made an impassioned plea to the American Ford Foundation to defray the costs of reconstruction. For Eddy, Toynbee Hall was the "pioneer" social settlement, which begot not only other university settlements (especially Hull House) but the Workers' Educational Association, the Workers' Travel Association, the great sociological researches or the "floodlighting of East London," and the U.K. National Health Service (through William Beveridge).[65] Eddy even saw a bright future for its educational and social work in spite of the advent of the British Welfare State.[66]

The links with churches were more tenuous among American settlements than among their British counterparts. Nevertheless, they often worked closely with churches, especially as the city missions of churches began to falter late in the century. Jane Addams herself was one of the committee of five appointed to carry out the suggestions of W. T. Stead's Civic Federation for Chicago.[67] But her hope was also to place the work of the settlement on a *more scientific basis*, thereby making it a model for other similar American enterprises to come. Therein lay a dilemma. American settlement leaders were well aware of the British tendency to lose themselves "in the cave of their own companionship" in places like Toynbee Hall based upon class insularity,[68] but another type

64. Jane Addams, "Hull House (Chicago)," in *The New Encyclopedia of Social Reform*, ed. William Dwight Porter Bliss (New York, 1908), 587. See also note 108 to Chapter 4.

65. Application to Ford Foundation, 1 September 1951, p. 2, box 2, folder 2, Sherwood Eddy Papers, Yale Divinity School Library.

66. Ibid., 2–3.

67. Addams, *Twenty Years at Hull-House*, 160.

68. Ibid., 90.

of insularity was now setting in as a result of professionalism in social work. Charles Stelzle detailed the principal reasons for failure in American settlements in this regard:

> First, many of the residents do not come to settle but spend a limited number of months in the hope of doing a little and learning much. Second, nearly every settlement is compelled, through periodical statistical reports, to justify its existence in the eyes of outside subscribers. Third, from these facts of transient workers and tabulated reports there follows as a necessary evil the widespread tendency to employ machinery in order to produce effects. Although the number of so-called settlements has largely increased, we must not lose sight of the fact that many of them are training colleges, not settlements at all, and that no real attempt has been made to realize the settlement ideal except by a few scattered individuals.[69]

For those reasons Stelzle felt that church affiliation or a strong Christian Social component was essential for proper direction of settlement work. That is why he believed that "some of the strongest social settlements are founded upon a religious base."[70] In fact, Stelzle had focused upon perhaps the most important issue—the danger inherent in the secularization of church work. While social service work had progressively moved away from the conventional parameters of church work, it was, broadly speaking, still considered pastoral work. Now a fundamental change was starting to take place; a new slant or approach based exclusively upon scientifically verifiable "results" was emerging. This would later be reinforced by increasingly secularized social science. The undefinable qualities of older social service—individual contact, the transmission of values, and above all the understood, if not always articulated, religious experience of applied Christianity for both the worker and recipient—were leaching away. Goals and methods changed, became secular, with modern social work eventually replacing pastoral work altogether. This was perhaps a clearer break with the past than most contemporaries or historians today would credit.

In Britain professionalism also came to be more important in social service work. But the well-established statistics-gathering techniques generated by the Condition-of-England question were also undergoing a metamorphosis. Meacham's point about social ends being an expression of a moral ideal in the settlement movement and other outreach enterprises had been progressively

---

69. Charles Stelzle, *Christianity's Storm Centre: A Study of the Modern City* (New York, 1907), 139.
70. Ibid., 140.

diluted through the efforts of those assisting in data collecting since the time of Mayhew. As Rosemary O'Day has pointed out in the case of the young Beatrice Webb (née Potter), who worked for the Charles Booth team in the late 1880s, a change occurred in her attitude, not only transforming her from philanthropic worker into social investigator but also dissuading her from the Booth approach of illuminating social problems in favor of the social activist approach. As O'Day has indicated, her divergence from Booth was chiefly "in her emphasis upon the historical development of the social problem."[71] The belief in the inevitable coming of collectivism was beginning to appear, displacing the older religious concept of the emerging Kingdom of Christ. Perhaps collectivism for some working in the field was the Kingdom. Reba Soffer's point about the ideal of the social scientist affecting the collection of data in British social science again holds true. This time a new secular philosophy or indeed almost a theology of collectivism would gain momentum.

This is not to say that social investigation could not continue to have a strong Christian social base to it. Seebohm Rowntree demonstrated this with his *Poverty: A Study of Town Life* (1901), which was the result of a detailed investigation of working and living conditions in York. Rowntree may well have provided the clearest definition to date of the "poverty line."[72] Fellow Quaker Edward Cadbury made an important but lesser-known contribution to social studies in his thoroughly researched *Women's Work and Wages* (1906). But Rowntree's more remarkable achievement was to publish a second study of York, *Poverty and Progress,* in 1941, based upon follow-up investigation in the 1930s, some thirty years after the original. The contrasts provided by the first and second studies of York were exceedingly useful, revealing continued deprivation that in many minds begged for intervention by the state.

As Standish Meacham and Asa Briggs would describe it, the transitional period, involving the conflicting concepts of a "social service state" and a "social welfare state," coincided mainly with the Edwardian years.[73] The results of social surveys of the period could be taken in many ways, depending on the lessons to be derived from them. Essentially it was a question of viewpoint and how evidence could be used to support it. Within the ranks of Social Christians and their associates further discussions took place concerning the root cause of social problems. For a time the advocates of advanced pastoral

---

71. Rosemary O'Day, "Before the Webbs: Beatrice Potter's Early Investigations for Charles Booth's Inquiry," *History* 78, no. 253 (1993): 241.

72. Edward Royle, *Modern Britain: A Social History, 1750–1985* (London, 1987), 86.

73. See Standish Meacham, "The Sense of an Impending Clash: English Working-Class Unrest Before the First World War," *American Historical Review* 77, no. 1 (1972): 1360.

work and the advocates of more state intervention had coexisted within the bosom of settlements and other agencies. But after 1900 it was increasingly obvious that a large proportion of the working classes were not making progress regardless of their attitudes, and more drastic action was prescribed. Things eventually came to a head over parliamentary investigation of the antiquated poor-law system and society's systemic unemployment problem.

Members of the Charity Organization Society who served as royal commissioners investigating the poor laws from 1905 to 1909 went some distance in agreeing that social services had to be extended to disadvantaged groups. But Octavia Hill and her COS compatriots were unwilling to go much beyond the framework of the existing poor laws. This brought a challenge, spearheaded by Sidney and Beatrice Webb, in the form of the Minority Report, which stressed social causes ahead of attitudinal questions and thence advocated the breakup of the Poor Law and its replacement by a comprehensive state policy on poverty and unemployment. What was significant was the support the Minority Report received not only from Fabians but also from New Liberals, including Gilbert Murray, J. A. Hobson, William Beveridge, and Charles Masterman, the last two being Social Christians.[74]

Perhaps the most symbolic episode was the cross-examination of R. H. Tawney by Commissioner Octavia Hill, which revealed the complete rift between old and young Social Christians over the relevance of moral character to social conditions.[75] Octavia Hill died not many years later, but by that time she seemed quite old-fashioned to most. As Charles R. Ashbee recorded in his journal after her death in 1912: "She belonged I think to that early and mid-Victorian mould out of which the Unitarians and positivists are made, and those others whose God is an abstraction but like many of those her enthusiasm was a very noble quality."[76]

In North America the welfare state did not loom as close, but social scientists were advancing in a direction that made many clergy feel increasingly out of place and unprofessional in their company. Nevertheless, church work or social service by religious institutions continued to be relevant, though frequently subject to criticisms and redirections by intellectuals unsympathetic to their ultimate goals and purposes. This situation moved churches to an even greater commitment to social service. Canada stands out as proceeding quite early with central social service bodies created by the Presbyterian and Methodist

74. A. M. McBriar, *An Edwardian Mixed Doubles: The Bosanquets Versus the Webbs: A Study in British Social Policy, 1890–1929* (Oxford, 1987), 301, 304.
75. Ibid., 268.
76. August 1912, Ashbee Journals.

churches. The Methodist Department of Temperance and Moral Reform, established in 1902, was among the earliest in the English-speaking world. Statistical studies of urban social problems were the particular strength of the department in its early years. Small wonder that its first secretary, S. D. Chown, was a strong supporter of sociology. Chown's support of the social sciences, of course, was indicative of a general movement, given concrete expression, for example, in the new Wesleyan Methodist Union for Social Service in England, which Chown first visited through the summer of 1907. In fact, historians feel that he began to confuse the aims of social science with those of religion at this stage as well as later, when he became general superintendent of the Canadian Methodist Church.[77] In urging other churches to amalgamate their efforts in the Dominion Moral and Social Reform Council in 1908, Chown certainly set aside any fears about the dilution of Methodism. According to Ramsay Cook, by the early twentieth century there had been among Canadian liberal Protestants a "substitution of theology, the science of religion, with sociology, the science of society."[78] In another sense, for Chown, "the perfect sociology" of Christ the social reformer was also the means, if perfectly applied, to the realization of "the Kingdom of God on Earth."[79]

In the United States Methodists were also in the forefront of church-organized social service. Influenced by the British Forward Movement, as were their Canadian counterparts, American Methodists were intensely interested in extending church influence in the cities. Frank Mason North, who had earlier involved himself in the New York City Church Extension Society and the Institutional Church League, founded the Methodist Federation for Social Service in 1907. In the years immediately thereafter he also helped to form the Federal Council of Churches, including its Social Creed. American Protestant ecumenism, as in Canada, also seemed to go hand in hand with the drive to extend social services. The perceived need to keep religious control over social services undoubtedly inspired the latter development.

In 1909 the newly formed Federal Council of Churches convened a Commission on the Church and Social Service. Meeting in New York in October 1909, the session, chaired by Frank Mason North, included such eminent figures as Josiah Strong and Charles Stelzle. Leading members expressed different viewpoints concerning the function of the commission. All agreed that coordinated action was necessary to the investigation of social problems and to the well-

77. According to A. B. McKillop, Chown's eschatology was that of a man uncertain whether he should be a clergyman or social scientist (*A Disciplined Intelligence,* 226).
78. Ramsay Cook, *The Regenerators: Social Criticism in Late Victorian Canada* (Toronto, 1985), 4.
79. S. D. Chown, cited in ibid., 195.

publicized dissemination of its results. The term *clearing house* was repeatedly used in reference to joint church organization.[80] One representative did express some pessimism regarding the capacity of churches to carry on social service, since "the churches at large were not interested, and . . . the ministers and other leaders could not be depended upon to carry out a concerted piece of social service."[81] However, the view of the majority prevailed, and the concept of a bureau of social service was later approved. The bureau established was to have representatives from both the commission and the Home Missions Council, and its functions were outlined as follows:

1. Its office equipment would provide a centre and source of united action in matters of common interest.
2. It would be in a position to encourage and to institute investigation of social questions in their relation to religion and the evangelization of the country.
3. It would serve as a clearing house for the distribution of information to all of the denominations.
4. It would aid in guiding and co-ordinating the social-religious work of all churches, and in correlating the work of the denominational agencies for social service.
5. It would make possible such a correlation of forces that duplication of efforts would be avoided and economy of resources secured.
6. Such a Bureau would afford a common ground for an exchange of views and for fraternal relations, with those who within the Church represent the purpose and plan for human betterment, and those who outside the Church are engaged in the effort for human uplift.[82]

Churches in the United States and Canada also helped to sponsor interfaith and secular conferences on social work, as occurred in Canada just before World War I.[83] In fact, social work and church work seemed thereafter to become inseparable in the minds of some Social Gospel ministers, as witnessed in such publications as *The Socialized Church* (1908), edited by Worth M. Tippy.

80. Minutes of the Commission on the Church and Social Service, 5 October 1909, folder "Church and Labor," Frank Mason North Papers, Archives and History Center of the United Methodist Church, Drew University.

81. Ibid., Mr. Folks, 4.

82. Report of Committee on Organization of a Bureau of Social Service, 7–9 December 1909, 1–2, folder "Church and Labor," Frank Mason North Papers.

83. *Social Service Congress, Ottawa, 1914: Report of Addresses and Proceedings* (Toronto, n.d.).

Britain had also witnessed the appearance of centralized social service bodies among the churches in the decade before World War I. Was this crucial to the massive decline of the British churches in this century, as suggested by Jeffrey Cox? Most certainly it was a contributing factor. On the other hand, it would have been out of character and out of the chain of recent thinking by Social Christians suddenly to reverse the order of things and emphasize church attendance, for example. Studies sponsored by church-related bodies, such as that reported in C.E.B. Russell's *Social Problems of the North, London and Oxford* (CSU, 1913), though they might yield recommendations for church-related remedies such as settlement work, increasingly were devoted to collecting and displaying data in much the same way as secular-inspired studies. With the increase in statistics gathering, from the Asquith government onward, it seemed ludicrous to duplicate the work of government statisticians. A similar trend would occur later in the United States and Canada, where figures on unemployment from departments of labor proved to be particularly useful.

For Britain the great agenda for social service during the interwar period had been framed by COPEC on one end and the Malvern Conference on the other. The latter, of course, was a more specifically Anglican meeting (see Chapter 1), though it was as influenced by politics as it was concerned with a renewal of theology. On the other hand, COPEC, which was led by William Temple and also had considerable Anglican input in other ways, was designed to be a general meeting of the best Christian minds to develop strategies for attacking social evils. Before the meeting (1,400 delegates assembled at Birmingham in the spring of 1924), much preparation had gone into amassing data from questionnaires in the good old tradition of statistics gathering. The meetings themselves focused upon every aspect of work and leisure in a Christian setting. The eventual commission reports were published in twelve volumes.[84]

Edward Norman's extensive analysis of COPEC portrays it as an attempt to pull together a body of assorted ideas that in many ways reflected the "ragbag" of attitudes in the Labour movement of the time. He believes its most lasting consequence was the rise of Temple as leader of the Church of England.[85] Adrian Hastings, like Norman, has doubts about the immediate significance of the week's meetings and of the reports issued. However, he goes slightly further than

84. Vol. 1, *The Nature of God and His Purpose for the World;* vol. 2, *Education;* vol. 3, *The Home;* vol. 4, *The Relation of the Sexes;* vol. 5, Leisure; vol. 6, *The Treatment of Crime;* vol. 7, *International Relations;* vol. 8, *Christianity and War;* vol. 9, *Industry and Property;* vol. 10, *Politics and Citizenship;* vol. 11, *The Social Function of the Church;* vol. 12, *Historical Illustrations of the Social Effects of Christianity.*

85. Edward R. Norman, *Church and Society in England, 1770–1970: A Historical Study* (Oxford, 1976), 306, 313.

Norman, who maintains that the conference promoted a corpus of social teaching and imparted a "progressive bias to a lot of Church social opinion";[86] Hastings states that the conference weaned clerical and lay leaders of the church "from high Tory attitudes" and maneuvered them into "an acceptance of the Christian case for massive social reform and the development of a welfare state."[87]

Whatever the degree of impact upon the Church of England or the churches in general, COPEC obviously caused many to reflect upon issues of substance: the direction of future social policy in church and state and how to achieve it. It seemed quite in order, therefore, to hear statements such as that of an archdeacon at the 1938 Church Congress, that all ordination candidates should be trained in a parish "or in some centre of social service."[88]

On a more general level COPEC also inspired an interplay of church policy with that of the secular state. Overtly Social Christian social scientists were increasingly marginalized not only because of dwindling numbers but also because of divisions within the ranks. R. H. Tawney's break with the older generation during the poverty hearings of 1909, as I have shown, placed him and those who admired him on the collectivist path. Yet his political pursuit of equality was not completely understood by paternal Social Christians, or perhaps even by William Temple,[89] and did not lead to inevitable triumphs in state policy.[90]

The settlement movement, of course, was far from dead. In the 1920s Fr. Basil Jellicoe and his St. Pancras Housing Association made some effort to correct the paternalism of the Toynbee Hall approach (see Chapter 4). Jellicoe was successful not only in building large tenement houses but in bridging the culture gap between well-intentioned upper- and middle-class patrons and the working classes. Bishop George Bell's St. Richard's Housing Society was similarly effective in southern rural areas during the Great Depression, as were techniques of social service, such as the distinctive allotment system, introduced by the Quakers.

But the issue of isolation from the intellectual climate of the times remained. This may well explain the new Christian sociology of the Christendom Movement and its offshoot, the Chandos Group.[91] Christian sociology was transpar-

86. Ibid., 306.

87. Adrian Hastings, *A History of English Christianity, 1920–1985* (London, 1986), 179.

88. The Venerable L. Owen, "Training for the Ministry," in *Report of the Proceedings of the 66th Church Congress, Bristol 4th–7th October 1938,* ed. Maurice H. Fitzgerald (London, 1938), 257.

89. See the discussion on the issue in John Kent, *William Temple: Church, State, and Society in Britain, 1880–1950* (Cambridge, 1992), 17.

90. See Meacham, *Toynbee Hall,* 188–89.

91. The group met originally at the Chandos restaurant in London in 1926 to discuss the sociological direction of economic thinking, especially Social Credit. Its membership included

ently not sociology, nor did it attempt to be. Its prescriptive tone probably offended many social scientists, but it is doubtful whether many would have been attracted to the call in any case.

The isolation worried some who still sought a rapprochement with social science. As the Reverend W. Rowland Jones wrote in the *Sociological Review* concerning the Anglo-Catholic movement: it was "rapidly becoming identified officially with the nonsociological point of view already established in the Church, and [was] in danger of missing the ideal of true catholicism by spelling it always with a capital letter."[92] For Jones it was necessary to find a "unifying element" fusing "place, work, and folk." Jones's fear was that social science groups would move further away from organized religion, carving out for themselves a substitute for religion or an amorphous amalgam of psychology and sentiment.[93]

British seminaries made nominal accommodations to social science but continued to emphasize traditional aspects of theological study. Knowledge of society was best left to later, practical pastoral experience. In a few seminaries such as the Methodist Wesley House at Cambridge, seminary students mingled freely with other students and were encouraged to study other disciplines in the wider university. Other Methodist seminaries often listed comparative religion, psychology, and social questions in the curriculum timetable but placed more weight upon Biblical studies.[94]

In North America more movement was evident in the training of ministers. In Canada S. D. Chown, as superintendent of the Methodist Church, had pushed for the introduction of more social science into the training of ministers.[95] In the United States the contour of the debate was more complicated in the interwar period. Fundamentalists and other religious conservatives stymied innovation in some church circles by questioning the overemphasis of social ministry as against traditional biblical training. A classical conflict took place even at the liberal Union Theological Seminary between Harrison Elliott and Sloane Coffin.[96] The presence of clergymen in the ranks of professional association members was greatly diminished after 1903.[97] This may well have indicated a

---

Maurice Reckitt and V. A. Demant. They produced a number of books, including *Coal: A Challenge to the National Conscience* (1927).

92. W. Roland Jones, "Sociology and the Church of England," *Sociological Review* 17 (1925): 135.

93. Ibid., 131.

94. See *The Ministry in the Making: An Account of the Training of the Wesleyan Methodist Ministry During the Year 1931–1932* (London, 1932), 27.

95. "Sociology Course," 50a, 50b, n.d., box 2, S. D. Chown Papers, United Church Archives.

96. See Morgan Phelps Noyes, *Henry Sloane Coffin: The Man and His Ministry* (New York, 1964).

97. See Ross, *Origins of American Social Science*, 172, citing Edward T. Silva and Sheila A. Slaughter, *Serving Power: The Making of the American Social Science Export* (Westport, Conn., 1984).

declining prestige of clergy in American society as much as a lack of expertise. The older generation of professional Christian social scientists were dying off or entering a quieter, less productive phase, as in the case of Richard T. Ely. However, the continued presence of some prominent Christians in the professional ranks was still reassuring. Charles A. Ellwood, in his *Reconstruction of Religion: A Sociological View* and *Christianity and Social Science*, argued that liberal Protestants and social scientists could continue as partners in the 1920s. And undoubtedly studies such as *Middletown* (1928), by Robert S. Lynd and Helen Merrell Lynd, kept religion in a prominent place. In the tradition of Shailer Mathews, Harlan Douglass (trained in sociology at Chicago) directed the Institute of Social and Religious Research in the 1920s and early 1930s. Funded by church organizations and the Rockefeller Foundation, Douglass commissioned numerous surveys and published volumes designed to assist the interdenominational church work in locales neglected by the churches. The Lynds' study of Muncie, Indiana, was the institute's most famous product.[98] According to Martin Marty, the Lynds had a bias against the continued relevance of the churches in daily life. Certainly the first study and its 1937 follow-up established that the churches had no monopoly in religion.[99] But in the area of social service the results of their studies were particularly disconcerting. As they stated: "The churches of Middletown, also, are less conspicuous in local charity today. As in the case of health, the trend toward secularization is an outstanding characteristic of Middletown's charity in the last twenty-five years."[100]

The significance of this trend was undoubtedly not lost on Helen Merrell Lynd. She later noted, in *England in the Eighteen-Eighties* (1945), the contribution of a revived Christian Socialism to the aroused social conscious of the late-Victorian middle classes. Now in the United States, as in Britain, that influence was clearly much diminished, as was the position of the clergy, who by emphasizing social science over theology had lessened their basic stature as authority figures—a point realized by theological conservatives quite early.

Liston Pope of the Yale Divinity School produced his acclaimed sociological and historical study of the strike-bound textile town of Gastonia, North Carolina, *Preachers and Millhands*, in 1942. His ambivalent judgments concerning

98. R. Laurence Moore, "Secularization: Religion and the Social Sciences," in *Between the Times: The Travail of the Protestant Establishment in America, 1900–1960*, ed. William R. Hutchison (Cambridge, Mass., 1989), 238.

99. Martin E. Marty, *Modern American Religion*, vol. 2, *The Noise of Conflict, 1919–1941* (Chicago, 1991), 17–20.

100. Robert S. Lynd and Helen Merrell Lynd, *Middletown: A Study in American Culture* (New York, 1929), 462.

the churches' mediating role in labor disputes raised uncomfortable questions. So too did the *Social Sources of Denominationalism* (1929), by Richard Niebuhr. While attempting to advance a Christian perspective in first-rate social scientific theory, he may have in fact inadvertently undermined the very cause to which he aspired, in spite of his message that churches ought not to surrender a leadership role in the social and economic life of the nation.

Whether these intellectual dilemmas had much effect on the course of the social service conducted by the churches is doubtful. The process seemed almost inevitable, as witnessed in the changes at Toronto's "Haven," where, from the 1870s to 1930, professional social workers gradually replaced religiously inspired charity dispensers.[101] By the 1930s the U.S. Federal Council of Churches could produce works such as *The Social Work of the Churches: A Handbook of Information* (1930), edited by F. Ernest Johnson, works that were the American Social Gospel equivalent of the evangelically inspired *Charities of London*, by Sampson Low, published almost a century earlier.

Among the advances with such improved and systematic social work was greater attention to racial issues and rural questions. A group of Northern Social Gospelers (later to be associated with the Fellowship of Southern Churchmen) designed and launched the Delta Cooperative Farm project to address both these issues. In spite of harassment by local authorities (including the jailing of an investigative team by local sheriffs) and suggestions that sympathetic blacks might die of a "sudden pneumonia" or lynching in one impoverished area of eastern Arkansas, the project was born after a cursory social survey of rural conditions in selective areas of the Deep South in the mid 1930s.[102] Led by Sherwood Eddy, the celebrated YMCA organizer, and with an illustrious board of trustees including Reinhold Niebuhr as chair, the project took shape on a farm site of 2,138 acres purchased in Bolivar County, Mississippi, in 1936. This Delta Cooperative Farm was founded upon four principles:

1. Efficiency of production and economy in finance through the cooperative principle.
2. Participation in the building of a socialized economy of abundance in the midst of the present poverty. We uphold the right of collective bargaining, especially as applied to the Southern Tenant Farmers Union, and hope to see an end put to the lawlessness and violence recently manifested in Arkansas.

101. See J. R. Graham, "The Haven, 1878–1930: A Toronto Charity's Transition from a Religious to a Professional Ethos," *Histoire sociale—Social History* 25, no. 50 (1992): 283–306.

102. See "The Delta Cooperative's First Year," *Christian Century* 3 (February 1937): 139.

3. The principle of interracial justice. Without raising the question of "social equality," the teaching of which is specifically forbidden by the laws of Mississippi, we endeavour to enable both races to cooperate and solve their mutual economic problems together, instead of being pitted one against the other in fatal economic competition, as in the past.

4. Realistic religion as a social dynamic. We believe in the return of Christianity to its prophetic mission and its identification with the dispossessed and the poor with whom it began.[103]

Though point 3 seemed to fall short of the goal of complete racial justice, black sharecroppers did benefit from arrangements more equitable than usual. Beset with regional conservative opposition, financial difficulties, and even questions raised by the Southern Tenant Farmers Union about the condition of workers, the Delta Cooperative was in deep trouble by 1940. The major ingredients in its decline were undoubtedly those listed, but correspondence also revealed resentment over the paternalistic aloofness of the leadership. As tenant farmer George Smith stated: "The Trustees think of us as a bunch of poor sharecroppers to whom they were giving a wonderful opportunity. They do not know how we feel, and they have not thought very much so far about how we might feel."[104] These complaints were reminiscent of accusations of early settlement leaders' condescension to the working classes of cities in Britain and the Northern United States.

Reinhold Niebuhr, who was deeply involved in the affair, continued to uphold the value of social work based upon informed social science methods. As he stated in 1928 to the National Conference of Social Work meeting in Memphis: "We assume people to be good or bad, and do not realize how bad good people can be in certain situations. We need more science, more intelligence, to guide men in their group contacts."[105] But Niebuhr also believed in the centrality of religion in providing direction to social work.[106]

For Niebuhr, however, social ills were also to be rectified in the political quest for social justice. Other figures in the 1920s and 1930s, such as Harry F. Ward, had come to believe in what was increasingly a political social ministry of the Left. George Coe, the educational psychologist and Social Christian, would

103. Ibid..

104. Report of Meeting of Members of Delta Cooperative Farm, 6 February 1939, 4, Delta Cooperative Papers, container 4, Reinhold Niebuhr Papers, Library of Congress.

105. *Proceedings of the National Conference of Social Work at the Fifty-Fifth Annual Session Held at Memphis, Tennessee, May 2–9, 1928* (Chicago, 1928), 53.

106. Reinhold Niebuhr, *The Contribution of Religion to Social Work* (New York, 1932), 68.

have agreed with this broad conjunction of social and political objectives. This was a path taken even earlier by Norman Thomas and J. S. Woodsworth in Canada in their formal abandonment of church ministry by the end of the Great War.

In Britain social work and politics had already been combined much earlier in the acceptance of the general path to collectivism. Charles Masterman had come to such acceptance before World War I, and it had informed his political activity on behalf of the New Liberalism. The same was true of R. H. Tawney in relation to Fabian socialism. William Temple was also broadly political, tilting always to collectivism. He developed a working relationship with social scientists who were not professed Christians, such as John Maynard Keynes, while retaining older ties with Christian Socialists such as Tawney. The extent of Temple's contribution to the development of the post-World War II welfare state is debatable, but his attempt to place the church at the center of an emerging consensus in that direct was a shrewd tactic on behalf of an institution that could easily have remained on the fringes of the discussion. Temple's purpose, from the Interdenominational Conference of Social Service Unions in 1919 to COPEC five years later, was to ensure that the churches retained a central role in the guidance of social service and social science. COPEC's first report, *The Nature of God and His Purpose for the World,* even attempted a theological basis for the effort. An old Toynbee Hall resident and friend of Temple, William Beveridge, is regarded as the principal architect of the modern welfare state. His famous 1942 report on national social insurance attacked the five giant "evils" of want, disease, ignorance, squalor, and idleness. Unlike Tawney he had no ultimate vision of a completely egalitarian society. As he stated his opposition to absolute equality of income before the Rochester Diocesan Conference on 10 November 1942: "It attaches expressive importance to material things and treats envy as our master passion."[107] He thought a national minimum was quite sufficient.

In Britain the emerging welfare state had made the social services of the Church of England and other churches appear redundant. In North America this was a slower process before 1945, but the pattern of the transformation was emerging. Beveridge had even made a tour of the United States to promote an understanding of the Beveridge plan.[108] But the fusion of the social service mission of the churches with that of the public sector was hardly a reliable

107. File "Rochester Diocesan Conference," box IIb, William Beveridge Papers, British Library of Political and Economic Science, London.
108. Box XI, file 31, contains material on Beveridge's visit to the United States in 1943, Beveridge Papers.

measurement of the decline of religious influence in general. After all, it had been the goal of Social Christians of three generations in the English-speaking world and beyond to alleviate the distress of the masses by whatever means possible short of revolutionary violence. Social service had been the original and credible method, employing the tools of social science where possible, in a vacuum of governmental and upper-crust indifference. In time, through an aroused social conscience, this was replaced by secular concepts of social welfare. To quote Canada's J. S. Woodsworth, when he was himself experiencing his own gradual transformation from a church minister-agent of social service to his eventual role as apostle of a cooperative commonwealth: "Should we mourn that the Church is losing ground or rejoice that her life is now pulsating in a hundred new organizations?"[109] It is true that the churches and church-related organizations may have been weakened as institutions in the process, but it is also clear that many Social Christians, albeit with some misgivings, were prepared to pay the price for the redemption of society.

109. James Shaver Woodsworth, *My Neighbor* (1911; Toronto, 1972), 109.

# 4

## MODES OF TRANSMISSION

The great social literature before 1880 reveals the gathering of the forces. To discover the issue was the work of that period. To face it is the work of our own.
—Vida Scudder, *Social Ideas in English Letters*

Social Christians were not satisfied with ministering to the converted. In order to effect the change they desired in society it was necessary to expand their influence throughout the general public. A wide group of sympathizers, if not believers, could pressure government and other secular agencies to serve the cause. Inactivity on this front was inexcusable because it might yield leadership in the field of social justice to groups, such as Marxists, hostile or indifferent to Christianity and perhaps even risk significant loss of existing support to the opposition. It was imperative to reach the minds of both those who might work on behalf of Social Christianity and the potential recipients of its benefits. This was all part of the interaction with the wider community that Social Christians demanded of themselves.

Communication also had a deeper significance. In a sense, from the very beginning, F. D. Maurice, J. M. Ludlow, and the earliest Christian Socialists had argued that the actual objective of Social Christianity was improved dialogue. This was also part of the associationism linked to the earliest cooperatives, settlements, and adult education.[1] The empowerment of the individual, not the rousing of a class, was the objective. Through multifarious forms of

1. See J.F.C. Harrison, *Learning and Living, 1790–1960: A Study in the History of the English Adult Education Movement* (London, 1961), 92–93 and 155–172, and Thomas Kelly, *A History of Adult Education in Great Britain*, 2d ed. (Liverpool, 1970), chap. 12.

communication between social classes, Social Christians would blaze the trail to the promised land of social harmony.

Often B. F. Westcott was accused of speaking and writing on the nature, ideals, and objectives of Christian Socialism with a good deal of vagueness. But he argued with unusual clarity that the quest for dialogue, not social conflict, was at the heart of the movement. As he stated on behalf of the CSU: "To take part in class movements on class grounds will be impossible for those who believe that the highest welfare of the body is the highest welfare of all the members."[2] The behavior of Marxist socialists, however understandable in its origins, was not acceptable in the form of class warfare, which contributed to discord, not dialogue. The high road, for Westcott, the road leading to a society at peace with itself, was the promotion of mutual understanding among individuals of all classes. It was the way to a true and lasting sense of community.[3]

As Jürgen Habermas (of the Frankfurt school) has argued, the processes of communication, which can be complicated, are important in determining the social thought and behavioral norms of a society.[4] Though they are important in themselves and not merely reflections or appendages of productive processes dominating society, processes of communication can be affected by social relationships that frequently distort the meaning of language. Habermas has distinguished two operations at work in discourse. One is "communicative action," which is designed to encourage "reciprocal understanding." The second, "strategic action," involves controlling others through forceful direction or deception. In the case of Social Christianity perhaps both underlay, to varying degrees, the attempts of its leaders and major practitioners to give direction to society. In general, the message was a complicated one. While early Social Christians departed from the line of argument, used by some churchmen, that justified the current social and economic situation, they hardly advocated the rejection of the existing social order. To use Habermas's terminology, their motive for engaging in "communicative action" was evident, but their method often entailed a degree of paternalism that bordered on "strategic action."

Before the Social Christians became well established in the world of communication, Evangelicals in particular had worked vigorously on behalf of their multifaceted causes. The latter had been more ambitious in their attempt to

---

2. Brooke Foss Westcott, *The Christian Social Union* (Oxford University Branch, London, 1895), 9–10.

3. Brooke Foss Westcott, *The Incarnation Visitation: A Revelation of Human Duties: A Charge delivered at his Primary Visitation, November 1892* (Cambridge, 1892), 35.

4. See Jürgen Habermas, *Communication and the Evolution of Society* (Boston, 1979).

create an uncompromising, uniquely Christian culture. The regimen of public, home, and private prayers in Victorian daily life was designed to reinforce the beliefs cherished by those who accepted the evangelical vision of the world. These daily and weekly rituals were supplemented by a deluge of devotional pamphlets and books produced by the religious press for the literate, semiliterate, and illiterate. Some even dabbled in the genre of the novel, though more serious-minded early Victorian Evangelicals withheld thorough approval of this technique.

In contrast to Victorian Evangelicals, Social Christians gave little emphasis to private and family prayer as well as other sustaining rituals. There was no plan to create an enveloping culture that would supply comfort and explanation in all circumstances. Success in Social Christian enterprises demanded improved communication in all possible forms, precisely because they were part of this world. Some secular influence was inevitable in such an approach, especially when formal and informal preaching, the dissemination of practical social data, and entertainment intermingled. Yet the quest for the New Jerusalem was felt to be worth the risk of condemnation by other Christians for adopting too fully the ways of the world.

To some extent Social Christians and Evangelicals were the same. Neither developed any truly distinctive art forms. Until the 1920s tradition had firmly linked religion and painting. Social Christians made no special contributions in this tradition, though a few, such as Eyre Crowe, were known to be artists. However, the artistic ideas of a secular figure, John Ruskin, were introduced by his close associate, Octavia Hill, into some of her English Christian Socialist endeavors quite early. Hill's teaching at the London Ladies' Guild and Working Men's College gave the notion of art for the people practical effect and satisfied her desire to see that the aesthetic needs of the masses were ministered to. Those associated with the Guild Socialist medieval revival of the 1920s and 1930s made a more conscious effort to link religious art forms with the cause of Social Christianity, but this revival was the unique preserve of British Anglo-Catholics.

As with art, music was traditionally associated with religion. Here the Evangelicals made significantly greater contributions through their nineteenth-century gospel hymns. Perhaps the Social Christians' best claim for originality came with "Where Cross the Crowded Ways of Life," composed in 1903 by the New York City pastor Frank Mason North. It is believed to be the first hymn to emphasize the social strife of the modern city,[5] truly reflecting a distinctive concern of Social Christianity.

5. Eric Routley, *An English-Speaking Hymn Guide* (Collegeville, Minn., 1979), 96 n. 813.

The much wider range of evangelical hymns followed from the much wider range of emotions unleashed by their performance, especially at the revivals that swept both sides of the Atlantic. Many Social Christians had harsh words for the emotionalism of the older generation, notably Charles Spurgeon and other great evangelical preachers. Though some praised the ability of Dwight Moody and Ira Sankey to move the masses, few imitated their methods. The Canadian-born Stitt Wilson remained a unique figure in his attempt to stage Christian Socialist revivals in Britain and the United States.[6] Without the necessity of forging strong emotional bonds among their members, Social Christians felt little incentive to produce hymns on a large scale.

Besides art and music the theater of popular sports also provided a venue for dialogue with the multitudes. The subcult of muscular Christianity, born within the bosom of the Broad Church, had direct applications in this regard. Charles Kingsley, in novels such as *Westward Ho!* and in his general idea of the perfectibility of the whole man, had certainly been its earliest proponent. But it was Thomas Hughes who actually embraced the term, developing both the notion of the links between ancient games and the church, and the central Social Christian belief that sports could bring about a better understanding among individuals of diverse social background.[7]

Hughes, of course, circulated his ideas most effectively in *Tom Brown's School Days* (1858), employing as a model Thomas Arnold's headmastership period at Rugby.[8] But the message was complex, combining a gospel for the working class with radical social thought and a leadership idea for the middle class. Hughes also lectured and traveled in the United States, attempting to extend his ideas throughout the English-speaking reformist community, and in 1880 established the Rugby colony in Tennessee, which was designed as a sort of living model of the combined ideals of old Rubgy and English Christian Socialism. Its inhabitants engaged in industrial pursuits (canning) as well as athletic activities (lawn tennis) and, of course, worship at Christ Church Episcopal Chapel. Though records stretch into the first decades of the twentieth

6. Peter d'A. Jones, *The Christian Socialist Revival, 1877–1914: Religion, Class, and Social Conscience in Late-Victorian England* (Princeton, 1968), 426–430. Wilson conducted at least one social crusade in England. There are reports of large gatherings at Browroyd Congregation Church and St. George's Hall at Bradford, Yorkshire, in February 1900 as well as in London. *Brotherhood* 7, no. 11 (1900): 169, and ibid., no. 12 (1900): 182–83.

7. See William E. Winn, "Tom Brown's Schooldays and the Development of 'Muscular Christianity,' " *Church History* 29, no. 1 (1969): 70, and Peter Gay, "The Manliness of Christ," in *Religion and Irreligion in Victorian Society*, ed. R. Davis and Richard J. Helmstadter (London, 1992), 102–16.

8. See Asa Briggs, "Chapter 6: Thomas Hughes and the Public Schools," in *Victorian People: A Reassessment of Persons and Themes* (Harmondsworth, Middlesex, 1954).

century, the colony's influence was minimal, largely due to its remoteness and its overtly English character.[9]

The cult of muscular Christianity had ramifications for sports activities and the manliness ideal on both sides of the Atlantic.[10] William Herbert Perry Faunce, president of Brown University, could lecture to Yale Divinity students in 1908 that "the clergyman as depicted in the popular novel or on the modern stage is frequently not a virile or attractive person."[11] Perhaps for that reason, as Grier Nicholl has pointed out, the physically rugged minister was an image specifically conveyed in most Social Gospel novels.[12] Although muscular Christianity sprang from the same roots as English Christian Socialism, its effects were too diffuse to be of any particular advantage to Social Christianity. It was as easily employed by Evangelicals or even Roman Catholics.

Sermons were the mainstay of ministry for Social Christians, just as they were for Evangelicals. From the earliest days, Social Christian preachers such as Charles Kingsley or Frederick W. Robertson evoked as much hostility as approval. The liberal theology underlying many of these sermons may have been one root cause of consternation. Robert F. Horton thought that he provoked much enmity toward himself in his Hampstead Baptist Church by publishing his *Inspiration and the Bible* (1888).[13] Certainly his assistant, Basil Martin, thought conservatives strongly disapproved of this perceived heresy of secular accommodationism. As Basil's son, Kingsley, recounted, concerning Basil Martin himself: "Once, he tried to comfort a man whose son had committed suicide. He suggested that God's mercies might cover such cases, and that the boy might have a better chance in the next world. The sorrowing father was furiously angry at the suggestion that his son was not in hell."[14]

Robert Horton, however, placed as much or more emphasis upon the negative reactions to his identification with "labour and democracy" as to his

9. Ibid., 174. See also Edward R. Norman, *The Victorian Christian Socialists* (Cambridge, 1987), 91–92, and Thomas Hughes, *Rugby, Tennessee: Being Some Account of the Settlement founded on the Cumberland Plateau by the Board of Aid to Land Ownership Ltd.* (London, 1881). The Rugby Colony Papers, 1872–1942, lie in the Manuscript Section, Tennessee State Library and Archives, Nashville.

10. For Canada, see David Howell, "The Social Gospel in Canadian Protestantism, 1895–1925: Implications for Sport" (Ph.D. thesis, University of Alberta, 1980), and David Howell and Peter Lindsey, "Social Gospel and the Young Boy Problem," *Canadian Journal of History of Sport* 17 (May 1986): 75–87.

11. William Herbert Perry Faunce, *The Educational Ideal in the Ministry* (New York, 1919), 5.

12. See Grier Nicholl, "The Image of the Protestant Minister in the Social Gospel Novel," *Church History* 37, no. 3 (1968): 319.

13. See Robert F. Horton, *An Autobiography* (London, 1917), 89–90.

14. Kingsley Martin, *Father Figures: A First Volume of Autobiography, 1897–1931* (London, 1966), 38.

liberal theology. But did this actually result in "alienating the rich from the church"?[15]

There is little evidence to suggest a sizable exodus of wealthy, conservative members from any churches. It could be grasped fairly readily that such pro-labor sermons were attempts to reach those largely alienated from the churches, especially when Horton and others were quick to point out the failures of older clergy such as Spurgeon in reaching the working classes.[16] An element within the wealthy laity always supported the call for social responsibility. By the 1920s the Social Gospel sermon had become so much of a set piece in many quite affluent congregations on both sides of the Atlantic that it would be difficult to imagine any passionate stirrings, for or against, by that time.

Many important sermons appeared in printed form, and ultimately it was propagation through print that acted as the main conduit of Social Christian communicative action until 1914. In that sense Social Christians took advantage of the mass religious culture already in print, created by the earlier generation of Evangelicals.[17] Innovative use of the print media had special priority, especially since many rival evangelical journals and books were already in circulation on both sides of the Atlantic. Indeed, F. D. Maurice himself had experience as both a journalist and editor with the *London Literary Chronicle* and *Athenaeum* prior to his ordination. Innovation appeared almost at once. Flouting the evangelical condemnation of fiction writing, he published a novel early in the century entitled *Eustace Conway; or, A Brother and Sister: "A Novel"* (London, Richard Bentley, 1834). From the literary scholar's point of view, *Eustace Conway* has little to recommend it, and Maurice's success as a novelist was probably less than that of Cardinal Newman, who was likewise not famous for fiction writing. From the historian's perspective, the novel served as the model for a future didactic tool of considerable importance to Social Christians. Maurice established the utility of fiction for Social Christians in the very act of writing his novel. The story concerns a young man who, after experiencing the various social philosophies of the 1820s and 1830s, comes to the ultimate understanding of human nature and of the possibilities to improve the human

15. Horton, *Autobiography,* 83.

16. Ibid., 90–91.

17. See Richard D. Altick, *The English Common Reader: A Social History of the Mass Reading Public, 1800–1900* (Chicago, 1957), 102, and Nathan O. Hatch, *The Democratization of American Christianity* (New Haven, Conn., 1989), 141–46. Two new books on the United States have been published—R. Lawrence Moore, *Selling God: American Religion in the Marketplace of Culture* (Oxford, 1994), and Leonard I. Sweet, ed., *Communications and Change in American Religious History* (Grand Rapids, Mich., 1994).

condition through acceptance of the Incarnate God. Eustace was thought to be Maurice's alter ego, and authors continued to produce similar alter-ego works until, by the later decades of the century, outright autobiographies came to be considered a better way of relating the lessons of a personal religious journey. *Eustace* was also in many respects a better sounding board for Maurice's view of human nature and society than his more-muddled theological discourses. The point that religion must be the teacher of society, the source of direction for true service to humanity rather than the servant of faddish public opinion, is also quite evident in this work.[18]

Maurice was not the only early Christian Socialist engaged in novel writing. Ludlow tried it years later but failed to produce one for want of basic technique.[19] Charles Kingsley did write fiction and became in many ways more famous as a writer than as a cofounder of the Christian Socialist movement. A clergyman like Maurice, Kingsley's primary objective was to preach through his fictional characters and story lines. His best work, *Alton Locke* (1850), was based upon the life of the Chartist poet Thomas Cooper, but much of it in Maurice-like fashion was really about Kingsley himself. Not only did he introduce a series of denunciations, especially in depicting the inertia of those in power, from Cambridge dons to bishops, who could do more to help the unfortunate, he also created a sympathetic picture of both working people and the forces that drove them to radical politics. The effect was not altogether positive. Speaking many years later, even the American Social Gospeler Washington Gladden, who like many of his fellow countrymen was thoroughly exposed to English novelists, could speak of Kingsley's "offence against respectability; his sympathy with the toiling classes was too quick and keen."[20] But Kingsley's advocacy added a spark of life to the rather introverted soul-searching of the intellectual life as depicted by Maurice in *Eustace*. It also made the Christian Socialist novel an important species of the emerging genre of the social novels.

18. John Frederick Denison Maurice, *Eustace Conway; or, A Brother and Sister: "A Novel"* (London, 1834), 2:173. See also Olive Brose, *Frederick Denison Maurice: Rebellious Conformist* (Athens, Ohio, 1971), 30–31, 281. Brose believes many of Maurice's attitudes revealed in *Eustace* remained with him till his death.

19. Transcription of Memoirs of John Malcolm Ludlow, 1821–1911 (prepared 1952), supplement A, "Couldn't-Have-Beens and Might-Have-Beens," J. M. Ludlow Papers, Cambridge University Library. This is printed in *John Ludlow: The Autobiography of a Christian Socialist*, ed. A. D. Murray (London, 1981), 316. It indicates that Ludlow felt pride in his ability as a literary critic and disappointment at not being asked to be an editor (*John Ludlow*, 316–17).

20. "Charles Kingsley," sermon 324, 22 January 1888, 49, Washington Gladden Papers, Ohio Historical Society.

In the second half of the nineteenth century, concerns about the social regeneration of society, based upon moral concerns, became a predominant influence upon the purveyors of culture within the English-speaking world. This is evident in the wider circulation of the earlier social or industrial novels of Dickens, Disraeli, and Gaskell, as well as the writings of a Kingsley. It was partially, as Stefan Collini has coined it, a culture of altruism, similar to that in English-speaking Canada between the late nineteenth century and the First World War.[21] A reading of American writers of the period reveals the same trend, in part influenced by slightly earlier writers in Britain.

The formal collapse of the first Christian Socialist movement by the 1860s did not bring about a concomitant disappearance of the Christian Socialist novel. Indeed, the novel was the main conveyor of the Christian Socialist legacy to the public; cooperatives and adult-education activities serviced rather limited sectors of the population. Thomas Hughes produced *Tom Brown at Oxford* in 1861, which kept alive the earlier ideals of Christian Socialism. In this sequel to *Schooldays at Rugby* (1858), the hero Tom is now a troubled undergraduate at Oxford. As a matriculant at St. Ambrose's College, Tom notes that among the best men are the "diligent readers of the *Tracts for the Times*."[22] One of these High Churchmen, Grey, a history and theology reader, points out that "Carthage was the mother of all hucksters" and hopes "the Church would yet be able to save England from sharing the fate of Tyre and Carthage, the great trading nations of the world."[23] This observation upsets Tom, and in his second year this, together with an encounter with the agrarian social problems in the village of Englebourn, propels him into serious reading on Roman plebeian demands, agrarian laws, and the politics of ancient Athens, "shaking many old beliefs, and leading him whither he knew not."[24] While he comes to the conclusion that the world follows the ways of the devil, most notably in the principle of laissez-faire, he remains skeptical of the ability of the church to solve the problem, at least in its closed, exclusive sense as interpreted by the Tractarian Grey. His ongoing radical struggle with the wider devilish influences in the world and his continued association with Grey (eventually a London parson to the poor) highlights the dilemmas of the age both in social and religious circles.

21. Stefan Collini, *Public Moralists: Political Thought and Intellectual Life in Britain* (Oxford, 1991), chap. 2; Ramsay Cook, *The Regenerators: Social Criticism in Late Victorian Canada* (Toronto, 1985).

22. *Tom Brown at Oxford: A Sequel to Schooldays at Rugby* (New York, 1861), 3.

23. Ibid. 99, 100.

24. Ibid., 396.

Dilemmas also abound in the novels of Mary Ward (Mrs. Humphry Ward), who was to become the leading Christian Socialist novelist. Ward was enormously successful in that over one million copies of *Robert Elsmere* (1888) were sold worldwide. Her success coincided with the great British middle-class awakening to social problems in the 1880s. As the granddaughter of Thomas Arnold (the living inspiration for the Rugby ideal of Tom Brown), Mary Ward was well situated in the upper echelons of London society and the reigning intelligentsia. As Jane Lewis has recently pointed out, Mary Ward believed herself to be primarily a novelist.[25] But Ward also saw this dedication to the art and business of novel writing as a vehicle for the discussion of important social and political issues.[26] Mary Ward once described her situation as follows:

> The root difficulty was of course the dealing with such a subject in a novel at all. Yet I was determined to deal with it so, in order to reach the public. There were great precedents—Froude's *Nemesis of Faith*, Newman's *Loss and Gain*, Kingsley's *Alton Locke*—for the novel of religious or social propaganda. And it seemed to me that the novel was capable of holding and shaping real experience of any kind, as it affects the lives of men and women. It is the most elastic, the most adaptable of forms. No one has the right to set limits to its range. There is only one final test. Does it interest?—does it appeal?[27]

In *Robert Elsmere* a young Anglican clergyman, influenced by Professor Grey at Oxford (no relation to Tom Brown's Grey), dedicates himself to the service of the poor through pastoral work in the East End of London. It is not easy to endure the hostility of secularists as well as the moral and physical conditions of the laborers and the destitute. The exhausted Elsmere eventually dies.

The success of *Robert Elsmere* was extraordinary, and neither Ward nor any of her imitators were ever able to equal it. Certainly the book appeared at precisely the right moment for audiences aroused by a succession of public exposés of the Condition-of-England question. But its story also touched a nerve underlying social service—the Victorian Crisis of Faith. At Oxford, Elsmere had been inspired by Professor Grey, a T. H. Green–like figure, but he had also been exposed to German Higher Criticism, after which his faith was

25. Jane Lewis, *Women and Social Action in Victorian and Edwardian England* (Stanford, 1991), 194.
26. Ibid., 197.
27. Mrs. Mary [Humphry] Ward, *A Writer's Recollections* (New York, 1918), 2:66.

never the same. As Ward stated in *A Writer's Recollection:* "I wanted to show how a man of sensitive and noble character, born for religion, comes to throw off the orthodoxies of his day and moment, and to go out into the wilderness where all is experiment, and spiritual life begins again."[28] Ward's realistic depiction of the Crisis of Faith in fact earned hostile reviews by evangelical and even some moderate clergy and laity.[29] The story of *Robert Elsmere,* however, was accessible to the average reader, and Mrs. Ward probably succeeded more as a novelist than as a social moralist. Her work established enduring dialogue with readers throughout the world.

In North America the British Christian Socialist novelists captured a substantial audience for themselves at the same time that other great Victorian writers were being acclaimed. Frequently the British influences fused in their impact upon early Social Gospelers such as Washington Gladden, who wrote sermons inspired in equal measure by Dickens and Mary Ward. The American market had very early displayed a thirst for religious novels and for those rooted in religious concerns, such as *Uncle Tom's Cabin* (1852). Until the 1890s, on balance, American writers tended to exemplify the same mixture of religion, social concern, and entertainment as found in Britain. One genre, however, that emerged first in America and reverberated back upon British Social Christian audiences was the utopian novel.

In the midst of the watershed 1880s Edward Bellamy produced *Looking Backward* (1888), the most significant of all the utopian novels of modern times. In 1935 John Dewey, Charles Beard, and Edward Weeks named *Looking Backward* as second only to *Das Kapital* in its world influence over the previous fifty years.[30] On the British side, R. C. K. Ensor states that *Looking Backward* was one of the inspirers of the Independent Labour Party and contributed, along with Gronlund's *Co-operative Commonwealth,* to the utopian and idealistic qualities of modern English socialism.[31]

Bellamy may have been motivated partly by his own religious convictions, but he was also disturbed by the recent wave of strikes and other serious signs of social unrest in the United States and by the related problems of poverty and social injustice. He responded by writing about what the society could be if it followed the right prophets. He developed a story, unique at the time, of a

28. Ibid., 67.

29. See Bernard Lightman, "Robert Elsemere and the Agnostic Crisis of Faith," in *Victorian Faith in Crisis: Essays on Continuity and Change in Nineteenth-Century Belief,* ed. Richard J. Helmstadter and Bernard Lightman (Stanford, 1990), 283–311.

30. Robert C. Elliott, *The Shape of Utopia: Studies in a Literary Genre* (Chicago, 1970), 153.

31. R. C. K. Ensor, *England, 1870–1914* (Oxford, 1936), 334.

person (Julian West, a wealthy young Bostonian) who is put into a hypnotic trance (30 May 1887) and later discovered and resuscitated by a physician (September of the year 2000). The late-Victorian vision of the future that unfolds for West is one of national cooperation in which disparities of wealth are eliminated and replaced by a credo of "public capitalism," or service for "the common fund."

*Looking Backward* was as successful as *Alton Locke,* one million copies being sold. As a result of its success, imitations of Bellamy's ideals, the utopian approach (in novel form or otherwise) and even particular literary techniques contained in its pages, appeared on both sides of the Atlantic. So-called Nationalist clubs also appeared in many American cities in the years that followed. The extraordinary impact of what might be described as the "sugar coating" of a social agenda in the form of the novel was clear.

A year before his death, Bellamy completed *Equality* (1897), the lesser-known sequel to *Looking Backward.* In many ways *Equality* is a much fuller exposition of Bellamy's theories. The revolutionary change from the old America to the new, according to Dr. Leete (Julian West's guide in both novels), was based upon economic equality, "the cornerstone of our state" and the "only adequate pledge of these three birthrights—life, liberty and happiness."[32] Later, in reference to the full emancipation of women, West's guide explains that "[e]quality is the only moral relation between human beings. Any reform which should result in remedying the abuse of women by men, or working men by capitalists, must therefore be addressed to equalizing their economic condition. Not till the women, as well as the working men, gave over the folly of attacking the consequence of economic inequality and attacked the inequality itself, was there any hope for the enfranchisement of either class."[33]

On the cultural side, Bellamy revealed his shortcomings in overlooking the continued workings of racism within his utopia of the future. When West expresses the old concern over a possible "closer commingling of the races" in the new system of economic equality that now embraces the "colored race" of the southern States, Dr. Leete replies: "So we read, but there was absolutely nothing in the new system to offend that prejudice. It related entirely to economic organization, and had nothing more to do than it has now with social relations. Even for industrial purposes the new system involved no more commingling of races than the old had done. It was perfectly consistent with any degree of race separation in industry which the most bigoted local

32. Edward Bellamy, *Equality* (New York, 1897), 17.
33. Ibid., 133–34.

prejudices might demand."[34] Racial reform was clearly not part of Bellamy's
Great Revolution of the twentieth century.

Bellamy's economic-social interpretation of and solution to the problems of
America not only influenced Progressive writers such as Charles Beard but also
led many to conclude that Bellamy's Nationalist movement was nothing more
than socialism. In the introduction to the revised *Co-operative Commonwealth*
Lawrence Gronlund claimed that his frank exposition of socialism had led to
"Mr. Bellamy's *Looking Backward,* the novel which without doubt has stealth-
ily inoculated thousands of Americans with socialism, just because it ignored
the name and those who had written on the subject."[35]

Gronlund (like other socialists) found some small faults with Bellamy, including his concept of equal pay.[36] There was undoubted rivalry in proposals for
change and organizations, but Gronlund and other socialists also generally
agreed that Bellamy's thoughts were well intentioned.

The religious dimension in Bellamy was quite important. In contrast with
Gronlund, who believed in not much more than "a Will of the Universe" as a
basis for future religion,[37] Bellamy approached social issues from deeply held
religious convictions. Son of a Baptist minister, he migrated from orthodox
Calvinism toward the liberal theology of Henry Ward Beecher, along the way
picking up a healthy infusion of Comptean ideas best expressed in the title of
his unpublished 1847 manuscript, "The Religion of Humanity." He allied himself strongly with the early Social Gospel movement; much of his year-2000
society, as Joseph Schiffman has pointed out, appears to contain qualities of the
millennium foretold by the Hebrew prophets.[38]

In *Equality* he revealed the full extent of his ethical designs, linking the
application of the Golden Rule to his economically egalitarian society. Shortly
before the revolution that formed the basis of the new society came the Great
Revival, which produced "a religion which . . . dispensed with the rites and
ceremonies, creeds and dogmas, and banished from this life fear and concern
for the meaner self; a religion of life and conduct dominated by an impassioned
sense of the solidarity of humanity and of man with God; the religion of a race
that knows itself divine and fears no evil, either now or hereafter."[39]

34. Ibid., 365.
35. Lawrence Gronlund, introduction to *The Co-operative Commonwealth: An Exposition of
Socialism* (1884; reprint, New York, 1890), viii.
36. Ibid., viii and 51–72.
37. Ibid., 284
38. Joseph Shiffman, ed., introduction to *Edward Bellamy: Selected Writings on Religion and
Society* (New York, 1955), xxxiii.
39. Bellamy, *Equality,* 344–45.

Bellamy's vision was indeed of a religion of humanity in which the conventional practices of attendance had withered away, supplanted by the living reality of the Golden Rule. Such a sentiment smacked of the early acceptance of a secularization of religious life, which had grave implications for the continued role of the churches. Yet with a gift for clairvoyance, allied to an up-to-date knowledge of current technology, Bellamy predicted preachers would reach mass audiences with the gospel of humanity through the use of the telephone and the "electroscope."[40] Perhaps this surreptitious solution to declining church attendance, together with his comments upon the disgrace of those men of the cloth who had opposed the revolution,[41] may explain why large numbers of clergy supported his Nationalist societies.

On the other hand, many may simply have read Bellamy's utopian novels for their entertainment value, in much the same way that they would later read the works of H. G. Wells. After all, Bellamy had been a reasonably popular writer before producing *Looking Backward,* demonstrating in his first novel, *Six to One: A Nantucket Idyl* (1878), and in magazine pieces his ability to produce readable light fiction without any great social messages. Bellamy supposedly assisted the cause of the Social Christians on both sides of the Atlantic, but it is not clear how much they ultimately benefited from this alliance. Certainly those who rejected his vision, such as William Morris (in *News from Nowhere*), used the same genre but in the service of an agnostic socialist utopia—albeit with medieval trappings in Morris's case.[42]

In the late 1890s a new fiction genre emerged, a genre that has best been described as the Social Gospel novel. The endeavors in this genre were more formula-ridden and less introspective than any of their predecessor "Christian Socialist" novels. However, they undoubtedly reached a more plebeian readership. In their desire to influence and control the reader, they were also, following Habermas's theories, better examples of "strategic action." It was perhaps essential that they be so, since by that time the readership for religiously connected periodicals and books was in decline on both sides of the Atlantic in spite of the success of religious fiction such as *Quo Vadis?* (1897), by Henry K. Sienkiewicz.[43]

40. Ibid., chap. 31.
41. Ibid., 342–43, 383–86.
42. See Trevor Lloyd, "How to Write a Utopia: William Morris's Medieval Interests and *News from Nowhere*," *Historical Reflections* 2, no. 1 (1975): 89–108.
43. For the United States, see Dennis V. Voskuil, "Reactions Out: Protestantism and the Media," in *Between the Times: The Travail of the Protestant Establishment in America, 1900–1960,* ed. William R. Hutchison (Cambridge, Mass., 1989), 72–92. For a broader picture of publishing in Britain, see Joseph McAleer, *Popular Reading and Publishing in Britain, 1914–1950* (Oxford, 1992).

By far the most famous and successful of the Social Gospel novels was *In His Steps* (1897), by the Kansas Congregationalist minister Charles M. Sheldon. Sheldon's work contained most of the elements of later Social Gospel novels and perhaps a slightly greater degree of taste than found in the generally tasteless representatives of the genre. Sheldon, an activist working in a variety of projects for the dispossessed, used the central figure, Henry Maxwell, to express his concerns. These coincided very much with the mainstream views of most Social Gospelers at the time, which can explain in part Sheldon's success. Maxwell is not an overly dramatized tragic hero, as are the heroes in many Social Gospel novels that followed, but rather one who experiences a sustained conversion throughout the story. The initial conversion comes at the hands of a dying tramp who disrupts the Sunday service of the fashionable First Church in the mythical industrial city of Raymond to exhort parishioners actually to practice their pious Christian platitudes. The Reverend Maxwell then takes up the challenge, followed by fifty members of the congregation, and together they try to determine and do "what Jesus would do" in Raymond.

The result is a predictable flurry of social service involving the enlistment of others, including a notable number of women, to the idea of reaching the destitute in the poorest section of Raymond. Settlements arise, replete with references to Toynbee and East London, though the earliest activity seems devoted to the cause of temperance and Sabbatarianism.[44] Maxwell's work then abruptly shifts to Chicago, where an even greater contrast between rich and poor in urban life is evident. The reader is also repeatedly reminded of the difficulties most ministers have in speaking to those below the affluent class. Lurking in the background, toward the end of the novel, is Carlsen, the nonbelieving socialist leader, who once blurts out, "The trusts and monopolies have their greatest men in the churches. The ministers as a class are their slaves."[45] While Sheldon preaches the value of the organization in bringing Christian compassion to the poor, he also emphasizes the personal element in Christian discipleship, in which each believer must individually follow in Christ's steps to achieve overall social justice.

This blend of elements was a spectacular success. In the seventy years following its appearance in 1897, it was reissued by seventy publishing houses in the United States, Canada, and Britain. Sheldon had obviously touched the very soul of the Anglo-American readership. His other works were not as popular, perhaps because of their special concerns such as the treatment of

44. Charles M. Sheldon, *In His Steps: What Would Jesus Do?* (Toronto, 1897), 140.
45. Ibid., 266.

women workers and anti-Semitism. *Of One Blood* (1916), with an African American central hero, skillfully combated the baneful effects of racism. Later Social Gospel novels by imitators clearly established that this was an enduring genre, but by restoring the didactic approach to Social Christian fiction writing, they descended to a cruder assertion of the moral authority of the movement. Just why *In His Steps* was such an outstanding success has been thoroughly dissected and debated, with Paul S. Boyer most notably suggesting that it was really about a troubled American middle-class conscience, rather than religion or social reform.[46] Against this, a case might be made that Sheldon's literary style had a reasonably wide appeal that, after all, included a following in Britain even larger than that in the United States.[47] The positive elements in Sheldon's message were not overshadowed by the fear of social tension represented in comments on socialism and trade unionism in the book's pages.

Perhaps what is even more significant is that *In His Steps* reflects the essence of Social Christianity itself, with its various nuances and, at times, seeming contradictions. In Britain the book produced some debate about its lack of theological rigor.[48] While in harmony with their secular fellow travelers on the quest for social improvement, and conscious of the challenge of militant socialism, the fictional heroes of the novel follow a path to reform involving large numbers of altruistic individuals responding to the call. Like Social Christians in the real world, they are conscious of their middle-class limitations and yet are emboldened to overcome them through the process of religious conversion to the full meaning of Christ's message.

Slightly earlier and independent of the Social Gospel fiction writing in the United States, a less significant but quite similar genre appeared in Britain, heralded by the novel *Stephen Remarx* (1893). The book's author, the Reverend James Adderley, a socialist and Ritualist, believed that the Reformation had needlessly separated religion from theatrical art forms, thus effectively rejecting, for example, the Passion play. The result was that "the modern Church is almost the only institution that has not understood the power of the drama or the value of the appeal to the imagination."[49] A very heavy dose of drama was certainly evident in *Stephen Remarx*. Though the manuscript endured numerous rejections, the published work ultimately went through twelve editions,

46. Paul S. Boyer, "*In His Steps:* A Reappraisal," *American Quarterly* 23 (April 1971): 60–78.

47. Timothy Miller, *Following in His Steps: A Biography of Charles M. Sheldon* (Knoxville, Tenn., 1987), 83–84. For the impact on British Social Christians, see James Adderley, "A Voice from Kansas," *Goodwill* 1, no. 1 (1899): 82–83.

48. Miller, *Following in His Steps*, 83–84.

49. James Adderley, *Slums and Society: Reminiscences of Old Friends* (New York, 1916), 166.

including an American one. The central hero, Stephen Remarx, like his North American counterparts, is a parson who involves himself with the laboring class of his parish. In Kingsley-like fashion, however, a wealthy lay patron forces Remarx's resignation because of his alleged socialism. Remarx then joins a society dedicated to the service of the poor, while his successor, the Reverend Bugsnoter, empties Remarx's old church with dull support of the status quo. Adderley then produces a convention used in many Social Gospel novels—the tragic ending. While stumbling in the street as a result of philanthropic over-work, Remarx is hit by a cab. In the final deathbed scene, however, Remarx, through his own lifetime exemplification of the truth of the Incarnate God, succeeds in converting Oxenham, the secularist labor leader. Oxenham is a more central figure than Carlsen in *In His Steps* but likewise personifies the dangerous alternate path that society might take if the Social Christian message is not accepted.

Adderley declared *Stephen Remarx* to be a "tract." Here the author's own description worked to his disadvantage in some circles; as he explained: "Newspaper critics always say that I disarm criticism by calling my novels 'tracts.' Perhaps I do. It is rather a good dodge, and succeeds in getting readers."[50]

Although Adderley argued that the publisher had labeled *Remarx* a novel for purposes of sales,[51] he also appeared to have a good idea of his market: " 'Stephen Remarx' came out just when slumming was the fashion among religious people of the upper classes, and socialism of a very mild type was beginning to be indulged in even by duchesses. It was also rather an 'unsec-tarian' kind of book, and appealed to the Nonconformists, though written by a supposed ritualist."[52]

Hall Caine, a socialist and New Theology associate of R. J. Campbell, produced a novel along much the same lines four years later—*The Christian*. It received a harsher reception from critics, though Adderley had revised some of the proofs.[53] The hero, John Storm, son of a peer and nephew of the prime minister, is nonetheless a hardworking socialist vicar. Though concerned with slum dwellers, the book devotes much space to the comfortable decadence of the wealthy—including the popular Canon Wealthy of Belgravia. The novel then becomes utopian, or millennial, with the predictable social disintegration of London before the Second Coming. The disintegration eventually brings

50. Ibid., 169.
51. Ibid.
52. Ibid., 170.
53. Ibid., 176.

down the affluent except "the Jews on the Exchange, who held their peace and profited by their infidelity."[54] This anti-Semitic theme is unusual in British Social Christian writing but has some parallels in contemporaneous populist writings in the United States, where such views were not uncommon. It is also interesting that the hero is a Ritualist, a member of the Society of the Holy Gethsemane, a fictional descendant of the Oxford Movement. Traces of anti-Semitism can be found in the later writings of the Anglo-Catholic Conrad Noel, vicar of Thaxted, and perhaps, according to some, more than traces in those of the Anglo-Catholic layman T. S. Eliot.[55] In any case, the Social Gospel novel remained a largely undeveloped literary form compared with its North American counterpart.

Halfway between the British and American writing traditions, and truly an Anglo-American, stood the Reverend W. J. Dawson. Originally a Nonconformist minister in London, Glasgow, and Southport and an active figure in Christian Socialist circles (such as the Minor Prophets Society founded at Mansfield College, Oxford), Dawson assumed the pastorate of a Presbyterian church in Newark, New Jersey, in 1906. In his later years he was as well known for his poetry and fiction writing as for his Social Christian sermons. Shortly after establishing permanent residence in the United States, he published one of his more famous works—*A Prophet in Babylon: A Story of Social Service* (New York, 1907). The impact was considerable. Washington Gladden even made it the subject of one of his sermons.[56]

Dawson reflected a number of American and British Social Gospel trends in his writing. Didactic in purpose, Dawson frequently criticized American greed and competitiveness as well as the fact that churches had become a phenomenon of Fifth Avenue largely to the neglect of poorer areas.[57] *A Prophet in Babylon* begins with a crisis for Dawson's hero, John Gaunt, minister of fashionable Mayfield Avenue Church. Gaunt inadvertently offends Mrs. Somerset, a powerful church member bedecked with big gold bracelets, by making some mildly critical comments concerning the complacency of the wealthy

54. Hall Caine, *The Christian* (London, 1897), 360.

55. For example, Conrad Noel, in "The People's Life of Jesus," *Crusader* 3, no. 52 (1922), makes the point that though both Jews and Christians were monotheistic, only the latter were persecuted because of their social criticism. As he states, "[H]ow is it, then, that the liberal Jew throughout the Empire refused to burn incense to Caesar and were [sic] promptly exempted from doing so? Obviously because the liberal Jew was a friend to the Empire and the Christian an enemy" (ibid., 11). For the debate concerning T. S. Eliot, see Christopher Ricks, *T. S. Eliot and Prejudice* (London, 1988).

56. 8 December 1907, sermon no. 1144, f. 691–717, Washington Gladden Papers.

57. W. J. Dawson, *A Prophet in Babylon: A Story of Social Service* (New York, 1907), chaps. 2 and 6.

toward the plight of the poor. This criticism, together with a decline in church attendance due to the declining market value of Gaunt as a "seller of rhetoric," leads to Gaunt's departure from the church. In his youth, as a seminarian, Gaunt had been concerned with economic inequalities, but such thoughts had been laid aside as youthful indiscretions when he opted to serve the comfortable pew. Now such thoughts are rekindled and fortified through acquaintance with an elderly theologian named Paul Gordon. As happens to Maxwell in *In His Steps*, circumstances of the cold, cruel world, channeled through the life story of another figure, lead to Gaunt's conversion to the true principles of Christ.

In his day Gordon had been a great preacher and then an equally great seminary professor. Unfortunately, his comments indicating knowledge of German biblical criticism led to a heresy trial. While many supported him, Gordon had to leave his post, surviving on his religious publications, while using most of his time and energy in the service of the poor of New York. He eventually stopped publishing and was forgotten.

Through his friendship with this old prophet, Gaunt is inspired by a new goal of founding a great interdenominational organization called the League of Service. He collects support from many, including allegedly godless socialists who he believes are at root religious. His plan of action derives from the original ideas of Christ, ideas that existed before theology or a church had developed.[58]

Later, Gaunt delivers a sermon at Madison Square Garden that launches the league on a path of early and great successes. Then, in Adderley-like fashion, with a touch of American violence, the hero is assassinated by a former pugilist shooting from a saloon recently closed by the league. It is a double tragedy, since the occasion also marks Gaunt's attendance at Gordon's funeral! Here again is suggested the danger of violence, anarchy, and social disintegration attributable to an enemy of the cause, though this time an enemy more to the Right.

As a significant genre the Social Gospel novel had really disappeared from Britain by 1914 and would disappear from the United States in the next decade or so. The novels had often been penned by parsons, and James Adderley suggested, at least in the case of Britain, that the clergy were no longer prominent in writing because they "ceased to spend much time in composing sermons."[59] Americans such as Harold Bell Wright remained to round out a more Western, Southern, and rural rendition of the original urban genre or combine the two, as in Wright's *Shepherd of the Hills*. Progressive writers in the

---

58. Ibid., 226–28.
59. Adderley, *Slums and Society*, 187.

United States, such as Robert Herrick, could continue to preach through novels such as *Clark's Field* (1914), but the message was increasingly secular reformist. Social Gospel novels began to merge with social concern novels, and all in turn could be taken solely for their entertainment value.

In Canada the Social Gospel novel had also become an important literary trend and perhaps survived there somewhat longer, thereby helping to keep the genre alive south of the border through the copublication of Canadian writings. Two of the most significant Social Gospel novelists in Canada, Agnes Machar and Ralph Connor, have recently received close scrutiny by literary scholars and historians. Machar was a master of diverse forms of literature, though chiefly in the area of fiction. A dedicated Christian and, according to Ruth Brouwer, well read in socially oriented works of British and American writers,[60] Machar published *Roland Graeme Knight* in 1892. This early date, together with a plot that would become familiar in some later Social Gospel novels, would certainly qualify Machar for the title "pioneer." However, the crisis of faith found in the central character, Roland, is reminiscent of the older Christian Socialist works. Like W. J. Dawson (in his later work), Machar used the novel as a vehicle for criticizing the collaboration of the traditional churches with American capitalism and set the scene in a fictional American industrial town (though Machar's hero is Canadian). This site may also have been chosen to increase sales, since the book was copublished in New York. The solution to the woes of society comes in the form of legislative control of factory abuses, a cooperative factory, and a general spirit of social harmony based upon Christ's teachings, all of which Roland advocates, though he maintains his pure Christianity by remaining outside the church.

Machar, whose work compared favorably with the cruder work of later Social Gospel novelists, was thus a reasonably sophisticated apologist of Christian Socialism. But the more famous of these two Canadian writers was Ralph Connor, who published very popular works from the 1890s to the 1930s. Ralph Connor (the pseudonym for the Reverend Charles W. Gordon) was one of the most prominent Social Christian figures in the Canadian Presbyterian Church in the early part of the twentieth century. Connor's works included muscular Christian variations on the Sheldon theme of courageous ministers, but frequently it is the enormity of the social problem that brings both clergy and laity, including many women, to the realization that old theology and old economics will not work. In works such as *The Sky Pilot* (1899) he would make the

---

60. Ruth Compton Brouwer, "The Between-Age Christianity of Agnes Machar," *Canadian Historical Review* 65 , no. 3 (1984): 306.

American bestseller list as well. In *Arm of Gold* (1932) he even revealed a possible appreciation of the activities of Social Catholicism by attributing to the activities of fictional Presbyterian ministers in Cape Breton qualities that were remarkably similar to those of the Antigonish Movement, which in reality operated in precisely the same locale. David Marshall gives considerable credit to Connor's ability to deliver his religious message through both his novels and the associated genre of "biblical fiction."[61] But much of his writing could be considered pure adventure, explaining in part the relative longevity of his works compared with the brief tenure of other Social Gospel novels. Mary Vipond believes that in only one work, *To Him That Hath* (London, 1921), were the concerns of the Social Gospel fully developed.[62] The book's labor strike and its resolution were clearly based on the author's own experiences as a skilled arbitrator in labor disputes. In that sense the careers of Charles Gordon and Ralph Connor intersected on that occasion.[63]

Less well known for his fiction writing was the venerable patriarch of Canadian Methodism, the Reverend Albert Carman. Carole Gerson finds his novel *The Preparation of Ryerson Embury* (1900) to be a well-written analysis of socioeconomic conflict and the role of religious institutions in such conflict.[64] It is interesting that Carman's theological conservatism did not inhibit him from identifying with the frustrations of those suffering within the industrial-capitalist system or from employing a literary form commonly associated with those firmly within the Social Christian fold.

However, by the late 1930s, it undoubtedly was through the continuing profitable sales of novels like those of Ralph Connor and Harold Bell Wright (and cinema adaptations of their works) as well as reprints of older works such as *In His Steps* that the Social Gospel genre continued. Indeed, Henry May is probably correct in seeing the novel as the Social Gospel's "most successful medium."[65] Between works of fundamentalist religious literature on the one side and works of pure entertainment on the other, the Social Christian fiction was eventually wedged into an uncomfortable position.

Indeed, the readership of any religious or semireligious works was never completely certain. Even the Unitarian professor Francis Greenwood Peabody

61. David Marshall, *Secularizing the Faith: Canadian Protestant Clergy and the Crisis of Belief, 1850–1940* (Toronto, 1992), 140–45.

62. Mary Vipond, "Blessed Are the Peacemakers: The Labour Question in Social Gospel Fiction," *Journal of Canadian Studies* 10 (1975): 37.

63. See his *Postscript to Adventure—The Autobiography of Ralph Connor* (Toronto, 1975).

64. Carole Gerson, *A Purer Taste: The Writing and Reading of Fiction in English in Nineteenth-Century Canada* (Toronto, 1989), 143–44.

65. Henry R. May, *The Protestant Churches and Industrial America* (New York, 1969), 207.

of Harvard believed that his well-known academic apologies for Social Christianity were in fact read by evangelical ministers in both the United States and Britain "to derive from them what are excellent 'seed thoughts,' which may be like a caraway seed, put in to give a taste."[66] Even more superficial would be the reading of works of fiction. It is also interesting that the Chicago publisher Fleming H. Revell, which produced so much of the domestic Social Gospel literature and copublished some British works in the same category, had fundamentalist roots.[67]

Some works of nonfiction approached the readability of novels. By the twentieth century autobiographies appeared with increasing frequency, including works by major Social Christian figures from James Adderley to Ralph Connor. Some of these, such as the one by Robert F. Horton, could relate inner soul-searching, a perspective on politics and contemporary social questions, and even the hostility of wealthy churchgoers in a very direct, authentic way.[68] However, they were usually retrospective, written safely some years after the events. Vida Scudder, the American socialist and socialist Christian, in writing *A Listener in Babel* (1903), experimented with a collected series of pieces she later called "semi-fiction, semi-autobiography." As she stated, "I threw it into a favorite literary form of mine, imaginary conversation."[69] The advantage of such a form was that Scudder did not have to face the ultimate criticism of others who would scrutinize real policies and past actions. As in other works of fiction, characters had to be true only to the story line of their actions in the context of fictionalized people and situations. The technique was in a sense manipulative, if not deceptive, in competing with a wider, real world of viable alternatives.

Beginning in the 1880s the real rival to the novel was sensationalist religious journalism. *The Bitter Cry of Outcast London* (see Chapter 2) appeared as an anonymously written pamphlet in 1883. There had been earlier examinations of social problems, and the approach was not particularly original. However, the public reaction was extraordinary. Though the pamphlet was prepared for the London Congregational Union, its impact was felt more in politics and society as a whole than in church circles, because it implicitly questioned whether mid-Victorian self-improvement was of any use in helping the destitute. The older evangelical church efforts that relied on self-help assisted by Christian philanthropy also appeared to be repudiated.

---

66. Peabody to his publisher, Roger L. Scaife of Houghton Mifflin, 14 January 1922, Francis Greenwood Peabody Papers, Houghton Library, Harvard University.

67. See Vernon E. Mattson, "The Fundamentalist Mind" (Ph.D. diss., University of Kansas, 1971), 14.

68. See Horton, *Autobiography,* 83, 90–91.

69. Vida Scudder, *On Journey* (New York, 1937), 181.

The device of the exposé was now exploited to the fullest by Social Christian writers. The approach was twofold. On the one hand, authors mustered all possible literary techniques to maximize the shock value of revelations. On the other, they carefully managed the release of data to the public in order to achieve the desired effect. It was obvious that ideas unpopular with affluent, conservative congregation members were better expressed through studies or surveys, which were ostensibly objective. Since the publication of the 1851 Census of Religious Worship, surveys conducted by most major churches had revealed the diminishing base of working-class support. This was now exploited. Those interested in furthering the cause of particular Nonconformist churches or the Established Church could often be persuaded to accept Christian Social ideals as part of the approach to the problem of the unchurched. This conception was rather the reverse of the early-nineteenth-century argument that churchgoing would result in the improvement of the lot of the working class in general; social action now would bring them to the church, as corroborated in the pages of the *British Weekly*, for example, which conducted its own religious census of London in 1886.

An infinitely more impressive statistical barrage came from Charles Booth's *Life and Labour of the People of London*, which included, in its third series, "Religious Influences," published mainly in 1902–3. Some of the material was certainly useful to the Christian social cause, though, as Rosemary O'Day has pointed out, such material formed part of a larger body of diverse views culled from the perceptions of ministers rather than their people. As O'Day also notes, raw data did not always yield up clear support for progressive sermons.[70]

Some Christian writers availed themselves of unlikely tools, including manipulation. The correspondence of Richard Mudie-Smith, chief organizer of the *Daily News* Census of Public Worship in London (1902–3), provides insight into the use of this device. Seeing advantage in the publication of bleak statistics for his work, the Nonconformist minister Scott Lidgett wrote to Smith from the Bermondsey Settlement concerning the census results, saying that it was "the glory of Christianity that it can face unpleasant truths."[71] George Cadbury, the Quaker philanthropist, also thought the results would arouse the churches "to a sense of the very small hold they have upon the population of London."[72] But in other correspondence concerning the release of such information, Cadbury wrote: "I am most anxious in the comments and returns that we avoid any

70. Rosemary O'Day, "Interviews and Investigations: Charles Booth and the Making of the Religious Influence Survey," *History* 74 (1989): 361–77.
71. Lidgett to Mudie-Smith, 20 November 1903, Richard Mudie-Smith Papers, British Library of Political and Economic Science, London.
72. Cadbury to Mudie-Smith, 15 December 1902, Mudie-Smith Papers.

disparaging remarks as to the Anglican Churches, but that we should keep our minds steadily on the one point that all the churches combined are accomplishing so very little."[73] That is why he encouraged Mudie-Smith to publish the results of a district where the Anglican Church predominated, since publication would "disarm some of the opposition from them."[74]

Lidgett and Cadbury clearly understood that statistics could be used for their shock value, and thus appreciated both aspects of the exposé. Following publication of *The Bitter Cry*, however, the unchallenged master of shock value on both sides of the Atlantic was W. T. Stead. A provincial English Congregationalist imbued with a Nonconformist conscience, Stead first gained national attention with his stirring editorials in the Darlington *Northern Echo* during the Bulgarian Horrors agitation of the late 1870s. After becoming editor of the *Pall Mall Gazette*, the very year *The Bitter Cry* was published, he quickly caught the public eye with his flare for sensationalism, creating events instead of simply reporting and commenting upon them, as in his Marden Tribute crusade. Increasingly associated with Social Christians, he finally left the *Gazette* in 1890 to found *The Review of Reviews*, modeled after American illustrated magazines, repaying his inspirers by also founding an *American Review of Reviews*, with Albert Shaw, a year later. Though the American version was filled with reprints from its British counterpart, Stead spent much time in the United States, becoming as famous in that country as in his own. He was truly a transatlantic figure, advocating closer cultural and political unity between the English-speaking giants[75] and ironically dying on the Titanic during its maiden voyage to America in 1912. His success in religious journalism was unequaled.[76]

Before his death, however, Stead produced a large number of books and pamphlets, some culled from his pieces in the *Review of Reviews*. His most celebrated work was *If Christ Came to Chicago!* (1894), published in the heyday of the Social Gospel novel. The timing was perfect. Stead had already established a reputation in America as a moral crusader, a proponent of the advancement of women, a disciple of James Russell Lowell,[77] and a publicizer of the

73. Ibid., 6 December 1902.

74. Ibid., 4 December 1902.

75. See William T. Stead, *The Americanization of the World; or, The Trend of the Twentieth Century* (New York, 1902).

76. By comparison, see B. B. Benson, "A Social Gospel Experiment in Newspaper Reform," *Church History* 33, no. 1 (1964): 74–83, for Charles Sheldon's less successful foray into newspapers in the United States..

77. For Lowell's ideas, see Claire McGlinchee, *James Russell Lowell* (New York, 1967). For Stead's view of Lowell, see William T. Stead, *James Russell Lowell: His Message and How It Helped Me* (London, 1891).

Chicago Columbian Exposition of 1893. His prolonged visit to Chicago in 1893 resulted a year later in *If Christ Came to Chicago!* an impassioned call for a unified politico-religious effort to improve civic government and social services based upon the application of Christ's teaching. Placing Christ in America's greatest city had its desired effect on urban America and to a lesser degree on Britain, though Stead's Civic Federation, formed in Chicago, did less well elsewhere. Nevertheless, what success the pamphlet enjoyed demonstrated how important had been the author's groundwork. His Central Music Hall meetings in November of 1893 and his revival-like addresses to trade unionists created an intense prepublication public appetite for the pamphlet, an appetite unabated by his later public gaffes and the opposition of his colleague Albert Shaw.[78]

Shaw had curiously ambivalent feelings toward British figures. Shaw's collaboration with Stead in editing the *American Review of Reviews* left little doubt of his admiration for British Social Christians. Yet his words to Stead a month after Stead's visit to Chicago were harsh. Shaw wrote on that occasion, advising him that he needed years of experience in order to write with authority on the American scene, and added:

> Hugh Price Hughes was not mercenary like Matthew Arnold, but he seriously believed that it was more important that he should instruct us than that he should learn anything about us or anything from us, and consequently he went back knowing nothing whatever about the United States excepting that he did not like our hotel cooking. Fairbairn and Horton of course came over under definite engagement to give lecture courses in theological seminaries. Their opportunities of observation were better and were better used. Nonetheless I think both of them made the mistake of all distinguished English visitors of feeling obliged to instruct rather than to observe, and that they went back regarding America as a place where they had left impressions rather than a place where they had received any.[79]

Shaw's observations may have reflected the resentment of a segment of the American intelligentsia toward their British tutors. On this particular matter, of course, he was wrong about the outcome of Stead's foray into Chicago's social distress.

78. See Joseph Baylen, "A Victorian's 'Crusade' in Chicago, 1893–1894," *Journal of American History* 51 , no. 3 (1964): 418–34.

79. Shaw to Stead, 30 December 1893, box 177, Albert Shaw Papers, New York Public Library Annex.

Before this, Stead, by helping with the production of General William Booth's *In Darkest England and the Way Out* (1890), had already demonstrated his ability not only to bestir the public conscience but also to help provide the emerging Salvation Army with their own plan for the social rejuvenation of Britain. As he wrote to Shaw:

> In concluding this letter, let me tell you to look out for the Salvation Army's new Scheme for dealing with the unemployed. You know what Carlyle wrote in *Past and Present?* All that Carlyle proposed that should be done, General Booth is now girding up his loins to do. For the next fortnight, I am immersed up to the eyes in getting his book ready for the press, in which he explains his scheme. I will send you a copy of it as soon as it is out, and would strongly recommend that you describe it in the *Century*. Henry George told me, the other day, he regarded it as the most remarkable thing he had seen since he left America.[80]

As demonstrated elsewhere in this book, the ideas of W. T. Stead and Herbert Stead on urban problems, politics, and religious unity were highly creative, though not quite so creative as their ideas devoted to the development of religious journalism into the early part of the twentieth century. No period after the 1890s could boast a phenomenon to rival this new journalism in its impact on the dissemination of the views of Social Christianity to the reading public of the English-speaking world. With the demise of this major tool of communication, no period thereafter was to enjoy the same bounty of celebrities shared on both sides of the Atlantic.

By 1900, of course, new methods of propaganda were beginning to be examined, principally in the improved areas of technology, public relations, and advertising. In the first area, W. T. Stead himself, for example, was quite anxious to see the "bioscope" used widely to enhance the impact of Christianity.[81] A 1900 "photo play" of *In His Steps*, consisting of one hundred and fifty transparencies, was possibly the first photographic screen adaptation of an American novel. Unfortunately, it was not until 1936 that an actual cinema version was produced, in spite of the strenuous efforts of Sheldon himself. *Sons of the Children* bore little resemblance to the novel.[82]

In the area of public relations, the cinema also proved to be a threat as much as a tool. In 1932 F. W. Norwood, the famous London minister, remembered that

80. Stead to Shaw, 2 September, 1890, box 177, Shaw Papers.
81. Stead, *Americanization of the World*, 181.
82. Miller, *Following in His Steps*, 91, 92.

an equally famous preacher had proclaimed Charlie Chaplin, the first significant cinema star, to be better known than Jesus.[83] But by that time the creation of celebrities was also the domain of the churches. Well before World War I, supporters of R. J. Campbell had experimented with an embarrassing array of tricks intended to build a popular image for their New Theology leader, including the *R. J. Campbell Birthday Book*.[84] Such ploys were already part of public relations activity at the Salvation Army, whose correspondence reveals great care over the timing of General Booth's appearances, over reporting these appearances in their own newspapers, and over the solicitation of favorable reporting in the press as a whole. Where necessary, the tricks of the music hall, such as the "Magic lantern," continued to be employed.[85]

By the interwar period image building became a standard practice, greatly assisted by the appearance of radio and motion pictures. Dick Sheppard became the radio priest of the early 1930s in Britain, and his counterparts were Harry Emerson Fosdick in the United States and Bible Bill Aberhart in Canada (even through his later Social Gospel phase).[86] Publicity was actively sought by Social Christian figures, who stood somewhat apart from their particular denominations. But these figures, despite their fame, were national rather than international celebrities.

By the early 1920s even William Temple had cultivated a public image, assisted by the media's preference for someone who was already high in the hierarchy of the Established Church and who was quite early seen to be the almost inevitable choice as primate. Building upon his great traditional skills as a preacher, Temple embraced the microphone and camera early in his career. Though in the Social Christian circle, he did not allow his utterances to be clouded by the less-than-popular rhetoric of the predominant Anglo-Catholic faction. Temple spoke through the secular medium. In suggesting good historical fiction to capture the human aspects of the Industrial Revolution, for example, he chose the novels *Inheritance* (1932) and *Manhold* (1942), by Phyllis Bentley, and *The Crowthers of Bankdom* (1940), by Thomas Armstrong, rather

83. F. W. Norwood, *Indiscretions of a Preacher* (London, 1932), 195.

84. Jones, *Christian Socialist Revival*, 430.

85. Bramwell Booth to William Booth, 22 January 1895, "Your Welcome Home and Next Campaign," folder no. 11, Letters, William Booth Collection, Salvation Army Heritage, Salvation Army Headquarters, Judd Street, London.

86. Of the three, Harry Emerson Fosdick (1878–1969) most consistently proselytized the Social Gospel. A disciple of Walter Rauschenbusch, he was a Baptist minister when he founded the Riverside Church in New York, which he transformed into a nonsectarian institution with expanded social services in the 1930s. He had earlier incurred the wrath of theological conservatives with his famous printed sermon "Shall the Fundamentalists Win?" (May 1922). See William R. Hutchison, *The Modernist Impulse in American Protestantism* (Cambridge, Mass., 1976), 274–87.

than any earlier Christian Socialist piece.[87] Though of the Left politically, his early formal resignation of his Labour Party membership allowed him to earn the respect of even the quite secular-minded Conservative Winston Churchill. He did indeed become a national prophet by the end of the 1930s, and the outpouring of grief at the time of his sudden death in 1944 was huge. Temple never declined an opportunity to speak in new ways to vast numbers of people, whether at ecumenical meetings, secular gatherings, or in the privacy of their own homes, where he reached them through best-selling pamphlets. But there was more to Temple than the cult of personality. The views he expressed were rooted in sincere convictions molded by theology and social philosophy, though, as John Kent has pointed out, Temple's pursuit of some ideas and not others is sometimes difficult to explain.[88] But this was partially the nature of his role; to him, the overall guidance in the spirit of national oracle was more important than any specific action. Servicing of his public persona constituted a significant portion of Temple's activities, which explains how historians can write so much about the man and so little detail about his private attitudes, a practice roughly similar to the present-day treatment of the inner lives of politicians.

Though both Britain and the United States saw significant advances in popular image making by Social Christians, the latter witnessed a peculiarly rapid adaptation of advertising techniques for the cause. It was perhaps inevitable that this should occur in the United States. By 1900 advertising had ceased to be merely the vehicle by which manufacturers could inform an existing market of their products.[89] Now the actual *creation* of markets and its attendant psychology had begun to appear. These American developments were increasingly greeted with hostility by the British press, which viewed commercial culture as a function of Americanization, a phenomenon associated with vulgar materialism undermining traditional culture.[90] Such an attitude was not helpful in the continuation of Anglo-American Social Christian intellectual exchanges.

Susan Curtis, in *A Consuming Faith* (1991), has argued that the textbooks on advertising written by Social Gospelers Francis Case and Charles Stelzle were signposts on the path to the modernization of American life through the

---

87. William Temple, *Christianity and Social Order* (Harmondsworth, Middlesex, 1942), 118 n. 10.

88. John Kent, *William Temple: Church, State, and Society in Britain, 1880–1950* (Cambridge, 1992), 168–90.

89. David Potter, *People of Plenty: Economic Abundance and the American Character* (Chicago, 1954), chap. 8, "The Institution of Abundance: Advertising," 166–88.

90. D. L. LeMahieu, *A Culture for Democracy: Mass Communication and the Cultivated Mind in Britain Between the Wars* (Oxford, 1988).

establishment of a consumer society. Certainly there is some support for Curtis's contention that Stelzle wanted to sell—at times by stealth and the admixture of religion with entertainment—the message of church attendance.[91] Gone was the heavy hand of strategic action, as Habermas would call it, in the message. After 1913 Stelzle also operated a Madison Avenue advertising agency that specialized in helping churches. Though he supported the Institutional Church movement, his approach was diametrically opposed to that of W. S. Rainsford, who shunned advertising and emphasized communication on the immediate neighborhood level.[92] This was a serious difference of opinion over what constituted Christian neighborliness.

Notwithstanding Curtis's evidence that Stelzle believed the church no longer had a monopoly as sounding board for Christianity, Stelzle nonetheless continued vigorously to defend the church's unique role as "the best and highest expression of Christianity."[93] Stelzle's realization that the church had competitors in secular humanitarianism or even diffusive Christianity (those Christian believers beyond the pale of formalized religion) was not very different from Charles Masterman's view that "ethical advance is accompanied (as it seems) by spiritual decline." Like Stelzle, Masterman also addressed his appeal to the middle classes, for he saw them as "the centre and historical support of England's Protestant creed" and hence held them responsible for the ultimate decline of the churches.[94]

Stelzle, at least from his work as chairman of the Presbyterian Home Missionary Society in New York, believed that the church must advantageously display itself in a competitive marketplace. Later in his life this belief simply took the more professional form of his consulting services for churches. His *"Report of the Publicity Operations" by Plymouth Church of the Pilgrims in Brooklyn* did suggest the use of speakers, newspapers, and radio to capitalize on the Plymouth Rock celebrations.[95] In that sense there is much to Curtis's claim that Stelzle saw the church more as a "season's sensation, a fast-moving article."[96] However, Stelzle never lost sight of the religious element. In his 1920 report on the parish of the Church of the Saviour, an old Manhattan congregation, Stelzle

91. Susan Curtis, *A Consuming Faith: The Social Gospel and Modern American Culture* (Baltimore, 1991), 254, 260.

92. W. S. Rainsford, *The Story of a Varied Life: An Autobiography* (1922; reprint, Freeport, N.Y., 1970), 208.

93. Charles Stelzle, *Principles of Successful Church Advertising* (New York, 1908), 13.

94. Charles Masterman, *The Condition of England* (London, 1909), 274, 269.

95. Box 9, Charles Stelzle Papers, Rare Book and Manuscript Room, Butler Library, Columbia University.

96. Curtis, *Consuming Faith*, 265.

realistically assessed the changing social composition of the surrounding neighborhood and urged a less doctrinal approach so as to involve many who were not of the church's persuasion. In suggesting a "social service revival," however, he argued that a round of meetings emphasizing the social obligations of the church must be conducted with "a deeply religious fervour that would win the very best men and women in the community and in the city."[97] In reference to Columbia House, originally part of the chapel but now increasingly a community center, he suggested that attempting no religious teaching was "debatable." Rather, he thought a broad religious teaching should be reintroduced with the help of Roman Catholic priests.[98]

In his reports on specific congregations such as Grace Chapel, Madison Avenue, or on entire cities such as Atlantic City, New Jersey, and Wilkes-Barre, Pennsylvania, Stelzle admittedly stressed the social club atmosphere in churches.[99] But Stelzle saw these entertainments as a means by which to link the working class in particular to the church. While some of his comments may well have been made to middle-class church ministers and elders, Stelzle's commitment to the working class was bona fide. As the title of his autobiography indicated,[100] Stelzle was a son of the Bowery; he had started as a factory hand, had educated himself, and had eventually attended the Moody Institute in Chicago. During his first pastorate in St. Louis, Stelzle saw the possibility of a nonpolitical link between the labor movement and the church. Later, in his home missionary work in New York, he founded both the Labor Temple (1910) and "Labor Sunday" (1904), which came to be observed by churches across the United States. He remained an active member of the International Association of Machinists most of his life. Though he moved firmly to the Social Gospel, Stelzle never forgot the influence of Moody's simple approach to Bible preaching. He described his preaching to working people as follows: "Let me [as preacher] get away from churchly things and ecclesiastical manners and go down to some big shop at the noon hour, having secured permission from the owner, and give the men a simple, practical talk on a Bible theme."[101]

Stelzle usually supplemented his talk with slides of the outcast of the city. Later in his life he would try to organize radio broadcasts and sponsor

97. Report, 7, Folder "Surveys," box 16, Stelzle Papers.
98. Ibid., 3.
99. "Preliminary Study of Atlantic City, N.J., 3 May 1915," "Preliminary Study of Wilkes-Barre and Surrounding Communities, 7 March 1914," Folder "Surveys," box 16, Stelzle Papers.
100. Charles Stelzle, *A Son of the Bowery: The Life Story of an East Side American* (New York, 1926).
101. Charles Stelzle, "Preaching to Workingmen," *Interior,* 22 January 1903.

films.[102] He was far ahead of British figures such as Basil Jellicoe, who produced propaganda films to sell housing projects in the 1920s, and J. Arthur Rank, who used film to sell Christian values a decade later.[103] Stelzle was always interested in exploring the best media for reaching people of his own background. The *Primitive Methodist Leader,* describing his tour of Britain in 1909, noted that his ways were "daring," easily outstripping church methods in that country. His ability to attract working people to the church made him in their eyes "the livest wire in present-day organized Christianity."[104] However, his later Madison Avenue advertising techniques were never important enough to influence trends in secular advertising and were undoubtedly regarded as gauche by the Social Christian intellectual elite. Those associated with the leading seminaries in the country, such as Harvard's Francis Greenwood Peabody, could worry even before the First World War about the effects of the hurried life of the telephone and motor cars, not to mention modern advertising, upon the thought patterns of their students.[105] Nevertheless, Stelzle's efforts to reach and organize women and black Americans in the cause of Social Christianity were exemplary. In a fast changing, competitive world a restrictive approach to the dissemination of the message was a fatal mistake in Stelzle's eyes.

In Britain the lines of communication between workers and Social Christian leaders were tenuous at best. F. D. Maurice, in assuming leadership of Working Men's College, had emphasized the teaching function of Social Christianity.[106] Octavia Hill's rent collectors were supposed to engage in the same activities as did university residents at Toynbee Hall, a middle-class approach whose shortcomings Standish Meacham has brought out in his book on Toynbee Hall.[107] It is true that at Toynbee much of the activity, from picture exhibitions to handicraft schools to soirées, reeked of middle-class paternalism. But in time the settlement movement widened its base, guided by other socioreligious groups that were less elitist. Such a movement always ran the risk of being taken over by non-Christians equally committed to bridging the gap between the middle and

102. See *Preliminary Plan for International Community Pictures Inc.,* n.d., "Plans" file, box 9, Stelzle Papers.

103. See David Jeremy, *Capitalists and Christians: Business Leaders and the Churches in Britain, 1900–1960* (Oxford, 1990), 350–51.

104. *Primitive Methodist Leader,* 11 March 1909.

105. Martin E. Marty, *Modern American Religion,* vol. 1, *The Irony of It All, 1893–1919* (Chicago, 1986), 291.

106. See note 1 to this chapter.

107. Standish Meacham, *Toynbee Hall and Social Reform, 1880–1914: The Search for Community* (New Haven, Conn., 1987).

working classes. As recounted in the last chapter, Stanton Coit, founder of Ethical Societies in both the United States and Britain, organized the Neighbourhood Guild system in New York, almost beating out the expansion of church-directed settlements from Britain to the United States.[108] Later the settlement movement successfully engulfed Coit's movement, bringing it back into cooperation with churches but at the same time, according to some historians, distorting its message toward an Americanizing campaign among inner-city ethnic groups.[109] The ultimate goal, however, was the reestablishment of an organic unity to society—something clearly recognizable to Social Christians.[110]

In general, paternalism guided Social Christian social service, but it could result in many benefits for the lower classes. Octavia Hill, for example, was as interested in the cultural life of her working-class charges as she was in inculcating proper attitudes toward work and family. She is remembered by many later critics for her stern company of female rent collectors. However, she also helped to found the National Trust and other enterprises, which introduced the beauty of nature to the dispossessed. It may be said that Hill's organizations did not touch the most destitute in society, but neither did most other organizations, church-related or otherwise. However, there is little doubt that she did reach the upper strata of the working classes of East London. William Temple, as president of the Workers Educational Association, also continued the venerable Social Christian tradition of adult education, believing that exposure to culture in the liberal tradition would ensure a fuller development of the individual.[111]

By the interwar period even the old approaches had seen some improvement. Basil Jellicoe, through the St. Pancras Housing Association in the 1920s, corrected techniques employed in earlier settlements by being less patronizingly middle-class in his social ideas. He also used all of the media tools to bring attention and money to the cause of working-class housing. Cinema was his particular fascination, and he counted "stars" as well as royalty and popular writers

108. See George Henry Staples, "Stanton Coit and the Neighborhood Guild: Ethical Idealism and Social Reform in New York City" (Ph.D. diss., City University of New York, 1990), 10. Coit's inspiration was Toynbee Hall.

109. Opinions vary on this question. Rivka Shpak Lissak argues that Americanization was not practiced so crudely, though it was more or less the ultimate goal. Lissak, *Pluralism and Progressives: Hull House and the New Immigrants, 1890–1919* (Chicago, 1989).

110. See Mina Carson, *Settlement Folk: Social Thought and the American Settlement Movement, 1885–1930* (Chicago, 1990).

111. See J. H. Sadler, "William Temple, the W.E.A., and the Liberal Tradition," *Journal of Educational Administration and History* 18, no. 2 (1986): 34–43.

among his personal friends.[112] The Prince of Wales's visit to Somers Town in 1926, for example, was particularly well exploited for the purposes of the society.[113]

Another approach to spanning the social chasm was the creation of the church "of the people," which, in a sense, the Salvation Army had already attempted by accepting the world of the working class and tailoring entertainments borrowed from musical halls for them. But by the end of the nineteenth century the notion emerged that remaking some of the churches into organizations specifically operated by the working classes would foster more rapidly the social and political objectives of Social Christianity. It was never clear how significant a role was envisaged for them by any prominent Social Christian leaders. This approach probably originated in the Scottish and English Chartist Churches of the 1840s. The Brotherhood Movement, organized by J. Bruce Wallace, attempted to band all socialist Christians together in a movement with some similarities to the earlier Christian Socialist Society, but the unifying factor was a socialism tantamount to theodicy. Though its ideas were circulated in Britain and North America, largely through its periodical,[114] it achieved little.

John Trevor's Labour Church was far more ambitious, an actual alternative to the existing churches.[115] The culture of the working class was respected, but the purpose of the church was mainly political. The movement appeared in North

112. A film was prepared by the society for publicity purposes. However, more advantage accrued from use of established literary and cinema stars, such use as the celebrity cricket match between authors (John Drinkwater, Evelyn Waugh), captained by J. B. Priestley, and actresses (Gertrude Lawrence, Flora Robson, Celia Johnson), captained by Gladys Cooper, on 20 June 1933 in aid of the St. Pancras Housing Improvement Society. "Publicity Material 1930–37," brochure, Records of St. Pancras Housing Improvement Society, Archives of St. Pancras Housing Association, Camden, London.

113. For reports of the visit, see "Prince in Somers Town," *Daily Telegraph,* 16 December 1926, and "Royal Lead to Crusade Against Overcrowding," *The People,* 19 December 1926, in vol. "Prince of Wales Visit, December 1926, Newspaper Clippings," Records of St. Pancras Housing Improvement Society. A discussion of the tactical advantage of publicity—to rouse public sympathy and to approach politicians, such as Neville Chamberlain—took place at a meeting of the Society's Advisory Council, 17 December 1926, minutes, vol. I (1925–32), 60, Records of St. Pancras Housing Improvement Society.

114. *Brotherhood,* the weekly paper and main organ of the movement, edited by J. Bruce Wallace, was published from 1887 until the First World War. Among its contributors were North Americans such as George D. Herron and J. Stitt Wilson, as well as British figures such as Samuel E. Keeble and E. D. Girdlestone. Their main headquarters was the Brotherhood Church, Southgate Road, London.

115. See K. S. Inglis, *Churches and the Working Classes in Victorian England* (London, 1963), chap. 6; see also Stephen Yeo, "A New Life: The Religion of Socialism in Britain, 1883–1886," *History Workshop Journal* 4 (1977): 45–56. As John Trevor, the founder, stated, "The fundamental concept of the Labour Church and the First Principle in its Constitution is THAT THE LABOUR MOVEMENT IS A RELIGIOUS MOVEMENT" (*Labour Prophet* 5, no. 56 (1896): 124. In the same address Trevor denied that the Labour Church espoused Christian Socialism.

America, most notably in Canadian variations such as "the People's Church," after World War I. The American branches met with little success, though one branch in the Boston area achieved a considerable following under the former Canadian Methodist preacher Herbert Casson. Apparently the lack of clear theological underpinnings and the sectarian warfare between socialists led to the collapse of this enterprise in spite of the more vigorous religious leadership of Casson.[116] Linking these "congregations" to the mainline churches was ever a problem, but such a link had to be accomplished in the ultimate vision of social harmony. It should be noted that the leadership of Social Christianity remained with the clergy of these mainline churches.

The creation of ideal communities specifically dedicated to Social Christian ideals was another route to the same end of social unity. The idea of such communities can be traced to Fourier, Owen, and others. Comte was secretary to Saint-Simon, another advocate of the idea. General Booth's colonies were founded on such a notion, as was Thomas Hughes's small Christian Socialist community in Rugby, Tennessee. But the most notable communities, as described in Chapter 2, were those created by Quaker philanthropists near Birmingham and York, which, though not fully Christian Socialist, had social ideas and a goal of Christian cooperation that was closely akin to Christian Socialism. The Garden City Movement, which spread to the United States from Britain, also had strong links with Social Christians, the Reverend W.D.P. Bliss being the American founding father. These experiments met with limited success among selected groups in creating support for Social Christian ideas, in part because the Social Christian message was so dilute. The most successful were usually those most weakly linked with Social Christianity. The public wrote the majority off as failed utopian experiments—the New Harmonies of the twentieth century.

The development of new approaches to the working classes also entailed considerable debate about the acceptance or rejection of their habits—especially drinking. Stewart Headlam campaigned against the "Puritanism" of the Edwardian era. He believed that temperance and other evangelical fetishes stood in the way of dialogue in the service of Social Christian goals. For Headlam positive Christian attitudes were essential to winning the working class. Music halls and popular entertainments should therefore be joined to the movement.[117] Headlam's views were soon vindicated, when Pleasant Sunday Afternoons, church

116. Leslie Wharton, "Herbert N. Casson and the American Labor Church, 1893–1898," *Essex Institute Historical Collections* 117, no. 2 (1981): 719–837.

117. See John Richard Orens, "Christ, Communism, and Chorus Girls: A Reassessment of Stewart Headlam," *Historical Magazine of the Protestant Episcopal Church* 49, no. 3 (1980): 233–48, and Edward R. Norman, "Victorian Values: Stewart Headlam and the Christian Socialists," *History Today* 37 (April 1987): 27–32. For his views against temperance and Sabbatarian legislation, see

picnics, and the like, as well as sermons as a form of entertainment, ceased to hold the interest even of staunch middle-class churchgoers.

In his later writings James Adderley echoed Headlam's points. Seebohm Rowntree, in his second survey of York, noted that it was "common knowledge" that there was a drastic decline in church activities since the first survey of 1901 due to "counter-attractions" of cinema and dances.[118] In the 1920s Basil Jellicoe adopted the same attitude toward popular entertainments, especially drinking, by establishing a pub at his St. Pancras housing estate. This was in sharp contrast to the conduct of Charles Stelzle in New York, who still believed drink to be a major impediment to the rehabilitation of the working class and the poorest regions of the country.[119]

English Nonconformists and many prominent American and Canadian Social Gospelers in such organizations as the Women's Christian Temperance Union (WCTU) continued for the most part to stand with the temperance cause into the 1920s and 1930s. For Social Christians such as S. D. Chown, leaders in Canadian Methodism, temperance provided new grounds for an active state. Given the enormous amount of time, energy, and money invested, temperance propaganda and organizations did reach many people. But the connection between temperance and Social Christianity was tenuous, the subject itself was divisive, and ultimately the crusade was co-opted by twentieth-century fundamentalists. The Prohibition of the 1920s did not serve the cause of the churches very well with regard to the general American public, though the nation was dotted with pockets of support for it.

In North America as a whole Social Christianity continued to have some popular appeal into the 1930s. The onset of the Great Depression brought new life to organizations, such as the Institutional Churches, providing relief measures to the destitute. With regard to the United States this seems to corroborate Bryan Wilson's argument that churches tended to be secularized from within.[120] Given the slow progress of the American welfare state, the churches, in their more progressive church work, continued to attract support for essentially nonreligious reasons. In this line of thinking, Social Gospelers' collective urging for more governmental action to alleviate economic distress could threaten their ultimate importance for society if government took up their call. Yet at

---

Stewart Headlam, *Municipal Puritanism* (London, 1905).

118. Seebohm Rowntree, *Poverty and Progress* (London, 1941), 425.

119. On the latter point, he stated in *Why Prohibition!* (New York, 1918), 178, that "[p]rohibition didn't make the South poor. It found the South poor and it's going to help make the South rich." His other well-known tract on this subject was *Liquor and Labour: A Survey of the Industrial Aspects of the Liquor Problem in New Jersey* (Newark, N.J., 1917).

120. Bryan Wilson, *Religion in Sociological Perspective* (London, 1982), 152.

least one survey from the period indicates that clergy held more liberal views on economic and social matters than most laity.[121] People stuck to the churches for more than bread alone.

Fundamentalism, of course, was strong in the Protestant population of the American South. It also held considerable influence in the Northeast, Midwest, and even in California. While sympathetic to the plight of the dispossessed, fundamentalists were not apt to confuse a short-term political cause, especially of the Left, with the ultimate goal of personal salvation. Fundamentalist criticism of the Social Gospel could be strident on both a philosophical and a practical level.[122] Canada also had its share of fundamentalists, such as T. T. Shields of Toronto, who would either fight against encroaching liberal humanism within the churches or withdraw from the broader issues of the general culture.[123] As Martin Marty, quoting Walter Lippman, has said of the period, there were millions who did care if Adam was created at 9 A.M.[124] Certainly Social Christian activists such as Reinhold Niebuhr were popular, but primarily in intellectual circles and in seminaries. The political recruitment of their followers tended to bolster the socialist, Communist, and other leftist parties rather than churches and congregations. A silent majority probably gave them a more mixed reception. However, some young people were brought somewhat to churches, and to Social Christianity, indirectly through organizations such as the YMCA, under Sherwood Eddy's guidance, and to some degree through the Student Christian Movement in all countries. In turn, college-age students often became affiliated with pacifism through organizations such as the Methodist Youth Organization of the 1930s that were closely linked with Social Christianity.[125] The problem was, What was the message of Social Christianity in all of this?

In Canada Social Gospelers engaged more actively in depression politics, many of them within the newly formed Cooperative Commonwealth Federation (CCF). Indeed, the culture of the Left, especially in rural, western Canada, seemed to be synonymous with the Social Gospel under J. S. Woodsworth as

121. Norman L. Trott and Ross W. Sanderson, *What Church People Think About Social and Economic Issues: Report of an Opinion Survey Made in Baltimore Under the Baltimore Rauschenbusch Fellowship of the Council of Churches and Christian Education of Maryland and Delaware* (New York, 1938).

122. See George M. Marsden, *Fundamentalism and American Culture: The Shaping of Twentieth-Century Evangelicalism, 1870–1925* (New York, 1980), pt. 3, 141–83.

123. See John G. Stackhouse Jr., *Canadian Evangelicalism in the Twentieth Century* (Toronto, 1993).

124. Marty, *Modern American Religion*, 2:162.

125. Memorandum on Developments of F.O.R.—U.S. for Percy Bartlett, 1947, by A. J. Muste, 2, International Fellowship of Reconciliation, series 4, box 1, Records of Fellowship of Reconciliation, Swarthmore College Peace Collection.

both a regional prophet and national prophet of the Left. This was in marked contrast to Britain, where, according to Chris Waters, the Left had fallen out of touch with popular culture by 1914.[126]

In Britain some felt the declining influence of the churches, but such decline was without visible effects upon the continued strength of Social Christians in church leadership circles. The seeming stability of church membership, for example, in the Church of England, may have bred complacency. However, the Methodist Church leadership in particular was concerned with the Socialist Sunday schools and the more aggressive proletarian Sunday schools in their agnostic grab for the minds of youth.[127] Alan D. Gilbert points to this period as crucial in that the loss of outside recruits contributed to the ultimate decline of the churches later in the twentieth century.[128] But the real culprit was indifference, not conversion to a religion substitute learned in a handful of Socialist or Proletarian Sunday Schools. As Percy Dearmer described the situation for the 1920s: "Young people avoid the churches, not as once with a sense of misgiving but in a kind of happy innocence. They have as a rule no quarrel with organized religion and are untroubled by theological problems; they even in a vague way like to think that services are going on, so long as they do not have to attend them."[129]

The enclave of Anglo-Catholicism was also an important element within the British Social Christian movement at this time. Under Charles Gore and the Community of the Resurrection, Anglo-Catholicism seemed too aesthetic, somewhat popish, and rather hard-line on questions of birth control and divorce early in the century. Christian sociology as devised by Anglo-Catholics in the 1930s was more positive, though very prescriptive. Leaders of the Christendom movement attempted to guide people toward the Guild movement as a means of dealing with economic dysfunctions within the broader context

126. See Chris Waters, *British Politics and the Politics of Popular Culture, 1884–1914* (Stanford, 1990).

127. Henry Carter, a Methodist Social Christian leader, felt that the church must not only work to overcome social problems in its quest to encourage church attendance but must also train youth in Sunday schools to attend. See Henry Carter, *The Church and the New Age* (London, 1911), pt. 2, chap. 3, "Non-Church-Going," 225–35. Concerning the agnostic threat, see "Proletarian Sunday Schools," a report by Reverend J. Williams Butcher, 31 March 1922 meeting, International and Industrial Relations Committee, MA 182, Division of Social Responsibility, Methodist Archives, John Rylands University Library of Manchester.

128. See Alan D. Gilbert, *The Making of Post-Christian Britain: A History of the Secularization of Modern Society* (London, 1980), 78–80. See also Robert Currie, Lee Horsley, and Alan D. Gilbert, *Churches and Churchgoers: Patterns of Church Growth in the British Isles Since 1700* (Oxford, 1977), 64–74, 79–90.

129. Percy Dearmer, *The Church at Prayer and the World Outside* (London, 1923), 177.

of their desire to restore a sense of community. Conrad Noel tried to recapture religious art and folklore for the ordinary people at Thaxted as well as lead what was called the Catholic Crusade. The goal of this communicative action was the organic unity Noel and his peers thought existed in the Middle Ages. Like A. J. Plenty, a contemporary architect and friend, Noel believed in social renewal through the revival of medieval notions of craftsmanship. As Noel's sermon notes "Salient Points from the Official Literature of the Catholic Crusade" (n.d.) state:

> The Crusade is not merely concerned with politics and economics, nor could it possibly be so if it is a Catholic society, any more than it could claim the name of Catholic if it were not, among other things, directly concerned with politics and economics. We, therefore, consider it essential, as Christians, to attack falsity and shoddiness in the literature, music, architecture, and other arts, of the Church and Nation. We regard this as an essential part of the political fight.[130]

V. A. Demant too made interesting arguments about safeguarding the ecology of the planet against the destructive effects of capitalism—a line of argument predating that of modern environmentalists by many decades. Much of this fell upon deaf ears. Ordinary Englishmen were simply uncertain about the merits of the "Catholic ideas" in particular. When, at the beginning of World War II, the Anglo-Catholics launched their most ambitious project, the *Signposts*, a twelve-volume series on their teachings as applied to everyday life, even some of their former colleagues broke ranks. T. S. Eliot, for example, saw these writers as a younger breed compelled to formulate a new religious mode but essentially lost at sea. He could not blame them for seeking bits of inspiration in Thomism or papal encyclicals, but at the same time, it was clear that the Anglican tradition stretching down to Gore was now being broken.[131]

Anglo-Catholics were defensive about the possible challenges not only of modernism but also of resurgent Evangelicalism. The American Evangelical Frank Buchman's First Century Christian Fellowship spread to Britain and Canada and was soon called the Oxford Group Movement. The movement's "house parties," which sprang up in the 1930s, made inroads among most mainline churches and even Social Christian circles. However, reactions were

---

130. Files ⅔, "Notes for Sermons," Conrad Noel Papers, Brynmor Jones Library, University of Hull.

131. T. S. Eliot to P.E.T. Widdrington, 9 January 1940, Maurice Reckitt Papers, University of Sussex Library.

quite mixed, many Anglo-Catholics believing that it reintroduced old evangelical ways at the expense of a social conscience.[132] Until the death of Buchman in 1961, the movement continued to have considerable and divisive influence in Britain. Here and elsewhere it would ultimately be known as Moral Rearmament.

Anglo-Catholics, therefore, followed the path blazed by Evangelicals a generation earlier; they retreated into a protected enclave withdrawn from the mainstream of society. Social Christianity, in terms of its general influence in Britain, became much more the work of individuals: Dick Sheppard within a largely secular pacifist crusade, R. H. Tawney in academic circles, and William Temple as national prophet. It is significant for Christianity as a whole that D. L. LeMahieu's *Culture for Democracy* (1988) has almost nothing to say about religion, let alone Social Christianity, in the emerging "middlebrow" British national culture of the interwar period. Certainly no one can overlook the literary importance of T. S. Eliot, who joined both the Church of England and Social Christianity in 1927. However, his influence was limited to the intellectual circles of the English-speaking world, and his Anglo-Catholicism limited his impact in religious circles. Earlier, G. K. Chesterton, in James Adderley's view, had been Social Christianity's "biggest asset" in his overall impact on national life.[133] But his departure from Anglicanism also coincided with his move to the fringes of social thought.

That Social Christianity had a significant cultural role to play in the societies of Britain and North America until the First World War there can be little doubt. But the efforts of Social Christians on both sides of the Atlantic to deliver their message to the general public seemed to meet with increasing difficulties thereafter. In Britain, for example, this may explain why one of the COPEC reports devoted considerable space to the need to reform the press.[134] Much of the difficulty also came from weakening bonds between Britain and America. No longer were there Anglo-Americans in the sense of a W. T. Stead. And within each country there was no agreement on the best means to garner public support for Social Christian ideas. For example, the slow but steady mastery of modern media, especially of mass entertainment, by rival Evangelicals in North America, probably contributed to the erosion of Social Christianity's support. More important, Social Christians never had a clear idea of what constituted victory in the struggle to capture the hearts and minds of

---

132. Extensive notes were taken by Conrad Noel on Oxford Group Movement meetings, 1932–36. See Files ⅔, Conrad Noel Papers.

133. Adderley, *Slums and Society*, 180–81.

134. *Politics and Citizenship* (report presented to the Conference on Politics, Economics, and Citizenship at Birmingham, 5–12 April 1924, vol. 10) (London, 1924), chap. 5.

people. In the United States Susan Curtis has suggested that by the 1930s the Social Gospel became supportive of the growing belief that the "ethos of consumption" could deliver "abundance, justice and meaning to American life."[135] While having strong religious roots, the Social Gospel was understandably willing to become subordinate to changes that more or less facilitated the goal of social justice. In that sense the Social Gospel removed itself from mainstream culture or at least abandoned any hope of dominating it. In Britain the general expectation of a rising standard of living could likewise have called for Social Christianity to take a subordinate role. As each society moved to eradicate many of the evils that had spurred Social Christians into action in the first place, it in essence eradicated the reasons for them to continue rousing the public conscience. Social Christians, of course, continued to make attempts to keep religion in a central place within national life. Stelzle clearly understood this in persistently urging American churches to modernize in order to keep pace with the rhythms of modern life.[136] But most Social Christian theoreticians, with the exception of some Anglo-Catholics, had never sought to dominate national life as they believed the church had done in the Middle Ages. In a sense, they would have been satisfied to accept a Durkheimian notion of religion as an aspect of a wider culture, provided that culture increasingly reflected the essential social teachings and harmonious relationships advocated by Christ.

135. Curtis, *Consuming Faith,* xiii.
136. See Charles Stelzle, "The Church and Modern Efficiency," in *American Social and Religious Conditions* (New York, 1912), chap. 13, 210–11.

# GALLERY OF SOCIAL CHRISTIANS

## British

F. D. Maurice

Thomas Hughes

Charles Kingsley

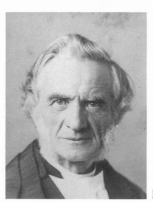

B. F. Westcott

Hugh Price Hughes

Mrs. Mary [Humphry] Ward

T. H. Green

R. H. Tawney

Charles Gore

Samuel Barnett

Conrad Noel

William Temple

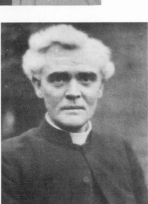

R. J. Campbell

## Americans

Washington Gladden

Lyman Abbott

Walter Rauschenbusch

Frank Mason North

Charles Stelzle (with Calvin Coolidge)

Richard T. Ely

George D. Herron

Henry George

Vida Scudder

George Coe

Sherwood Eddy

Norman Thomas

Harry F. Ward

Reinhold Niebuhr

## Canadians

J. S. Woodsworth

S. D. Chown

Charles Gordon
(pseudonym Ralph Connor)

# 5

## CHURCH, STATE, AND RECONCILIATION

> The community which we call a State stands more than
> ever in need of being directed and controlled and domi-
> nated by the moral sense of the community. In other
> words, the State must have a conscience as well as a will
> and a mind. That community will be best governed in
> which the moral sense of its members has most authority.
> —W. T. Stead, *If Christ Came to Chicago!*

The theme of unity was an enduring one in the history of Social Christianity.
The unity of church and state was implied in the desire to break down the
barriers between the sacred and the secular. However, the ability effectively to
build social harmony not only demanded the cooperation of government but
also a lessening and eventual elimination of denominational rivalry. The Kingdom of Christ was a unified Kingdom—"let them be one."

Bryan Wilson has seen the movement toward ecumenism in the early
twentieth century as part of a defensive reaction of the churches—a symptom of
their increasing weakness in the face of encroaching secularization.[1] On the
other hand, Social Christians on both sides of the Atlantic realized that there
were certain religious precepts they held in common regardless of their particular churches. As I have shown with regard to social service activities, particularly in North America, ecumenism had arisen through a coordination of
efforts. The attempt to reach the dispossessed also made church leaders focus
upon the need to control and guide the apparatus of the earthly Kingdom with
its potential for largesse far exceeding that of privately funded social service.

---

1. Bryan Wilson, *Religion in Secular Society: A Sociological Comment* (London, 1966), 128.

The unitive tendencies within Social Christianity were evident from its very inception.[2] The Broad Church circle was influenced by the thought of Samuel Taylor Coleridge and especially Thomas Arnold. In *The Constitution of Church and State* (1830) Coleridge argued that the Church of England was both catholic in its appeal and the moral guide to the nation through its educated clergy and laity (clerisy). A supporter of the established Anglican Church, Coleridge nonetheless argued that the church was primarily concerned with broad moral principles and good works and could, therefore, be a rallying point for unity among denominations. Rather than merely defend the crumbling ancien régime and justify the present social order,[3] Thomas Arnold, in his *Principles of Church Reform* (1833), developed more fully the Romantic theme of the Church of England as a great national institution, the expression of the best in English civilization. Toward this goal Arnold's religious Liberalism led him to argue against rigid dogmatism in an effort to reunite all English Protestantism. His scheme of comprehension also involved a revitalized link with the state. Arnold's arguments were urgent; he believed in the imminent severing of the ties between church and state and the inauguration of government uninformed by a Christian conscience. Both Coleridge and Arnold were fathers of the Broad Church circle, which would soon pass into the hands of F. D. Maurice and other prophets of Christian Socialism. The Broad Church circle, the party that identified most with Maurice's cause within the Established Church, was least concerned with dogmas and most concerned with getting on with others in the wider society. Toward the objective of getting on with others they found in the ideas of Coleridge and especially Thomas Arnold a way of ending the scandal of a divided Christianity. A revitalized, comprehensive National Church could accomplish reunification of the churches as well as guide the maintenance and progress of Christian civilization in general.

Many Broad Churchmen, for the above reasons, also opposed disestablishment. To their minds much could be done to revitalize, even radically reform, the Church of England, but they saw its disestablishment as a retrogressive step toward the triumph of the Philistines and the downfall of a national Christian culture.

2. Much of the material in the first part of this chapter is taken from my article "The Concept of a National Church in Late Nineteenth-Century England and America," *Journal of Religious History* 14, no. 1 (1986): 26–37. For other treatments of the National Church concept, see R. T. Shannon, "John Robert Seeley and the Idea of a National Church," in *Ideas and Institutions of Victorian Britain,* ed. R. Robson (London, 1967), 236–67, and M. A. Crowther, *Church Embattled: Religious Controversy in Mid-Victorian England* (London, 1970), chap. 5. For a comparative discussion of church-state relations in North America from a British perspective, see Edward R. Norman, *The Conscience of the State in North America* (Cambridge, 1968).

3. See Robert Hole, *Pulpits, Politics, and Public Order in England, 1760–1832* (Cambridge, 1989).

The National Church concept continued to surface throughout the period, for example, as the topic of a chapter in *Essays and Reviews* (1860).[4] Laymen such as Thomas Hughes also kept the cause alive, allying it to schemes of national revitalization or of the preservation of culture, as those of Matthew Arnold. T. H. Green, in an interesting speech at Merton College, Oxford, in December 1881, discussed the subject of church reform. For Green "sacerdotal ideas" within the Established Church presented a pressing problem insofar as such ideas were inhibiting men with active religious consciences from serving fully in the Church. To Green's way of thinking, disestablishment would only embitter social relations further and make clergymen mere priests or preachers rather than leaders "in useful social work, and in the administration of such public business as is not directly administered by the state." The solution was "to congregationalize the Church," to create congregations with control over the appointment of clergy and over ceremony (including the possibility of ordination without declaration of specific beliefs). Green defined congregations broadly, excluding no residents of the local community from the fold.[5]

The most complete formulation of the National Church idea appeared in the writings and activities of the Reverend W. H. Fremantle, particularly, of course, in the highly successful *World as the Subject of Redemption* (1885), which was more widely read and greatly appreciated in American circles than in Britain itself. (The general ideas contained in these reprinted Bampton lectures are described in Chapter 1). What was also significant about this book and about other areas of Fremantle's thought and action was the specificity given to the Nation Church concept, from his own implementation of an elected non-denominational parish council as a local embodiment of the unified Christian commonwealth to his participation in the earliest international ecumenical gatherings of Protestants. For Fremantle, public worship, the family, and like gatherings were also associated with the larger, divinely inspired *nation*. Such a concept made it more clearly necessary for people to engage in social improvement as part of the general redemption of the whole community, encompassing individual salvation along the way. It also made distrust of the encroaching power of the state irrelevant, for the state was merely another aspect of the same nation-church entity. In these formulations Fremantle went much further than Maurice in identifying the nation with the church in the cause of Social Christianity.[6] He could also hope that such a concept would both eradicate

---

4. H. B. Wilson, "Séances Historiques de Genève—The National Church," in *Recent Inquiries in Theology, by Eminent English Churchmen being "Essays and Reviews"* (London, 1860), 145–205.

5. "Church Reform," no. 3, pp. 3–4, T. H. Green Papers, Balliol College, Oxford University.

6. Owen Chadwick, *The Victorian Church* (London, 1970), pt. 2, 280.

denominationalism and make Christianity the directing force behind the social policies of government. His positive attitude toward government is clearly reflected in his comments opposed to Herbert Spencer's individualism: "It appears to me much truer to think of the state, not as a hostile power imposed on us, but according to the idea expressed in the noble term 'commonwealth.' We are all sharers in it, and have power over its action, it partakes of the nature of a brotherhood, of an enlarged family."[7]

Fremantle's list of friends and associates was impressive. His greatest disciple was his former curate at St. Mary's, Marylebone, Samuel Barnett, the celebrated founder of the settlement movement. Barnett once described the National Church idea as "at once an effective charity organization society [which Fremantle earlier had helped to found], and the means of spiritualizing state action."[8] Like Fremantle, Barnett did not believe there was a sacred and a secular; they were one in the Christian nation. He fully realized that the various educational and philanthropic activities of the churches were as yet valuable, but he also saw that in time they would become redundant in the advancing the Christian commonwealth. As he wrote concerning the "church's opportunity":

> The Church exists not for the Church but for the nation, it is established not to secure its property, its position, or its reputation, but to serve the people. It diverts its strength when it turns that strength from Christianizing the State to the foundation of sectarian societies. There is no object in keeping up the stays when the ship is launched, it is then wiser to man the ship. There is no object in using effort to protect a Christian preserve when the whole country is under Christian influence.[9]

Barnett was understandably a driving force behind the National Church Reform Union of the 1880s, whose membership included John Robert Seeley, Thomas Hughes, T. H. Green, Sidney Ball, Arnold Toynbee, and Sir William J. Ashley. The Reform Union wanted in effect to see the nationalization of the Church of England's facilities, forming the core of the new church. Disestablishment and disendowment were rejected and Nonconformists invited to join, enticed by an offer of equitable arrangements for their particular services.

7. William Henry Fremantle, "Individualists and Socialists," *Nineteenth Century* 41 (February 1897): 318.

8. Samuel A. Barnett, "A National Church and Social Reform," in *Church Reform*, ed. Albert Grey and William Henry Fremantle (London, 1888), 159.

9. Samuel A. Barnett, "The Church's Opportunity," *Contemporary Review* 68 (July–December 1895): 357.

This National Church, committed to social action, would be a national agency for the improvement of the English people. According to Fremantle's emphasis on parish councils, the details of fusing the churches were best worked out in the "little nation" of the local community. Home rule, or democratic self-government, was the prime vehicle to achieve this "fresh reformation."[10] The method of immediate implementation Fremantle had suggested was straightforward, and typical of mid-Victorian "improvers"—a movement fashioned after the followers of temperance.

But within Anglican circles generally the Christian Social Union was the main conduit for propagandizing the idea of a National Church. As Fremantle's ideas became more widely respected by the 1890s, many in the CSU took up the cause. Edward Norman has stated that the CSU was within the mainstream of English social thinking, being "central, respectable and vague."[11] The CSU membership was influential, large, and committed to Christian Socialism. The National Church ideal was supported by Henry Scott Holland, founder of the CSU, who once stated that "Churchmanship ought to be co-terminous with the nation."[12]

Bishop Brooke Foss Westcott, president of the CSU and the most visible spokesperson for Christian Socialism at the end of the century, was an enthusiastic supporter of the National Church concept. As early as 1872 Westcott argued for the "great spiritual power leavening the whole nation" in the form of the Church of England, which had a unique power to bring the nation together against the "subtle power of materialism."[13] While believing that the people would support the Church of England if disestablished,[14] he warned politicians of the importance of the church-state connection, contrasting England with the dangerous political power of the state in France.[15]

Almost thirty years later Westcott could write of a new social era replacing the post-Renaissance period, in which individualism had been emphasized.[16]

10. See Samuel A. Barnett Papers, MSS 1463, 1464, 1465, Lambeth Palace Archives. This organization should not be confused with the Church Reform League formed in 1895, which included Social Christians such as Charles Gore and Henry Scott Holland but no prominent Broad Churchmen. Its minute books are held at the General Synod of the Church of England Archives, Westminster.

11. Edward R. Norman, *Church and Society in England, 1770–1970: A Historical Study* (Oxford, 1976), 180.

12. Henry Scott Holland, "The Church of England," *Progressive Review* 4 (January 1897): 324.

13. Brooke Foss Westcott, *The Idea and Work of the Church of England* (London, 1872), 9–10.

14. Ibid., 6.

15. Ibid., 9.

16. Brooke Foss Westcott, *"The National Church and the Nation": A Speech by the Right Reverend The Lord Bishop of Durham in Westminster Town Hall, 14 May 1891 at annual meeting of Church Defence Institution* (London, 1891), 1.

As he stated: "We are preparing for the fulness of corporate life in a higher form than that which characterized society in the middle ages. We acknowledge on all sides that a nation is something more than an arbitrary association of those who combine for their mutual advantage." Westcott made it clear that in this evolved society the Church of England and nation were entwined: "If, then, our nation is indeed a complete body, it must have an adequate spiritual organ; and such an organ is the National Church. A National Church witnesses that the corporate life of the society is a divine life."[17]

The major initial impact of Fremantle's ideas, at least in terms of gaining new converts, was, however, felt in North America rather than England. In the preface to the 1895 edition of *The World as the Subject of Redemption,* Fremantle in fact credited the lectures' ultimate success in the English-speaking world to their early, favorable reception in the United States.

Just why they were so well received by Americans is difficult to explain. In a general way the notion of a National Church was similar to the corporate view of church and society found in Horace Bushnell's *Christian Nurture* (1847). As Theodore Munger said of Bushnell's background:

> It has been a special characteristic of the New England ministers that they have fostered all the interests of the towns in which they are settled. The separation of Church and State was only formal until the churches of the "Standing Order" were swamped in a multitude of sects, and the ministry lost its permanence and became a migration from parish to parish. Before this change, the minister was the leading man in the community, and shaped its affairs often down to the most practical details.[18]

There was an undoubted nostalgia for such a unitive picture. Certainly the widespread American endorsement of F. D. Maurice's ideas, as well as those of other earlier figures connected with the first wave of English Christian Socialism, can explain much. But Maurice's view of the existing Church of England functioning as a type of welfare agency and his prediction that America would embrace Anglicanism in the form of an establishment were both awkward ideas for Americans to swallow. The ecumenical aspect of Fremantle's National Church concept was more attractive to North Americans, allowing for a broad-based effort to advance the social role of the churches. In addition, Fremantle's emphasis upon parochial cooperative initiatives in realizing his goal could

17. Ibid., 2.
18. Theodore T. Munger, *Horace Bushnell: Preacher and Theologian* (Boston, 1899), 368.

appeal to the democratic localist impulses within the American political tradition.

It was the work of specific Episcopalians, however, that was largely responsible for Fremantle's initial success in America. Fremantle's ideas were immediately taken up by Professor Richard T. Ely, then of Johns Hopkins University, who was soon to become a very influential economist at the University of Wisconsin. Perhaps with the added zeal of an Episcopalian convert, Ely endorsed the idea of the National Church as part of his overall acceptance of Social Christianity. Ely believed that his only spiritual inspiration was to be found in the English Christian Socialists. In spite of his German education, Ely rarely, if ever, cited or communicated with German Christian Socialists, with the possible exception of Bishop Ketteler. The anti-Semitism of some central European Christian Socialists was repugnant to him.[19]

Concerning the idea of a National Church, in particular, Ely believed that Fremantle's notion that "the real English Church . . . is the English nation"[20] was adaptable to the North American scene. The state, as he viewed it, was a morally neutral institution with a great potential to increase the common good. A National Church built upon a strong state could provide the direction necessary to create a progressive religious culture that was "persuasive and not coercive." In the United States, he once wrote, "it could occupy the same large and liberal ground as does the public school."[21] In such an effort the National Church would have to enlist the great intellects of the time, and at one stage, Ely advocated a Coleridgean clerisy as governors of a new society.[22]

Ely obviously borrowed heavily from his English mentors, especially Fremantle. He felt such tutelage was fully justified, given what he believed was the success of the Church of England among the industrial working classes. But he was also influenced by his German teachers more than he realized in his admiration of the state as the nucleus of the National Church. This emphasis upon the state in Ely's thought went beyond the same tendency to be found in the writings of English Broad Churchmen.

Ely was not the only Episcopalian to accept the National Church concept, much less Christian Socialism. W.D.P. Bliss, founder of the American Society of

19. Ely was briefly exposed to German Social Christians in Berlin. The strident anti-Semitism of their leader, Dr. Stöcker, the court chaplain, thoroughly disgusted him. See Robert T. Ely, *French and German Socialism in Modern Times* (New York, 1903), 256–57.

20. Robert T. Ely, "Church and State" (lectures at the Hartford Theological Seminary), *Hartford Courant,* 17 April 1890.

21. Robert T. Ely, "Church and State," *Hartford Courant,* 18 April 1890.

22. "A Plea for an American Aristocracy," n.d., additions, box 8, R. T. Ely Papers, Wisconsin State Historical Society.

Christian Socialists and the American Fabian Society, appears to have been converted to Episcopalianism itself because of the National Church concept.[23] As Bliss once remarked of the Protestant Episcopal Church, "[I]t represented, at least, more nearly than any other in this country, the original Catholic idea of combination and union in the name and life of Christ, rather than denominational self-seeking and division."[24] This remark is reminiscent of Maurice's comment that "the Americans are craving for something which is Catholic and not sectarian."[25] Bliss helped to found the American branch of the CSU in 1891 and in doing so became its principal organizer and publicist.

Though many non-Episcopalians were sympathetic to the idea of interdenominational cooperation in the area of social reform, the supporters of the National Church idea tended to be liberal Episcopalians (or American Broad Churchmen). Their hopes were not deterred by the constitutional separation of church and state. They were clear that their objective was not the creation of a church establishment on older, European lines. They were also encouraged by the modern transatlantic Anglican ecumenical movement, which was launched by their own American Episcopal priest William Reed Huntington.

Since the publication of his first major work, *The Church-Idea* (1870), Huntington had been devoted to the reunion of the Protestant churches—in the tradition of a number of earlier liberal Anglicans and Episcopalians on both sides of the Atlantic. He was the inspirational figure immediately behind the famous quadrilateral statement on church unity issued by the American Episcopal Church in 1886. The statement's vision of a united Protestant Christianity could also be linked to the general pastoral efforts of the Social Gospelers of his day.[26] Huntington chose to emphasize the goal of unity above Christian Socialism and all else in his quest for a National Church, or "Church of Reconciliation."

Huntington's main achievement was the development of a specific blueprint for the realization of a National Church. In this plan Huntington went much further than Ely, for example, who could only suggest a religious amendment to the United States Constitution.[27] Modeling the new church upon the federal

23. See Bernard K. Markwell, "The Anglican Left—Social Reformers in the Church of England and the Protestant Episcopal Church, 1846–1954" (Ph.D. diss., University of Chicago, 1977), 211. See also James Dombrowski, *The Early Days of Christian Socialism in America* (New York, 1966), chap. 9.

24. William Dwight Porter Bliss, "The Origin and Organizing of the Church of the Carpenter," *The Dawn* 5, no. 5 (1893): 1.

25. John Frederick Denison Maurice, *The Kingdom of Christ* (London, 1842), 154.

26. John F. Woolverton, "William Reed Huntington and Church Unity" (Ph.D. diss., Columbia University, 1963), 266–68.

27. Ely derived this idea from the National Reform Association. Robert T. Ely, "The Church and the State," 157, additions, box 40, Ely Papers.

government system found in the United States, Huntington advocated a territorial system of local, state, and national bodies. The local churches and pastors, as in Fremantle's conception, would retain their autonomy and thus would determine much of their own policy.[28] Unlike the English Broad Churchmen, however, Huntington was ostensibly committed to the complete independence of church and state, though he felt the church would be so important as to influence the ideas and actions of the mass of society. In time, he was even prepared to abandon the notion that the Episcopal Church would be the nucleus of the American National Church. What he consistently argued for, however, was the "Americanization" of the various ethnic groups as a prerequisite for the success of the National Church.[29] "Americanization" essentially meant the cultural predominance of the English language and civilization. It would eliminate such foreign forces, destructive to the national fabric, as Communism and Romanism. This cultural role derives more from Coleridge than from Fremantle.

Perhaps Huntington was not too specific in his point that the wall between church and state should be preserved. In the mid-1850s Philip Schaff had observed in *America: A Sketch of the Political, Social, and Religious Character of the United States of America* (New York, 1855) that the separation was quite incomplete. In fact, evangelical opinion in the 1870s had lobbied, through the National Reform Movement, for the sort of constitutional amendment approach, albeit of much broader scope, that Ely suggested for a national church.[30] As Huntington once stated:

> To sum up this brief exposition of the practical workings of a non-established Anglicanism, I would wager that while there may be much to be said against autonomy there is more to be said for it. True, anyone who supposes that autonomy, or disestablishment, carries with it, or can possibly carry with it, a complete severance of Church and State takes but a surface view of a deep question. The two institutes are like a pair of interlocked rings, each has an identity and an integrity of its own, and yet the moment an attempt is made to pull them quite apart, they become tangent.[31]

In English Canada, the movement for a National Church also made some headway. Here the ideas were a blend of English and American influences, with

28. William Reed Huntington, *A National Church* (New York, 1898), 55–60.
29. Woolverton, "William Reed Huntington," 281.
30. See Norman, *The Conscience of the State in North America,* 78.
31. "Autonomy in the United States," n.d., 14, W. R. Huntington Papers, Episcopal Divinity School, Cambridge, Mass.

the latter predominating. The concept of church union ultimately took concrete shape with the formation of the United Church in 1925. Professor John Grant believes that Huntington's *National Church* (1898) was a highly important influence in bringing about union.[32] Ironically, of course, Canadian Anglicans were not included in the ultimate union, although most of the early momentum toward union was theirs. At various meetings held in the 1880s and thereafter,[33] it was clear that a number of Anglican clergymen, such as James Carmichael,[34] were enamored of the concept of the National Church in their efforts to achieve church union. Most of these clergy had time only to emphasize the importance of ecumenism, with social reform receiving somewhat less attention, in the fashion of Huntington. However, a consistent blending of the concept of the National Church with Social Christianity, similar in pattern to that advocated by groups in England and the United States, was maintained. Principal J. P. Sheraton of Wycliffe College, Toronto, for example, was a strong supporter of the Canadian branch of the Christian Social Union and shared his concerns for the promotion of Social Christianity at the University of Toronto with other Anglican clergy and laity within the faculty.

One highly respected voice within this academic circle during the late 1880s and early 1890s was Professor William J. Ashley of the University of Toronto's Political Economy Department. While a student at Oxford, Ashley had learned of the National Church concept as a member of the National Church Reform Union. In North America he established a strong friendship with Ely, sharing both the experience of conversion to Anglicanism as well as adherence to the German historical school. After his appointment as the first professor of economic history at Harvard in 1892, Ashley continued his advocacy of Social Christianity, acting as chairman of the American CSU's publications committee; and back in Britain after 1901, he displayed, both in thought and action, an abiding interest in advancing the social role of the Church.[35]

32. John W. Grant, *The Canadian Experience of Church Union* (Toronto, 1967), 29–30. The Methodist architect of church union, S. D. Chown, in one address certainly described a federal union similar to Huntington's design. See *Christian Guardian*, 13 February 1901.

33. The Anglican Church in Canada initiated meetings on union in 1881, the most celebrated being the Toronto Conference on Christianity Unity in 1889. See T. R. Milman, "The Conference on Christianity Unity, Toronto, 1889," *Canadian Journal of Theology* 3, no. 3 (1957): 165–74.

34. See James Carmichael, *Organic Union of Canadian Churches* (Montreal, 1887); J. P. Sheraton, *The Idea of the Church* (Toronto, 1896); Ashton Oxenden, *The Unity of the Church* (Hamilton, Ont., 1875); and John De Soyres, *Christian Reunion* (St. John, N.B., 1888).

35. In 1901 he returned to Britain after his appointment as first professor commerce at the University of Birmingham. See Bernard Semmel, *Imperialism and Social Reform: English Social-Imperial Thought, 1895–1914* (London, 1960), chap. 11.

The most outstanding spokesman for the entwined causes of the National Church and Christian Socialism in Canada as a whole was undoubtedly the Reverend Herbert Symonds, rector of St. Luke's Church, Ashburnham (Peterborough), Ontario. Even before he began his crusade for church unity late in the nineteenth century, Symonds appears to have been deeply influenced by the writings of Maurice and his followers while a student at Trinity College, the University of Toronto.[36] Like Ely, he believed that the Church of England had succeeded in reaching the masses through the inspiration of "the Broad Church school of thought."[37] While he fully supported the practical church-confederation efforts of Huntington, at the core of his thought the nation and church were one, in the fashion of Fremantle. Closely associating the National Church ideal with the implementation of Christian Socialism, he stated on one occasion: "The goal of the Church is not the perfection of liturgy, or of organization, it is not found in any of those multitudinous forms of ceremonies which we call means of grace, but it is the achievement of the perfect man, in the perfect society."[38]

It greatly disturbed Symonds (who was, at one stage, president of the Canadian Society of Christian Unity) that Anglicans, once in the forefront of the church union movement in Canada, should lose the initiative to other churches. Shortly before his death in 1921, he founded an Anglican study group on church unity in Montreal, with the intention of reconciling the episcopally based union advocated by the Lambeth Conference with the church order advocated by the Presbyterians and others. The Reverend D. V. Warner, a member of the same group, shared Symonds's desire to link Social Christianity with the National Church cause.[39] The formation of the United Church in 1925, including Methodists, Congregationalists, and some Presbyterians, caused Anglicans with convictions similar to those of Symonds to lament that the National Church idea had not been fully achieved. It was perhaps of some comfort to them, however, that the term *National Church* was used repeatedly in the articles of union and that those involved in the inception of the new church showed a general commitment to the Social Gospel.

South of the border, Episcopalians were not eclipsed by other churches in their efforts to obtain a National Church and a greater degree of social justice. Under Ely's leadership, the Christian Social Union included some of the best

---

36. Herbert Symonds to George Wrong, 10 October 1900, box 3, George Wrong Papers, Fisher Rare Book Library, University of Toronto.

37. Herbert Symonds, *The Broad Church* (Montreal, 1907), 10.

38. Herbert Symonds, *Lectures on Christian Unity* (Toronto, 1899), 63.

39. See D. V. Warner, *The Church and Modern Socialism: An Essay* (Truro, N.S., 1909).

Christian Social thinkers in America. Most were Episcopalians, though members of other denominations, such as the Congregationalist Robert Woods of Boston, were attracted to their fellowship. The concept of the National Church was not accepted by all, but it consistently surfaced. It also stimulated socially active clergy and laity in other churches to think along similar lines. Leighton Williams, for example, once pastor of New York's Amity Baptist Church and a cofounder, with Walter Rauschenbusch, of the Brotherhood of the Kingdom, advocated a confederacy of national churches built around the various ethnic communities. As an Episcopalian convert, he was, however, quick to add that "we of English descent very naturally would fashion our National Church after the model of the Church of England."[40]

Better known among non-Episcopalians were the church unification efforts of Washington Gladden and W. T. Stead, both inspired in part by Fremantle. Gladden, the celebrated Ohio Congregational pastor, eventually embraced the notion of a municipal church as part of his advocacy of the Social Gospel. Gladden argued that the essential business of Christians was consolidation of their resources for the betterment of their immediate society—city, town, or village. As he stated, "[T]here can be but one Christian church in any community."[41] For Gladden, national denominational organizations might continue, but at the parochial level, local boards or councils should direct the churches in a great coordinated effort to achieve social salvation. Gladden's emphasis upon the local community as the place to begin the movement for unity was reminiscent of Fremantle's suggestions and actions in his own pastoral work. Indeed, Gladden had visited Fremantle in England as early as 1884 and was deeply impressed by the practical work of both Fremantle and his disciples in East London—Canon Barnett and Octavia Hill.[42]

W. T. Stead, the well-known journalist who championed a number of causes dear to the hearts of Social Christians on both sides of the Atlantic, argued in the columns of his celebrated periodical, *The Review of Reviews,* for the necessity of a "Civic Church." Using Benthamite-sounding phrases about the greatest good for the greatest number, Stead, like Fremantle, portrayed this church as the embodiment of a coordinated effort on the part of the denominations to bring about "the regeneration of the whole

40. Leighton Williams to the editor of the *Churchman,* 1917, box 1, Marlborough Papers, American Baptist Historical Society, Colgate-Rochester Divinity School.

41. Washington Gladden, "The Municipal Idea of the Church," *American Review of Reviews* 6 (August 1892–January 1893): 307. See also "Church Unity," c. 1911, sermon no. 1286, Washington Gladden Papers, Ohio Historical Society.

42. Gladden to his children, 12 and 26 June 1888, Correspondence Series I, box 2, Gladden Papers.

community,"[43] not merely the salvation of individual souls. Perhaps predictably for the author of the famous tract *If Christ Came to Chicago!* he was particularly interested in marshaling Christian forces within the cities of his native Britain and the United States. He suggested that "the Civic Church is the spiritual counterpart of the town council, representing the collective and corporate responsibility of all the citizens for the spiritual, moral and social welfare of the poorest and most neglected within their borders."[44] Apart from a "New confession of Faith," his concept on a practical level was not very different from that of Gladden. His brother, the Reverend F. Herbert Stead, developed a fuller plan of church federation leading to the formation of a "National Church," though district churches would remain autonomous in many areas of activity. Adopting a transatlantic outlook similar to that of his brother, he also looked forward to a confederacy of churches within the English-speaking world.[45] Fremantle, far from ignoring the work of these non-Anglicans, actively encouraged the advancement of concepts similar to his own on both sides of the Atlantic.[46]

By the 1890s Episcopal and non-Episcopal Americans were even helping the National Church cause in Britain itself. Ely, who was a frequent contributor to the CSU's *Economic Review,* had done much to support the idea outside as well as inside the United States. The third Lambeth Conference in 1888, by accepting Huntington's quadrilateral statement on church unity, had extended it to the entire Anglican communion. However, within the transatlantic exchange of ideas, the flow in this instance continued to be mostly from Britain to North America.

Though the National Church ideal remained an important element in the minds of many socially reforming Protestants within the North Atlantic Triangle even after the turn of the century and deserves much more attention from historians, it is clearly not a success story in itself. Despite the strenuous efforts of Fremantle, Barnett, Ely, Bliss, Symonds, and many others in the 1880s and 1890s, it was not fully realized in any country.

In Britain, for example, divisions within the ranks of Anglican Social Christians tended to weaken the linked causes of Christian Socialism and the National Church. The CSU was challenged by the smaller Guild of St. Matthew

43. William T. Stead, "The Civic Church," in *World's Parliament of Religions,* ed. J. H. Barrows (Chicago, 1893), 2:1209.

44. William T. Stead, "The Civic Church," in *American Review of Reviews* 8 (July–December 1893): 439.

45. F. Herbert Stead, *The English Church of the Future: Its Polity: A Congregational Forecast* (London, 1892).

46. For example, see Fremantle's reaction to Herbert Stead's ideas in ibid., "Letters from Leaders," 36–37.

over the issue of the National Church. For Headlam and other guild members, the concept of the "National Church" was so vague as to be detrimental to the realization of a truly socialist (and thereby Christian) society. Some Anglo-Catholics resented the implied debasement of Anglican dogma in a unified National Church.[47] From another quarter the Reverend Hastings Rashdall, later a well-known Modernist, writing in the *Economic Review,* conceded that there was a great similarity in purpose for both church and state in a Christian society. However, speaking for many in the CSU, he rejected fusion of the two, since it might produce the extreme of either Erastianism or papalism, depending on whether state or church predominated in the relationship. As he stated:

> There is one essential difference between Church and State which is ignored by thinkers of the Arnold School. There is no difference of sphere between Church and State, but there is a fundamental differ-ence of method. It is of the essence of the State to be compulsive. It is of the essence of the Church to be a voluntary society. Hence from its very nature the Christian society is ideally one which the individual must be free to join, free to leave, and from which he is capable of being expelled. Hence an absolute impossibility of complete fusion with a society whose essential attributes are compulsion and all-inclusiveness.[48]

Rashdall was more concerned with the role of the individual than the role of the individual church in such an arrangement. In his apprehension one notes some shades of an Orwellian future, when, in his words, "no department of human life can be regarded as wholly beyond the scope of the State's interest, if the State is to deal with life as a whole."[49]

Rashdall's criticism is interesting because it unfolds additional considerations concerning the National Church concept. Kitson Clark has noted an authori-tarian strain in the thought of both John Robert Seeley and T. H. Green, who supported the National Church idea.[50] F. D. Maurice in his day had believed that the state was divinely inspired—as indeed were other traditional institutions of the English nation. His state, however, had no mandate for collectivism. It was also somewhat distinct from the church. Seeley, on the other hand, in his

47. For example, see John N. Figgis, *Churches in the Modern State* (London, 1914), 133.
48. The Reverend Hastings Rashdall, "The Rights of the Church," *Economic Review* 6 (Jan-uary–October, 1896): 173.
49. Ibid., 174.
50. George Kitson Clark, *Churchmen and the Condition of England, 1832–1885* (London, 1973), 236–37.

acceptance of the fusion of church and state, invested the latter with a special moral authority. As Deborah Wormell has pointed out, Heinrich Stein's Prussia provided Seeley with the best model for a "harmoniously united nation state" in which the government would even take over certain cultural and spiritual functions from the church.[51] It is in Seeley's writings that one sees the best example of the tendencies feared by Rashdall.

Hegelian idealism in the doctrine of the positive state can also be seen in the work of T. H. Green, another member of the National Church Reform Union. However, Stefan Collini, Michael Freeden, and others have noted the limits placed upon state action by Green, making him less of a collectivist than some in the next generation whom he inspired.[52] Kitson Clark has argued that he was "too nearly a Christian to go far" in his support of the powers of the state.[53] But it is by no means clear that Christianity was the prime impediment to his worship of Caesar. I. M. Greengarten, for example, has suggested that Green's reservations about the power of the state were based primarily upon secular ideology—a continuing belief in the value of a regulated but essentially free market economy.[54] Furthermore, the fact that neither Seeley nor Green was a conventional Christian thinker renders them interesting secularizing factors at work within the support for the National Church idea (perhaps Matthew Arnold was a slightly earlier version of this).

Among the National Church advocates, of course, were many figures quite concerned with limitation of state power. Freeden has pointed out that Barnett worried about the effects of state socialism on individuality.[55] As Barnett stated in a letter written late in his career: "I found now more reason to believe in liberalism—not a party that is but in this principle whose aim is the development of freedom."[56]

Bishop Westcott, president of the CSU, shared many of the same views as Seeley, including, in time, his social imperialism. Westcott's advocacy of the National Church was important because he was a celebrated figure in Social Christian circles. Westcott's vagueness on the specifics of dealing with the evils

51. Deborah Wormell, *Sir John Seeley and the Uses of History* (Cambridge, 1980), 178.

52. Stefan Collini, *Liberalism and Sociology: L. T. Hobhouse and Political Argument in England, 1880–1914* (Cambridge, 1979), 44–47, and Michael Freeden, *The New Liberalism: An Ideology of Social Reform* (Oxford, 1978), 58–60.

53. Clark, *Churchmen and the Condition of England*, 237.

54. I. M. Greengarten, *Thomas Hill Green and the Development of Liberal-Democratic Thought* (Toronto, 1981), 5–6.

55. Freeden, *The New Liberalism*, 61.

56. Samuel A. Barnett to Stephen Barnett, 15 April 1913, F/BAR/4, Samuel Barnett Papers, Greater London Record Office.

of capitalism, once exposed, probably paralleled his vagueness on how to bring about a revitalized National Church. Westcott's positions in a sense represent the culmination of attempts to place the church once again at the center of national life. His advocacy of the National Church idea was tinged with the compromise he saw implicit in a situation in which the lines of the sacred and secular would be blurred. This posture of compromise could unite many in a common effort, but such views could also be profoundly disturbing, especially for those who had a special fondness for the historical church. Even some Broad Churchmen, perhaps harking back to Coleridge rather than Thomas Arnold, would still uphold the existing Church of England as opposed to the reconstructive proposals of the Arnold-Fremantle school, which laid aside special considerations of tradition.

For outright supporters of secular socialism within Social Christian circles, Westcott's approach provided other grounds for divisive squabbling. Among the most famous critics of Westcott and the CSU was first and foremost Stewart Headlam. As leader of the Guild of St. Matthew, Headlam was actively involved in proselytizing secular collectivism, believing that there was a Christian message inherent within the new socialist creed. As he wrote in a Fabian tract in 1892, exhorting Anglicans to support the cause: "[U]nite with socialists of every sort in their endeavor to seize the State and to use it for the well-being of the masses instead of the classes."[57]

In his appeal for action, however, Headlam was careful not to identify his church with the state. He spoke for the many High Churchmen and Ritualists who feared the dilution of doctrine and ritual implied in the National Church concept. As his periodical, *The Church Reformer,* stated in reference to Barnett and the Church Reform Union: "The Broad Churchmen would either practically get rid of the Church altogether with his talk about the Nation being the larger wider church: or would narrow it down into being the State organized for worship. As if worship was the only function of a Church: as if conduct personal, social, political, international had nothing to do with Churchmanship, and as if the Church was not a Society distinct from, though properly in harmony with the State!"[58] Later Fr. J. N. Figgis would say more or less the same thing, though his guild socialism led him to reject any meaningful role for the state at all.[59]

Unfortunately Headlam could also alienate many of his close colleagues. He did this not so much through his association with music hall entertainers or by bailing Oscar Wilde out of jail but by supporting disestablishment and thus

57. Stewart Headlam, *Christian Socialism: A Lecture,* Fabian Tract no. 42 (London, 1892), 9.
58. Stewart Headlam, editorial, *Church Reformer* 5, no. 2 (1886): 25.
59. John N. Figgis, *Churches in the Modern State* (London, 1914), 133.

rejecting any possibility of a National Church. This version of religious democracy, unlike the other version of religious democracy held by members of the National Church Reform Union, may have been his answer to the elitism of the church leadership, but it led to further divisions in the ranks of Christian Socialists. Thomas Hancock, for example, was in agreement with Headlam on almost every issue except disestablishment.

Fabianism and the early Labour Party made strange bedfellows; not only did Headlam have the pleasure of Nonconformist company within the early Labour Party, he also had the specter once again of the National Church idea. Stanton Coit, "minister" to the Ethical Society and later a parliamentary Labour candidate, wrote in the spirit of Coleridge in glowing terms of the efficacy of a National Church as a moral teacher. For Coit's democratized institution to materialize, however, a precondition was necessary: "Only when supernaturalism has been replaced by humanism can we know the meaning and interdependence of Church and State, and of both with the national life."[60] In this ethical National Church the ultimate secularizing trend, found in the position of figures such as Seeley, would find its fullest expression.

Within Nonconformist Social Christian circles the move toward acceptance of collectivism was also evident. Here the distance traveled from earlier in the century was greater than that for members of the Church of England, but the result was much the same—in fact, was accompanied by even more innovation in combining social concerns with those of Protestant reconciliation.

The concepts of the Broad Church circle had permeated some sectors of Nonconformity by the 1870s, as had the general tenets of Christian Socialism. For some the transition was difficult. Baldwin Brown, for example, though he was influenced by Maurice, still maintained ties with the Liberation Society. His fears about the Arnold-Maurice Christian Commonwealth were not unlike the later qualms of Anglicans such as Rashdall. He stated in 1870: "Instead of rejoicing that Christianity under the auspices of the Establishment will fall naturally and easily into the new order, we should pray earnestly to be delivered from an Endowed Democratic church, and contend strenuously for the freest play of the energies and activities of the religious life."[61]

Soon many concerned Nonconformists, however, would follow R. W. Dale's call for a more active role in the life of the nation. In his New Evangelicalism Dale pointed to a more positive attitude toward the state in the interest of social reform. Eventually he too could say that the "State is a Divine institution—like

---

60. Stanton Coit, *National Idealism and a State Church* (London, 1907), 67–68.
61. J. Baldwin Brown, "The English Church and Dissenters," *Contemporary Review* 16 (December 1870–March 1871): 320.

the family, like the Church."[62] His words were similar to those of Scott Holland, who, a bit later on, used the imagery of the extended family and the home in describing his best hopes for the state.[63]

Support for a rebirth of Christian Socialism within Nonconformity produced a host of figures and societies in the 1880s. The figure most conspicuous in espousing Social Christianity was the author of a work by that name, Hugh Price Hughes.[64] In his formative years Hughes was exposed to the ideas of the Broad Church circle and indeed formed a personal relationship with T. H. Green. Some of this influence is evident in his comments upon the need for a national religion that would dedicate itself to a spirit of social reform for the sake of the people. Hughes influenced many Nonconformists to shun the path of sectarian withdrawal in favor of social activism. Later he was even to share the social imperialist notions of Seeley and Westcott.

In subsequent years Samuel E. Keeble enlarged upon the Methodist commitment to collectivism imperfectly found in Hughes,[65] while earlier it had fallen upon the shoulders of General Booth to develop more fully the social machinery of the mission in Methodism. Booth, of course, combined the objectives of dealing with social problems, reaching diffusive Christianity, and ending or at least sidestepping denominational conflict through the Salvation Army. As he wrote in 1882: "Warned by the failure of John Wesley of maintaining his unsectarian position, we are striving to avoid what we think were his mistakes. . . . Instead of insisting upon attendance on any church, even for the Sacrament, we teach our people to spend all their leisure time with the Army, to visit churches only as corps by invitation, so as to promote general godliness and harmony, and to avoid as the very poison of hell all controverted questions."[66]

It should be no surprise that Booth had many imitators. It should also be noted that the Church of England made some efforts at incorporating the Salvationists into their ranks before launching the Church Army. The gesture

62. R. W. Dale, *From Fellowship with Christ and Other Discourses* (London, 1896), quoted in John Kenyon, "R. W. Dale and Christian Worldliness," in *The View from the Pulpit: Victorian Ministers and Society,* ed. Paul T. Phillips (Toronto, 1978), 202.

63. Henry Scott Holland, "The State," in *The Church and New Century Problems* (London, 1901), 45, 51.

64. See John Kent, "Hugh Price Hughes and the Nonconformist Conscience," in *Essays in Modern English Church History,* ed. G. V. Bennett and J. D. Walsh (London, 1966), 181–205, and William McGuire King, "Hugh Price Hughes and the British 'Social Gospel,' " *Journal of Religious History* 13, no. 1 (1984): 66–82.

65. See Samuel E. Keeble, *Industrial Day-Dreams: Studies in Industrial Ethics and Economics,* new ed. (London, 1907).

66. William Booth, "What Is the Salvation Army?" *Contemporary Review* 42 (July–December 1882): 175–82.

was made by Broad Churchmen with the blessing of Archbishop Tait (who also believed in the National Church concept).[67] The particular lure here was the opportunity to reach diffusive Christianity, which at this time concerned so many Broad Churchmen, from Fremantle to Westcott.

Other forms of dialogue were possible beyond the idea of co-opting organizations or indeed whole denominations into the older churches. John Clifford, one of the leading Baptist Social Christian ministers of the period, worked closely with Headlam and other Anglicans on behalf of the Fabian Society. In such associations he argued forcefully for the merits of an interventionist state: "[T]he ideal we need and must have is in the unity of English life, in the recognition that man is complete in the State, at once a member of society and of the government—'a ruler and yet ruled'; an ideal that is the *soul* at once of Collectivism and of the revelation of the brotherhood of man in Jesus Christ our Lord, Son of God and Son of men."[68] Clifford also appears to have given credit for much of the new religious spirit to Broad Church ideas on church and state, believing that the state "is essentially a spiritual organism" and that "Dr. Arnold's ideal for the English Church has been accepted and adopted as the working ideal of the British State."[69]

However, in conceding these worthwhile changes from the early-nineteenth-century age of laissez-faire, when the social impact of religion seemed to him abstract and remote, Clifford still argued against the fusion of church and state as envisaged by Arnold's intellectual heirs. In a spirit of friendship he believed that disestablishment would ensure that the Anglican Church might remain exempt from encroachments by the state, as was the case for Nonconformists.[70]

In rebuttal, Fremantle, as the leading representative of the Arnold school, viewed Clifford as one who would make the old Church of England into a sect and moreover impede its larger work through the state. Clifford, according to his logic, had only come halfway in freeing Nonconformity from its chains of separatism, seeing the world still divided between the sacred and the secular, reclusive religion and social science.[71]

But Fremantle formed a better ecumenical bridge to Clifford than could other members of the Church of England through socialist politics. For every Angli-

67. See note 54 to Chapter 3.
68. John Clifford, *Socialism and the Teaching of Christ*, Fabian Tract no. 78 (London, 1897), 11. See David M. Thompson, "John Clifford's Social Gospel," *Baptist Quarterly* 31, no. 5 (1986): 199–217.
69. John Clifford, "Religion and the State," *Contemporary Review* 67 (January–June 1895): 439, 443.
70. Ibid., 449–50.
71. William Henry Fremantle, "Dr. Clifford on Religion and the State," *Contemporary Review* 67 (January–June 1895): 714–20.

can who extended the hand of friendship was one in whom lingered denominational hostility. The Reverend Conrad Noel, for example, could not forgive
Nonconformity for its associations with plutocracy and laissez-faire.[72] His
suggestion was that right-thinking Nonconformists might come to Anglicanism
because the Established Church was more clearly the home of Christian
Socialism. While allowing for latitude in areas of service at the parish level, his
vision of church unity was essentially based upon an Anglo-Catholic require-
ment of acceptance of "the Eucharist, symbol and bond of fellowship."[73]

While differences in doctrine and church order were very much alive for
socialists such as Noel, clergy such as Charles L. Marson preferred to cast off the
yolk of the past and proceed without reference to "sacerdotal" considerations.
In urging that the essential message of the Gospel be accepted, Marson had
little patience for theological hairsplitting. As he stated concerning the Bible:
"If we are wise we shall extract the eternal element, and not lose our tempers
because facetious persons conclude that Usher's dates are misplaced."[74]

Through the columns of the *Christian Socialist* and his other writings Marson
did much to launch the Christian Socialist Society, which espoused to unite
socialists of all denominations in the late 1880s. Though joined by Anglicans
and, even more, Nonconformists of similar views, the society eventually was
bedeviled by bickering over the ideas of Laurence Gronlund and Henry George
and over the issue of moving beyond "sectarianism" by ceasing to call itself
Christian—this change being urged by an increasing number of members. By
the early 1890s cohesion became impossible.[75]

A fellow Anglican worker for the socialist cause, the Reverend Percy Dearmer, thought he had found the answer to most of these problems in his
insistence that the very success of Christian Socialism was contingent upon
unification of the churches. For Dearmer undivided Christianity would not
tolerate the inequalities and class divisions in society for very long and would
seek to establish a "Christian democracy" along inferable from the teachings of
the "Divine Democrat of Nazareth."[76] The results of Dearmer's pleas were even
less impressive than those of Marson. Like many others who had called for
unity, Dearmer did not appreciate the fact that such discussions could reignite

72. See Peter d'A. Jones, *The Christian Socialist Revival, 1877–1914: Religion, Class, and Social Conscience in Late-Victorian England* (Princeton, 1968), 301.

73. Conrad Noel, *Socialism in Church History* (London, 1910), 282.

74. Charles L. Marson, *God's Co-operative Society: Suggestions on the Strategy of the Church* (London, 1914), 120.

75. See d'A. Jones, *Christian Socialist Revival*, 308–30.

76. Percy Dearmer, "Social Work of the Undivided Church," in *The New Party*, ed. Andrew Reid (London, 1894), 287.

theological controversy—the net result being quite the opposite of what was intended.

Nonconformity, while continuing to exhibit sectlike withdrawal symptoms in the eyes of Fremantle and others, did make more attempts to reach diffusive Christianity than did those in the Established Church. Congregationalism, in particular, seems to have generated more than its fair share of experiments (with due respect to Methodism's help in spawning the Salvation Army, as mentioned earlier). Here, of course, so-called advanced theology such as that preached by R. J. Campbell was helpful, but more helpful still was the flexibility of the Congregational system itself. In *The English Church of the Future* (1892), for example, the Reverend F. Herbert Stead described the ultimate solution for the reorganization of socially conscious Christian denominations as follows: "The Christians of a given village or district would unite in a village or district Church; the churches in a given town or county would federate in a town or county Church; the churches in a given nation would federate in a National Church."[77] Such a plan was not unlike that of the National Church Reform Union but articulated no relation between church and state and so displeased Fremantle in that regard.

Herbert Stead's more famous brother, W. T. Stead, also did his best, through advocacy of a Civic Church, to encourage an ecumenical approach to Social Christianity. In the columns of the *Review of Reviews* he spearheaded a movement to unite churches in order to wage "a guerrilla war" against the social ills of urban life. The Civic Church would establish goals, but would ultimately hand over to the state the performance of tasks the church initiated. Stead, like Hughes, saw the final proof of a Christian nation in its statute books. For Stead, the duty of this church was always to be "the pioneer of social progress, to be the educator of moral sentiment."[78] The actual amalgamation of existing churches would occur only at the committee level, in the "civic centre," a number of which were attempted in various English and Scottish cities in the 1890s.

Stead also publicized the ecumenical religious conferences at Grindelwald and Lucerne in 1892 and 1893 respectively, organized on the theme of reunion by the Reverend Henry S. Lunn on behalf of the Free Church Council. Though Fremantle was an active supporter of these efforts, it was clear that they assisted Nonconformist churches themselves, rather than Anglicanism and Nonconformity, in moving together. The merger also reflected the general

77. F. Herbert Stead, *English Church of the Future*, 19.
78. William T. Stead, "The Civic Church," *American Review of Reviews* 8 (July–December 1893): 440.

consolidation of various denominations going on in the period. The ultimate result was the formation of the National Free Church Council, which, as its name suggests, excluded the Established Church, though the original intent had been to include the Anglicans.

Federation rather than organic union was the approach of these Nonconformists. The design was best described by the Unitarian James Martineau in his arguments in favor of church federation.[79] Sensing that many Nonconformists were uneasy with Liberationists' earlier, misguided demands for disendowment of the Established Church, Martineau stressed that the object of Christian merger should not be accomplished through the dismantling of Anglicanism. By removing any parliamentary statutory control over the Anglican Church, that church would be left to determine its own destiny without an Act of Uniformity or elected parish councils filled with interfering non-Anglicans. In the inevitable re-sorting of the national religious life Nonconformist churches of sufficient antiquity and size would be permitted to share in the revenues of the pre-Restoration estate, ultimately federating with the Anglican Church in the new "Church of England." Such a National Church could also merge its resources in reclaiming the unchurched. Unity of faith rather than unity of organization was the goal. It is also interesting to note that Martineau argued against disendowment on the grounds that such a move could assist the forces of secularization—a point similar to that made by the National Church Reform Union.

Throughout these times of ecumenical experimentation Nonconformity remained resourceful in its attempts to reach diffusive Christianity. The Pleasant Sunday Afternoon Societies, for example, quickly led to the Brotherhood Movement, in turn producing J. Bruce Wallace's Brotherhood Church, which in turn was linked once again with Social Christianity. In contrast, Anglican figures interested in combining these objectives, such as Percy Dearmer and Stewart Headlam, figures other than the upholders of the National Church idea, had at hand no such devices and had instead to avail themselves of such meager opportunities as invitations to speak to the theologically starved Labour Church (which should have offended at least Headlam's High Church principles).

The efforts to combine the goals of Christian Socialism, ecumenism, and reunification of diffusive Christianity within the bosom of "legitimate" churches would seem compatible, if not attainable, in an age in which the word *brotherhood* appeared frequently. In the course of pursuing these goals, however,

---

79. James Martineau, "The National Church as a Federal Union," *Contemporary Review* 51 (January–June 1887): 408–33.

church leaders discovered new dilemmas involving the relationship of religion to a society experiencing accelerated "secularization." The debate over the role and nature of the state became a major problem that cut across denominational lines, a problem raised questions about the role and nature of the Christian Church itself. In the midst of all of this, aroused in particular by talk of unity, the issues of theological doctrine and traditions of church order could also rear their heads from time to time in spite of the general tendency of Social Christians to set them aside in the interest of their socially relevant agenda.

In the United States, some of the reasons for the failure of the cause were similar to those in Britain. Some responsibility can certainly be placed upon organizational problems within the American CSU, especially the dispute between Ely, the founder, and Bliss, the popularizer. Bliss believed that the membership must be exclusively Episcopalian, whereas Ely saw such an approach as retrogressive, putting back the day in which denominationalism would cease in American society.[80] There were also some within the CSU who harbored a philosophy not unlike that of socialist Christians, such as Headlam in Britain. Vida Scudder, for example, divorced her churchmanship from support for secular socialism. Some "Left-inclined" members were undoubtedly coming to the position of George D. Herron, who had given up on the churches as agencies of constructive social reform.[81]

The climate of public opinion had also turned hostile toward socialism of all types, including that of the Christian Socialists, after the mid-1890s. Academics, such as Vida Scudder, John R. Commons, and especially Ely, became targets of a "Red Scare." The result, according to Dorothy Ross, was to make such intellectuals more circumspect.[82] Most of the momentum for Christian Socialism, and the National Church with it, was lost or subtly redirected in this sensitive period.

In the decade of the 1890s ecumenism was not lost, of course. The Columbian Exposition's World's Parliament of Religions inspired Philip Schaff, Josiah Strong, and others to suggest that the best, most immediate and practical step to unity was church federation rather than union. Already the cooperative practical efforts of church workers in cities was working in this direction. A major spokesman for the cause after 1900 was to be John R. Mott, whose primary

80. This can be seen in Ely's correspondence during the period and in the records of the American CSU, additions, box 61, Ely Papers.

81. Herron made an early declaration of his disillusionment in a letter to Ely, 29 March 1891, correspondence, box 6, Ely Papers.

82. Dorothy Ross, "Socialism and American Liberalism: Academic Social Thought in the 1880s," *Perspectives in American History* 11 (1977–78): 7–79.

interests had been in the missionary field. The predominant flavoring became increasingly Social Christian, however. As Martin Marty has indicated concerning the 1914 Conference on Social Needs, "[T]he liberal ecumenical and social Gospels were fusing."[83]

Certainly the Federal Council of Churches, established in 1908, was intimately involved with the improvement of church social services. In the years following its establishment progress beyond a cursory federation was slight. Protestant Evangelicals anxious to deny state aid to Catholic schools were for that reason opposed to any formal attempts to bridge the gap between federated churches and the state.

As both Robert Handy and Martin Marty have pointed out, it was World War I that generated movement toward a stronger bond with the state.[84] But the bond was in many ways one of junior partnership with concentration upon chaplaincy services and supportive propaganda. That was much the same situation in Britain and Canada. Roman Catholic agencies tended to act in these cooperative functions alongside their Protestant colleagues. Though it became clear that all churches had much in common in this situation and that individual, congregational, and denominational opposition to war could arise sporadically anywhere without disturbing the overall commonality of interests, this did not mean that a National Church was about to be born. No image of the National Church had included Roman Catholics. As Robert Handy has pointed out in *Undermined Establishment* (1991), by the 1920s the informal church-state relationship within the United States begged some fundamental rethinking. No longer could the major Protestant denominations take for granted their cultural hegemony over the nation, including its government.

While a minority, those who so vehemently condemned the moral authority of the government in waging total war also revealed through the futility of their protests that the power and momentum of government was its own legitimizing force. Pacifism brought forth the ugly side of enlarged government power to those who believed in the merger of church and state. For some the militarism of Britain, the United States, and Canada was veering toward the same path as had been taken by Germany. Older figures such as Sir William Ashley grew fearful of the state's destructive power.[85] Second thoughts began to be expressed about the positive social engineering that could be carried out by such

83. Martin E. Marty, *Modern American Religion*, vol. 1, *The Irony of It All, 1893–1919* (Chicago, 1986), 274.

84. Robert T. Handy, *Undermined Establishment* (Princeton, 1991), chap. 7, and Marty, *Modern American Religion*, vol. 1, chap. 13.

85. See William J. Ashley, *The Christian Outlook* (London, 1925).

an amoral state. By war's end prominent Modernists had become distrustful of broad-front collectivism. Anglo-Catholics and Evangelicals in Britain were never keen on Erastianism, though the former believed that a properly guided state could affect interventions in the service of Christian social goals.

For this reason Anglo-Catholics and others fought hard to free the hands of the Church of England in providing more guidance. The Life and Liberty Movement, begun in 1917, demanded reforms and changes in the church; at the same time, a study of church-state relations by an archbishops committee recommended more church self-government. The Enabling legislation of 1919 resulted in a National, or Church, Assembly of three houses (bishops, clergy, and laity) that could recommend legal changes in the Established Church. For Anglo-Catholics it gave the church new life, retreating from Erastianism. For more moderate, politically astute figures such as William Temple, it represented a middle path that allowed for the retention of a valuable link with the state but introduced more flexibility in church governance. For Hensley Henson it represented the end of the ideal of a comprehensive National Church. As he argued, until this time membership in the Church of England was identical with a Christian's residency in England. In future, membership would be contingent on specific tests. "The possibility of a National Church, wide enough to embrace all the varieties of English Christianity," would now disappear. Henson added: "To these whose lives have been coloured and guided by that ideal it matters little that Parliament should permit the sectarianized Church to retain possession of the national endowments."[86]

By 1923 Henson had begun to reflect increasingly on the question of the National Church. Seeing the manipulation of the Church Assembly by the Anglo-Catholics, or "Gore's Crowd," he felt that insistence on Apostolic Succession and other touchstones was making the maintenance of the Established Church unrealistic even for the benefit of the Anglican minority in the country. The Church of England was also in a vulnerable position in relation to Parliament, as evident in the Prayer Book controversy, "the to be or not to be of the Church of England as an autonomous or independent church."[87] Henson came to the view that he must support disestablishment if only to rid the church of Anglo-Catholic control.[88] Before this Henson already believed that "[t]he Nation is now completely indifferent to the Church."[89]

86. Letter to the *Times of London,* 15 December 1919.

87. Henson to the archbishop of Canterbury, 22 February 1923, vol. 103, letters, Hensley Henson Papers, Dean and Chapter Library, Durham.

88. Henson to the Reverend Alfred Fawkes, 26 December 1928, vol. 109, letters, Henson Papers.

89. Henson to Canon Cremer, 5 May 1923, vol. 103, letters, Henson Papers.

W. R. Inge, the Modernist dean of St. Paul's who frequently disagreed with Henson, had much the same view of what had happened to the Church of England as a result of Anglo-Catholic initiatives. As he wrote in 1921: "Our present isolation in Christendom is the work of a faction, which, though it is now dominant, is not in the mainstream of the Anglican tradition. It has shut the door on the Wesleyans, who ought to have been the backbone of Evangelical Churchmanship; and it has used its unrivalled power of organization to capture the machinery of Church government."[90]

For Anglo-Catholics the church-state link was still a valuable conduit for their espousal of Christian Socialism, though they also participated in ecumenical conversations, albeit at the instigation of the Lambeth Conference statement of 1920 on Christian reunion. But in contrast to Hastings Rashdall, who concentrated on dialogue with Nonconformists in the 1920s, Anglo-Catholics expended much energy on the so-called Malines conversations with the Roman Catholic Church in the same period.[91] The Malines conversations complicated relations with Evangelicals and Low Churchmen, and indirectly complicated relations with Nonconformists outside the Church of England as well, given the poisoned atmosphere of the mid-1920s Prayer Book controversy.[92] Inclusion of Roman Catholics not only was an unrealistic objective at this time but had never been part of the National Church dream on either side of the Atlantic. Exclusion of Roman Catholics notwithstanding, the Lambeth statements had envisaged something like organic union and had rejected the alternate path of federation.

Before the Lambeth Conference appeal, Nonconformists and Anglicans had met in dialogue. The Mansfield College Conference of 7–9 January 1920 had called for reunion involving the mutual acceptance of the validity of ministers and admission to divine service as well as interchange of pulpits. James Vernon

90. William Ralph Inge, "Fellowship with Other Communions," *The Record*, 13 January 1921, clipping, f. 83, vol. 59, Cosmo Lang Papers, Lambeth Palace Archives.

91. Actually, the Association for the Promotion of Unity of Christendom, founded by Roman Catholics and Anglicans in 1857, was the oldest of all Christian unity societies. Some Ritualists had also been impressed with the past record of the Roman Catholic Church in relation to their social ministry. See James Adderley, *Monsieur Vincent: A Sketch of a Christian Social Reformer of the Seventeenth Century* (New York, 1901).

92. See Walter Frere, bishop of Truro, to archbishop of Canterbury, 30 April 1927, box 3.1, folder "Malines Conversations January–June 1927," Frere Papers, Community of the Resurrection Papers, Borthwick Institute, York. Within the ranks of Anglican Social Christians, Charles E. Raven, who favored union of "reformed" churches, was hostile to the Roman Catholic Church, which he considered "committed to an immutable system of doctrine which is becoming every year less easy of sincere and intelligent acceptance." Raven, "The Church's Task in the World," in *The Church Today*, ed. P. Gardner-Smith, F. C. Burkitt, and Charles E. Raven (Cambridge, 1930), 367.

Bartlett, professor of church history at Mansfield, had emphasized the prophetic character of original Christianity. In the tradition of A. M. Fairbairn he had also enlisted the help of fellow Nonconformists such as Scott Lidgett in alliance with Anglicans such as Charles Raven, persons liberal in theology and in favor of Social Christianity. The Mansfield College manifesto sparked a strong negative reaction from Gore and other Anglo-Catholics, leading to the "Pre-Lambeth" Oxford Conference on Reunion later in June, which now included W. H. Frere, superior of the Community of the Resurrection, as well as all the major denominations of Scotland.[93] Lambeth cooled the prospects of any swift plan of reunion that might set aside High Church doctrine.

The King's Weigh House church meetings between Anglicans and Nonconformists, meetings initiated by the correspondence between W. E. Orchard and the archbishop of Canterbury in response to the Lambeth Appeal of 1920, came closer than had previous meetings to a loose fusion of interests. Orchard noted in a letter to the archbishop that it would be good if the Church of England could make more efforts to free itself from the state, with an eye to complete control of its facilities. He believed that "twenty or thirty years from now it is no inconceivable thing that we might have a government in power so hostile both to religion and to the Church, and so in need of money, that it might demand complete disendowment as well as disestablishment, and perhaps the sequestration of all cathedral and parish churches to the state."[94] During meetings in earlier years, in 1923 and 1924, Nonconformist leaders had advised Anglicans to go slow on the Malines conversations. These meetings also featured dialogue between Anglican and Nonconformist Social Christians such as Scott Lidgett.

Momentum built, and by the 1930s the Sub-Committee on Union with the Free Churches, or the "Bridge Committee," had made some additional progress. At a meeting at Lambeth on 15 January 1932 the Nonconformists W. F. Lofthouse, Scott Lidgett, and A. E. Garvie had many exchanges with William Temple on the necessity of joint social evangelism in the spirit of COPEC. The bishop of Worcester suggested in one statement that "it is reasonable to claim that the Free Church Ministers are not merely 'prophets,' but are in the true Pauline succession. We—i.e. Evangelicals—would regard the case of St. Paul as absolutely vital when dealing with the argument from Scripture." Probably

93. "Oxford Conference on Reunion, Pre-Lambeth," Varia, box 4, Darwell Stone Papers, Pusey House, Oxford.

94. Orchard to archbishop of Canterbury, 4 November 1927, box 2, folder "Correspondence Between the Archbishop of Canterbury and Dr. W. E. Orchard," Frere Papers. The Reverend W. E. Orchard, a leading figure among Congregationalists, stood very much in the Social Christian tradition, preaching at King's Weigh House the necessity of applying Incarnational theology through a policy of social justice.

against the criticism of High Churchmen, he asserted, "Our claim is that no one can be a disloyal Anglican who in *the cause of re-union*, for *a deliberate purpose*, and for a *recognized period of time*, in *a day of decisive importance*, prefers to follow the example and practice of the earlier Reformation Divines. It is along that line that we believe Reunion can best be served."[95] Bishop George Bell of Chichester, however, though an outstanding ecumenical leader and Social Christian, was still puzzled by what constituted "union."[96] The polity question indeed remained central. The final confidential memorandum of the Free Church members of the Sub-Committee urged a union that would incorporate Episcopal, Presbyterian, and Congregational forms of governance. But it was critical of the Anglican position; it argued that "the Church must be spiritually FREE—that is, its courts and officers must be under no civil or other secular control so far as concerns faith, order, worship and discipline. The relation of this to the English 'establishment' is a large and complex matter into which it is impossible here to enter; but the principle itself is, for the Free Churches, one which they cannot compromise."[97]

William Temple, in cooperation with others, became the most conspicuous spokesperson for ecumenism in the period, of course. But his continued belief that the establishment was useful in maintaining the central role of the church as teacher to the nation was very much linked to his espousal of an assertive interpretation of Social Christianity. For him, the Oxford World Ecumenical Conference of 1937 was not only a pivotal event on the road to the establishment of the World Council of Churches but an opportunity to come together with the likes of Reinhold Niebuhr in a general reaffirmation of faith in social action and a denial of individualism. The World Council of Churches not only would embrace North Americans and continental Europeans outside the Roman fold but was, as John Kent has pointed out, "not so much a step towards complete unity, as a device which would enable the Protestant Churches to draw attention to their view of the rapidly worsening economic and political crisis."[98] In England the vision of a true National Church had all but disappeared, except insofar as the propagation of such a vision served some communicative purpose. Church unions were no guarantee of happy endings for Social Christianity. To the north, the 1929 reunion of the Scottish Presbyterian Church,

95. Memorandum of April 1932, 4, box 1, "Union with Free Churches," Frere Papers.
96. Bell to archbishop of Canterbury, 11 April 1932, Frere Papers.
97. "The Place of Episcopacy, Presbytery, and Congregation in a United Church," October 1932, Frere Papers.
98. John Kent, *William Temple: Church, State, and Society in Britain, 1880–1950* (Cambridge, 1992), 96. See Joseph H. Oldham, *The Oxford Conference Official Report* (Chicago, 1937).

which had been linked to the cause of Social Christianity, actually led to a decline in social activism in the 1930s.[99] It was in fact left largely to William Temple, whose roots were Broad Church, to redefine the implementation of the National Church idea along new lines. By treating the positive impulses in church and state as though they formed parts of an integrated movement toward the realization of the Kingdom, with himself as the pilot, Temple treated the National Church as a fait accompli. This may explain his strenuous efforts on behalf of ecumenism as well as social justice in the interwar period. By the late 1930s Temple was able to dominate the three earlier movements of ecumenism (Faith and Order, Life and Work, and the International Missionary Council) in order to stand on an equal footing with John R. Mott in the foundation of the World Council of Churches. He also eclipsed, in the popular media, the significant contributions of Joseph H. Oldham and George Bell, who was more direct in his quest to define more clearly the relationship between church and state.

In the United States and Canada interchurch steering organizations such as the Federal Council of Churches gave the illusion that federation was at hand. In the case of Canada the prominence of the United Church after 1925 stood out as the best prospect for Protestant unification in spite of the clear and considerable theological and ecclesiological obstacles for Anglicans. The furtherance of the Social Gospel in Canada was intimately associated with that development, but so also was the trend of accommodation to the forces of secularization, according to David Marshall.[100]

A few years after union, George Campbell Pidgeon, first moderator of the United Church (and formerly a Presbyterian leader), indicated, in a somewhat combative mood, the continuing association with the Social Gospel:

> Unquestionably one of the major objections to Union was the dislike and dread felt by certain interests for our aggressive policy of moral and social reform. Our struggles and sacrifices for these principles did not end with the coming of Union; rather the increase in influence which Union brought made the reaction against the advocacy of our principles the more severe. The fact that our advocacy of these principles involves sacrifice commits us more unreservedly to them.[101]

99. Stewart J. Brown, "The Social Vision of Scottish Presbyterianism and the Union of 1929," *Records of the Scottish Church History Society* 24, pt. 1 (1990): 77–96.

100. David Marshall, *Secularizing the Faith: Canadian Protestant Clergy and the Crisis of Belief, 1850–1940* (Toronto, 1992), 154–55.

101. "The Message and Mission of the United Church of Canada," 1928, 18, Address no. 2072, Sermons and Addresses, box 52, George Campbell Pidgeon Collection, United Church Archives.

Social Christianity, in any case, was linked to the unitive efforts of most church leadership groups in North America and Britain and to the emerging World Council of Churches. But the idea of a truly National Church remained, as it had been at the time of F. D. Maurice, a dream. The realization of an organically unified society, an accord between the sacred and secular, was for some Social Christians also achievable through the political goal of state intervention.

# 6

## PATHS TO INTERVENTION

The famous comment attributed to Sir William Harcourt, that "we are all socialists now," a comment made in reference to the more interventionist role of government envisaged by many politicians and aspiring politicians in Britain from the 1880s until the Great War, has become perhaps the most quoted political axiom of that period. Its applicability to the United States and Canada in roughly the same time frame adds to its legendary quality. But like any dictum it contained an encapsulation of what was in fact a rather complex set of developments involving the interplay of political thought and action on both sides of the Atlantic. Social Christianity was part of this picture, though historians have tended to gloss over its presence. As I have shown, many Social Christians supported a unitive approach to the problems of the age. This unitive approach involved not only a close companionship between church and state but also an organic wholeness that eschewed individualist social and economic thinking in favor of a cooperative commonwealth. At bottom, the approach was based upon a moral revulsion found in F. D. Maurice and early Christian Socialism against Mammon and the social disintegration that accompanied it. Immanentism, Incarnationism, and Postmillennialism necessitated concern over the deteriorating social landscape in defiance of individualism. This was the particular viewpoint of Social Christianity. Certainly A.M.C. Waterman and Edward Norman may argue with some justification that there was nothing inherent in the basic beliefs of Christianity that necessitated a collectivist position, though most Social Christians would have felt the individualism of market economics was highly unchristian![1] Social Christian teaching also blurred the lines of distinction between the sacred and the secular. Beginning in the 1880s, if not before, the agency of state intervention seemed increasingly appropriate for the task of social reconstruction, though it was not clear such concepts necessitated political activism. Whether political developments acted upon Social Christianity or vice versa is also difficult to determine, for it has never been very clear what sparked the public social conscience of the 1880s. What is known is that many Social Christians did enter the arena of politics.

Perhaps more apt than the comment made by Harcourt was that made by the Reverend Philip H. Wicksteed in 1885: "Those who look forward with hope to the new era of legislation are those who believe that there is such a thing as *collective injustice*, for which society is *collectively responsible* and which it can collectively remedy."[2] Under such circumstances it was rather difficult for prominent Social Christian leaders to make a case against political activism in the service of noble political goals. Clergy of most churches had been active in politics for centuries, of course. In that sense nothing was new. In fact, it appears to have been easier to bridge the gap between religion and politics than, for example, that between religion and business.[3] In the minds of many clergy, political parsons were defensible within Social Christianity, though in practice they were sometimes questioned for their participation and were not actually very numerous. Politics could be clearly linked to social conscience. Yet there were perplexing difficulties for Social Christians in the real world of politics.

These difficulties probably arose with the early Christian Socialists. They themselves had been stirred by political movements of the 1840s, such as Chartism, and to assert their Christian Social agenda may have considered a political response logical. But Maurice's misgivings about political activity, which may have increased Maurice's ultimate standing as a prophet, undoubtedly diminished some opportunities for action and eventually proved to be the

1. See A.M.C. Waterman, *Revolution, Economics, and Religion: Christian Political Economy, 1798–1833* (Cambridge, 1991), 3, which also refers to Edward Norman's position. Even some of the more advanced political activists, such as James Adderley, argued that socialism was not the diametric opposite of individualism and that it was "more in accordance with the mind of our Lord" than something mandated by theological dogma. Adderley, "Christian Socialism," *Goodwill* 2, no. 1 (January 1895): 10.

2. Philip H. Wicksteed, *Our Prayers and Our Politics* (London, 1885), 9.

3. See David Jeremy, *Capitalists and Christians: Business Leaders and the Churches in Britain, 1900–1960* (Oxford, 1990), chap. 4.

kiss of death for the first attempts to organize politically. Maurice, of course, consistently maintained that Chartism, Owenism, and the like, arose out of the aggregate social ills of the laboring masses, which were themselves the result in part of a flawed relationship between church and society. Before everything else a new mentality had to be nurtured in the church and the general public, and politics itself had to be placed on new footing. He conceived of his movement's role as largely educative. Many years later E. V. Neale wrote that Maurice's catholicity did not require even outward Christian belief of the members of the original flock under the early Christian Socialist leaders.[4] What was called for was dialogue between themselves and with the dispossessed. This was in keeping with his final efforts in adult education and his general abhorrence of political radicalism. However, Maurice contributed to confusion over the term *Christian Socialism* in his persistent avoidance of political discussions (even in *Politics for the People*) and ultimately rejected use of the term altogether.

This confusion over a term was in keeping with the general confusion in Britain concerning the specific ideals of socialism. The "English school" of socialism, which traced its roots to William Godwin, among others, had an individualistic bent toward anarchism. The strong assertion that workers are entitled to the full fruits of their labor[5] resulted in an early and pointed criticism of the unearned increment, which fell into the hands of the propertied classes. On the basis of this criticism the American Henry George later developed his "single tax" proposal (which may explain George's unusually strong appeal in Britain). In 1890 Alfred Russell Wallace, in a letter to Richard Ely, took George's points further by arguing for land nationalization with a view to the reduction of the landed aristocracy.[6] Wallace, unlike George, was a professed collectivist.

Owenite socialism, which arose in the same general period as Christian Socialism, was boldly denounced by Anglican and Nonconformist clergy, some of whom took pains to point out the difference between the two.[7] Followers of Maurice later mingled with Owenites in the cooperative movement of the 1850s and 1860s, which injected utopian socialism into the discussion. Older English and French socialist ideas were subsequently superseded by those of the German writers at midcentury. Thus, long before the 1880s, problems abounded

4. Neale to Ely, 6 July 1885, box 4, R. T. Ely Papers, Wisconsin State Historical Society.

5. See H. S. Foxwell, ed., *Bibliography of the English Socialist School* (London, 1976).

6. Wallace saw the aristocracy as the instigator of the class system (21 October 1890, box 5, Ely Papers). He came to his collectivist views through the reading of Edward Bellamy, *Looking Backward* (1888) (Wallace to Ely, 6 December 1889, box 4, Ely Papers).

7. J.F.C. Harrison, *Learning and Living, 1790–1960: A Study in the History of the English Adult Education Movement* (London, 1961), 110.

concerning the definition of both Christian Socialism and English socialism itself. About all that could be agreed was that all were dissatisfied with the evils produced by the existing economic and social order.

In Britain, as stated earlier, the early Christian Socialists such as F. D. Maurice had no explicit political program other than the quest for social harmony. Fifty years later the political objectives within mainstream Christian Socialism had not necessarily moved much beyond that position. Bishop Westcott, president of the Christian Social Union, in a famous address to the Church Congress in 1890,[8] fully endorsed the idea of socialism and its goal, "the common well being of all alike through conditions which provide for the fullest culture of each man." Westcott's philosophy of society was suffused with ideas from Albrecht Ritschl and other continental philosophers, even Marx. He decried the evils of competition, upheld the idea that labor should be rewarded in proportion to "its actual values as contributing to the wealth of the community," and openly espoused a state that would create a position of stability for those who had nothing save their labor. Yet Westcott has been cited by Edward Norman, Geoffrey Best, and others as essentially a Liberal or Burtist,[9] never a socialist. This undoubtedly was the result of his refusal ever to go beyond his theoretical conclusions or to be "committed to any one line of action." Indeed, Christian Socialism did not necessitate membership in a socialist party. Since Social Christianity was originally a religious movement, many clergy and laity in its ranks did not see themselves as primarily of the Left. However, the social involvement of Social Christians frequently made for close associations with those actively espousing various forms of interventionism.

Some Christian Socialists were, of course, less reluctant to become involved with the everyday world of politics. Scott Holland, Charles Masterman, and others (many in Westcott's own CSU) were associated with the more radical or progressive wing of the Liberal Party. More important than these, however, was T. H. Green. I. M. Greengarten has asserted, contrary to Melvin Richter, that politics was at least as important an influence in Green's life and thought as religion.[10] While admitting that religion increased Green's sensitivity to certain

8. Brooke Foss Westcott, "Socialism" (reprinted from *The Official Report of the Church Congress* [London, 1890]), in *Religion in Victorian Society,* ed. Richard J. Helmstadter and Paul T. Phillips (Lanham, Md., 1985), 460–66.

9. Geoffrey Best, *Bishop Westcott and the Miners: The Bishop Westcott Memorial Lecture for 1966* (London, 1967), 22. Thomas Burt (1837–1922), president of the Miners' National Union, was first elected to Parliament in 1874 as a Liberal. He later migrated to the Labour Party.

10. I. M. Greengarten, *Thomas Hill Green and the Development of Liberal-Democratic Thought* (Toronto, 1981), 6–7; see also Melvin Richter, *The Politics of Conscience: T. H. Green and His Age* (London, 1964), 15.

problems of the age, Greengarten argues that Green attempted through all of his writings to develop an elaborate defense of the liberal capitalist system. While arguing the right of the state to appropriate personal property for the good of the collective whole, Green still argued for a market economy—albeit guided by a *regulated* contractual system. His real enemy was the long series of inheritances that withheld most land and other forms of property from the capitalist economy. Such a view accorded with C. B. Macpherson's notions of the origins of liberal democratic thought.[11] Green's influence upon Christian Socialism, therefore, was at base antithetical to notions of collectivism.

Examination of the treatises of various Social Christians on the sacred right to property seems to corroborate such an interpretation of Green's influence,[12] yet perhaps this interpretation portrays Green's thought as less ambivalent than it truly was in the political area (it did have collectivist intentions). This view of Green also tends to downplay the very important ethical impact Green had upon the thinking of many Liberals, Labourites, and members of the so-called Progressive movement.[13]

The New Liberalism associated with L. T. Hobhouse and others was very much inspired by Green.[14] These Liberals, like Green, believed that wealth, especially unearned increment, should be made socially responsible. This path toward a form of collectivism was inspired by Green's social ethics as much as anything else. At the end of the nineteenth century many in the Christian Social Union and other organizations still felt that political liberalism could produce the most satisfactory mixture of the new collectivism and the old ideas of freedom as an alternative to scientific or atheistic socialism.

In the United States nothing inherent forbade political movements among the earlier evangelical Protestants of the mid-nineteenth century.[15] For the most part, the popular social philosophy of individualism was so entwined with Evangelicalism that it worked against group activity. However, the antebellum period in America not only produced abolitionism but also some activism in the area of social reform, and pastors such as Henry Ward Beecher represent a

11. See Crawford B. Macpherson, *The Political Theory of Possessive Individualism: Hobbes to Locke* (Oxford, 1962).

12. For example, see the Reverend Henry Scott Holland, "Property and Personality," in *Property: Its Duties and Rights: Historically, Philosophically, and Religiously: Essays by Various Writers, with an Introduction by the Bishop of Oxford, Charles Gore* (London, 1915).

13. See P. F. Clarke, "The Progressive Movement in England," *Transactions of the Royal Historical Society*, 5th ser., 24 (1974): 162.

14. Ibid. See also L. T. Hobhouse, *Democracy and Reaction* (London, 1904).

15. Political activity often reflected Nativist, anti-Catholic feelings at certain elections. Otherwise, according to George Marsden, dispensationists tended to view politics as very subordinate to spiritual issues, *Fundamentalism and American Culture*, 66–67.

transitional group moving toward a Social Gospel.[16] In the late nineteenth century the outcry against the excesses of plutocracy began to move many Americans, religious or otherwise, toward social reform policies with implications of state action. When Progressivism began to emerge, so did a Social Gospel, heavily influenced by the Christian social revival in Britain as well as by revulsion toward the gospel of wealth. As James Kloppenberg has pointed out for the United States, there was a "strong identification of reform with religion."[17]

For a number of American historians, especially Richard Hofstadter,[18] the status theory is a key element in any explanation of the rise of Progressivism and, by implication, the Social Gospel. According to this much-disputed theory, older traditional elitist elements such as large landowners, professionals, and the clergy, as well as other groups, were resentful of the enhanced power of big business in the second half of the nineteenth century. Their status anxiety about diminished power found its ultimate expression in a number of late-nineteenth-century reform and radical political movements that were critical of the new barons of wealth. The extension of this theory to the clergy by Hofstadter, who saw them as the most "conspicuous losers" in this situation, raises questions about the purity of motive behind the political actions of Social Gospelers. Professor William R. Hutchison has done much to discredit a crude application of this theory to liberal Protestants engaged in social reform;[19] Hutchison points to insignificant social background differences between the conservative and the liberal clergy (the latter actually being a bit more plebeian than the former). Nonetheless, clergy as a whole did come from backgrounds less commonly associated with business. Certainly their increasing professionalism and questionable social standing in urban America made them lament the passage of the older America at the hands of the pilots of change— businesspeople. They were no longer the virtual leaders of the community as in the New England of Bushnell's youth.

16. Henry Ward Beecher (1813–87) was important in disseminating the view that religious ideals must adapt to the needs of contemporary society. While conservative on such questions as poverty, he was a vigorous antislavery campaigner and defender of women's rights. Beecher was a Congregationalist minister, the son of the famous and equally controversial New England preacher Lyman Beecher, and the brother of Harriet Beecher Stowe. He was pastor of Plymouth Church, Brooklyn Heights, New York City, for forty years and was succeeded in that appointment by Lyman Abbott.

17. James T. Kloppenberg, *Uncertain Victory: Social Democracy and Progressivism in European and American Thought, 1870–1920* (Oxford, 1986), 264.

18. See Richard Hofstadter, *The Age of Reform: From Bryan to F.D.R.* (New York, 1955), 131–73.

19. William R. Hutchison, "Cultural Strain and Protestant Liberalism," *American Historical Review* 76, no. 2 (1971): 386–411.

Some parallels can be drawn with historians' views of Christian Socialists in England. R. A. Levitas, following the theory of Karl Mannheim, has explored the relationship between "carrying groups" and social ideas with regard to early British Christian Socialism.[20] He noted that not only were most of the 1848–54 leaders Anglicans, they were also professionals (clergy, lawyers, architects, doctors) of the landed interest, "being downwardly mobile sons or grandsons of the landed upper classes."[21] Levitas also sees a schizoid quality to the whole endeavor of being "Christian" and "socialist;" with the Christian aspect finally predominating in Maurice's singular support for the Working Men's College at the expense of the socialist-appealing cooperative activities urged by J. M. Ludlow and E. V. Neale. Maurice's noblesse oblige toward workers represented the view of the idealized old order as well as the essence of this Christian movement. Levitas sees the socialism part of Christian Socialism arising out of the urban working class, which was "largely areligious,"[22] with Ludlow making the unsuccessful attempt using Anglican paternalism to appeal to it through their common opposition to the emerging industrial order. In the end it was impossible to find a course of action acceptable to the different social groups, Anglicans and the working classes—despite Peter Berger's theory, cited by Levitas, that ideas extrinsically linked to carrying groups can be adopted by others, detaching themselves from their original social roots.[23] In any case Edward Norman's indictment of Maurice's social ideas as a reflection of Tory paternalism seems to be reinforced.[24] Here strong parallels might also be drawn with the status theory of Hofstadter.

Between the activism of the 1850s and the renewed social consciousness of the 1880s lies a political gulf, however. The revival of Christian Socialism in the 1880s involved virtually all Protestant denominations on both sides of the Atlantic. Until that time, the remnants of the original Christian Socialist group in England had largely been engaged in adult educational work or in the cooperative movement. Yet from the outset of the 1880s there was a widespread movement into politics. How did this come to pass?

The explanation is twofold—the growing interest of Social Christians in political science and the growing involvement of Social Christians in municipal politics. The former can be seen in the intense discussions of social philosophy

20. R. A. Levitas, "Social Location of Ideas," *Sociological Review* 243 (1976): 545–58.

21. Ibid., 547.

22. Ibid., 552.

23. Ibid., 556.

24. Edward R. Norman, *Church and Society in England, 1770–1970: A Historical Study* (Oxford, 1976), 171–72 and chap. 5 passim.

that spilled over into political theory and in T. H. Green's contributions to the New Liberalism of the period. The latter is abundantly clear in city politics from London to Toledo, Ohio.

In England Nonconformity belied its previous adherence to economic individualism by actively supporting municipal socialism of the 1870s onward. R. W. Dale's Gospel of Civic Improvement itself was born of Nonconformist Liberal pride in the achievements of the reformed councils since the late 1830s.[25] Dale was an acknowledged inspiration to Joseph Chamberlain and other younger Liberals advocating a theological departure from old Evangelicalism as well as a Christian duty of political action to remedy social ills. Of course, state intervention contradicted the normal Nonconformist scruples about such activity at the parliamentary level. Nonetheless, state intervention at the local level was very apparent throughout Britain in the last decades of the century.

Dale argued that the conscientious Christian must embrace, not avoid, political activity. As he stated: "The true duty of the Christian man is not to forsake municipal and political life because it is corrupt, but to carry into municipal and political activity the law and the spirit of Christ."[26] Dale also made the same point for the United States, even going so far as to suggest that the high degree of corruption in American city government might itself have been a product of political indifference on the part of professional and business classes.[27]

In the United States the crusade against morally corrupt city politicians gained increasing momentum in the last decades of the nineteenth century. Washington Gladden agreed with Dale that in America, in marked contrast with Britain, the poorest type of men served in civic government.[28] Certainly Gladden's visit to Dale's Birmingham impressed him with its clean streets and public order. Gladden felt that the city was "probably the best governed city in the Kingdom."[29] Indeed, like his Nonconformist cousins, Gladden was even prepared to countenance the ownership of utilities in the interest of the public good: "Whatever we may think about it, it is plain that the principle of what is known as collectivism must increasingly prevail in municipal governments."[30]

25. See Asa Briggs, *Victorian Cities* (Harmondsworth, Middlesex, 1968), chap. 5, and E. P. Hennock, *Fit and Proper Persons: Ideal and Reality in Nineteenth-Century Urban Government* (London, 1973), pt. 2.

26. R. W. Dale, *Laws of Christ for Common Man* (London, 1884), 204.

27. See R. W. Dale, *Impressions of America* (New York, 1878), 49–50, and John Kenyon, "R W. Dale and Christian Worldliness," in *The View From the Pulpit: Victorian Ministers and Society,* ed. Paul T. Phillips (Toronto, 1978), 202.

28. Washington Gladden, *Social Facts and Social Forces* (New York, 1897), 189.

29. Gladden to "friends at home," 10 June 1888, Gladden Papers, Ohio Historical Society.

30. Gladden, *Social Facts and Forces,* 165.

Albert Shaw, Frederic Howe, and other American observers of the British city had more or less come to the same conclusion in the 1890s. However, as Bernard Aspinwall has demonstrated, examples such as the Glasgow tram system, which linked the working-class city center with the middle-class suburb, presented alternatives to actual socialism.[31] Indeed, Gladden saw public ownership as a means of applying Christian ethics to public issues, much as he and others hoped the government would regulate the drink trade.

Municipal collectivism was of particular importance in applying Social Christianity to politics. In its blending of traditional and socialist-inclined politics in the more controlled atmosphere of the city council, secular ideological challenges to Christian social principles could be more easily contained. Progressivism on both sides of the Atlantic seemed to be a useful concept particularly well suited to local government. The Progressives on the London County Council of the 1890s included an interesting mixture of New Liberals and more collectivist-inclined politicians.[32] As Edward R. Pease stated, a Progressive is a "practical socialist," and so he could include within that fold both Lord Rosebery ("an undoubted member of the Progressive party") and Sydney Webb.[33] City governments in the United States also were frequently inclined toward the tutelage of Social Christianity. In American cities, however, the complications of ethnicity could work against the patrician outlook often evident in Progressive leaders, as did those which created difficulties for Jacob Riis in his association with Mayor William L. Strong of New York in the late 1890s, though occasionally, as in the case of Henry George, ethnicity could strengthen a candidacy.[34]

In the United States and Canada, in particular, temperance offered another great hope as an organized means of serving the political interests of Social Christianity in the late nineteenth century. Here was an area that could gain the support of Evangelicals for government intervention—normally resisted due to the individualistic ethos strongly linked to that religious position. Moral reform could easily progress toward social reform, addressing in the process the wider social ills of society.

31. Bernard Aspinwall, "Glasgow Trams and American Politics, 1894–1914," *Scottish Historical Review* 56, no. 162 (1977): 64–84.
32. See Paul R. Thompson, *Socialists, Liberals, and Labour: The Struggle for London, 1885–1914* (London, 1967).
33. Edward R. Pease to Richard T. Ely, 8 March 1894, box 6, Ely Papers.
34. See James B. Lane, "For Good Government: Jacob A. Riis' Urban Reform Activities in New York City, 1895–1897," *Societas* (1973), and David C. Hammack, *Power and Society: Greater New York at the Turn of the Century* (New York, 1987), 174–76.

Frances Willard's Women's Christian Temperance Union (WCTU), for example, did much to inspire political reforms (as well as support for Christian
Socialists such as W.D.P. Bliss) in both the United States and Canada and
encouraged similar moves in Britain by WCTU affiliates.[35] The official organ of
the movement, *The Union Signal,* described the process by which Christian
Socialism would be realized: "Edward Bellamy's vision, as given in 'Looking
Backward,' is exerting a wonderful fascination over many minds. But, the only
possible avenue to Bellamy's Elysium must be entered through the prohibition
gate—that is, through the rescue of public affairs from the grip of the saloon.
The battle for prohibition is on, and it must be fought out to a victorious finish
before any other battle can be won."[36] Among a later generation of disciples
was Nellie McClung, a figure of central importance in women's political rights in
Canada, whose efforts were firmly linked to Christianity. In the United States
the overall advancement of women's rights was not on the main agenda of the
Social Gospelers, according to Martin E. Marty.[37] In Canada temperance was
quite early linked to moral reform in general. It provided a useful unifying issue
for leaders as diverse theologically as the two superintendents of the Canadian
Methodist Church—Albert Carman and S. D. Chown.

Chown in fact started as secretary of the Temperance and Moral Reform
Department of the church, which quickly became the innovative social service
of Canada's most important Protestant denomination. From that position
Chown eventually became superintendent of the church (jointly with Albert
Carman for a few years after 1910) and pursued a Social Gospel policy, in
imitation of British and American figures, without an overt break with the old,
evangelical, theologically conservative elements that had supported Carman in
earlier days.[38]

In the United States temperance was blessed from most Social Gospel pulpits
and was usually linked to the cause of political reform. Such open espousal was

35. Lady Henry Somerset was Frances Willard's British counterpart. William T. Stead had a high
regard for both and wondered whether Britain or America would ultimately lead the great
"temperance, moral reform." Stead to Albert Shaw, 26 April 1893, box 177, Albert Shaw Papers,
New York Public Library Annex.

36. *Union Signal,* 17 October 1889, 1.

37. See Martin E. Marty, *Modern American Religion,* vol. 1, *The Irony of It All, 1893–1919*
(Chicago, 1986), 286, 291–94. Occasional gestures were made in that direction; see, for example,
William Dwight Porter Bliss's periodical *The Dawn* 2, no. 6 ("A Woman's Number") (1890).

38. On one occasion Carman allegedly stated that Chown had "killed and disgraced" Methodism by taking it in new directions (Chown to Carman, 6 February 1908, box 10, file no. 209, S. D.
Chown Papers, United Church Archives). However, this was not an accurate portrait of Chown, who
skillfully manipulated older evangelical elements along with liberal-minded, even radical, Social
Gospelers in pursuit of legislative goals.

less conspicuous in Britain, except in some Nonconformist circles. Even Hugh Price Hughes once stated that the liquor trade was the greatest of all existing hindrances to the progress of the Gospel in England.[39]

The government interventionism linked with demands for temperance legislation was a useful prelude not only to Prohibition in the interwar period but more particularly to the general regulation of behavior that was a feature of "war socialism"[40] in World War I. This consequence obtained on both sides of the Atlantic.

Temperance, however, was not the central issue in the political agenda of Social Christianity. It served more of a midwife function between the womb of the evangelical world of self-improvement and the world of societal regeneration. Social Christians were for the most part not single-issue in their politics, though they could lobby from time to time for very specific items, as Ludlow and Neale did for limited liability to protect cooperatives,[41] or as these two, along with Fabians, did in support of the striking London matchgirls or even in trying to get friends elected to the London School Board in 1888.

No Christian Social political party ever emerged in Britain, Canada, or the United States. In this perhaps Maurice—in defining the role of prophet or teacher for society above the hurly-burly of mainstream politics—had greater influence than one might have imagined. Ultimately, however, the failure to organize politically was due not so much to the minuscule number of clergy willing to engage in practical politics as to a concentration upon theory and education of the public to the allegedly right issues of policy. Walter Rauschenbusch reflected this attitude very well in his statement to the Baptist Congress in 1892: "The best time to preach on political questions is before they have become political questions; before they have been thrown into the general wrangle and snarl of politics."[42]

This explains in large measure the unusual amount of time British and American Social Christians spent on political theory—particularly the terminology and substance of "socialism." In Britain, as I have shown, socialism can

39. Hugh Price Hughes, "Sermon XII: Our Duty in Relation to the Licensing Clauses of the Local Government Bill," in *Social Christianity: Sermons Delivered in St. James's Hall, London* (London, 1890), 167–68.

40. The term refers to the controlled, or command, economy and regulation of attendant behavior that became a feature of total war. The term may well derive from a 1916 speech by Winston Churchill. See Alan J. P. Taylor, *English History 1914–1945* (Oxford, 1965), 65.

41. See Boyd Hilton, *Age of Atonement: The Influence of Evangelicalism on Social and Political Thought, 1795–1865* (Oxford, 1988), 265–66.

42. Walter Rauschenbusch, "The Pulpit in Relation to Political and Social Reform" (20 May 1892), in *Tenth Annual Session of Baptist Congress for the Discussion of Current Questions, Philadelphia, May 19–21, 1892* (New York, 1892), 128.

be traced back to the early nineteenth century, but the 1880s led to a fresh reappraisal. As Gertrude Himmelfarb has demonstrated, in this period socialists were as confused about what constituted socialism as Christian Socialists were about what constituted Christian Socialism.[43]

W. T. Stead, for example, boldly asserted that Mrs. Booth, wife of General Booth of the Salvation Army, was a socialist. Yet he quickly pointed out that her socialism "was the socialism of the Sermon on the Mount, and of the Epistle of James." Stead added: "The Salvation Army takes no part in party politics. It is indirectly, no doubt, a profoundly conservative force in the best sense of that term. But, in essence, it is an army of revolt. Every Salvationist is a soldier enlisted in a holy war against all that is opposed to God's will in the existing order."[44] Hugh Price Hughes and John Clifford wrote about socialism on the Nonconformist side as did a number of Anglicans from their point of view. They tended to mold secular socialism in a manner that reflected Social Christianity. The basic and very broad view that socialism constituted a rejection of individualism was probably widely accepted, though even here many Social Christians, such as W. H. Fremantle, set down certain caveats.[45]

Westcott's vagaries of definition convinced Stewart Headlam that the CSU was not sufficiently committed to the practical realization of the goals of Christian Socialism. Headlam may have been right, but then, he worked the side of the street opposite Maurice, that is he strove to socialize Christianity. In so doing he in essence rediscovered that the Christian Church was intended "mainly and chiefly for doing on a large scale throughout the world those secular, socialistic works which Christ did on a small scale in Palestine."[46] Headlam may have done more than any Social Christian of his time to begin the process of encouraging politicians of the Left to employ the services of church organizations for their own purposes. Headlam wrote pamphlets for the Fabian Society and sat in its inner councils. However, he opposed the Labour Representation Committee, remaining a Liberal. Membership in any party with

43. See Gertrude Himmelfarb, *Poverty and Compassion: The Moral Imagination of the Late Victorians* (New York, 1991), bk. 5.

44. William T. Stead, *Life of Mrs. Booth: The Founder of the Salvation Army* (New York, 1900), 198, 197.

45. William Henry Fremantle, "Individualists and Socialists," *Nineteenth Century* 41 (February 1897): 311–24.

46. Stewart Headlam, *Christian Socialism: A Lecture*, Fabian Tract no. 42 (London, 1892), 6–7. For a discussion of Headlam's relationship to Fabianism, see William L. Sachs, "Stewart Headlam and the Fabian Society," *Historical Magazine of the Protestant Episcopal Church* 45, no. 2 (1976): 201–10. For comparisons with Marx's analysis of society, see Irby C. Nichols, "Stewart Headlam and the Guild of Saint Matthew: A Christian Socialist Looks at Marx," *Consortium on Revolutionary Europe, 1750–1850: Proceedings* 18 (1988): 405–26.

socialist aspirations was in a sense redundant, since he believed that being a Christian constituted membership in a socialist society. His knowledge of secular socialism was somewhat limited and confused, befitting the times. He based his hopes for society largely upon the belief that the teachings of Henry George (whose writings circulated in Britain years before the English translation of Marx's *Kapital* appeared [1887]) would accomplish the goal of restoring property to the people.

The theories of Henry George, which successfully buffered Social Christianity from the scientific materialism of the Marxist alternative, were acceptable to many Christian Socialists.[47] As the Fabian William Clarke confided to the American Henry Demarest Lloyd in 1883:

> One of the chief features in English affairs just now is the undoubted spread of Socialist ideas. I do not mean that there is any definitely formulated programme advocated by any special party as in Germany, but I mean that there is quite a revolution going on as to interference with private property, relations of labour and capital, and a very great spreading of the doctrine of nationalization of the land. The old political economy of Ricardo has gone to the wall, and Henry George's book has had a most enormous sale. This called forth more popular interest than any work I can recollect in my short life.[48]

It is revealing that in the 1906 survey of important authors read by the fifty-one Labour M.P.'s Henry George stood out as among the most influential, along with Ruskin and Carlyle.[49]

Not all American writers were seen as prophets, of course. While Richard T. Ely's writings on economics and political theory had admirers among Christian Socialists, he also had his detractors. Sydney Webb, for example, found his form of "progressive conservatism," allowing for distinctions between social reforms and restrained nationalization on the one hand and socialism on the other, to be a false dichotomy. As Webb stated concerning Ely's *Socialism and Social Reform* (1894): "If I had to criticize your book I should say that I do not recognize your division between Socialism and Social Reform—any more than I could a classification between Christianity and Social Reform. Collectivism, to me, is a principle, not a system. All *your* social reforms are based it seems to me on

47. See Peter d'A. Jones, *Henry George and British Socialism* (New York, 1991) chap. 9.
48. Clarke to Lloyd, 23 May 1883, box 2, series J, Correspondence, Henry Demarest Lloyd Papers, Wisconsin State Historical Society.
49. Forty-five replied to "Character Sketches, : The Labour Party and the Books That Helped to Make It," *Review of Reviews* 33 (January–June 1906): 568–83.

Collectivism, and so I agree with them."[50] But some within the British Labour movement called for a more pointed socialist direction. The "religion of socialism," in the spirit of the Brotherhood Movement of Bruce Wallace, was one answer. Another was the notion, espoused by Stewart Headlam, that socialism was the embodiment of basic Christianity itself. The Marxist H. M. Hyndman, leader of the Social Democratic Federation (SDF), found the Independent Labour Party worth watching but was conscious of different tendencies within its ranks and the need for it to evolve into better form. As he stated in an 1894 letter: "It is of course very strange, and not a little ludicrous, to hear the great jumble of Asiatic mysticism and supernatural juggling which we call Christianity put forward by Keir Hardie and Tom Mann as the basis of a social and economic propaganda."[51] Hyndman's criticism of Hardie and Mann was based on his belief that "untheological" leaders would eventually emerge within the party. An inspection of correspondence, such as the Keir Hardie Papers in the Independent Labour Party Archives, however, reveals the importance of both clerical and lay supporters, including the Labour Church at the local level.

Virtually all Labour M.P.'s had church affiliations, according to the compilers of the 1906 survey. James Adderley, for example, wrote to Ramsay MacDonald that the transplanted American Ethical Society leader, Stanton Coit, would be an unsuitable parliamentary candidate for East Birmingham. As Adderley stated concerning Coit: "I believe he is a very good man but I am sure he will *not* do here, because he holds peculiar religious beliefs. The people are *anti*-agnostic here and I am sure we should lose heaps of votes if it were known that he is not orthodox."[52] Adderley, threw his support to the young George Lansbury, future leader of the Labour Party in the 1930s.

It is true that Hardie stated that socialism was "the embodiment of Christianity in our industrial system,"[53] but in the same article he stated that out of moral obligation the church must act politically rather than try to develop an unsophisticated argument likening early Christianity to socialism.[54] Though not a Social Christian, he once stated in very Social Christian terms:

> The question is frequently put—what is the duty of the Christian Church in relation to Socialism? I reply that the Church has no special

50. Webb to Ely, 19 September 1894, box 15, Ely Papers.
51. Hyndman to Ely, 28 September 1894, box 15, Ely Papers.
52. Adderley to MacDonald, 28 February 1907, Labour Party General Correspondence 12/11, Labour Party Archives, London.
53. Quoted in Himmelfarb, *Poverty and Compassion*, 335.
54. James Keir Hardie, "Socialism," *British Weekly*, 18 January 1894.

attitude which it can assume towards this or any other question. Truth is truth, whether in the realm of economics or any of the absolute sciences. It is the duty of the Christian to find out where the truth lies, and to advocate that. This is true of every question. If the present industrial system aggrandises the strong and selfish, and crucifies the meek and lowly of heart, it is anti-Christian. If Socialism tends toward the development of brotherliness and good-will and peace on earth, it is the Kingdom of God.

W. Reginald Ward has observed that one of the principal reasons for the failure of Christian Socialism was that it viewed problems "too much from the top of the social pyramid ever to create a foothold for the church in the world of labour."[55] Hardie was well aware of this difficulty, arguing on one occasion that while there was no fundamental antagonism between Christianity and Labour, some in the movement were repulsed by a church in which "the rich and comfortable classes have annexed Jesus and perverted his Gospel."[56] On occasion Hardie could come frighteningly close to the image of a seventeenth-century Christian egalitarian, as he did shortly before the Coal Strike of 1912, when, in argument against the mine owners, he pointed out that no private property existed in the early Church.[57]

Hardie's frequent jibes against clergy sometimes made his political opponents paint a picture of him as a latent atheist. Yet anticlericalism was not a strong factor in the Labour movement or in affiliated socialist circles.

Hardie's exchanges with the New Theologian R. J. Campbell concerning the latter's support for the Labour Party in 1905 are especially illuminating. After an initial interview with Robert Williams, who thought Campbell was actually a Tory, Campbell had a letter exchange directly with Hardie in which he indicated his general sympathy with the ideas of the party (even raising the idea of being a Parliamentary candidate), though he admitted he had no understanding "of the life of the poorer classes from the inside."[58] In reply Hardie related the following story:

55. W. Reginald Ward, "The Way of the World: The Rise and Decline of Protestant Social Christianity in Britain," *Kirchliche Zeitgeschichte* 1, no. 2 (1988): 301.

56. Address at Browning Hall, 5 May 1910, box 25 (2), James Keir Hardie and Emyres Hughes Papers, deposit 176, National Library of Scotland.

57. "What Think Ye of Christ?," *Pioneer,* 20 January 1912, box 25 (6), James Keir Hardie and Emyres Hughes Papers.

58. Campbell to Hardie, 24 December 1906, box 25 (3), James Keir Hardie and Emyres Hughes Papers.

I am afraid that you have not quite realized what joining a Socialist Organization may mean to you personally. I remember some years ago a Dr. of Divinity and a popular London preacher joined the party, much as you now propose doing. I advised him as I now advise you to first of all make sure that he had fully counted the cost, but in his enthusiasm he was prepared to meet any difficulties that might arise. In less than twelve months however, he had to resign his church and leave London. So long as a man in your position merely talks from the pulpit his Deacons and Elders rather like it, but the moment he attempts to apply his principles especially in the sphere of politics his action assumes quite another aspect in their sight.[59]

Overt involvement in socialist politics was beyond the pale of tolerance. Whereas wealthy laypeople were prepared to live with the seemingly eccentric views of Social Christian clergy as espoused from the pulpit, socialism on the hustings was unacceptable. As the young Charles Gore wrote to his mother in the 1890s: "I cannot quite say that the clergy ought *never* to take part in politics. I think there are circumstances where justice is at stake, then it is duty to speak out."[60] But most clergy, save lone figures such as Stewart Headlam, a priest without a living, were not active politicians. William Temple found it better to resign from membership in the Labour Party after World War I to preach Social Christianity. Sherwood Eddy described his Social Gospel activities while a YMCA organizer under J. R. Mott as follows:

Just as I warned them [YMCA International Committee Executive], as soon as I began to preach the social gospel and men like Judge Geary, President of the U.S. Steel Corporation, saw the garbled reports on my talks, they threatened not only to cut off all support from the YMCA but to induce other capitalists to do the same. Mott as a master strategist would play John D. Rockefeller, Jr. against Judge Geary, outmaneuver the latter and refuse to let me resign. I had to work thus under fire for some years until I retired at the age of sixty. The next day, I joined the Socialist Party, not having felt quite free to do so in the spell as a money raiser.[61]

59. Hardie to Campbell, 4 January 1907, box 25 (3), James Keir Hardie and Emyres Hughes Papers.

60. Gore to his mother, 12 February, no year, 12-1-9 Letters to Mother, 1883–97, Correspondence, Charles Gore Papers, additional deposit 12, Papers of the Community of the Resurrection, Borthwick Institute, York.

61. Sherwood Eddy to E. Brewer Eddy, Reinhold Niebuhr, 9 June 1942, box 2, folder 35, Sherwood Eddy Papers, Yale Divinity School Library.

In the United States it was perhaps in deference to the delicacy of the situation that the Socialist Party in its years before 1908 made little reference to religion in spite of the known affiliation of hundreds of clergy.[62]

Back in Britain, though Campbell did not emerge as a Labour candidate, his sympathies lay with the movement. By the end of first decade of the new century most churches saw the appearance of some sort of socialist society in their ranks. Smaller denominations such as the Theosophists and the New Church (perhaps for special theological reasons) seemed to have an inordinate number of socialists in their membership.[63] One review of *Looking Backward* even suggested that the concept of equal incomes actually rested upon a Swedenborgian religious precept: "Regarded as a moral principle, the law of equal incomes receives, it seems to me, a support from the doctrines of the New Church, which Mr. Bellamy has been unable to give it."[64]

Church members were not uniformly in agreement with the progress of socialist thought within their folds, of course. Indeed, a staunch Nonconformist Anti-Socialist Union was formed in 1909, principally composed of Wesleyan Methodists and Baptists, in response to such organizations as the Sigma Club (dedicated to evolutionary socialism), which was led by figures such as Henry Carter and S. E. Keeble.[65] Besides the Sigma Club, it also targeted for criticism Lloyd George, the Nonconformist political hero, for socialistic tendencies and political shortcomings, though perhaps declining religious belief was a more relevant concern as applied to Lloyd George and many other politicians.

From the opposite perspective, committed socialists in the churches felt that their leadership was indifferent or lukewarm to the cause. Stewart Headlam quarreled with the CSU over many matters.[66] He was followed by figures such as Joseph Clayton, who argued that "[t]he Bishops of the Established Church do

62. David A. Shannon, *The Socialist Party of America: A History* (Chicago, 1967), 59–60.

63. See Peter d'A. Jones, *The Christian Socialist Revival, 1877–1914: Religion, Class, and Social Conscience in Late-Victorian England* (Princeton, 1968), 353–67. On Theosophy and politics, see Anne Taylor, *Annie Besant: A Biography* (Oxford, 1992). For one interesting figure who combined a social conscience, psychical research, and the ILP, see E. I. Champness, *Frank Smith, M.P.* (London, n.d.). See also note 40 to Chapter 1.

64. J. Howard Spalding, *New Church Magazine* 9, no. 102 (1890): 257.

65. Pamphlets and handbills of the Sigma Club and the Nonconformist Anti-Socialist Union dating from 1909 and 1910 can be found in MA 234, Records of Division of Social Responsibility, and folder 6 in S. E. Keeble Papers, Methodist Archives, John Rylands University Library of Manchester.

66. See the editorial by Scott Holland in *The Commonwealth: A Christian Social Magazine* 7, no. 1 (1902): 18, which discusses Headlam's problems with the CSU.

not support the Socialist movement. Some of them criticize it; most of them ignore it or oppose it."[67]

Those committed to the religion of socialism were not declining with the declining Labour Church. Indeed, in 1901 the Socialist Sunday School movement appeared. Following a line suggestive of Stanton Coit's position on the Education Act of 1902,[68] the movement was dedicated to the ideal that "all public education should be secular in character"[69] and that all children should be indoctrinated with the ideals of socialism in their own Sunday schools. The rubric that Sunday schools would include hymns as well as supporting literature such as *The Young Socialist* developed as the movement spread. The national conferences reported in *The Young Socialist* showed the link with the Labour Representation Committee (LRC), especially through the Independent Labour Party (ILP). The tenuous link with Christianity was maintained, however.[70] After the Great War the more militantly socialist Proletarian Sunday Schools appeared, with a slightly more atheistic direction, no doubt inspired by earlier apostles such as Annie Besant and Robert Blatchford. Nonetheless, on occasion even the Proletarian School Series or their magazine, *The Red Dawn*, published after the Great War, made sympathetic statements about figures such as John Wycliffe who had attempted to overturn the established order in the past.

Those Social Christians traditionally sympathetic to the advance of Labour had doubts about directions within the movement. Thomas Hughes confided to Ludlow in 1893, in the patrician way of the old generation of Christian Socialists: "I still hope for better things through Cooperation and the influence of the army of good Christians (as most of them I hope are) who are taking a hand in the labour question and (I trust) lifting the working class out of their blind and selfish materialism; but it seems to me quite in the cards that the coming democracy may turn out as tyrannical, selfish and short-sighted as the worst of Kings and oligarchies in the past."[71]

67. Joseph Clayton, *Socialism for Bishops: Why Do Bishops and Curates Ignore Socialism?* Pass On Pamphlets no. 18 (n.p., n.d.), 1.

68. Coit to Ramsay MacDonald, 26 November 1903, LRC 11/437, Labour Representation Committee correspondence, Labour Party Archives, London. Coit argued in the letter that "the Labour Party is as keenly interested in the Educational as well as the economic emancipation of the people."

69. Preface to *The Socialist Hymn Book: For Use in Socialist Sunday Schools and Labour Meetings Generally* (Huddersfield, Yorkshire Socialist Sunday School Union, 1907); found at Edmund and Ruth Frow Library, Salford.

70. For example, see Allen Clarke, "Two Sights in Manchester," *Young Socialist* 15, no. 7 (1915), 106, where he poses the question, "If Christ Himself came to Manchester as a poor man, what would be his fate?"

71. Hughes to Ludlow, 23 October 1893, J. M. Ludlow Papers, Cambridge University Library.

The elderly Samuel Barnett found the issues of Edwardian politics between the Liberals and Labourites not fearful but confusing. The Labour Party lacked coherence and good leadership, while the Liberals foundered in poor tactics, though its basic philosophy was good.[72]

There was considerable strength in Barnett's desire to see the blending of liberal freedoms and collectivism in an effective political party. P. F. Clarke, in a highly interesting essay, has described the development of the Progressive movement in England at the end of the nineteenth century.[73] Similar to its American counterpart of a slightly later period, the Progressive movement was wider than any particular political party and clearly included within its ranks the so-called New Liberals, many of whom were apt to define "true socialism as a special case of liberalism."[74] Progressives were certainly inspired by the writings of T. H. Green and others associated with Christian Socialism, and included within their working membership many committed to the ideals of Social Christianity. In the columns of its journal, *The Progressive Review,* many articles argued for an end to sectarian conflict between Nonconformists and Anglicans in the interest of the greater battle to transform society from wasteful competition to a magic blend of collectivism and individual freedom.

Progressives on the whole were a very loose alliance including New Liberals, Fabians, and members of the Independent Labour Party, as displayed in the London County Council. The Progressive period may have been the most significant period of Social Christian influence in politics. According to P. F. Clarke, it was in fact the issue of war—first the Boer War and then, more dramatically, World War I—that produced the cleavage between Liberals and Fabians, ending for practical purposes the Progressive movement.[75] What is interesting here is that a similar cleavage appeared within the ranks of the Christian Socialists over imperialism, with B. F. Westcott and John Robert Seeley as social imperialists and Charles Gore, Scott Holland, and Conrad Noel as vehement anti-imperialists. According to Peter d'A. Jones, the Boer War produced some strong opposition to imperialism, including a strain of anti-Semitism observable in the New Church periodical *Uses* and somewhat in the CSU.[76]

72. Samuel Barnett to Stephen Barnett, 15 April 1913, F/BAR/4, Samuel Barnett Papers, Greater London Record Office.

73. P. F. Clarke, "The Progressive Movement in England." For the links with American Progressivism, see Arthur Mann, "British Social Thought and American Reformers of the Progressive Era," *Mississippi Valley Historical Review* 42, no. 4 (1956): 672–92.

74. Ibid., 171.

75. Ibid., 165–67, 177.

76. See Peter d'A. Jones, *Christian Socialist Revival,* 362.

The Fabian Society itself was a product of disgruntled young Liberals of the 1880s. It is frequently forgotten that the Fabian Society arose from a group called the Fellowship of the New Life, led by Thomas Davidson. Davidson believed that the reformation of society should be spearheaded by a fellowship dedicated to the application of pure intelligence to social problems, with an emphasis upon personal regeneration. According to the Davidson papers, the Fabian Society was to occupy itself primarily with temporal concerns and would act in concert with the Fellowship of the New Life, which would occupy itself with spiritual questions and overall direction.[77] As Stanley Pierson has noted, the Fabians, at least in their early period, continued to claim Davidson as their leader and founder.[78] While Davidson (who had emigrated to New York, where a branch of the fellowship had been founded) began to suspect the intentions of the Fabians, he maintained that the two groups constituted one movement for moral and ethical rejuvenation. As he stated of the fellowship: "What is the function of a church? Its function plainly is to cultivate the pure intellect or the faculty which grasps the universe in its ideal unity."[79]

In this sense Davidson regarded the fellowship as a church. The Fabians, clearly, did not conceive themselves in this way. However, as A.M. McBriar has noted, their most successful tracts were those written by the clergy: Stewart Headlam, Percy Dearmer, and John Clifford.[80]

Similar to the blending of New Liberals, Fabians, and Labourites in the Progressive movement was that in the "Rainbow Circle" operating from 1894 to 1931. Though it grew out of a number of roots, including the ethical movement, its early membership included Christian Socialists such as Percy Dearmer. Some of its members founded the British Institute of Social Service, which later expanded into the National Council of Social Service. A strong agnostic influence animated its membership, however.[81] As Progressivism faded and more overt gestures were made toward socialism, the divisions of secular socialism began to permeate the ranks of Social Christians. Some earlier divisions over Henry Georgism persisted, though by focusing upon the evils of unearned income, organizations such as the Christian Socialist League could unite the Baptist John Clifford with the Anglican Charles L. Marson. Guild socialism

---

77. See Thomas Davidson, "Fellowship of the New Life," box 47, folder 49, Thomas Davidson Papers, Sterling Library, Yale University.

78. Stanley Pierson, *Marxism and the Origins of British Socialism: The Struggle for a New Consciousness* (Ithaca, N.Y., 1973), 112.

79. See Thomas Davidson, "The Function of a Church," 11, box 47, folder 49, Davidson Papers.

80. A. M. McBriar, *Fabian Socialism and English Politics, 1884–1918* (Cambridge, 1966), 154–55.

81. See Michael Freeden, ed., *Minutes of the Rainbow Circle, 1894–1924*, vol. 38 of *Camden Fourth Series* (London, Royal Historical Society, 1989), 441.

began to be popular in certain Christian Socialist circles, though in 1912 the *New Age*, ignoring its syndicalism, described this socialism as "industrial democracy" within "self-contained units," in contrast to collectivism or state socialism. In 1913 the Christian Socialist League endorsed it—reviving the old associationism of Ludlow, Maurice, and Kingsley—as a line of thinking that had been sustained a little earlier, according to Peter d'A. Jones, in the Brotherhood Church.[82] George, Bellamy, and Gronlund continued on the whole to precede Marxism. The *Church Reformer* expressed a view of the situation in the 1880s, which was probably still valid by 1914, when it described *Das Kapital* as a "most valuable collection of figures and facts" and a useful indictment of laissez-faire while discounting its general impact on British society.[83]

The goal of merging socialism and Christianity under the auspices of the church was confidently proclaimed by one wing of Social Christianity, especially Anglicans such as Conrad Noel, before World War I. The *Christian Socialist* (June 1891) implicitly contrasted themselves with Maurice when they announced, "We are endeavouring not to Christianize socialism but to socialize Christianity," and added, "We are Socialist-Christian socialists, and therefore neither revolutionary nor atheistic . . . but we are undoubtedly socialist, and we have nailed our colours to the mast." There was too much ambition in such pronouncements and in similar hopes for the guidance of socialism. In the same year, William Clarke wrote in a private letter to his American friend Richard Ely, "I quite feel that some blending of the economic with the religious element is what society must need. But there were scarcely any of your socialists here who take that view for skepticism has gone very deep into English cultivated society and into the most intelligent section of the working classes."[84] Clarke was himself somewhat of a skeptic, being opposed to organized religion, though associating with Christian Socialists in the cause of Fabianism.[85]

In the case of the emerging Labour Party, Social Christians did have some influence. But the Labour Party itself was not admitted to the corridors of power before the Great War. For the most part the traditional parties predominated, and the traditional role of the churches still superseded any social roles advocated by Christian Socialists. The notion of the Church of England as the Conservative Party at prayer and of the Nonconformists as the backbone of the

---

82. Peter d'A. Jones, *Christian Socialist Revival*, 442.

83. "Lassalle and Marx," *Church Reformer* 3, no. 10 (1884).

84. Clarke to Ely, 20 May 1891, box 6, Ely Papers.

85. See Peter Weilmer, "Wm. Clarke: The Making and Unmaking of a Fabian Socialist," *Journal of British Studies* 14, no. 1 (1974): 88.

Liberal organization, with Roman Catholics somewhere in between, still contained much truth before 1914. Though some Nonconformists had shifted their support to the Labour Party, the Victorian pattern of denominational animosities and allegiances carrying over to traditional politics persisted. Political squabbles such as that over the 1902 Education Bill demonstrated clearly the traditional church-party allegiances. Hensley Henson, for example, resented the organized efforts of prominent Nonconformist leaders, including Social Christians, to defeat the Conservative legislation. As he stated in a letter to Hastings Rashdall in 1902: "The agitation against the Education bill is supremely exasperating. There is a strong case against the Bill but it is not the case which Clifford and his fellow fanaticks put forward: *their* incessant beating of the Protestant drum ecclesiastick is wholely disgusting."[86]

Lloyd George, at the time of the Liberal budget crisis some years later, still believed that "Nonconformity alone" could bring "the middle class to our aid." On the question of legislation, whether in education, licensing, or even disestablishment, he wrote: "The destruction of the veto of the Lords means so much to the Free Churches that I cannot help thinking that they will realise that it is their special business to make the greatest concerted effort they have ever put forth."[87]

Though figures sympathetic to Social Christianity (though not necessarily Social Christians themselves) could be found within the higher circles of political power—such as Charles Masterman, Lord Rosebery, Lloyd George, Lord Randolph Churchill, and Arthur Balfour—it is clear that before 1914 the movement was of secondary importance in their considerations of the churches. Charles Gore's belief that the Christian Social Union had sufficiently influenced public policy was self-delusionary. Indeed, W. Reginald Ward's contention that Christian Socialists never exercised "practical influence on the policies of government" is probably closer to the truth.[88]

In the United States the pattern of Social Christian activity from the 1870s to 1914 was similar. In fact, this was truly the heyday of the American Social Gospel, as in Britain. Very much a part of this North Atlantic phenomenon, English Canada also experienced a great stirring of the Social Gospel in the same period, though its political heyday went well into the interwar period. Undoubtedly the Gospel of Wealth and widespread acceptance of Social

---

86. Henson to Rashdall, 14 October 1902, MSS English letter d. 359/27, Hastings Rashdall Papers, Bodleian Library, Oxford University.

87. Lloyd George to Nicoll, 9 September 1909, f. 52, letters, Sir William Robertson Nicoll Papers, National Library of Scotland.

88. Ward, "The Way of the World," f. 52, 301.

Darwinism (as interpreted by wealthy churchgoers) in the United States made American Social Christians seem more revolutionary than the British. Fear of godlessness or Romish influences among the massive number of immigrants, as well as the labor strife of the 1870s and 1880s, also tended to inculcate American Social Christians with a sense of urgency. Given the example of Standard Oil, among other emerging business giants, there was also an obsession with the dangers of *big* business. British reformers made less of an issue of monopoly, some socialists even regarding it as a convenient stage in hastening state ownership. However, as Henry Demarest Lloyd, author of *Wealth Against Commonwealth* (1894), wrote to a British friend: "I thoroughly disbelieve in the policy of some socialists of letting everything drift into the hands of trusts with the idea that we can then by a coup d'economie change masters from monopolist to democracy. Just as we are about to shake ourselves for this grand transformation, we may find, that the process of preparation has annihilated us."[89] The message of achieving social harmony through lessening the excesses of capitalism was similar to that of their English counterparts.

American Social Christians, however, were perhaps driven to postures of greater militancy by the frustrations experienced in attempting to voice their concerns. Gaining admission to the inner councils of government and party was a frustrating business, but even more infuriating was the high degree of corruption they perceived in public life. This, therefore, led to interest in new political parties, as in Britain, and, unlike in Britain, crusades for morality in public life. This latter activity made American Social Christians appear more puritanical than their British counterparts.

British Social Christians visiting America commented in particular upon the oppression of workers in what seemed to be aggressive, resurgent capitalism in the closing decades of the nineteenth century.[90] From the other direction, many American ministers and laypeople feared the emergence of a hostile working class unconnected with the churches. As seen in Chapter 2, C. E. Ordway, W. S. Rainsford, C. M. Morse, and others wrote literature warning of Christianity's loss of the urban working class, literature every bit as alarmist as anything produced by late-Victorian English writers confronted with an even more crucial situation. Class war in cities was regularly predicted by figures such as

89. Lloyd to Arthur G. Symonds, 29 December 1898, box 10, series I, correspondence, Henry Demarest Lloyd Papers, Wisconsin State Historical Society.

90. See, for example, "The Progress of Socialism in the United States," *Economic Review* 1 (January 1891): 57–85, and John Trevor, *An Independent Labour Party,* Labour Church Tracts no. 2 (London, 1892), 5. For personal observations, see Samuel Barnett MS Diary of "Trip to America," 1867, F/BAR/559, Canon Samuel Barnett Papers, Great London Record Office.

Josiah Strong.[91] This threat, perhaps, together with the flood of Continental immigrants, may explain Americans' higher degree of anxiety over the challenge of Marxism.

At the early Lambeth conferences American Episcopal bishops took a decidedly more conservative line on political reform than did their not-very-radical British counterparts. At the 1888 conference the bishop of Manchester could see that the aims of Christian Socialism and of secular socialism were much the same and that this association was legitimate—that these bedfellows were not thrown together merely out of fear of "democracy" or competition from Social Catholicism. Yet the bishop of Mississippi could find in the very word *socialism* "a kind of horror, because there is connected with it the idea of anarchy." He urged that the church bind itself to no specific doctrine of government or property.[92] At the 1897 meeting the bishop of Rochester (England) and the bishop of Hereford encouraged those engaged in socialist enterprises for the common good, while the bishop of Washington supported only traditional philanthropy in dealing with problems such as poverty. As he stated: "[T]he Church will only multiply sources of evil instead of overcoming evil with good if she opposes the greed and selfishness of the rich by siding with the greed and selfishness of the poor."[93]

At the 1908 Lambeth Conference the bishop of Hereford felt that the English Church was now "face to face with a new democracy, that is to say, a democratic awakening to a new sense of power," which included the political emergence of the working class with an educated leadership dissatisfied with existing social and economic conditions. One of his solutions was to urge support of the ILP in the Commons.[94] Individuals on the American bench appeared to have moved considerably toward recognition of the urgency of political support for social reforms. The bishop of Connecticut in fact was willing to concede that the plutocrats of his country were a greater threat to social democracy than the aristocrats of England (who were imbued with a greater sense of public service)

91. Josiah Strong, *The Challenge of the City* (New York, 1907), 158.

92. Proceedings of the Lambeth Conference, 1888, minutes, vol. 2, 6 July 1888, LC 19, ff, 81–95, Lambeth Palace Library. The reaction of Social Christians was mixed. Stewart Headlam's *Church Reformer* ("Bishops on Socialism" [September 1888], 200) described the statements on socialism as a "curious muddle of sound exhortation with trivial or ridiculous practical suggestions."

93. Proceedings of the Lambeth Conference, 1897, minutes, vol. 2, 9 July 1897, subject VII, "The Office of the Church With Respect To Industrial Problems," LC 39, f. 164, Lambeth Palace Library. The statements by the bishops of Rochester and Hereford are found in ff. 190–96 and ff. 149–60 respectively.

94. Proceeding of the Fifth Lambeth Conference, 1908, minutes, vol. 2, "Morning Session: The Moral Witness of the Church in Relation to (a) the Democratic Ideal, (b) Social and Economic Questions," 8 July 1908, f. 4, 7, Lambeth Palace Library.

were to social democracy in that country. Plutocracy, as well as political apathy and corruption, had to be opposed by the American church. Notwithstanding all of this, he added, "The democratic idea, as I understand it, is threatened again by the rising cloud of Socialism, so far as that menaces personality; and the Church ought to confront socialism."[95]

This is not to say that all churchmen on the British side welcomed the increasing number of leading figures expressing a friendly attitude toward socialism. As the *Church Times* critically summarized the political views expressed by Social Christians at the 1908 Pan-Anglican Congress:

> The church is viewed as a philanthropic association, or as a branch of the Independent Labour party. Very little is said about sin (other than that of the capitalist), very little of the need of stern self-discipline and the individual battle for holiness. We know how Dissent has lost ground among its best members by the transformation of its pulpits into political platforms. Yet is not the beam in our own eye, while our people are harangued Sunday by Sunday, on "social questions," on wages, housing, sweating and the rest?[96]

The American Episcopal Church was by no means overly reactionary compared with other churches. American church congresses from the very beginning, in 1875, concerned themselves with the conditions of the working class, and later with the relations of capital and labor (1878), communism and socialism (1879), and the clergy and politics (1891). Indeed, Henry George addressed one session in Detroit in 1884 on the subject "Is Our Civilization Just to Workingmen?" Similar congresses were held, often in imitation of the Episcopalians, by other churches. For example, the Reverend E. H. Johnson of Providence, Rhode Island, instituted the Baptist Congress for the Discussion of Current Questions in 1882. Early annual meetings dwelt on temperance and social aspects of Christianity. However, by the late 1880s much time was devoted to theoretical issues of politics, including socialism.

The American religious press printed a seemingly endless discussion of the definition and morality of socialism. Washington Gladden's belief that social ills must be addressed by the entire community led him to sanction not only the extension of the regulatory powers of government but also government ownership of large utilities. However, Gladden always maintained that inner direction came first, that the socialization of the individual came before the socialization

95. Ibid., f. 14.
96. "The Church and Social Problems," *Church Times*, 14 August 1908, 194.

of society: "That some improvements can be made and must be made in the form of industrial and social organization I do believe; that these improvements will take the general direction of what is known as scientific Socialism I have no doubt; nevertheless, the deepest need is not a change of focus but a change of aims and purposes and tempers."[97]

Somewhat later Walter Rauschenbusch also became convinced that the society was headed for collectivism, largely in response to the excesses of plutocracy. In fact, protection of individual economic rights against abuse by monopolistic Robber Barons necessitated it, or as he put it, "Laissez-faire today means public ownership."[98]

Rauschenbusch, like Gladden, gave no specific timetable but was clear in favoring a gradual approach. Fearful of class warfare, he argued that "it is to the interest of all sides that the readjustment of the social classes should come about as a steady *evolutionary* process."[99] His view of the path to the Kingdom had more of Darwin than of Marx in it. But Rauschenbusch did not become a party member in spite of a close association in his thought between socialism and Christianity.[100]

Such discussions, though rather restrained, were bold enough for their times. Many clergy had associated the word *socialism* with a Continental movement at odds with the very essence of Christianity. Others saw the differences as profound, but requiring a modus vivendi for the sake of social progress. Edward S. Parsons, after a lengthy discussion of such a need, concluded: "The two cannot work together as collaborators. Christianity must be the teacher, and Socialism the pupil."[101]

Some American Social Christians, like their British cousins, also believed in engaging directly with the socialist movement. American socialism, of course, had stronger Continental roots than the British. But native pragmatism and the fate of third parties moved many toward ideas not unlike those found in late-nineteenth-century Britain. The American Fabians, perhaps inspired indirectly by Thomas Davidson's residence in the United States, are one important example. They came to be led in part by the Reverend W.D.P. Bliss, the Boston Episcopal clergyman who modeled himself very much upon the early English

97. Washington Gladden, *Christianity and Socialism* (New York, 1905), 147.

98. Walter Rauschenbusch, *Christianizing the Social Order* (New York, 1912), 433.

99. Walter Rauschenbusch, *Christianity and the Social Crisis* (New York, 1907), 410.

100. See Jacob H. Dorn, "The Social Gospel and Socialism: A Comparison of the Thought of Francis Greenwood Peabody, Washington Gladden, and Walter Rauschenbusch," *Church History* 62, no. 1 (1993): 82–100.

101. Edward S. Parsons, "A Christian Critique of Socialism," *Andover Review* 11 (January–June 1889): 611.

Christian Socialists, who had wanted to Christianize socialism. In fact, Bliss and fellow New England Episcopalians introduced a Christian Socialist circle into the United States, paralleling the British developments of the 1880s. George and Bellamy eventually inspired him to work toward socializing Christianity, and in 1890 Bliss left the ministry to found the Mission of the Carpenter and to publish the *Dawn*.

Bliss's activities became increasingly secular after 1900, as he moved from the Christian Socialist Fellowship into the Socialist Party. This move reaffirmed an earlier position in which he had expressed doubts about allowing existing old parties to "bid for the Collectivist vote," believing that in their corrupt state, "if they undertook to Nationalize or Municipalize any monopolies, they would do it wrongly and poorly and make a failure of it, and then let all the foes of Collectivism say we told you so." Rather he had urged a slower pace "working towards a new party."[102] In this he provided a model for later clergy who would follow the same path, such as the New York Presbyterian pastor Norman Thomas. Bliss used terms such as *scientific socialism* and once stated that "private wealthy subverted Christian morality."[103] But he rejected doctrines of class violence and extremes of the greatest of "scientific socialists"—Marx. Hence, the influence of Bellamy as well as the gradualist views of the British Fabian Sydney Webb can be seen in figures such as Bliss. He also believed that clergy, like other Social Christians, should actively engage in politics.

A noted disciple of Bliss was the academic Vida Scudder. Scudder in many ways was a better guide to the essence of Blissian socialism than Bliss himself, except that she viewed Bellamy's utopia as Philistine. With a blend of Christian (Episcopalian) fervor and social evolutionary theory, she believed that a socialist society was the next stage in a higher, more progressive, and more Christlike civilization. In a way, Christ's religion was the religion of the future because it was socialistic. Socialism was basic; it shifted "supervision of physical needs and responsibility for physical support which now falls upon the individual, to the collective whole, that is, to the state."[104] But there was also a strong streak of Christian individualism in her thought. The axiom "Take no thought for the morrow," from Christ's teachings, would lead in a future collectivist welfare society to concentration upon moral self-perfection. As Scudder stated, "Char-

102. Bliss to Ely, 30 March 1891, box 6, Ely Papers.

103. Arthur Mann, *Yankee Reformers in Urban Age: Social Reform in Boston, 1880–1900* (Cambridge, Mass., 1954), 93. See also Richard B. Dressner, "William Dwight Porter Bliss's Christian Socialism," *Church History* 47, no. 1 (1978): 66–82.

104. Vida Scudder, "Socialism and Spiritual Progress," *Andover Review* 16 (July–December 1891): 59.

acter only emerges as we escape from the barren individualism of the savage state."[105]

Scudder, like Bliss, deplored class violence, arguing that "[s]ocialism is no demand for a destructive evolution, but the next step upward in the journey of the human race. This is made evident whether we look at the teachings of science or of faith."[106] These Christian Socialists were middle-class, and their appeal by and large was in that direction, revealing considerable gaps in their knowledge of the working class in spite of their selected agitations for shorter working hours and the improvement of other aspects of the workplace.

One disciple of Bliss, Herbert Newton Casson, attempted to remedy the lack of dialogue with the working classes, however. Formerly a Methodist minister in Canada, Casson had journeyed to Boston in the 1890s and had become an assistant editor on Bliss's *Encyclopedia of Social Reform.* Seeing both his own power of persuasion with the working people (leading the so-called Boston Common Riot of 1893) and fearing the growing influence of Marxist socialism, Casson decided to adapt the ideas of the British Labour Church to the American scene. According to Leslie Wharton, Casson's Labour Church was closer to Trevor's dream than what had been accomplished in Britain.[107] Totally rejecting conventional churches and conventional Christian Socialism, Casson refused to admit anyone but bona fide laborers. Though he rented three halls, his church in Lynn was the most successful in attracting a working-class following. His writing consistently defended trade unions.[108] Taking a leaf from the book of some American populists and the German Christian Socialist Adolf Stöcker, he unfortunately indulged in some degree of anti-Semitism to attract attention. In a famous pamphlet entitled *Red Light,* which attacked capitalists and financiers, he announced: "Shakespeare has been revised, and Shylock is now the hero of the play. Portia's plea for mercy is revolutionary, and Bassanio is a repudiator. After centuries of contempt, the money-lending Jew is having his revenge upon the world. Once his trade was the most disreputable in Europe, but today he is the master of nations."[109]

His son's biography argues that Casson later departed from such thoughts, working among Russian Jews in New York as well as engaging in other work at

105. Ibid., 49.
106. Ibid., 66.
107. Leslie Wharton, "Casson and the American Labour Church," *Essex Institute Historical Collections* 117, no. 2 (1981): 122–23.
108. Herbert Newton Casson, *Organized Self-Help: A History and Defence of the American Labor Movement* (New York, 1901).
109. Herbert Newton Casson, *Red Light* (Lynn, Mass., Lynn Labour Church, 1898), 10.

the Ruskin Colony in Tennessee.[110] He is also credited with writing a book for Sam "Golden Rule" Jones of Toledo on behalf of the eight-hour workday. By the end of the century the Lynn church had disappeared, and by 1915 Casson had started a new and final career in England as a leader of the Efficiency Movement, which sought a solution to social ills through a better-run economy based on superior social organization.[111]

Casson had made the most pointed attempt to reach the industrial working class. But while his message was radical in approach, in theory it proceeded not much further than Bliss's. The figure who set the theoretical limits of American Social Christianity was George D. Herron. Chair of Christian Sociology at Iowa (later Grinnell) College and founder of the American Institute of Christian Sociology, Herron attempted to broaden the academic interests of his followers to include immediate political matters. Though John R. Commons, Graham Taylor, and some other professors could associate with his institute and its quasi-academic pursuits, other Social Christian academics such as Albion Small attacked him for confusing political activism with real social science (and true Christianity).[112]

Herron's Kingdom Movement, which he jointly launched with Iowa College president George A. Gates, aimed at rousing the churches, especially Congregationalist, to the social issues of the 1890s.[113] Throughout the period he grounded his public utterances in Christian rhetoric, even at times in traditional Protestant Evangelicalism.[114] His attacks upon Spencerianism and its capitalist underpinnings ultimately led him to equate individualism with sin. But the strident nature of his denunciations, in spite of their religious phraseology, shocked and offended. His views about the evolving nature of politics left little to the imagination. As he stated in the mid-1890s, "A pure social democracy is the political fulfilment of Christianity."[115]

Herron's activities were not confined to the theoretical. Rejecting the gradualism of figures such as Bliss, Herron believed in immediate action. He was involved with Midwestern populism, gave qualified support to Henry George,

110. Edward E. Casson, *Postscript: The Life and Thoughts of Herbert N. Casson* (London, c. 1952), 28–29.

111. See Jose Harris, *Private Lives, Public Spirit: A Social History of Britain, 1870–1914* (Oxford, 1993), 231.

112. Small to Ely, 15 June 1894, box 14, Ely Papers.

113. See Robert T. Handy, "George D. Herron and the Kingdom Movement," *Church History* 19, no. 2 (June 1950): 97–115.

114. See George D. Herron, *Social Meanings of Religious Experiences* (1896; reprint, New York, 1969).

115. George D. Herron, *The Christian State: A Political Vision of a Course of Six Lectures Delivered in Churches in Various American Cities* (1895; reprint, New York, 1968), 75.

and later gave public support to the Social Democrats and the Socialist Party. This, together with his published view of the inevitability of class revolution (though he abhorred such an event) and his thorough knowledge of Marx, made him a suspect figure to middle-class Americans. His correspondence with Morris Hillquit, the socialist leader, reveals that he bickered with other Christian Social figures such as Stitt Wilson, the Canadian-born Social Gospel revivalist and eventual socialist mayor of Berkeley, and Walter Rauschenbusch, whom he regarded as a parasite on the socialist movement because he wrote not for the working class but "in the interests of the church."[116] His direct knowledge of French and German socialist circles was considerable, affording him the means to produce a devastating critique of British and Continental Social Christians.[117] But because of an attempt by college trustees to remove him from his teaching post at Iowa, a divorce, and his departure for Europe, Herron faded from the American political stage after 1901.

The Red Scare of the 1890s did much to limit the overt support among prominent Social Christians for political socialism. The trials not only of Herron but more particularly of Richard T. Ely and John R. Commons, among others, may, according to Dorothy Ross, have turned their overt political activities away from socialism and toward the more acceptable "liberalism" of the Progressive era.[118] They may have also inhibited figures such as Rauschenbusch from engaging in direct political activity at all in spite of increasing disenchantment with the prevailing social order. In any case, as Martin Marty has indicated, Social Gospelers on the whole were aloof from socialism (in spite of the Social Gospel rhetoric of Eugene Debs), which as a political force peaked with only 6 percent of the vote in the 1912 election.[119] In that election the four major presidential candidates all represented to varying degrees the general assumptions of the Social Gospel, merged with general reformism.[120]

Progressivism, as espoused by respectable Republicans and Democrats, was an important conduit for Social Christian ideas. As such it attracted many moderate Social Gospelers to its ranks. In turn they often gained limited access to the corridors of political power. Lyman Abbott would make the best case study of these relationships. Successor to Henry Ward Beecher as pastor of

116. Herron to Hillquit, 5 February 1908, box 1, Morris Hillquit Papers, Wisconsin State Historical Society.

117. Ibid., 21 December 1907.

118. Dorothy Ross, "Socialism and American Liberalism: Academic Social Thought in the 1880s," *Perspectives in American History* 11 (1977–78): 7–79.

119. Marty, *Modern American Religion,* 1:294.

120. Oscar Handlin, *The Americans: A New History of the People of the United States* (Boston, 1963), 348.

Brooklyn's famous Plymouth Church, Abbott had already achieved considerable recognition as editor of the *Christian Union* (1876–1912)—renamed *Outlook* in 1893). A theological liberal, Abbott also encouraged liberal political
reforms. His attitude toward socialists was expressed early on in his pastorate at
Plymouth when he contrasted their idea of societal reform with "the change of
character rather than of environment" allegedly prescribed by Christ.[121] Much
later, social ethician Francis Greenwood Peabody argued a similar line, emphasizing the need to address the moral flaw in humankind in his rejection of the
mechanical approach of the socialists.[122]

Abbott's appetite for political and social reform did not abate with his
rejection of formal socialism. Indeed, he was a principal architect of Progressivism, that peculiar blend of reformist ideas that in the United States, as in Britain,
provided the best opportunity for Social Christians to influence government
policy directly. As I have shown, by the 1912 presidential campaign virtually all
candidates claimed to be Progressives. But the earlier formulation of the
Progressivism came out of the cooperation of national, state, and local politicians with ministers and others concerned with reform. Theodore Roosevelt
emerged earliest as the national champion of Progressivism, and Abbott
became a close adviser. Abbott's reflections conveyed to Roosevelt concerning
political change in 1908 really summarized the essence of Progressivism:

> From the doctrine of our fathers that every individual is able to take
> care of his own interests, and that government should confine itself to
> the protection of persons and property and leave the individual to look
> after his own concerns, we have advanced to the faith that society is
> able to care collectively for its common interests and is to be encour-
> aged so to do. The first doctrine is individual democracy; the second is
> social democracy. They are not inconsistent, but they are not the same.
> The second is an evolution from the first.
>
>     This, at least, is my interpretation of the present world movement,
> and an understanding of it is necessary in order to comprehend the
> change which has taken place in both the Republican and the Demo-
> cratic parties.[123]

Roosevelt's trust-busting programs received vigorous support from Abbott.
In this opposition to monopoly both men revealed a strong belief in the power

121. Lyman Abbott, "Christianity Versus Socialism," *North American Review* 148 (1889): 453.
122. Dorn, "The Social Gospel and Socialism," 86.
123. Abbott to Theodore Roosevelt, 10 July 1908, Abbott Papers, Bowdoin College.

of the state over the menace of plutocracy. Abbott's views, however, were often subjected to criticism. As he wrote to Roosevelt: "I believe that I have been reported to be everything, theologically, in disguise, from a Jesuit to an atheist; and everything, sociologically, from a paid advocate of capitalism to a wild-eyed anarchist."[124]

Abbott, in spite of criticism, became the model for large numbers of Social Gospel ministers who publicly endorsed national, state, and municipal politicians claiming to be Progressives in the decades before World War I. His correspondence included letters from a variety of Social Gospelers seeking influence and advice in the realm of politics. These included even the Reverend Charles Sheldon of Topeka, Kansas, celebrated author of *In His Steps*, who once wrote to Abbott concerning Roosevelt's political stance toward temperance:

> I have never been able to find out from anybody whether he [Theodore Roosevelt] believed in local option, in high license or simply in moral suasion, and regarded the liquor business as entirely outside of politics. I have wondered whether you would be willing to tell me what his exact convictions in the matter are? I have felt at times as if Mr. Roosevelt represented great causes for which I could become very enthusiastic but I have never gotten over my bewilderment at the absolute silence he maintains on what seems to us is a tremendous evil.[125]

Before World War I Progressivism seemed the political notion most representative of mainstream Social Gospelers in the United States. From Gladden to Rauschenbusch to a host of lesser figures in the movement, all sought to influence Progressives. Lyman Abbott occupied a special niche in that regard because of his degree of access to the corridors of power. In recognition of this, Methodist leader Shailer Matthews wrote to Abbott in 1914: "I wish it were possible for you to say in your volume [*Reminiscences*] how much the country owes to you for leadership in the liberalization and vitalization of religion."[126]

It is quite possible to argue that, as in Britain, there was much self-delusion in the idea that Social Gospelers on the whole had influenced the body politic. Certainly some historians, such as Paul Merkley, would adhere more or less to

124. Ibid., 8 September 1908.
125. Sheldon to Abbott, 28 May 1912, Abbott Papers.
126. Matthews to Abbott, 26 January 1914, Abbott Papers.

this line in arguing that the claim that the Social Gospel had informed and fused with the national purpose was false. The Social Gospel, to Merkley, reflected rather than produced Progressivism.[127]

In the political sphere the concerns of Social Gospelers remained narrow. According to Martin Marty, "few pages of the Social Gospel" were given over to creativity on behalf of visible minorities.[128] Informed by British and European models, Social Gospelers had been largely intellectual, mostly confined to groups at the top of society though with the occasional foray, as in Europe, directly toward the urban working classes. The black question remained largely nonpolitical at this point, as confirmed even by sympathetic foreign visitors such as Edward Grubb, the British Quaker socialist, who saw it largely as a Southern social problem needing educational and social work initiatives.[129] But some Social Gospelers viewed the condition of African Americans as a national problem and had taken action. The Reverend Joseph Roy, writing in *The Kingdom* in 1896, felt that by raising the economic status of black Americans a foundation for racial harmony could and must be established. As he stated, "[P]aying taxes makes men conservative."[130] Eugene Debs could say more or less the same thing seven years later,[131] there having been no tangible achievements in the interim.

In Canada organized socialist political activities on the part of clergy were somewhat restricted before the Great War. This may partially have been the result of the mainline Protestant Church leadership's early political activism on behalf of Social Christianity. The situation in the largest of the Protestant denominations—the Methodists—is a case in point. Certainly the power brokerage of Albert Carman seems to have predominated into the early twentieth century. Harassing both plutocrats and godless socialists, he built powerful links to major national and provincial party organizations.[132] The Liberal Party,

127. See Paul Merkley, "The Vision of the Good Society in the Social Gospel," in *Historical Papers* (Ottawa, Canadian Historical Association, 1987), 138–56.

128. Marty, *Modern American Religion*, 1:294.

129. Edward Grubb visited America in 1901, 1904, and 1907, according to his manuscript autobiography (Temp. MSS box ³⁵⁄₆, Friends' House Library, London). His 1901 trip was reported in the *British Friend* 10, no. 3 (1901). In 1904 he discussed the race problem with both Booker T. Washington and President Theodore Roosevelt (MS autobiography, ibid., 133–35). However, his main concerns over the treatment of blacks were in the context of penal administration in the southern states.

130. The Reverend Joseph Roy, "The Negro Problem," *Kingdom*, 7 August 1896.

131. Eugene Debs, "The Negro and Class Struggle," in *Writings and Speeches of Eugene V. Debs* (New York, 1948), 65.

132. Carman's involvement in politics at the federal and provincial levels can be seen in his extensive correspondence with politicians (Carman Papers, United Church Archives), especially Liberal leaders from the 1860s to 1914.

with its urgent prodding toward a more rigid temperance policy, was a particularly useful conduit in this regard. William Magney indeed sees the Methodist Church as mainly responsible for a "National Gospel" suffusing many areas of public life with ideals of moral improvement and social service before 1914.[133]

Carman's successor as general superintendent before the war, S. D. Chown, displayed more openly the liberal theology and activism in social reform associated with the Social Gospel. In so doing Chown was temporarily able to keep more radical political activists such as J. S. Wordsworth within the fold, delaying the formation of the People's Churches until after the First World War. Moving away from Carman's overt political alliances, Chown preferred to apply the force of Christianity using single-issue pressure tactics through the Department of Evangelism and Social Service.[134] His friends included younger, socially concerned politicians such as the Chicago-trained W. L. MacKenzie King.

In Chown's travels abroad he not only met great British Social Christians, such as R. J. Campbell, but also observed the social reform program of David Lloyd George within the Asquith government and stated that it was "the most perfect expression of the Sermon on the Mount that ever reached the statute books of any country."[135]

Politically, he aligned himself with a conventional middle-class reformism, as did supporters of Progressivism to the south. Though he understood the grievances that generated labor unrest, he opposed Labour Churches, believing that "[t]he Christian must be greater than a class."[136] Indeed, without a creed of public service, the "rude arrogance" of some working-class leaders offended him as much as wealth.[137] He never really understood socialism, but pronouncements such as "We must Christianize our democracy and democratize our christianity at one and the same time or accept the failure of both" seemed to satisfy most progressive clergy and laypeople concerning his intentions.[138] His own record in the field of welfare legislation as well as temperance reform was exemplary. He was unusual in his strong support for the rights of native peoples.[139]

133. William H. Magney, "The Methodist Church and the National Gospel, 1884–1914," *The Bulletin* (United Church of Canada), no. 20 (1968).

134. Chown tended to concentrate on single issues in his politics, but he had a host of political contacts, such as Sir Leonard Tilley and W. G. Martin, Ontario minister of public welfare. He also used the print media to apply pressure on his political friends.

135. Chown, address at Wesley College, *Saskatoon Phoenix,* 7 June 1913.

136. "Notes for an Address on Canada and the United States," n.d., p. 18, box 1, file no. 22a, Chown Papers.

137. "Conference Address, 1912," 12, addresses, Chown Papers.

138. "Industrial Address," n.d., 7, addresses, Chown Papers.

139. "Lo, the Poor Indian!" box 9, file no. 191a, Chown Papers.

The First World War introduced a particularly difficult set of issues for the Social Christians on both sides of the Atlantic. In Canada Protestant church leaders initially gave enthusiastic support to the cause of empire. This was in keeping with recent history where Canadian Social Christians had not been conspicuously divided over the Boer War. Indeed, Goldwin Smith wrote to James Bryce in 1902, denouncing all of the churches, except the Baptists, for their overt support for the imperial cause.[140] With strong patriotism exhibited from the pulpits of English Canada, the pattern again generally held true. As a khaki-garbed Chown announced in 1916 concerning military service: "It is immoral for any man to enjoy the blessings conferred by the community, and not contribute his utmost to its welfare."[141]

His tour of combat zones and camps during and after the war changed many of his views. After visiting Vimy Ridge, he commented that "the ruins once seen can never be forgotten."[142] Following the war the man who had worn khaki denounced militarism. David Marshall sees his tour of battlefields as the beginning also of serious reservations about the "modern emphasis on social salvation,"[143] reservations that built upon some slighter prewar doubts. Liberalism as philosophy or theology, with its highly optimistic view of human nature, was gravely shaken by the war. Some Social Christians would go further; Canadian pacifism took a significant leap toward a more integrationist movement, away from the influence of isolated church groups.[144] For Woodsworth the war was the last straw, though it was not the only factor in his departure from formal church ministry,[145] which poised Woodsworth for political leadership in a new and vital chapter in the history of Canadian Social Christianity following the war.

In Britain, as in Canada, enthusiasm for the war was strong among most church leaders at its outset. But the Boer War had politically divided prominent Social Christians in Britain more than in Canada, also shattering the already

140. Smith to Bryce, 11 January 1902, Goldwin Smith Papers, microfilm copy, Cornell University Library.

141. "National Service: Letters to Members and Adherents of the Methodist Church on War, 29 December 1916," p. i, box 10, file 221, Chown Papers.

142. "The Story of My Life," n.d., p. 84, box 10, file no. 211, Chown Papers.

143. David Marshall, *Secularizing the Faith: Canadian Protestant Clergy and the Crisis of Belief, 1850–1940* (Toronto, 1992), 179.

144. See Thomas P. Socknat, *Witness Against War: Pacifism in Canada, 1900–1945* (Toronto, 1987).

145. For a consideration of the late Victorian crisis of faith as applied to this Canadian figure, see Mark D. Johnson, "The Crisis of Faith and Social Christianity: The Ethical Pilgrimage of James Shaver Woodsworth," in *Victorian Faith in Crisis: Essays in Continuity and Change in Nineteenth-Century Religious Belief,* ed. Richard J. Helmstadter and Bernard Lightman (Stanford, 1990), 315–79.

shaky solidarity between Liberal imperialists (who were so often social re-
formists) on the one side and many socialists and ILP members on the other.
In Britain, possessing one of the oldest pacifist movements in Europe, a
host of secular figures, mainly of Liberal background, in organizations such as
E. D. Morel's Union of Democratic Control, now joined traditional opponents of
war such as the Quakers. Individuals such as George Lansbury and Clifford
Allen, with Social Christian leanings, were among those Labour Party leaders
to stand with the minority supporting Ramsay MacDonald in opposition to
the war.[146]

Many Social Christians stood for the war effort or at least stood on the
sidelines, not disputing the public church support for the cause. But the goals of
Social Christianity were decidedly relegated to the file on future plans. Before
the war Evan Thomas (brother of Norman Thomas), a young American student,
had traveled to Britain to study theology and social service concepts of the
Presbyterians in Edinburgh. Following a period of admiration for British Social
Christianity, pessimism set in with the outbreak of the war. As he noted in a
letter to his mother: "People in larger or smaller audiences flock to churches for
intercessory services where they pray for victory, like ignorant 'heathen' or silly
puppets."[147] About a year earlier he had written to his sister-in-law: "Tell
Norman after talking with one or two of the ministers I have practically given
up my social survey plan. In the first place the war is the one and only thing of
any account in the land at present. In the second place the ministers won't tell
what they really think about social problems, and in the third place it wouldn't
do me much good if they would."[148]

British war leaders' inability to regulate drink coupled with their propensity
to talk of conscription made them seem particularly hypocritical to the young
Thomas. After 1916 the social restrictions of "war socialism," which included
regulating pub hours, came too late for young Evan Thomas, who returned to
the United States a pacifist.

Albert Marrin and Alan Wilkinson have written good studies of the Church of
England in its response to the war, and the latter author has reversed the
picture somewhat by supplying an additional good study of pacifists in all the
churches during and after the war.[149] What was significant was indeed the

146. See Arthur Marwick, *Clifford Allen: The Open Conspirator* (Edinburgh, 1964).

147. Evan Thomas to his mother, 10 December 1916, series VIII, subseries A, reel 85, Norman
Thomas Papers, microfilm edition, New York Public Library.

148. Evan Thomas to his sister-in-law, 17 November 1915, ibid.

149. See Albert Marrin, *The Last Crusade: The Church of England in the First World War*
(Durham, N.C., 1974); Alan Wilkinson, *The Church of England and the First World War* (London,

waning of religious initiative compared with the enhanced influence of secular forces. Social Christians could interpret the coming of collectivism as the fulfillment of their earlier hopes for state intervention on behalf of the oppressed. Certainly by-products such as the Whitley Councils, devised in part by the Quaker Malcolm Sparkes, proceeded along the lines of the dialogue between labor and capital long urged by many Social Christians. The corporatism of these years would encourage those dedicated to the professional ideal in the postwar period, as Harold Perkin has described it, including Social Christians such as R. H. Tawney.[150]

However, for many others the war represented an extension of capitalist power through state-directed militarism. As George Lansbury wrote to the Reverend Dick Sheppard in the midst of the war:

> If the churches are to be saved they must tackle this problem and must proclaim to the whole world that competition for bread, competition for markets, scrambling for the rich places of the earth and covering it over with what Cecil Rhodes would call an excuse based on unctuous rectitude, only makes all of us partners in the hideous mockery. And at this juncture because the State orders men to go and fight for a country they do not own, it is considered that we must all obey the State and conscience is not allowed to come in. But even if this question were properly dealt with there would still remain the great problem of riches and poverty and this crusade, if it is to be of any worth must have clear-cut opinions as to how the gulf between rich and poor is to be bridged.[151]

Woodsworth had come to roughly the same conclusion in Canada, and indeed so did both Norman Thomas (who left the ministry) and his brother Evan in the United States. As Evan stated in a letter to his mother, through nonresistance a man "once and for all frees himself from moral responsibility for this present social order."[152] By the postwar period British Quakers had

---

1978); and idem, *Dissent or Conformity: War, Peace, and the English Churches, 1900–1945* (London, 1986).

150. Perkin calls Tawney "the prophet of professional society." Harold Perkin, *The Rise of Professional Society: England Since 1880* (London, 1989), 336.

151. Lansbury to Sheppard, 18 December 1916, Lansbury file, Hugh Richard Lawrie Sheppard Papers (in possession of the Right Honorable Lady Richardson of Duntisbourne).

152. Evan Thomas to his mother, 28 April 1917, series VIII, subseries A, Thomas Papers.

actually linked the issues of peace and a Christian social order inextricably within a church department.[153]

In the United States the issue of the war was more complex, even though American participation lasted scarcely more than a year. Social Gospelers had been more fundamentally divided over the Spanish-American War and the Philippine insurrection than their British and Canadian counterparts over the Boer War. While Josiah Strong strongly backed the assertion of Anglo-Saxon power, most Social Gospelers opposed war as an instrument of national policy.

The circumstances of America's entry into World War I appeared quite idealistic and thus less divisive. Some former pacifists actually supported President Wilson. Social Christian pastors such as Gerald Beard of Bridgeport, Connecticut, delivered innumerable sermons on the moral righteousness of America's cause against German militarism.[154] As John Piper Jr. has detailed in his *American Churches in World War I* (1985), the Federal Council of Churches engaged in a massive expansion of services, many of which fell under the rubric of social ministry. Robert T. Handy has pointed out that their president, Frank Mason North, adopted a policy not of patriotism but of getting on with the special duties of the churches in these circumstances.[155] Interchurch cooperation leapt ahead on an unprecedented scale. But Handy has also noted the serious reflections engendered at war's end concerning the expanded regulatory power of the state.[156]

One reaction to such developments was to embrace this expanded power of the state for Social Christian ends. That path led logically to Prohibition in the 1920s. Others worked toward the sharper definition and protection of civil liberties against intolerant, arbitrary state power. By 1918 serious division between Social Gospelers began to emerge over these issues.

The Fellowship of Reconciliation could be found on both sides of the Atlantic (the American branch forming after a joint meeting in 1915). In their pacifist activities some Social Christians were to find considerable satisfaction, reclaiming moral authority for themselves, which they feared was falling to their secular humanitarian colleagues.

The First World War had demonstrated to all Social Christians how rapidly the powers of the state could be extended in times of national emergency. This

---

153. The War and Social Order Committee was established in 1915. It was replaced by the Industrial and Social Order Council in 1928, which finally disbanded in 1957.

154. "The Fight for Democracy," 15 July 1917, box 14, sermon no. 1136, file 206, series II, manuscript group no. 65, George H. Beard Papers, Yale Divinity School Library.

155. Robert T. Handy, *Undermined Establishment* (Princeton, 1991), 168.

156. Ibid., 190.

encouraged them to hope that social justice on a more collectivist basis was achievable in the near future. But the state had also demonstrated Its incredible power to control and set its own priorities regardless of the support or opposition of the churches. In this Social Christians found themselves ironically in a position, rather new to them, not unlike that which had always been experienced by their German counterparts.[157] The path to the interventionist and politically responsive New Jerusalem had become altogether more complicated and potentially hazardous.

157. W. Reginald Ward, *Theology, Sociology and Politics: The German Protestant Social Conscience, 1890–1933* (Berne, 1979), 36.

# 7

## THE WIDENING WORLD OF POLITICS AND THE KINGDOM

Diversity, bordering on confusion, was characteristic of the political role of Social Christianity after 1918. Whereas before the war many Social Christians were confident in their support of a growing state interventionism as well as a generally optimistic, progressive view of the future, things now had changed. Collectivism in league with authoritarianism could produce results that might serve vested interests rather than social justice, war rather than international social harmony. The New Jerusalem must not be confused with Hobbes's Leviathan.

The shaken confidence of the pre-World War I era was beneath the surface, however. In the United States the "social creed" approach prevailed, even taken up in spirit by the Roman Catholic bishops in their program of social reconstruction in 1919. The same could be said of Canada. In Britain the midwar National Mission of Repentance and Hope ended at war's end with *Christianity and Industrial Problems,* a report issued by an archbishops' inquiry committee that included CSU bishops, R. H. Tawney, and the politician George Lansbury. Other denominational documents, such as the Quakers' Foundations statement, were equally impressive in declaring that churches had an obligation to move into the area of public affairs to remove social ills resulting from economic injustice. According to David Jeremy, 1918 marked the beginning of two decades in which the churches, largely spearheaded by Social Christians, were to throw themselves with great vigor into the operations of business and the actual workings of the economy.[1] These efforts led quickly to the formation of the Industrial Christian Fellowship as well as COPEC. They also led some to realize that the aims of Social Christianity might be achieved in a more indirect way—for example, by a redeemed, socially responsive capitalism that in concert with an emerging welfare state would raise the standard of living. Politics was bound to become more complex under such circumstances.

Juxtaposed with these developments was the impression of the declining social influence of the churches in the public life of the nation in the same period. One was not necessarily a function of the other, but the situation did raise questions about the actual impact of Social Christianity. In Britain the roots of church decline predated the Great War; in fact, in numerical terms there was no dramatic evidence of change in membership or attendance, especially for the Church of England, in the interwar period.[2] In North America numerical decline was even less evident, given the rising tide of fundamentalism. In North America it was perhaps the influence of clergy, Social Christian or otherwise, that was in doubt. The clergy were no longer prime purveyors of information and guidance for the world about us. The position of the intellectual, liberal-minded clergyman was now rivaled by the government bureaucrat and social scientist. The more down-to-earth, social pastor was being crowded out by the social worker and, to a lesser degree than in Britain, the trade union official. Opinion polls also indicated that liberal, socially concerned pastors could annoy as many churchgoers as they could inspire.[3] Keen politicians could sense these things. The Social Gospel minister was no longer to be displayed on the election platform as a supportive trophy. Yet in both Britain and North America politics remained a vital area for Social Christians, perhaps even more so given their declining fortunes in social service, social science, and modes of communication by the second decade of the twentieth century, as revealed in Chapters 3 and 4.

For many Social Christians their political ways returned to business as usual, albeit with some caution. For them the goal of social harmony remained. For a considerable minority, however, new paths had to be taken and new prophets had to be sought. Could social harmony always achieve social justice? In some instances class conflict was now to be embraced. The resulting political picture

---

1. See David Jeremy, *Capitalists and Christians: Business Leaders and the Churches in Britain, 1900–1960* (Oxford, 1990), chap. 5.

2. David Butler and Jennie Freeman, *British Political Facts, 1900–1967,* 2d ed. (London, 1968), chap. 21, and Edward Royle, *Modern Britain: A Social History, 1750–1985* (London, 1987), 336.

3. See below and note 121 to Chapter 4.

would become more complex, further complicated by the machinations of politicians. Equally important, secular reformism was also changing, and in ways peculiar to each country. The result was a disparity between political results in Britain and those in North America, as well as widening disputes on the very fundamentals of the role of Social Christians in politics. Political experience would become so fractured that by the end of the period little would remain of an Anglo-American framework of political discussion for Social Christians.

## New and Old Directions in the Twenties

The juxtaposition of opportunities for the advancement of Social Christianity with incipient threats to its continued existence lay at the base of much that would follow. The perilous nature of this situation was undoubtedly realized by many Social Christians and helps to explain the curious mixture of the new with the old in policies for the postwar years. Insecurity goes far to explain the renewed political emphasis upon temperance in North America and to some extent even in Britain.

Prohibition received most attention in the United States, and with the ratification of the Eighteenth Amendment the manufacture and sale of intoxicants was prohibited from January 1920. For some Social Gospelers this represented a singular national triumph, which made them the envy of their counterparts elsewhere. Its effect may have been additionally positive insofar as it directed energies away from the turmoil of the Red Scare immediately after the war.[4] But the early 1920s in fact represented a period of intense uneasiness for American Social Christians. According to Paul Carter, the Social Gospel in many respects was at odds with normalcy following the demise of Progressivism.[5] More than one historian has indicated that Prohibition acted as a surrogate for the Social Gospel during the decade.[6] If so, it can help to explain the political inertia of the 1920s. To the radical Social Gospelers the Red Scare of the immediate postwar years was a scandal. Protests were raised over this and the treatment of labor but to no avail.

4. Martin E. Marty, *Modern American Religion*, vol. 2, *The Noise of Conflict, 1919–1941* (Chicago, 1991), 66–72.
5. Paul Carter, *The Decline and Revival of Social Gospel: Social and Political Liberalism in American Protestant Churches, 1920–1940* (Hamden, Conn., 1971), 31.
6. Sydney E. Ahlstrom (quoting Paul Carter), *A Religious History of the American People* (New Haven, 1972), 902.

Norman Thomas rose to leadership of the Socialist Party in 1926, after his departure from the Presbyterian pulpit, a departure similar to J. S. Woodsworth's in Canada. Earlier he had worked for the Fellowship of Reconciliation as editor of the *World Tomorrow*. In his pacifism he anticipated the direction many Social Christians would take by the end of the decade. In helping to found the Civil Liberties Union, he helped to defend the interests of the more militant political radicals within Social Christianity. Thomas, of course, was hemmed in, on the one side, by those moving toward Marxism and, on the other side, by more moderate Social Gospelers who believed that they still held influence over the major political parties in spite of Woodrow Wilson's death and William Jennings Bryan's defection to fundamentalism and then his death. This was the decade of ascendant Republicanism, with Harding, Coolidge, and Hoover in the White House. One is struck by the large number of clergy who corresponded regularly with Thomas in the interwar period.[7] This may well have followed from the demise of Progressivism. They had no real political home. Normalcy was the order of the day. The middle class seemed less interested in the message of social woes that streamed from their periodicals in the 1920s. Perhaps the many wanted a purer religious message, disentangled from politics. Fundamentalism was also on the rise, contributing to the so-called Great Reversal from social concerns expressed through politics. As George Marsden has said of the diverse assemblage of fundamentalists, their one unifying factor was "the overwhelming predominance of political conservatism."[8]

In Canada temperance legislation had been achieved in every province by virtue of the war, making almost realizable a prime goal of social reconstruction held by a majority of prewar Canadian Social Gospelers. Recent federal legislation was used by a number of provinces to prohibit liquor crossing their provincial boundaries in the years immediately after the war. Political radicalism and tendencies toward class warfare were also evident in various parts of the Dominion by 1919, especially in Winnipeg, and this tended to split Social Gospel ranks in a potentially serious way. Canada, of course, was ripe for some waves of protest, given the comparatively primitive state of social legislation before 1919 and the economic dislocations of the postwar period. As it turned out, in the sequence of developments that would follow, the temperance triumph was to do the churches less good and the class unrest less harm than anticipated.

7. General correspondence, series I, October 1905–October 1933 (reel 1), Norman Thomas Papers, microfilm edition, New York Public Library.
8. George M. Marsden, *Fundamentalism and American Culture: The Shaping of Twentieth-Century Evangelicalism, 1870–1925* (New York, 1980), 92.

Social Christians had for all intents and purposes used temperance to unify advocates of different types of Christian social engineering as well as to diminish the gulf between themselves and older, conservative Evangelicals in the mainline churches. In the period after the war the cause of Prohibition peaked and then rapidly declined. It reached its peak not only because of the cooperation of federal and provincial governments but because labor and women's groups seemed also to espouse the cause so vehemently before 1920. However, once in place, the opposition arguments that crime increased under Prohibition, that individual liberty was infringed, and, in some cases, that liquor control worked better than Prohibition seemed to gain ground by the early 1920s. Referenda in the same period indicated that a majority of Canadians (perhaps immigrant populations could be included here) were no longer supportive. By the end of the 1920s all provinces except Prince Edward Island had legislatively retreated from full prohibition.[9]

Richard Allen has noted the lack of enthusiasm among Anglicans for Prohibition.[10] There were also divisions between Social Gospelers, such as that between Ernest Thomas and A. J. Irwin, about the efficiency of Prohibition, as opposed to educational enterprises, in wooing public support to the cause. There were also the concerns of S. D. Chown and others about the need to Canadianize the immigrant population,[11] a need even more acute in their eyes in the turbulent postwar period, which could again explain the subordination of temperance. For more settled areas, areas less affected by immigration, Ernest Forbes has described how Prohibition became divorced from social reform in the public mind by the end of the 1920s, becoming an archaic throwback of "censorious fanaticism."[12] The coercive power of the state was to be avoided in this no less than in the settling of labor matters and other questions.

On the labor front, the churches had moved before the end of the war from concern to action in an effort to restrain unregulated capitalism. The Social Service and Evangelism Committee of the Methodist Church issued a report in 1919 advocating government economic planning. The 1916–17 reports summarizing the results of annual meetings of committees had focused upon rural problems. As the 1919 report stated: "We believe the fundamental problem of the country is Economic. The constant exodus of the country folk to the city is

9. See Richard Allen, *The Social Passion: Religion and Social Reform in Canada, 1914–28* (Toronto, 1971), chap. 17.

10. Ibid., 274.

11. "Canadian Civics, Lecture I," n.d., p. 7a, box 2, file no. 49a, S. D. Chown Papers, United Church Archives.

12. E. R. Forbes, "Prohibition and the Social Gospel in Nova Scotia," *Acadiensis* 1, no. 1 (1971): 36.

but a symptom of the underlying economic disease."[13] The practical recommendations included nationalization of the land and the railways and government control of combines.[14]

The rural aspect of the Social Gospel assumed special importance in the postwar period. Indeed, the rising militancy of farmers owed much to the ideas of the Social Gospel, and the rhetoric of organizations such as the United Farmers of Alberta reflected that debt. The West now seemed to become the hub of radical Social Gospel activity, with Winnipeg at its center. Since the decade before World War I, radical Social Gospelers such as Salem Bland, while espousing socialism, had helped to forge a link between workers and the church. There was even a Socialist Sunday School by 1917, though it was obviously aligned more closely with Christianity than were its British counterparts.[15] In the summer of 1918 this leftist drift culminated in the formation of a Labour Church by William Ivens.[16]

Ivens, later to be joined by J. S. Woodsworth, certainly aided and abetted trade union militancy in the city. Unfortunately, matters were now complicated by pro-Bolshevism, which temporarily enveloped Western social democratic circles through the Western Labour Conference called in Calgary in 1919. About the same time, strikes swept the Dominion. Finally, the Winnipeg Strike, which began as a nasty dispute in the building trades, led to a sympathetic strike by the city's Trades and Labor Council. The thinking of authorities tended to fuse these influences, and they overreacted to the six-week strike. The result, ironically, was not any hastening of class warfare but the birth of J. S. Woodsworth's parliamentary political career.

Elected as a member of the Independent Labour Party for Winnipeg North in 1921, Woodsworth soon became a national spokesman for a variety of causes from the grievances of urban labor to pacifism. In donning the mantle of leader of the dispossessed he also attempted to forge an alliance with farmers in the Progressive Party, setting up bases in both the West and Ontario. After 1919 the Social Gospel became synonymous with rural Western protest through publications such as *Grain Growers' Guide* and *Western Labour News*. Woodsworth had already departed from the Methodist ministry, possibly through a crisis of faith, almost certainly in opposition to the church's support for the war.[17] However, he

13. "Christianization of Canadian Life, 14th Year, 1916–17," 40, United Church Archives.
14. Ibid., 41.
15. Allen, *Social Passion*, 83.
16. See James Shaver Woodsworth, *The First Story of the Labor Church and Some Things for Which It Stands* (Winnipeg, 1920).
17. Allen Mills, *Fool for Christ: The Political Thought of J. S. Woodsworth* (Toronto, 1991), 38–39.

did keep his contacts with the Methodist Church Department of Evangelism and Social Service throughout the 1920s.[18]

At the same time as Woodsworth's rise to the leadership circle of the Progressives, MacKenzie King became leader of the Liberal Party. Trained in labor relations at the University of Chicago, a resident of Hull House, and a friend of Mrs. Humphry Ward,[19] King earlier in his life liberally imbibed the wisdom of Social Christians in both England and the United States. In 1918 he even produced a book (entitled *Industry and Humanity*) advocating industrial democracy in an effort to eliminate the recurring labor disputes that were plaguing Britain and North America at the time.

In practice, however, King proved to be disappointing to Social Christians. More concerned with forging a national Liberal alliance of Anglophones and Francophones, and, of course, with the maintenance of power, King was cautious in his social policies. When no party had a majority in the 1925–26 Parliament, Woodsworth was able to force King to commit the Liberals to setting up an old-age pension scheme. King may well have seen this strategy as forging some kind of block, not unlike the Progressive alliance on the London County Council in the 1890s. Woodsworth also succeeded eventually in persuading a number of Progressives to join the Liberal fold. Nellie McClung and H. W. Dobson, among others, were Social Gospelers attached to provincial Liberal parties.

On the other side of Woodsworth were the extreme radicals. The Reverend A. E. Smith, for example, had been a Methodist pastor in both Nelson, British Columbia, and Brandon, Manitoba, and in fact had encouraged the young William Ivens to become a minister. Moved by the wave of strikes in 1919, he gravitated toward communism from socialism, departing from his comfortable church appointment at the same time. As Smith wrote: "I found Brotherhood. I found the answers to my questions in communism. I found the teachings of Jesus and the old Hebrew prophets surrender their truth only when interpreted through the light shed by communism."[20] Though very small in number, these ministers and laity were a reminder that more extreme prophets than Woodsworth could be found in Canadian politics.

In Britain the decline of Social Christian organized influence in politics was at hand, though it was not very apparent at the time because of the complicated adaptations related to the collapse of the Liberal Party, the economic and social

18. See Allen, *Social Passion*, 99.

19. Jane Lewis, *Women and Social Action in Victorian and Edwardian England* (Stanford, 1991), 214–15.

20. The Reverend A. E. Smith, *All My Life: An Autobiography* (Toronto, 1949), 22.

malaise of the 1920s, and the confusing redefinitions of the relationship between the body politic and the Established Church.

In the late Victorian era, Anglo-Catholics had been conspicuous in their
violations of the rules of rubric within the Church of England. Their legitimacy
did not depend upon statute but rather upon their historical view of themselves
as Catholics. Shortly before the war the process of establishing a parliamentary
committee to consider a greater measure of self-government for the Established
Church had been initiated, largely at the request of Anglo-Catholics. The 1917
report of the Selborne Committee favored ecclesiastical legislative autonomy in
the form of a representative church council. Though favorably received by the
hierarchy, fears of a delayed action spurred many clergy and laity to form the
Life and Liberty Movement, whose purpose was to secure early action in the
direction of self-government. The Life and Liberty Movement was mainly
supported by Anglo-Catholics and for that reason was treated with suspicion by
Evangelicals and others such as Hensley Henson, who called it the work of
"Gore's crowd."[21]

Anglo-Catholicism was not the only characteristic of the Life and Liberty
Movement. For the Reverend Dick Sheppard it was imperative to see home rule
for the Anglican clergy not only for the sake of more ritualistic and doctrinal
freedom but also to break governmental authority over the Church of England,
an authority that had recently led the church to condone war. On the other
hand, William Temple, who also added his charisma to the movement, made it
clear that he did not favor disestablishment, which some supporters of home
rule were accused of at the time. The Enabling Act was obtained from Parliament in 1919, thanks to the guidance of the primate, Randall Davidson, as well
as a welter of complicated political maneuvers in Lords and Commons.[22]

The act was not completely satisfactory to anyone except those Anglo-
Catholics who chafed under what they perceived to be Erastianism. Then there
were further worries about overly wide lay participation in the internal legislative functions of the Church of England that offended some Anglo-Catholics.
Charles Gore resigned his bishopric in part because of the decision to allow
the franchise for the new Church Assembly to the unconfirmed. On the other
hand, Sheppard, who had been a leader in securing the Enabling Act, felt
that even baptism was too restrictive as a condition for membership in the
Church of England.[23]

21. See Alan Wilkinson, *The Church of England and the First World War* (London, 1978), 272.
22. See David M. Thompson, "The Politics of the Enabling Act (1919)," in *Church Society and
Politics*, Studies in Church History Series, vol. 12, ed. Derek Baker (Oxford, 1965), 383–92.
23. Hugh Richard Lawrie Sheppard, *If I Were Dictator* (London, 1935), 68.

Anglo-Catholicism was now viewed as a menacing element by other elements within the church because of its alleged rising power, as demonstrated in passage of the Enabling Act. Soon some of these fears would be brought to a head in the Prayer Book controversy. By 1927 many bishops believed that the prayer of consecration should be restored to the Book of Common Prayer, partly as a means of restraining Anglo-Catholics from pushing toward full liturgical rebellion. In 1926, this tactic had already been seen in the decision to allow reservation of the Eucharist but no formal services of benediction of the Blessed Sacrament.[24] In the Prayer Book controversy, however, tampering with the Book of Common Prayer seemed like an attack upon the Protestant heritage of the Church of England. In spite of the cautions of Archbishop Davidson, the revisions were enthusiastically supported by other bishops such as Lang and Temple and both houses of the Church Assembly. This, however, reflected the wisdom of a variety of factions, by no means simply the Anglo-Catholics. A bill eventually reached Parliament, and was passed by the Lords but soundly defeated twice in the Commons, which was responding to widespread public Protestant condemnation.

Both Conservatives and Labour were evenly divided on the issue, though the overwhelming majority of Liberals opposed it (twenty-three against two). Prime Minister Baldwin's papers reveal that for quite a long time laypeople and some clergy of various churches expressed considerable bitterness toward the "Romish" prayer book. Pamphlets and letters condemned the practice of recruiting so many bishops from Anglo-Catholic ranks and threatened Baldwin politically if it continued.[25]

The picture was further complicated by the Lambeth Conference decision to allow local synods the option of voting on the informal, qualified use of the defeated Prayer Book. Anglo-Catholics could at times engage in complicated tactics, feeling they were not offered enough, and the issue of benediction of the host was again raised.[26] Such deliberations made for difficulties in ecumenical discussions with Nonconformists. Many Nonconformists still favored disestablishment, but also saw that it was the very link with Parliament that had saved their fellow Protestants in the Established Church. None of these divisions were helpful to the promotion of Social Christianity.

The issue of the church-state link remained troublesome. By the mid-1930s many felt it to be an impediment to effective social action. For Dick Sheppard there were no real reformers or prophets in the Anglican leadership. As he

24. Adrian Hastings, *A History of English Christianity, 1920–1985* (London, 1985), 203–4.
25. Collection in vol. 53, D. 4.4, Stanley Baldwin Papers, Cambridge University Library.
26. See reports of London and Liverpool Synods, *Manchester Guardian*, 9 and 10 January 1928.

wrote, "The Church of England as by law established is a frightened Church, playing for safety."[27] Yet by the 1920s, following the Enabling Act and the increased detachment from the state implicit in it, Anglo-Catholics and others committed to Social Christianity undoubtedly felt less obliged to defend the existing political order. As Bryan Wilson has argued, it is possible for such groups under such circumstances to develop their skills as social critics without any sense of a conflict of interest.[28]

The strong attraction many Anglo-Catholics felt to political socialism also raised issues beyond the confines of the Established Church. For Hensley Henson the Anglo-Catholics were too political in all senses of the word. As he wrote to the archbishop of Canterbury in the mid-1920s: "With respect to conservatives we have generally succeeded in making the clergy understand that they must not compromise their ministry by pressing party preferences. But this lesson has not been learned by clergy who have allied themselves with Labour."[29] He later supported disestablishment in opposition to Anglo-Catholics' growing influence, fearing that other parties were being stifled by Anglo-Catholic predominance in the governing circle of the Church of England. Outside the Church of England more political reservations were offered.

For Nonconformity the postwar years were extremely complicated politically. The terminally ill Liberal Party offered bleak prospects for the future. Though many Nonconformists, such as John Clifford, had been active in the Labour Party, for others it was a poor alternative. As the Reverend J. D. Jones noted in his autobiography: "The Liberal Party since 1918 has been a mere rump. Labour has become the alternative Party and young men despairing of any future for Liberalism have transferred their allegiance to it. The effect of all this upon a man like myself, brought up on the old Liberal tradition, is to make me care less and less for party politics."[30] David W. Bebbington has transposed the Great Reversal from the American scene to Britain in order to describe a similar withdrawal from politics on the part of many who were previously

27. Sheppard, *If I Were Dictator*, 18.

28. Bryan Wilson, "The Functions of Religion: A Reappraisal," *Religion* 18 (1988).

29. Henson to the archbishop of Canterbury, 9 June 1926, letters v. 106 (1925–27), f. 124, Hensley Henson Papers, Dean and Chapter Library, Durham. Henson probably remembered the letters written to the *Mail* in December 1918 by Charles Gore and some other clergy in support of the Christian principles espoused by the Labour Party. More immediately, the congratulations extended by over five hundred Anglican clergy to the Labour Party on becoming the official opposition in 1923 were probably what he had in mind. See Edward R. Norman, *Church and Society in England, 1770–1970: A Historical Study* (Oxford, 1976), 316.

30. The Reverend J. D. Jones, *Three Score Years and Ten* (London, 1940), 240.

concerned with it for reasons of social justice.[31] Withdrawal was certainly one possible response in the 1920s.

Charles Masterman, a Social Christian and influential figure in the Liberal Party, thought that only Labour had class appeal. His hope seemed to lie in a revived New Liberalism, possibly in the return of some form of the prewar Progressive alliance but with Nonconformist support. But he was also well aware, through his statistics gathering, of the underlying problems of the Free Churches—especially the 9.6 percent decline in Sunday school scholars from 1900 to 1923 even though church membership had risen by 6.8 percent in the same period.[32] Frank F. Smith, writing to Masterman, noted: "I suggest Lloyd George and Sir John Simon for another—a combination that I think would rally Nonconformity and give Liberalism the majority it gave Gladstone."[33] Masterman did not seem to respond to this suggestion as a real possibility. Other correspondence revealed the complicated viewpoints of those who advised in the highest Liberal circles, including Seebohm Rowntree and H. W. Massingham, whom the editor of the *Westminster Gazette* described as "three quarters Fabian."[34]

For most Nonconformist Social Christians at this time political party affiliation was a dilemma. For many the Labour Party now offered the best prospect of reaching the New Jerusalem. The appearance of prominent Nonconformists within the Labour Party leadership was comforting, as were the words of Ramsay MacDonald concerning the "moral cause" of his party, delivered in an address at Mansfield College in the early 1920s.[35] Issues, however, tended to bring out political action not always related to parties and frequently on a nondenominational basis, as witnessed in the activities of the Industrial Christian Fellowship (ICF) in the 1920s. The ICF, though heavily Anglican, crossed church borders in the interest of Social Christianity.

Among the churches, the Quakers were perhaps the best prepared to address the issues of the postwar world from a Social Christian perspective. Its leadership circle included philanthropist-capitalists such as the Cadbury family and

31. See David W. Bebbington, *Evangelicalism in Modern Britain: A History from the 1730s to the 1980s* (London, 1989), 214–17.

32. "Statistics of the Evangelical Free Churches of Great Britain in the Twentieth Century," A¾/8, C.F.G. Masterman Papers, Birmingham University Library.

33. Smith to Masterman, 6 February 1927, A½/8, Masterman Papers.

34. J. B. Hobman to Rowntree, 15 January 1923, A½/8, Masterman Papers.

35. Ramsay MacDonald, "The Labour Party in Relation to National Life," Junior Common Room Conference, 10 February 1921, "JCR Conferences," Mansfield College Archives, Oxford University. On this occasion, MacDonald reportedly argued that Labour was not a class party, or even the conduit of the majority opinion in the country, but the expression of a "National need," which was a "moral cause."

the capitalist-social investigator Seebohm Rowntree, all sympathizers with Social Christianity; members of the Quaker Socialist Society; and those with wartime planning experience, such as Malcolm Sparkes, who engaged in the organization of the wartime Whitley Councils. They saw themselves as already an expression of fellowship, linking the salvation of society with peace, and realized by their very social composition that they could be natural arbitrators between rich and poor. In the early summer of 1918 they issued their famous eight-point "Foundations" agenda for the postwar world. Announced in *The Friend* (7 June 1918), the points included statements on discrimination on the basis of race, sex, or class, on the state regulation of land and capital for the needs of people, and on the spirit of righteousness in industrial relations. The last point, of course, spurred their War and Social Order Committee in 1925 to sponsor subcommittees to investigate unemployment, vagrancy, and other social ills. It also placed the Quaker organizations very early into the conflicts leading to the General Strike of 1926.

The General Strike of May 1926 was rooted in the labor disputes of the coal industry in which mine owners wanted to institute a wage cut and longer hours and the Baldwin government was unwilling to involve itself any more to reorganize a foundering industry as recommended by the Samuel Commission. The decision by the Trades Union Congress (TUC) to organize a sympathy strike was not a revolutionary move but more a move of pressure politics. The government would not budge. The churches—given their recent publicly expressed concerns at COPEC, sponsored by the Industrial Christian Fellowship, and the general commitment of senior clergy to Social Christianity—seemed almost forced into intervention. They had no clear idea what route to take. But this was not the 1895 Durham miners dispute, which was mediated by Bishop Westcott,[36] or indeed the London Dock Strike of 1889 with Cardinal Manning as arbitrator. The nation as a whole was involved together, with all the complex web of political and economic factors and social classes as well as the impact of viewpoints of the combatants represented in the media (much of which was temporarily controlled by the government).

Most of the focus on the churches was directed at one person, Archbishop Davidson, who first appeared unsympathetic to the strikers in a speech to the House of Lords and then shifted considerably by setting his seal to a document entitled *The Crisis: An Appeal from the Churches,* which called for a return to

---

36. Hensley Henson, in a journal entry during this period (6 June 1926, vol. 40, 334, Henson Papers), wrote that he thought the Westcott intervention of 1895 was "the grand precedent for episcopal meddling in economic crises," which was unfortunate then and very bad for the 1920s, given the much more complex economic situation and the "markedly secularist" temper of Labour.

the status quo before the eruption of disputes that had produced the end of discussions between miners, owners, and government. The prime minister was prepared to live with this call with small reservations.

Behind the scenes dedicated Social Christians had already been busy. An ICF delegation of Canons Kirk, Woods, Woodward, Bishop Garbett of Ripon, and the Methodist ministers Scott Lidgett and Henry Carter had in fact urged the archbishop to put his name to *The Crisis* early in the General Strike. Social Christian leaders joined in interchurch solidarity, but the clergy as a whole felt much uneasiness about supporting class war. Those not part of the Social Christian circle tended to be hostile. Cardinal Bourne, the Roman Catholic archbishop of Westminster, supported the government. Bishop Hensley Henson's papers noted admiration for Bourne.[37] The Reverend F. W. Norwood of the City Temple stated that "the majority of the people believed it [the General Strike] was a menace to good government" and by its defeat "the moral stature of the nation was enhanced."[38]

The Reverend W. R. Inge perhaps best captured the inner mood of many clergy immediately before the Strike:[39]

> The long threatened labour storm is breaking over us, and heaven knows how it will end. It is no mere wages dispute, but an attempted Syndicalist revolution, like that planned for the autumn of 1914, and only averted by the outbreak of the Great War.
>
> I hear Henry Wagner, who died last week, has left Charlie and me £2000 each. I think I can manage to let Kitty have the motor car after which she hankers, unless we are all ruined in civil war.

During the strike, Prime Minister Baldwin received letters of support from clergy in many parts of the country, offering prayers and good wishes for the government side. As the Reverend George McNeal of Wesley's Chapel, London, wrote, "I have never given a Conservative vote in my life, but we all believe in the Prime Minister."[40] Letters from some laymen focused on the role of the church in general, as did that of W. Baker of West Wimbleton, which stated, "[T]he real cause of all the unrest in our beloved country is the misleading teaching of the church," and singled out the bishops, who "must

37. Henson to the archbishop of Canterbury, 9 June 1926, letters 106, f. 124, Henson Papers.

38. F. W. Norwood, *Indiscretions of a Preacher* (London, 1932), 240.

39. Diary, 30 April 1926, vol. 30, W. R. Inge Papers, Pepys Library, Magdalen College, Cambridge University.

40. McNeal to Baldwin, 17 May 1926, vol. 136, f. 87, Baldwin Papers.

give account."[41] The Modernist Henry D. A. Major of Ripon Hall, Oxford, stated to the *Times* editor (12 May 1926) that the archbishop's appeal made it appear that the General Strike should be called off only "conditionally," and in so doing, by offering public advice, was undermining the prime minister. For these reasons he could not sign the primate's appeal. As he stated: "[T]he impulse of our hearts is to sign; the reflection of our heads holds us back."

Admittedly it is difficult to gauge general church and public opinion at such times. Churches were divided internally, much as they were during the Winnipeg General Strike of 1919. Discerning individuals probably did not see the strike as class war. However, members of the cabinet, such as Winston Churchill and Hicks Beach (who later vehemently opposed the bishops on the new prayer book), certainly did. Neville Chamberlain, who kept a careful political diary through the 1920s and early 1930s, thought before the strike that the press had been "generally anti-government" over the coal problems.[42] However, aside from noting "a strenuous fight with the C. of E. over the Economy Bill,"[43] he made no mention of the role of the churches during the General Strike or thereafter. These varied perceptions may explain the labyrinthine thinking behind the decision not to broadcast the archbishop of Canterbury's appeal initially over the BBC.[44] Though a conscientious Anglican, Baldwin was also a political realist.[45]

The *Christian World* argued in its very cheerful rendition of the General Strike (20 May 1926) that the Free Churches and the archbishop had triumphed over the extreme "Mussolinis" of the government and "Lenins" of the trade unions in the proposals for peace. The effect of the archbishop's message was "said in labour quarters to have been very real. It brought assurance to the T.U.C. [Trades Union Congress] that the moral forces, represented by the Churches, were (as the Primate said in his St. Martin's sermon) neither apathetic nor helpless in their desire for a just and peaceful solution. As one of the T.U.C. officials said, 'It was the turning point in the struggle.' "

To others, even within the Social Christian fold, the triumph of the churches was not so apparent. As the Reverend Henry Carter, general secretary of the

41. Baker to Baldwin, 14 May 1926, vol. 135, f. 71, Baldwin Papers.

42. 9 August 1925, Political Diary and Journal, NC2/21, Neville Chamberlain Papers, Birmingham University Library.

43. 28 March 1926, ibid.

44. Julian Symons, *The General Strike* (London, 1957), 184–85.

45. For example, the advancement of divorce legislation only months after the Abdication Crisis obviously diminished the influence of the church. See G.I.T. Machin, "Marriage and the Churches in the 1930s: Royal Abdication and Divorce Reform, 1936–7," *Journal of Ecclesiastical History* 42, no. 1 (1991): 68–81.

Wesleyan Methodist Welfare Department, wrote to Samuel E. Keeble: "It simply doesn't matter whether or not the churches get credit for what is being done. Our work is that of reconciliation. Anyone can have the credit as long as the goal is reached."[46] In the same letter Carter went on to praise Keeble as the author of *Industrial Day Dreams* (1889) and other works:

> The almost dramatic intervention of the churches in this national industrial strife is an out-working of your pioneer teaching. Those of us in the Free Churches at any rate who are immersed in the present efforts to achieve industrial reconciliation owe our early inspirations and enthusiasms to you as to no other man. I have said this before, but I want to repeat it now, since we have reached a moment of such immense import in the application of Christian social influence and teachings.

For the remainder of 1926 the churches continued their political involvement with the coal dispute (or stoppage) after the conclusion of the General Strike. The ICF was now superseded by a Standing Conference of the Christian Churches on the Coal Dispute, which included Canon P.T.R. Kirk as well as William Temple (who had been ill and absent during the General Strike), seven more bishops, the aged Gore, and a group of activist Nonconformists. The Standing Conference, with the bishop of Lichfield as chief spokesman, now took the initiative of returning to the recommendations of the Samuel Commission, delivering a memorandum to the government on 16 July. The demands were not accepted by the government, and as a consequence divisions opened within the delegation over a further, one-sided alliance with the workers. Letters to the editor took various sides in the religious and secular press. On the whole, they were critical of the churches. One letter to the *Times* editor condemned the bishops not only for claiming to represent church opinion but also for probably prolonging the strike.[47] This was more or less the view of Seebohm Rowntree, who had published articles in the *Torch*, the publication of the ICF, and met with A. J. Cook on 29 July to bridge the gap between the mine owners and workers. Rowntree's condemnation extended to other clergy, including the Nonconformists. As Rowntree stated in a letter to Henry Carter:

> I read the letter which appeared in the Press this morning, and with my intimate knowledge of the attitude of the Government and of the

---

46. Carter to Keeble, 12 August 1926, folder 7/, S. E. Keeble Papers, Methodist Archives, John Rylands University Library of Manchester.

47. A. C. Gloucester, letter to the editor, Times (London), 27 July 1926.

Miners, I feel that the action of your Committee in pressing for the acceptance of the terms which you put before the Prime Minister, can have only one result, and that is to lengthen the present strike. You will fortify the miners in their effort to stick out for the four months as against the one month, and the subsidy as against a loan. I am sure that the Government will never accept either of these, and eventually the miners will have to give way. As evidence that I am not expressing my opinion carelessly arrived at, I may tell you that before the Bishops' manifesto appeared, I recommended my Board of Directors at the Cocoa Works not to buy any further coal, as we had four weeks' supply then, and I felt sure that we could get a settlement "within that time."[48]

On the whole, the brunt of criticism was directed toward the Anglican bishops. Perhaps the historian Keith Feiling made the most devastating summary in an article entitled "The Church and Civil Order" (*Times*, 6 August 1926):

To the future historical student of the early 20th century few things will appear so surprising as the attitude of the Anglican Church towards the General Strike of 1926. Stripping the question of the confusion introduced by the coal controversy, he will find that a number of those then leading the Church invited the Government of an ultra-democratic country to surrender to physical force a position from which neither votes nor reasoning process had dislodged them, and equated that elected Government for purposes of negotiation with a section of its subjects.

For Feiling, "none except those who reason from the Sermon on the Mount to Blue-books, will ask from a Church or Churchman a detailed exposition of the State, of political rights and social obligation." He did decide, however, to consult the writings of Cardinal Newman, "the most living force in the making of modern Anglo-Catholicism," and found no such applied creed. Rather in Newman he found an emphasis upon the essential spiritual role of the church and no distinction "between the views of Newman the Anglican and the Roman cardinal upon the relation of the Church to society, for no break is apparent in his social teaching." As Feiling concluded his comments on Newman:

48. Rowntree to Carter, 24 July 1926, "General Strike" file, B. S. Rowntree Papers, Joseph Rowntree Memorial Trust, Beverley House, York.

The authority which in matters doctrinal he found in a living Church, this in things of this world he appears to place in the accumulated age, wisdom, and rationality represented by an old civilization and a legal order. He held that religion, though it transcended, did not supersede the order established by the original endowments of man, and continued the Catholic teaching of the moral guilt incurred by those who take the sword to accelerate the operation of law.

The intention of Feiling's writing was not to affirm the "Toryism" of Newman, or the correctness of Cardinal Bourne's recent actions, but to call into question the whole line of political involvements by Anglo-Catholics since Gore. Recriminations followed in the other churches. Though the Quakers engaged in extensive relief projects in the coal fields, the majority of their monthly meetings rejected the eight-point Foundations of a True Social Order manifesto of 1918. A socially responsive elite nonetheless continued to meet and investigate social and economic problems for the remainder of the interwar years.

Reprisals against the Quaker socialist group were also not terribly pointed within the Society of Friends. In fact, Quaker socialists were still widely respected. Edward Grubb had lived out his years as a respected member of the Socialist Society, eventually retiring to Letchworth Garden City, which he regarded as a reasonably classless community. This was also probably true of socialists among the Baptists, a church that since Clifford's demise took a more cautiously progressive line on many political issues. Among the Methodists, however, an antisocialist group had been in operation since before 1914. This group believed that a socialist conspiracy existed, which belief cast doubt upon all efforts of the Division of Social Responsibility. Their concerns continued to be raised in the 1920s on such issues as the threat posed to youth by recruitment by the Socialist and Proletarian Sunday Schools. During the General Strike, prominent lay members questioned Henry Carter and others about violations of church procedures in their capacity as self-appointed spokesmen.[49] In spite of Carter's cordial communications with the strident Christian Socialist Samuel E. Keeble before and during the General Strike, it became clear after 1926 that Keeble was placed at arms length from the leadership. Keeble had already rejected social work for socialism.[50] His path now lay within the ranks of the

49. The issue of Methodist leaders' bypassing the Committee of Privilege in strike negotiations was raised, 12 May 1926, in the Representative Session of Second London Synod (Division of Social Responsibility Records, Methodist Archives, Rylands). See also Jeremy, *Capitalists and Christians*, 176.

50. Robert Moore, *Pit-Men Preachers and Politics* (Cambridge, 1974), 59.

Labour Party, though, unlike North American prophet-politicians such as Norman Thomas or J. S. Woodsworth, he remained a minister.[51] A subfork in the road had now appeared for many very advanced socialists on both sides of the Atlantic on the question whether the churches any longer were in the forefront of advancing Christianity. Perhaps the remnant of the antisocialist group merged into the Great Reversal trend and the Oxford Group Movement to place special pressures upon Carter and other leaders. Thus by 1929 electioneering activities for Methodists, and perhaps for many other Nonconformists, came to focus on a single-issue temperance campaign, though the new interdenominational Christian Social Council continued to discuss political issues, as did the ICF. This reversion to temperance was perhaps a mistake, harking back to the older "Nonconformist Conscience," which could no longer be supported so simplistically. As Peter Catterall has stated, "[T]he general strike of 1926 in particular seemed to seal the fate of the nonconformist conscience."[52]

Nonconformity was in a political shambles by 1929. Seebohm Rowntree, in the Masterman Liberal tradition, emphasized a Social Christian outlook that, when projected into politics, would head away from class politics toward a progressive, harmonious society. As he wrote in the *Aberdeen University Magazine* in 1927, Liberalism's fundamental principle was the pursuance of policies for the interests of the community as a whole, not merely one class.[53] In a later paper presented at the General Convention of the Protestant Episcopal Church held at Cincinnati in October 1937, he stated: "It is for open-minded, impartial, and public-spirited people to lead the way and to avert class war and industrial strife of any description by removing the reasons for it." This was an important point and one widely shared by many. Churches were for all social classes, and so also should be their political expression.

Rowntree staked his hopes on Lloyd George in the late 1920s. From 1926 to 1929 numerous weekend meetings at Churt yielded the *Liberal Yellow Book* and the report entitled "We Can Conquer Unemployment." As Rowntree wrote to Thomas Jones, Lloyd George's former secretary, in 1945:

> I don't know whether you remember what was in that little book, but it
> contained a number of proposals for work which might with great

51. Keeble continued to conduct a 6:45 A.M. service at the large Brunswick Chapel, Sheffield, at least into the late 1930s. See "A Note on 60 Years as a Methodist Minister, 16 July 1938," folder 10, Keeble Papers.

52. Peter Catterall, "Morality and Politics: The Free Churches and the Labour Party Between the Wars," *Historical Journal* 36, no. 3 (1993): 672.

53. "Liberalism in Industry," 26 September 1927, "articles on Liberal Party," ART/8, Rowntree Papers, Borthwick Institute, York.

advantage be undertaken by the nation with a view to providing work for the unemployed. Our ideas as to the amount of capital which might be found for this purpose were not as ambitious as those which have become popular, largely through the influence of Keynes's book, but had the proposals made in our report been carried out a very substantial contribution would have been made to the solution of the unemployment problem. L. G. took the most pains over this work and entered into the various proposals with keen interest.[54]

The results of the 1929 election were undoubtedly as disappointing for Social Christian Liberals such as Rowntree as they were for temperance advocates within the ranks of Nonconformity.

The political search to find a harmonious society was certainly not confined to Masterman or Rowntree in the 1920s. Though Anglo-Catholics had been seemingly prominent in supporting the cause of the working class and socialism, their views were usually broader and more diverse regarding the appropriate political instruments to reach their desired goals. Many moved into the Labour Party or the British Socialist Party (after the SDF), but so did Nonconformists of similar sympathies. Guild socialism, with a view of a renewed medieval corporatism, had appeared before the war and was generally more compatible with Anglo-Catholics' social philosophy. Much of the guild socialist tradition was found in the Church Socialist League, which worked closely with the National Guilds League. However, the Catholic Crusade's interwar notion of an organic unity was probably the fullest expression of this idea. The central figure in the crusade was Conrad Noel, who consistently linked his Catholic socialist political vision with his Catholic social vision found in Thaxted. He had helped to found the Church Socialist League in 1906, served as its secretary, and later was on the executive committee of the British Socialist Party. Noel was not reluctant to deal with concrete issues, as demonstrated by his outright support of Sinn Fein (including their flag in church), involvement with trade unionists during the General Strike, praise of the enlightened leadership of the Bolsheviks, attacks upon the imperialism of the Boy Scouts movement, and, in the 1930s, participation in the Oxford Group Movement. The Catholic Crusade, combining Anglo-Catholicism and socialism, in any case, came first.

The extreme Christian Socialist Left in Britain had not yet jelled by the 1920s, and for that reason there was much room for political maneuvering. The Christendom Movement of the same period was a more theoretical fellowship

54. Rowntree to Jones, 24 May 1945, Lloyd George letters, Seebohm Rowntree Papers, Rowntree Trust, York.

exploring the links between social policy, politics, and religion. One member, P.E.T. Widdrington, during the 1920s left the Labour Party and transformed the Christian Socialist League into the League of the Kingdom of God, with a broader social agenda and theological underpinning.[55] Another, Maurice Reckitt, along with Travers Somers, Philip Mairet, and Alan Porter, formed the Chandos Group on the last day of the General Strike.[56] Their initial purpose was to explore Social Credit more fully, feeling that its founder, Major Douglas, was too much of a technocrat. They not only prepared articles for the *New Age* on Social Credit but also published *Coal: A Challenge to the National Conscience* (1927)—partial vindication of the actions of the bishops, V. A. Demant's *Miners' Distress and the Coal Problem* (1930) and, in the political sphere, a composite work, *Politics: A Discussion of Realities* (1928).

Outside the Chandos Group, Social Credit gained support among Christendom people like William Temple and especially Hewlett Johnson, later a member of the Communist Party of Great Britain, who communicated with William Aberhart in Alberta and in the mid 1930s did a speaking tour of the province.[57] Other groups also continued to have discussions on political directions, mainly in conjunction with support for the Labour Party. The ICF was dynamically represented by the great preacher and former war chaplain "Woodbine Willy" G. A. Studdert-Kennedy. However, their council meetings, after the General Strike, became rather repetitious examinations of social and economic policy and the idealized role of the Christian politician in politics.[58]

# The Final Quest for a Just Society: The Thirties

The outset of the Great Depression represented a major turning point in Social Christian politics on both sides of the Atlantic. Since a proactive political stance on solving social and economic problems had largely failed in the 1920s, with the possible exception of the Progressive forces under Woodsworth in Canada,

55. Percy Widdrington started his career in the Anglican priesthood as a curate, with Conrad Noel, to William Edmund Moll, vicar of St. Philip's, Newcastle. He was from the beginning a "Catholic socialist." See Maurice B. Reckitt, *P.E.T. Widdrington: A Study in Vocation and Versatility* (London, 1961). A small number of papers are in the possession of Stephen Widdrington of West Hill, Ontario, but are chiefly wills and genealogical materials.

56. "The Story of the Chandos Group: 1926–1966," typescript in V. A. Demant Papers (in possession of Justin Demant, Oxford; copy courtesy of Ian Markham, Exeter University).

57. Hewlett Johnson, *Searching for Light: An Autobiography* (London, 1968), 136–37, and David Elliott, ed., *Aberhart: Outpourings and Replies* (Calgary, 1991), 162–63.

58. Council meetings, minute book 1928–35, ICF Archive, Sion College, London.

it was necessary that Social Christians exert their influence by supporting the best possible secular political force that might alleviate misery, reduce the danger of war, and set society back on a course bound for the New Jerusalem. In all countries creative ideas, individuals, and groups emerged. Notably, a significant portion of the affluent in both Britain and North America also accepted the necessity of renewed reformism given the dire economic circumstances of the times. This, of course, was helpful to Social Christians but not a prerequisite for their own actions.[59] In the United States major and minor political firebrands would rekindle the Social Gospel. In Canada the Social Gospel would continue to be highly relevant to politics. In Britain a national prophet emerged, but no mechanism to give full expression to Social Christianity in politics. Everywhere controversy would abound.

In the United States the informal and formal repeal of Prohibition and more significantly the tremendous impact of the Depression did much to create the circumstances that would resuscitate the Social Gospel. It was not to be the philanthropic Quaker Herbert Hoover but the quite secular-minded Episcopalian Franklin Delano Roosevelt who would provide the political opportunity for a positive expression of moderate Social Gospel thinking. Like earlier Progressivism in the United States, the New Deal seemed to reflect the positive, nonrevolutionary, Postmillennial approach to tackling social problems. Roosevelt, for his part, was also quite anxious to gain clerical support. In September 1935 a form letter was mailed out from the White House to over a hundred thousand American clergy, soliciting their opinion on the new Social Security legislation as well as social conditions and possible remedies in their locales. From the responses of over thirty thousand, Aubrey C. Mills made tabulations and passed the information back to FDR. Predictably, the vast majority favored Roosevelt's efforts, but a significant number within that majority offered further criticisms. Social Security came in for very high praise. However, many clergy seemed to feel actual "business conditions" were as bad as or worse than before the onset of the New Deal.[60] Professors Monroe Billington and Cal Clark have done thorough statistical analysis on the remaining evidence of the poll in the clergy files of the Roosevelt papers. In their more concentrated focus on certain states they believe in general that the clergy took a pragmatic, rather

59. In Australia, for example, Protestant churches generally supported conservative economic and social policy during the Great Depression. Part of the explanation, according to Paul Nicholls, lies in the relative weaknesses of liberal Protestantism and the absence of a strong Christian Socialist tradition. See Nicholls, "Australian Protestantism and the Politics of the Great Depression, 1929–1931," *Journal of Religious History* 17, no. 2 (1992): 210–21.

60. Report of Aubrey C. Mills on clergy letters to Stephen Early, 15 June 1936, "Clergy Letters," PPF21A, box 35, Franklin D. Roosevelt Papers, Franklin D. Roosevelt Library, Hyde Park, N.Y.

than ideological, stand on the role of government in the local community, supporting many Roosevelt programs but also criticizing unnecessary bureaucracy and aid to the irresponsible.[61] The strength of Social Gospel support is not entirely clear in this survey, since questions did not refer specifically to it.

A subsequent survey conducted by the Rauschenbusch Fellowship (*What Church People Think,* by Norman L. Trott and Ross W. Sanderson [New York, Association Press, 1938]) contained more-specific information on support for Roosevelt's programs, albeit on a sample that was geographically narrower but included Protestant laity as well as clergy. Based on Baltimore, two-thirds of whose registered voters were Democrats, the investigation focused on social and economic issues as perceived by churchgoers in the mid-1930s. Notes appended to some questionnaires included comments that "ranged all the way from individualistic pietism to unapologetic socialism, with a preponderance of statements assuming that social justice is an inevitable by-product of personal goodness" (p. 49). This was probably a good indication of how the New Deal would be received. The overall statistical result from the 1,153 questionnaires collected revealed that "the church occupies a middle-of-the-road position" on social and political issues, though the tabulations often indicated curious inconsistencies or even contradictions in several categories. The results of the first section of the questionnaire, indicating the percentage of affirmative responses to each statement (pp. 15–16), were as follows:

1. The church should help to establish worldwide communism—4 percent.
2. The church should favor socialism—7 percent.
3. The church should take sides in the class struggle by joining hands with the poor and destitute—38 percent.
4. If the church does not show greater concern about social and economic problems, it is doomed—35 percent.
5. The church should actively oppose sweatshop conditions, child labor, long hours of work, and the like—80 percent.
6. The church should acknowledge that our present economic system has failed to supply an adequate living for most of the people—47 percent.
7. Business and religion are closely related. The church cannot remain silent when the vital interests of either capital or labor are involved—56 percent.

61. Monroe Billington and Cal Clark, "Clergy Reaction to the New Deal: A Comparative Study," *The Historian* 98, no. 4 (1986): 509–24.

8. The church should take part in all human concerns and not hold aloof—73 percent.
9. The church should stand for equal rights and complete justice for all men in all stations of life—89 percent.
10. The church should attempt to find justice and preach righteousness without favor—84 percent.
11. It is the amount of Christianity in a government that counts. I do not think that either Capitalism or Socialism is better than the other in itself—59 percent.
12. The church should preach love and righteousness, but avoid mentioning local or specific matters, leaving these for each person to decide upon—38 percent.
13. Preach the gospel and let the problems of the world take care of themselves as individuals are made better—24 percent.
14. The church should give its attention only to the moral and religious training of the individual, and not try to solve general and economic questions—30 percent.
15. Religion has nothing to do with business and politics—17 percent.
16. Heaven is our real home, so why bother with earthly matters?—8 percent.
17. Ministers who teach socialism should be run out of the church—20 percent.

The "middle of the road" was probably safest under these circumstances. After all, Roosevelt's clever balancing act had managed to forge an alliance of urban labor, Northern middle-class liberals, the South, and even some Western farmers. Though he was received more enthusiastically than the previous Democratic candidate, the Catholic Al Smith, who had tried to build a broad urban alliance, Roosevelt was not endorsed by all Protestants. In fact, according to the poll of the Institute of Public Information, Protestants were divided, with 75 percent of Congregationalists voting for Landon in November 1936, though Roosevelt received a majority vote of "unenlightened Baptists." As *Radical Religion* (vol. 2, no. 1 [1936]) described the situation: "We say unenlightened Baptists because this heavy democratic majority must have been contributed by southern Baptists. In other words the regional influence of Republican, Congregational New England and of the Baptist, democratic south were more potent than the enlightenment of the pulpit."

Such a situation made Roosevelt do considerable tightrope walking, particularly in the area of racial reform. An alliance of Southern whites and Northern, urban non-Protestant ethnic groups, for example, would make liaison with the Social Gospelers somewhat difficult. Apart from the Fellowship of Southern Churchmen, Methodist, Baptist, and Presbyterian conventions and conferences in the South remained silent on social issues in the 1930s, with the exception of Prohibition.[62] This hostile attitude toward rum and Romanism made the Democratic alliance very fragile at times.

Some associated with the Social Gospel preached socialism, of course, especially into the 1930s. Norman Thomas, though no longer a minister, could attract the support of Social Gospel ministers, professors, and laity to the party. Whether endorsing the Socialist Party platform or advocating peace or liberties, he had the respect of many. As Ralph Harlow, a professor of religion at Smith College, noted in a letter to Thomas in 1933 concerning his own support of the Socialist Party: "I think that the vision which brought you into the socialist party and helped you to take your stand against the war was your loyalty to the Christ to whom I am trying to be loyal. No man has helped me more than you to see exactly what the implications of taking Jesus seriously are."[63] Again, support tended to be almost entirely Northern, though Thomas extended his concern to black sharecroppers in Arkansas in the 1930s. He had little to lose. As Howard Kester of the Fellowship of Reconciliation reported to Thomas, from Tennessee, there was no progress for the socialists in "this seething cauldron of racial, industrial and agrarian strife."[64]

Reinhold Niebuhr for one was attracted to socialism. Skeptical of Roosevelt's manipulative New Deal at its inception, Niebuhr veered toward socialism in the early 1930s. The right wing of the Social Gospel struck him as too moralistic and without any understanding of the real problems of justice in society. The left wing, on the other hand, seemed to Niebuhr realistic in "substituting the 'service motive' for the 'profit motive,' "[65] and it was this "general ethos of the Social Gospel" that led him to join the Socialist Party and the Fellowship of Reconciliation. Niebuhr's political support of the Socialist Party seemed to parallel his theological rejection of Protestant Liberalism, just as his *Moral Man and Immoral Society* (1932), with its argument against utilitarian compromise in politics, seemed to preclude support for the New Deal.

62. Ahlstrom, *Religious History of the American People,* 924.

63. Harlow to Thomas, 5 January 1933, general correspondence, series I (reel 1), Norman Thomas Papers.

64. Kester to Thomas, 22 October 1933, general correspondence, series I (reel 1), Norman Thomas Papers.

65. "The Politics of the 1930s," 6, Addresses/Writings File, container 45, Reinhold Niebuhr Papers, Library of Congress.

Paul Carter believes that Niebuhr did much to revive the Social Gospel of the Left and also to help give birth to a gospel of the "far Left."[66] Niebuhr did in fact contribute to journals and did participate in other forms of intellectual engagement in conjunction with those who could be termed Stalinists. By the 1930s he was calling himself a Christian Marxist. In this he departed from the approach of Norman Thomas, who battled Marxists within his own ranks. Niebuhr's "realism" led him into a search for appropriate workable political means to achieve his social goals. But an early experience in the New York teachers union led him to reject any experiments in United Front activities.[67] His interest in Marxism was almost theological, though he sharply criticized the ideology in practice.

His real political goal for much of the early 1930s (and again after 1945) was the establishment of a political party similar to the British Labour Party, which he believed had considerable input from Anglicanism and Methodism.[68] His friends ranged from George Lansbury to Sir Stafford Cripps, and he made frequent trips to Britain. However, the reluctance of the labor movement to move in large numbers to support the Socialist Party in the United States seemed a major stumbling block.[69]

This impediment, together with Roosevelt's foreign policy, eventually moved him back into a "realistic" reevaluation of the New Deal by the Second World War. It was, of course, the idealism of pacifists that he also found most distressing. In reaction to the pacifism of socialists, liberals, some Communists, and many clergy, as well as to the isolationism in the general public, he helped to form the Union for Democratic Action in 1940. Like that of his friend William Temple, Niebuhr's belief in original sin seemed ultimately to lead to criticism of "the idealists who were concerned with justice [but whose] primary concern was with their own purity."[70]

Niebuhr's eventual position on foreign and domestic policy was not so different from that of Charles Stelzle. Stelzle, by the late 1930s, supported "preparedness" as opposed to pacifism. He also endorsed much of the New Deal. But his progress toward these positions was different. Like Niebuhr he had urban pastoral experience, but much more of it. Because of his continuous involvement with the labor movement, he was more in tune with developments

66. Carter, *Decline and Revival of Social Gospel,* 156–57.
67. "Politics in the 1930s," 15.
68. Reinhold Niebuhr, "Britain," reprinted in *Worldview* 17, no. 7 (1974): 31.
69. Donald Meyer, *Protestant Search for Political Realism, 1919–1941* (Berkeley and Los Angeles, 1961), 224.
70. "Politics in the 1930s," 9.

there. An admirer of British-born Samuel Gompers, he argued for the continuance of trade unionism as opposed to industrial unionism, which he associated with socialism and Communism.[71] His solution to labor unrest and economic distress depended a great deal on goodwill between employers and employees. But his faith in democracy was steadfast. As he saw it, the various manifestations of democracy in religion, politics, education, social recognition, relations between the sexes, racial matters, and industry were all aspects of the same movement, always necessitating some struggle against the status quo.[72] In spite of his less radical political past, Stelzle had a great deal more to say about the plight of working women[73] and blacks than Niebuhr did. Niebuhr, of course, did much to encourage the improvement of the economic plight of African Americans by supporting the Mississippi Delta Cooperative project of Sherwood Eddy. But, as his biographer Richard Fox has indicated, Niebuhr regarded black Americans more as recipients of charity than as participants in a great reform movement.[74] Stelzle would have been more hopeful of their capacity to be equal allies in the struggle toward the full realization of democracy.

By the 1930s the mood of the country was shifting toward new models of inspiration for Social Gospelers. Sherwood Eddy, Niebuhr's friend, had been a leader of the YMCA, which had adopted the "Social Creed of the Churches" as policy in the interwar period. Conducting numerous seminars for leading American Christians traveling to Europe in the period, Eddy noted in the 1920s that the churches in Britain "were not as a whole awake to the social crisis, and that religion was not adequately functioning in Christianizing all of life and its relationships."[75] But later, in the mid-1930s, he stated: "In Great Britain I found old England sound at heart, with more real democracy, free speech, and effective parliamentary government than any country in the world." On the social front, Eddy went on to say that Britain was "steadily advancing in the socialization of wealth, in social insurance and the municipal control of utilities and industries." In his admiration of the country he also noted its situation "in the midst of a surrounding sea of dictatorships."[76] It was significant, however,

71. "Industrial Versus Trade Unionism," CBS broadcast, 18 January 1936, 10–11, folder "Radio Talks," box 10, Charles Stelzle Papers, Rare Book and Manuscript Room, Butler Library, Columbia University.

72. "The Human Element in the Labor Problem," WABC and the Columbia Network, 6 September 1937, 4, folder "Radio Talks," box 10, Stelzle Papers.

73. "The Human Element in Unemployment," CBS, 21 June 1937, 6–7, folder "Radio Talks," box 10, Stelzle Papers.

74. Richard Wrightman Fox, *Reinhold Niebuhr: A Biography* (San Francisco, 1985), 94.

75. Eddy to friends, 23 August 1927, manuscript group 32, box 3, folder 73, George Sherwood Eddy Papers, Yale Divinity School Library.

76. Eddy to Friends, 12 September 1935, box 4, folder 81, Eddy Papers.

that by the 1930s Eddy had nothing to say about the role of the churches, though he was a founder and leader of the moderate Fellowship for a Christian Order. As a prominent member of the League for Independent Political Action he did support Norman Thomas.

Secular models were increasingly the order of the day, with the Soviet Union as the New Jerusalem among the far Left, Christian Marxists. Harry Ward was perhaps the best example of this school of thought. In the interwar period Methodists in a variety of regional conferences as well as the National Council of Methodist Youth expressed increasing criticism of the existing political order, leading most of the other Protestant denominations in this respect. Some of the major figures in this leftward drift were members of the Methodist Federation for Social Service, of which Ward was secretary.

Ward was born into poverty in London and emigrated to Salt Lake City at the age of seventeen. After studying at the University of California, Northwestern, and Harvard, he began his career as a Methodist minister in Chicago. Even in the period before World War I he became interested in preaching politics, as it was said. He was also a dominant figure in the Methodist Federation for Social Service from its inception. Toward the end of the Great War, while a professor of sociology at Boston University theological seminary, he had delivered a number of speeches that had been critical of plutocracy and had spoken "apologetically once for the Russian Bolshevik, and once for the I.W.W.," according to Walter Burr, secretary of the Speakers' Bureau of the Council of Defense and U.S. Food Administration for Kansas. Burr recommended to the Committee on Public Information in Washington that Ward be "discouraged" from speaking until the end of the war.[77]

After moving on to Union Theological Seminary, Ward, along with Norman Thomas, was active in the Civil Liberties Union in the 1920s, until it failed to defend the rights of Communists. Though attacks on Ward's views at the end of the war could often be scathing, they were not unique for outspoken Social Christians. Walter Rauschenbusch's widow wrote to Ward of an attempt by a Cincinnati gunpowder manufacturer to remove her husband from his seminary post after publication of *Christianity and the Social Crisis*.[78]

At the beginning of the post–World War I period Ward wrote the following to Professor David Snedden: "The objective of my life work is two-fold: first, to promote these social changes which I conceive to be required by the needs of humanity, and the social ethics of Christianity; second, to promote these

77. Burr to Arthur E. Bestor (copy), 20 March 1918, box 8, folder 1918, Harry F. Ward Papers, Burke Library, Special Collections, Archive and Manuscripts, Union Theological Seminary.
78. Rauschenbusch to Ward, 3 April 1919, box 8, folder 1919, Ward Papers.

changes on the basis of scientific knowledge and by orderly processes of political and social evolution."[79]

By the 1930s, however, Ward had clearly embraced what is best described as Christian Marxism, anxious to ram through the transformation of society and less reflective of the original principles of Social Christianity. His admiration of the Soviet Union was also quite apparent. As chairman of the American Civil Liberties Union in 1932, he was reported as stating, concerning freedom in the Soviet Union and the United States:

> The difference between the two countries is not a choice between political and economic freedom, as is often stated. It is rather a difference in direction. In neither country is it possible to organize an opposition to upset the system. But under the Soviet system, life moves experimentally to discover what freedom is possible and real under the controls necessary for a planned social economy. The very nature of government as we know it is changed. Here, under the illusion of freedom, a failing system tries to block all attempts to check those powers and privileges which condemn millions to hunger and make impossible their development.[80]

The basis of Ward's social-ethical thought since the early 1920s had been what he defined as the "new school" of economics. This new school, led by figures such as Thorstein Veblen in America and J. A. Hobson in Britain, was "a science of human relationships, and therefore a social and moral science." The old school, which he believed was no longer acceptable to younger social scientists, saw economics "as a natural science," which "came to be mainly a justification of the existing order."[81] Ward's approach, slightly reminiscent of George D. Herron's social science, seemed to lead to scientific socialism or Marxism. He expounded little theology through the period.

In his leadership capacity within the Methodist Federation for Social Service and with the help of Bishop Francis J. McConnell and others, Ward was formally to affiliate the entire organization with the American League Against War and fascism, of which he was also secretary. Years earlier Ward had displayed dictatorial traits on the Executive Committee of the Federation. Worth Tippy of the Federal Council of Churches' Commission for Social Service, writing to

79. Ward to Snedden, 30 January 1919, box 8, folder 1919, Ward Papers.

80. Abstract of remarks made by Professor Harry F. Ward, chairman of American Civil Liberties Union, "Freedom in the U.S.S.R. and the U.S.A.," 8 October 1932, box 10, articles, file I, Ward Papers.

81. Ward to David Snedden, 7 February 1919, box 8, folder 1919, Ward Papers.

McConnell on 24 November 1920, indicated his desire to resign in opposition to reconstitution of the executive, which would then be composed "exclusively of persons who are in sympathy with Dr. Ward's policies." Tippy noted: "The program outlined by Dr. Ward on Monday appears to me to be fraught with danger to the Federation, to the Methodist church and to society; and to be based upon a mistaken estimate of the outcome of the present industrial and political movement. Dr. Ward's program is the one to follow if the revolution is sure and desirable, but not otherwise."[82]

In the 1930s Ward became the key figure behind the United Front attempts to woo liberal clergy into alliance with Communism.[83] He was one of those responsible for launching the New America movement (an organization complementary to the American League Against War and Fascism) in the early 1930s, whose goal was the establishment of "a society without class distinctions or divisions." In order to accomplish their ends, New America believed "a controlled mixture of education and coercion is always required," albeit as "the only possible preventive of destructive violence."[84] Publicity was to be avoided and in its place infiltration emphasized, controlled by "democratic centralism." It was also stated that "an open door must be kept toward the Communist groups. In the end either the Communists will come into this movement or capture it, according to which has more vitality."[85] By the late 1930s Ward seems to have taken an increasingly hard-line Stalinist approach, noting in one letter concerning a fellow member, Richard Babbitt, that he had "dangerous tendencies in his thinking habits" because "his prevailing thought pattern is still Socialist-Liberal" with an "occasional side order of Trotskyism."[86] Concerning religion, the New America manifesto stated:

> A revolutionary economic change inevitably develops corresponding changes in religion. It therefore becomes the task of those who seek to revolutionize the social structure and the economic organization to discover what forms of religious behaviour must be destroyed because they buttress the old order, and what forms will best express and aid the new. This movement therefore expects its members who belong to

82. Tippy to McConnell (copy), box 15, Methodist Federation for Social Service, folder 1, Ward Papers.

83. See Marty, *Modern American Religion*, 2:292.

84. Transcription, "The Need," on approval of committee, 20 December 1933, p. 10, box 14, New America, folder I, Ward Papers.

85. Ibid., 3.

86. Ward to Tom Wright, 4 December 1938, box 14, New America—correspondence, folder VI, Ward Papers.

religious organizations to work within them for the eliminations of anti-social elements.[87]

It is a small wonder, given the statements of many in movements such as New America and the League Against Fascism and War or the estimated number of sympathetic clergy outside these United Front activities, that it was widely believed that many Social Christian clergy were Communists. This certainly prompted the congressional Committee on Un-American Activities to question some prominent clergy later in the McCarthy period.

Clearly the far Left Social Gospelers had allowed politics to dictate to religion. And there are even more-extreme examples. George Coe, unable to support the trend toward theological orthodoxy and totally giving up on the capacity of churches to do anything constructive in the cause of ultimate equality, turned to a type of spiritual Marxism by the early 1940s. Like Ward, he tended to lump capitalism, Roosevelt, and fascism together, though he remained a staunch believer in individual liberty.[88] One of his consolations was the support of the Soviet Union shared with fellow Christian Marxists as well as kindred spirits in Britain such as Hewlett Johnson.[89]

In spite of the fact that the Fellowship of Socialist Christians (FSC), with Reinhold Niebuhr as its chief spokesman, upheld the "class struggle" rhetoric of Marxism in the 1930s, its religious underpinnings were far more evident. This in large measure was characteristic of the other interdenominational or denominational organizations of the Left as opposed to the far Left. Though by late 1934 the Fellowship of Socialist Christians required membership in a socialist party rather than merely support,[90] its basic approach was to work through local churches. As Walter R. Warner, secretary of the FSC, explained to Professor Edgar S. Brightman of the Boston University School of Theology concerning FSC assistance to Labour Churches:

> We wish to assist only those labour churches that measure up to two qualifications. We should rather that the church be a genuine church with all the usual activities of worship, education, and fellowship. We

87. Transcription, "The Need," pp. 13–14.

88. Coe to "Bonnie," 19 September 1939, box 2, folder 11, manuscript group no. 36, George Albert Coe Papers, Yale Divinity School Library.

89. Johnson once sent Coe a warm letter in response to Coe's defense of his book *Soviet Power,* which had received a hostile review by W. E. Garrison in the *Christian Century* (Johnson to Coe, 4 June 1941, box 2, folder 15, Coe Papers).

90. Circular letter of Reinhold Niebuhr as national chairman, 19 October 1934, box 3, Fellowship of Socialist Christians Papers, Robert T. Handy collection, Burke Library Special Collections, Archives and Manuscripts, Union Theological Seminary.

favor those ministers who have a deep philosophical and theological grounding to their socialist Christian ideas. We fear that a labour church that gives only labour education tinged with some emotional fervor, or that a minister that has thought no farther than just to make a religion out of his socialism, cannot build anything very permanent.[91]

Niebuhr himself, when searching for a comparable movement overseas in the 1930s, found it in the British Socialist Christian League, which corresponded "most closely to our Fellowship of Socialist Christians." This group was largely Nonconformist and affiliated with the Labour Party. He also admired the Christendom group, which he placed "in the category of a kind of Anglican Social Gospel," though he felt that because of their recent identification with Social Credit they could not be counted in the ranks of the "genuine left." He viewed the Catholic Crusade of Conrad Noel as containing many who were Trotskyites and "not strong numerically."[92]

Clearly the Social Gospel of the Left sought less from the actual model of the Soviet Union and more from what was of possible value in Marxism as a philosophy. By the 1930s other more mainline organizations, such as the Fellowship of Reconciliation (especially after absorbing the Fellowship for a Christian Social Order in 1928), had begun making explicit statements on social conditions and racial justice that aligned them more toward Norman Thomas socialism and the labor movement, although they were badly divided for a time in 1933–34 when Christian Marxists attempted to assert themselves.[93] Could members condone the use of force in the class struggle while at the same time condemning the violence of war? The United Council for Christian Democracy, founded in 1936, experienced broad divisions between liberal and socialist adherents on a variety of such matters.

Polls appeared throughout the period that indicated the strong appeal of socialist-inclined ideas to Social Gospel clergy. But the prospects of a breakup of the churches was a sobering one. On the other side a 1936 *Literary Digest* poll of 21,606 clergy of all descriptions suggested that 70 percent were actually opposed to the progressive politics of the New Deal.[94] Robert Miller, after surveying all Protestant periodicals, suggested that the vast majority favored

91. Warner to Brightman, 4 November 1935, box 1, folder B, Fellowship of Socialist Christians Papers.

92. "Radicalism in British Christianity," *Radical Religion* 1, no. 4 (1936): 7–8.

93. Robert Moats Miller, *American Protestantism and Social Issues, 1919–1939* (Chapel Hill, N.C., 1958), 96.

94. Ahlstrom, *Religious History of the American People*, 924.

Hoover in 1932 and a smaller majority Landon in 1936.[95] He also noted the lingering strength of Prohibitionism and anti-Catholicism, as opposed to unemployment and other pressing social issues, as subjects of editorials. In addition, fundamentalism had produced demagogues of the far Right, and rightward drift needed to be considered, if not controlled, by church leaders.

As the 1930s came to a close in a tense prelude to the Second World War, issues became more complicated. Stalin signed a pact with Hitler, and both invaded Poland in 1939. The Christian pacifism of earlier times seemed increasingly out of joint with the issues of the day. The deep division caused by pacifism in the Social Gospel ranks began to subside, as did isolationism. As Niebuhr described in his own case, the political manipulations of FDR began to appear to be political artistry.[96] The Federal Council of Churches' earlier informal backing of the New Deal began to look better and better.[97]

In Canada many Social Christians and conservative Christians generally believed that the churches were strong in their social influence. Nellie McClung could say in the midst of the Dirty Thirties (while noting that the churches must listen to the pews or perish): "The church is strong here, and enjoys the confidence of the people, even the people who are not enrolled in its ranks."[98] In Canada there was nothing quite like the New Deal that could act as a political conduit for the social ideas of the moderate majority of Social Christians. The rather sudden, pragmatic, and belated attempt by the Conservative prime minister R. B. Bennett, an old-fashioned Methodist, to introduce in the mid-1930s some social security and social planning legislation was unsatisfactory.[99] MacKenzie King, Liberal opposition leader, could offer only quibbles about the constitutionality of federal government actions on these questions, which would disappoint Social Christians with Liberal political sympathies. However, support was probably given to any major-party proposals that seemed progressive in the moderate Social Gospel spirit of the United Church and other mainline churches. But the cutting edge of Social Christianity's politics remained J. S. Woodsworth,

95. Miller, *American Protestantism and Social Issues*, 117–23.

96. "Politics in the 30s," passim.

97. Miller, *American Protestantism and Social Issues*, 88.

98. "What Have We Learned in 1937," 9/24, add. MSS, 10, box 26: Notebooks and Diaries, Nellie McClung Papers, Archives of Province of British Columbia.

99. See J.R.H. Wilbur, ed., *The Bennett New Deal: Fraud or Portent?* (Toronto, 1968). Certainly P. B. Waite's *Loner: Three Sketches of the Personal Life of R. B. Bennett, 1870–1947* (Toronto, 1993) reveals both the strong religious background of R. B. Bennett and his fear of socialism. In Britain at this time, Frank Hardie wrote to Conrad Noel, "I think some people today, like Bennett, the Canadian P.M., quite consciously intend to use Buchmanite revivalism to prevent a social revolution in the early Twentieth century" (Hardie to Noel, 24 August 1933, DNO 2/6, Conrad Noel Papers, Brynmor Jones Library, University of Hull).

who together with socialist intellectuals and farmer and labor groups founded the Cooperative Commonwealth Federation (CCF) in 1933 at Regina, Saskatchewan. Within the next few years CCF organizations spread throughout the country, and as a political party they formed the Official Opposition in the legislatures of Saskatchewan and British Columbia.

The platform of the CCF party called for a planned, or "socialized," economy and the "eradication of capitalism." But these were long-term objectives in the same way that the British Labour Party viewed them. Indeed the Labour Party and George Lansbury, in particular, were a model to Woodsworth.[100] In practice, the CCF functioned much as the Progressive group of the previous decade, prodding the conventional party leaders into further action on short-term matters. The CCF also embedded itself into the politics of Western farmers and, in a more qualified way, of labor, achieving what Norman Thomas's socialists had failed to do in the United States. This political culture was decidedly Social Christian of the Left, but not far Left, with the Christian Marxists having little voice, and in consequence perhaps frustrated the advance of a Canadian Communist movement (assisted by very repressive legislation). In 1942 Woodsworth's successor as M.P. for Winnipeg North was Stanley Knowles, another Social Gospel minister. M. J. Coldwell, a Western, British-born school teacher, was also prominent in the leadership; his Anglicanism raised hopes among British Social Christians that he might one day succeed Woodsworth.[101]

Social Christian politics in Woodsworth's Western heartland were somewhat confused by the Social Credit experiment under the populist William "Bible Bill" Aberhart in Alberta. Hopes for the experiment ran high with a number of Christendom Movement clergy, some Quaker promoters, and especially Hewlett Johnson, who actually campaigned for Aberhart in the province. But as another British clergyman observed: "The religious element of the movement is well known but it is not so well understood that it seems also to have a definitely fascist colour, claiming to be the only real bulwark against socialism."[102] Aberhart, of course, was rooted in fundamentalism and came to a moderate Social Gospel position only in his later religious thought.[103] His social and economic policies, however, became progressively more conservative with the passage of the 1930s.

100. Mills, *Fool for Christ*, 216, 276 n.112.

101. Canon Burgon Bickersteth, "Some Observations on the Present Political Situation in Canada, April 1936," confidential, vol. 141, Cosmo Lang Papers, Lambeth Palace Archives.

102. Ibid. The British origins and religious connections of Canadian Social Credit have been explored by John L. Finlay, *Social Credit: The English Origins* (Montreal, 1972), esp. chap. 10.

103. See David Elliott and Iris Miller, *Bible Bill: A Biography of William Aberhart* (Edmonton, 1987), 178.

The Catholic half of the population, however, constituted a much larger stumbling block to the influence of Social Gospel politics. Though the Antigonish Movement in the Maritime Provinces shared many of the same aspirations as the Social Gospelers, the politics of Social Catholicism were not as clear. Quebec, home to the largest Catholic population, was led both in church and in state by men suspicious of the motives of the CCF in particular, though Social Catholicism was also on the move. Woodsworth, unlike Norman Thomas, had little appeal beyond the Anglo-Saxon pale, having rather hostile attitudes toward immigrants and French Canadian Catholics, as well as exhibiting racism on occasion.[104]

In spite of these major limitations many historians continue to point to Woodsworth as the conscience in the politics of English Canada, as a rough equivalent to Temple in Britain. Through the League for Social Reconstruction and other associations, he had a wide circle of intellectual friends, including Frank Underhill (a Canadian equivalent of a Fabian),[105] Frank Scott, and Eugene Forsey. His influence transcended the relatively small representation of the CCF in the federal House of Commons. It is also significant that the Social Gospel tradition carried on to the 1960s with the transformation of the CCF into the NDP. Its leader, Tommy Douglas, a former Western Baptist pastor, frequently employed the metaphor of the New Jerusalem in political speeches.

In Britain of the 1930s nothing comparable to the New Deal (which had served the political ends of many American Social Christians with some success) emerged, nor did a parliamentary political force under the direction of a Social Christian, as had Woodsworth's CCF. William Temple emerged a rather great prophet figure but one who could not make his views more concretely felt through the instrument of a political party and specific policies. This is not to say that Social Christians were not active in the area of politics. However, Edward Norman's assessment that "very little was either proposed or done by the Church in the face of recession—a great contrast to the United States, where the 'Social Gospel' underwent a revival of popularity and prestige in these years"[106]—is, on the whole, well founded.

Norman's comments most directly apply to the Church of England, but Nonconformity was equally ineffective. To some degree the political influence of the latter was split in 1929 between a reconstituted Liberal Party under Lloyd George and Labour. Sectarian tensions also surfaced, as when the Conservative leader, Baldwin, attempted to solicit more Nonconformist (Baptist) votes—

104. Mills, *Fool for Christ,* 16–17, 36, 231–32, explores racist attitudes toward the native peoples.
105. See R. Douglas Francis, *Frank H. Underhill: Intellectual Provocateur* (Toronto, 1986).
106. Norman, *Church and Society in England, 1770–1970,* 340.

though Baldwin's respect for Nonconformists was appreciated.[107] And there were those who had reservations about politics altogether. The Free Church leadership, perhaps as a result of internal divisions over the General Strike, joined in making temperance a prime issue in the election of 1929. Even P.T.R. Kirk and Henry Carter, joint secretaries of the Council of Christian Ministers on Social Questions, indicated that "[t]he daily and weekly secular Press testify to the emergence of Temperance Reform as a foremost moral claim at the present election, largely as a result of the work of the young electors, enrolled in the Active Service Order. Certainly, Christian electors, irrespective of Party, should rejoice in this manifest quickening in the national movement for Temperance Reform."[108]

Candidates were interviewed on the issue, and high hopes were raised for a temperance and sabbatarian parliament. Among the political parties, the Liberals responded with a hundred-page temperance policy report, Labour supported a royal commission investigation, and the Conservatives sidestepped the issue. It is instructive that the Temperance Council of the Christian Churches, which received high profile in the election, was an elected body of laymen and clergy. Was it more representative of rank-and-file churchgoers? Some Social Christians acted as though they believed so. The Council on Social Questions was a clerical body, now also compelled to endorse the primacy of temperance. They did manage to issue a Social Christian statement on other issues, however, including "(1) International Peace; (2) Industrial Recovery, particularly in regard to the coal industry; (3) Slum Clearance; (4) Education—here the point urged is the raising of the school-learning age; (5) Unemployment."[109]

For Social Christians, however, the formation of a Labour government in 1929 was a potentially happy event. As James Adderley wrote to George Lansbury on 8 June 1929: "What a glorious time this is and now it makes one go back in mind to dear old Keir Hardie and his prophesies which have all come true. The Labour Movement is the only one that is a Movement, with an inspiration behind it."[110] Lansbury, the soon-to-be leader of the party, in many ways was Social Christianity's best hope. He became president of the Christian Socialist Crusade, which was started by a group of Labour M.P.'s who believed that the ethics of Jesus and of their brand of socialism were identical. According

107. See "Conservativism: The Baptists and the Church Times," *Baptist Times*, 14 February 1929.

108. Kirk and Carter, letter to editor, *Methodist Times*, 25 April 1929.

109. "From the Editor's Chair," *Methodist Times*, 18 April 1929.

110. Adderley to Lansbury, 8 June 1929, vol. 9, George Lansbury Papers, British Library of Political and Economic Science, London.

to the *Methodist Recorder* (19 March 1931), which reported on their conference in London, religion was what made Lansbury a socialist. It also noted that Methodist ministers at the conference seemed in the majority, though they "were apparently about equally divided in support and in criticism of the Crusade."

The *East Anglian Daily Times* said of the crusade (18 March 1931) that it was commendable if its purpose was to make a Christian out of the "more virulent" type of socialist. However, if out to capture the churches for socialism, then the crusade served Soviet Russia, "where Christ is repudiated." Nationalization, according to the *East Anglian Daily Times,* had to be restrained from fulfilling the desires of the "Robin Hood" mind of the full-blooded socialist. As the Ipswich paper noted, "[T]he ethics of Robin Hood are not the ethics of Christ."

The ravages of the Great Depression and tension with the Labour movement plagued the MacDonald government. Though writers such as the Christian Socialist R. H. Tawney argued that the Labour Party was not a class party, most of its support could in fact be found in the working class. The decisions concerning the Unemployment Fund and the events leading to the formation of the Conservative-dominated, so-called National Government shattered many pro–Labour Party Social Christians' hopes for social remedies through politics. Though support for the Labour Party came readily from those who had originally supported it, the defeat and division of the period were disillusioning. It should be remembered that Philip Snowden, who stood with Ramsay MacDonald in exile, had been popular with Social Christians, especially Samuel E. Keeble, who believed that he had brought Snowden to Christianity in the first place. However, Keeble sided with Arthur Henderson and the rest of the Labour Party. As he mused to a friend concerning MacDonald and his other formerly successful socialist leaders who defected to established power: "It is marvellous how many have climbed to power by its [socialism's] means—in France, Germany and England and then lost either their heads or their hearts and forsake the Cause. Think of Briand, Millerand, Vivani, Mussolini, Blatchford, MacDonald, Snowden, Thomas and others. How few can 'carry corn' or refuse the bewitchments of popularity or social position."[111]

Worries existed following the formation of the National Government. Seebohm Rowntree described the situation to an American friend in the early 1930s:

> The political situation here is only a fiasco with the so-called "National" Government, which is becoming more and more Conservative.

111. Keeble to Joyce Hinsworth, 24 July 1932, S, folder 10, ⅔, Keeble Papers.

Ramsay MacDonald is a figure-head, respected by none. He is ineffective, and we all feel that he is selling his soul. Liberals like Simon and
Runciman, who are in the Cabinet are, I think, lost to Liberalism, and
will probably join the Conservative party. They have done it in act
now; they will do it in word after a time. Labour is gaining in power
every day, and I think that at the next election, the Liberals will be
practically wiped out, and the Conservatives will only have a narrow
majority.[112]

Yet some clergy interested in social reform had faith in the National Government leadership. The Reverend Grenville Cooke, writing from Cransley Vicarage,
Kettering, urged the prime minister to stand up against the "Diehard" Tories:

At present your Government is supported by thousands like myself
*because* it has proved itself an idealistic team bent on practical measures. The march of opinion is inevitably away from narrow nationalis-
tic views towards a more Christian form of social service. The average
Englishman of the middle class dislikes "Reds" and Revolutions: and
he detests and scorns jingoism: *that* is why he follows you and trusts
you: he feels in his bones that you are "white" and incorruptible—an
idealist.[113]

Confusion once again was apparent within Nonconformity. Henry Carter, in
his last days, with the help of Keeble and Donald Soper, had gained the approval
of the newly formed Methodist Union for his declaration *Christian View of
Industry in Relation to the Social Order* at the conference of 1934. As David
Jeremy has indicated, its social advocacy once again may have stirred the
antisocialist feelings of many Methodists.[114]

For some Nonconformist Social Christians, however, a golden opportunity
now appeared in the Council of Action Campaign of 1935. Dissatisfied with the
Conservative (National) Government and the Labour opposition, the hopes of
some now focused on a third option, the aged Lloyd George. No longer leader of
the Liberal Party but still popular, Lloyd George made one last try at a political
comeback by combining his personal charisma, oratorical skills, reputation as a
social reformer in the last generation, organizer of the victorious war cabinet,

112. Rowntree to Leland Robinson, 26 May 1934, correspondence Leland R. Robinson, file 1,
Seebohm Rowntree Papers, Rowntree Trust.
113. Cooke to the prime minister, 10 February 1935, general correspondence, MS Simon 81, f.
244, Papers of John Allsebrook Simon, Bodleian Library, Oxford University.
114. Jeremy, *Capitalists and Christians*, 177.

and friend of the National Council of Free Churches to launch a "New Deal" set of proposals for government. After making speeches in the previous year or so that garnered considerable sympathy from pacifists as well as those in the major parties anxious for a remedy to unemployment, he approached cabinet late in 1934. Knowing that his actual political clout was limited, he then launched a "call to action" for his New Deal early in 1935, receiving considerable support from Nonconformist leaders, who formed a Council of Action. There was potential. As Sir John Simon wrote to Neville Chamberlain within the National Government, "I feel in my bones that the Lloyd George campaign is going to be a rather serious event for us."[115] Among supporters were prominent Social Christian ministers such as Henry Carter, Scott Lidgett, P.T.R. Kirk (secretary of the ICF), and R. E. Rattenbury. Philip Snowden also joined the Lloyd George–led campaign. But aside from some Liberals and Labourites, Conservatives of the most progressive type, such as Harold Macmillan and his "Next Five Years" Group, disappointingly remained at a distance.[116]

The manifesto "Peace and Reconstruction," issued in June 1935, called upon "men and women, irrespective of all party attachments, to pledge themselves to secure at the approaching general election the return of a Parliament whose members are committed to insist on measures that will apply to the problem of unemployment remedies commensurate with the magnitude of its dangers to the moral and physical well-being of the community." The manifesto demanded that "the state" put forth "a great effort of national reconstruction and . . . organize the full resources of our social and economic system for the revival of our industrial life and the provision of work on schemes of useful and necessary public development." Slums were to be cleared, further provision for "healthy recreation and amenities of the nation" established, and the countryside restored "to fertility." It even provided for the improvement of the highway system "to reduce its daily toll of death and injury." The manifesto also called for world peace through more creative methods and was framed as a politically nonpartisan appeal, with "the constraint of Christian obligation and of social responsibility" as its "sole mainspring."[117]

It was soon apparent that the Council of Action was in fact politically partisan. This deterred sympathetic politicians, such as Lansbury, from giving further support in the Labour Party. Likewise, Nonconformists with social

---

115. Simon to Chamberlain, 9 January 1935, correspondence, MS 81, f. 31–32, Papers of John Allsebrook Simon.

116. See Arthur Marwick, "Middle Opinion in the Thirties: Planning, Progress and Political Agreement," *English Historical Review* 79 (April 1964): 285–98.

117. "Peace and Reconstruction," *Christian World,* 13 June 1935.

conscience sympathies in the National Government, such as Walter Runciman, became suspicious. Clergy who signed the manifesto now had to defend their action or withdraw support. Methodism began to be badly divided. Many Baptists gave support, but powerful figures such as M. E. Aubrey objected, seeing it as primarily political: "The document [manifesto] made a great deal of missed opportunities and imputed a lack of zeal to Governments."[118] For Aubrey it was too political in not recognizing the positive achievements of the National Government. Soon a small exodus of clergy signatories took place. P.T.R. Kirk and the bishop of Rochester withdrew, ending any small interest there might have been among senior Anglican clergy. Carter's departure was a more serious sign for the almost completely Nonconformist phalanx that supported the campaign.[119]

Perhaps the most astute reflections came from the *Spectator* (5 July 1935) regarding the Free Churches and the Council for Action. Noting the frequent comments on problems touching politics by Church of England bodies such as the Church Congress, the *Spectator* conceded that "[t]he duty of the Churches to educate and inspire Christian citizens who make it their business to apply the tenants of Christianity in the field of citizenship is undeniable." However, it went on to state:

> The term Council of Action has no very encouraging associations. The proposed council can more easily agitate than act. If it means that the Free Churches are to be mobilized in advance behind a programme sponsored primarily by one militant political crusader, the effect on the Free Churches will be bad. If it means that the Free Churches are in any way to sever themselves from the Church of England on such issues as reconstruction and the League of Nations it will be much worse than bad.

The Council of Action campaign proceeded, however. Local councils were organized in England and Wales, and a progressively closer association was forged with the National Free Church Council. In September Lloyd George formally launched the campaign at a great meeting in Plymouth that included delegates from local councils, Nonconformist churches, temperance groups, and cooperative guilds. In the same month the National Free Church Council instructed local Free Church councils to assist the local councils of action,[120] thus

118. *Baptist Times*, 27 June 1935.
119. See "Not Non-Political," *Birmingham Post*, 1 July 1935.
120. Stephen Koss, *Nonconformity in Modern British Politics* (London, 1975), 207, 208.

adding to the credibility of the charge that they were being used by the politicians. Officially they were not to engage in party politics,[121] but the suspicions grew, as did resentment against the triumvirate of Scott Lidgett, S. W. "Sammy" Hughes, and F. W. Norwood, who dominated the actual affairs of both councils.

The final device of the campaign was equally controversial. Rather than field their own candidates, which would be too overtly political, the Council of Action submitted to all candidates of whatever party for the forthcoming election a questionnaire, the answers to which the council would use to determine which candidates to endorse. The questions were as follows:

1. Do you whole-heartedly support the policy for Peace and Reconstruction advocated by the Council of Action, as set out in its official statement, "Peace and Reconstruction," and do you pledge yourself, if returned to Parliament, to insist upon this policy being implemented by whatever Government takes office after the Election?

2. Will you, to whatever Party you belong, join an inter-Party Group of members similarly pledged, and undertake on all issues which concern the carrying into effect of this policy to act in consultation and co-operation with that Group to bring the utmost pressure to bear upon Government to implement the policy?

3. Do you pledge yourself that you will on all occasions consistently support and vote for this policy even should the Government of the day fail or refuse to carry it out?[122]

Such assurances from candidates posed questions of disloyalty to their own parties. The scrupulous would have hesitated. Liberals may have readily pledged themselves, thinking that the Free Church–backed, Lloyd George–led Council of Action was really an adjunct to the Liberal Party.

About one-half of the candidates answered the questionnaire, and ultimately 354 were deemed acceptable by the Council of Action. In a number of constituencies both Liberal and Labour candidates were approved. All Liberals were endorsed, but only sixteen National Government candidates. Shortly before the election Lidgett veered toward outright support of the National Government, causing last-minute difficulties for the council because of the large number of Labour candidates approved. Samuel E. Keeble, writing to Walter Tripp, thought "Scott Lidgett should be ashamed of himself—to go over to the so-

121. Ibid., 202.
122. *Morning Post,* 8 November 1935.

called 'national,' 'Tory' side."[123] Shortly before, on 7 and 8 November, the *Morning Post* disclosed that many of the Labour Party candidates and the handful of National Government candidates, stated by the council to have made full affirmations, had not done so.

The Council of Action was tied for the most part to the Liberals, and that party did not do well in the election. That the council had any significant effect on the election is dubious. The recriminations that followed in Nonconformist circles were significant. The Reverend W. H. Armstrong, writing in the *Methodist Times and Leader* (21 November 1935) noted that "the Free Churches were badly let down at the General Election." Blaming the executive of the Free Church Council, the Council of Action, and Lloyd George, Armstrong suggested that "the time has come for a cessation of manifestos, resolutions etc.," on great issues and that steps be taken to form a properly representative body for Free Church opinion. The Nonconformist presence in politics, much less their social conscience in politics, was virtually at an end.

It is conceivable that a British equivalent of the New Deal could have helped to restore the morale of Social Christians in the arena of politics, as it had in the United States. But Lloyd George was no FDR. Responsibility for the failure of a New Deal scheme for Britain cannot be placed solely at the feet of the churches or indeed Lloyd George, of course. Daniel Ritschel has challenged the notion professed by Arthur Marwick, Paul Addison, and others, that a shared consensus on planning in public policy was emerging by the early 1930s.[124] Only at the very end of the 1930s, in the Popular Front and other forms of dialogue between planners in the various parties, such as Harold Macmillan and G.D.H. Cole, was there any emerging consensus on a public policy in that regard. In the meantime the record of the National Government in dealing with many social problems was probably as good as Roosevelt's and did have the initial support of public Christians such as Clifford Allen. The period of real planning consensus was the next decade.

The desire to affect ends through the manipulation of politics was reasonable. The problem for the Nonconformist churches, and perhaps churches in

123. Keeble to Tripp, 20 November 1935, folder 8, 9, Keeble Papers.
124. Daniel Ritschel, "A Corporatist Economy in Britain? Capitalist Planning for Industrial Self-Government in the 1930s," *English Historical Review* 106 (January 1991): 41–65. Among those affiliated with Social Christianity, Seebohm Rowntree expressed doubts about Roosevelt's governmental interventions (Rowntree to Leland Robinson, 4 December 1933, Robinson file, Rowntree Papers, Rowntree Trust); at the other end of the political spectrum, Sir Stafford Cripps saw massive loss of support for the New Deal in America (untitled paper, $^{746}\!/_{558}$, Sir Stafford Cripps Papers, Nuffield College Library, Oxford University). For Marwick, see note 114 above; see also Paul Addison, *The Road to 1945* (London, 1975), 16–21, 35–44.

general, was that their overall influence was in a decline. The Council of Action was an unfortunate miscalculation. A New Deal already in motion might have been used to achieve social goals as the National Council of Churches did in the United States. But a New Deal conceived by the churches, or indeed by the Nonconformist churches for the most part, was beyond their capacity to sustain. The council was seen in the last resolve as a maneuver by Lloyd George and generally induced Social Christians to join their conservative, evangelical counterparts in Nonconformity in the Great Reversal from politics. This interpretation is supported by a greater number of articles and letters that appeared in the Nonconformist periodicals in the late 1930s criticizing political involvement.

Peter Catterall has written that Nonconformist socialists within Labour continued to be important in making party objectives reflect a moral imperative in the interwar period.[125] However, Catterall also made it clear that this influence—given the declining quality of chapel-trained leaders in competition with the leadership of secular organizations such as trade unions—was steadily diminishing. Beneath this was the institutional decay of the chapel itself, of course.[126]

The Church of England had also experienced a bumpy ride in the political arena after the General Strike and coal stoppage fiasco of the late 1920s. Apart from its suspicion of political Nonconformity and Lloyd George, this instability may have been a factor in the Church of England's clear reluctance to become involved in the Council of Action. Many Anglicans might have agreed with Hensley Henson's assessment of the effects of COPEC on church thinking,[127] stated in his manuscript journals for 9 August 1924:

> The parallel between "Christianity" as represented by 'Copec' and "Labour," as represented by its extremists is suggestively close in at least one important particular. They will not accept the general stream of human tradition and take their place within it; but must vindicate a separate point of view, a recognizable distinct influence and objective. The result is bad enough in the case of "Labour," for the particularist temper known as 'class-consciousness' obliterates the frontiers of right and wrong, and leads (as in the conspicuous case of Russia) to the most shocking violations of the Moral Law. Can the result be wholesome in

125. See Catterall, "Morality and Politics."

126. See Clyde Binfield, *So Down to Prayers: Studies in English Nonconformity, 1780–1920* (London, 1977), and Kenneth Young, *Chapel* (London, 1972).

127. Adrian Hastings believes that people listened to figures such as Henson "because the middle-class layman in the pew naturally agreed with what they had to say" (Hastings, *History of English Christianity,* 176).

the case of Christianity? Will not this passionate insistence on a
definitely "Christian" vision of every human concern carry those who
make it into the difficult business of life with minds closed to truth, and
obsessed with policies which are not in any genuine sense Christian at
all?[128]

This is not to say the Social Christians were completely deterred in political
affairs because of setbacks earlier in the 1920s. Percy Dearmer produced a
collection entitled *Christianity and the Crisis* in 1933, which included calls by
P.T.R. Kirk, among others, for church action in the economic depression beyond
the words of conferences. However, in reference to Keeble's offering, Dearmer
could still advise him, in a old-fashioned vein, that "it was worth reminding
people that the keeping of a day of rest is one of the great social reforms
of history."[129]

The extreme Left of Social Christianity, mostly Anglican, was perhaps busier
as an organization and in the production of literature in the 1930s. They also
had contacts with the Left of American Social Christianity, often collaborating
in various undertakings. One example was the collection *Christianity and the
Social Revolution,* edited by Robert B. Y. Scott and Gregory Vlastos and published by Victor Gollancz in 1936. Introduced by Charles Raven, it included
contributions by figures such as Conrad Noel, Gilbert Clive Binyon (a Yorkshire
vicar), Julius H. Heckler (a former New York Methodist minister at Moscow
University), and Reinhold Niebuhr. The political posture of the collection was
predictably of the extreme Left. The collection attempted to bring Christians
into dialogue with Communism. Seeing the goals of Communism to be laud-
able, most pieces envisaged the opportunity of an evolving Christianity and an
evolving Communism finding common ground. However, the collection, in
spite of its political intent, contained a surprising amount of theology. Charles
Raven's scholarly eye also ensured a devotion to historical accuracy and led to
the rejection of a number of essays, including a second one by Noel that seemed
to distort for present-day activist reasons such things as the attitude of early
Christians toward property.[130]

By the time *Christianity and the Social Revolution* was published in the
mid-1930s, Noel's Catholic Crusade had come to an end. The Anglo-Catholic
Christendom Movement was also somewhat divided on issues of pacifism, and
there was even recurrent interest in Social Credit. As W. G. Peck wrote to

128. Vol. 37, 141, Henson Papers.
129. Dearmer to Keeble, 19 January 1933, folder ⅞, Keeble Papers.
130. Raven to Noel, 11 January 1935, ⅔₂, Noel Papers.

Maurice Reckitt in 1938: "But I think that neither the Conservative, nor the Liberal, nor the Socialist ideology can provide the categories in which we are to think of the human relations likely to be shaped by the acceptance of financial realism. Indeed, I like to say that Social Credit will not so much determine new human relations, as allow them to be focused in human freedom; and that is why Social Credit is so clearly an instrument which Catholic philosophy ought to use."[131]

But Social Credit had also interested Hewlett Johnson, who was much more of a Low Churchman with a strong theologically liberal background. After his experience with Aberhart in Alberta, he quickly departed from the ranks of Social Credit supporters and moved rapidly to support hard-line Marxism. Johnson's change of direction was due not only to the fact that Aberhart was "not very forthcoming over his difficulties,"[132] but also to his need forcefully to resist the advance of fascism in the second half of the 1930s. A visit to the Spanish Civil War in 1937 convinced him of the need to identify with the Communist side in this and other struggles with fascist aggression. Johnson had been influenced by the Communist sympathies of Conrad Noel and Lewis Donaldson, vicar of St. Mark's, Leicester. It was this multiplicity of influences as well as the United Front promptings of the publisher Victor Gollancz (of the Left Book Club) that moved Hewlett Johnson to serve the cause of Moscow. After 1935 he became vice president of the Society for Cultural Relations with the USSR and worked not only with English figures but also with Americans such as Sherwood Eddy and Harry Ward, who believed that the Soviet Union was of central importance in stemming fascism and in providing an alternate model to corrupt capitalism in Western society. His first major book of praise for the Communist system, *The Socialist Sixth of the World* (1939)—followed by *Soviet Strength: Its Source and Challenge* (1942)—sold well on both sides of the Atlantic.

Johnson was not treated quite so derisively as in his later "Red Dean" period, when he was termed "nutty as a fruit cake." However, his sudden swing to Stalinism after Social Credit (the latter being viewed by many as moving quickly into the fascist camp) made him a mercurial, peripheral figure. As Edward Norman points out, his conversion was based upon a careful examination of Tawney's works as well as those of other English socialists until, quite systematically, he refuted the capitalist system in favor of Marxism.[133] His later notoriety in the 1940s and 1950s tended to obscure the intellect behind the public political postures of the 1930s.

131. Peck to Reckitt, 28 March 1938, ¹⁰/₇, Maurice B. Reckitt Papers, University of Sussex Library.
132. Johnson, *Searching for Light: An Autobiography,* 137.
133. Norman, *Church and Society in England, 1770–1970,* 353.

Samuel E. Keeble, the still-practicing Methodist minister, had come to a Communist position in roughly the same period. In spite of his association with non-Marxists (such as V. A. Demant on the Christian Social Council) in the 1930s, he held increasingly to a Marxist line. His disillusionment with the Labour Party progressed through the 1930s; he wrote in one letter: "It seems to have lost its Socialistic and Christian soul. When will it regain it? It began in 1931 with the defection of MacDonald and Snowden, and has continued with its immersion in materialistic and not idealistic pursuits."[134] As he wrote and lectured, he came to believe more and more that even in the Soviet Union the materialist philosophy of Communism was eroding[135] and that Christian Socialism was "the only Socialism which has a lasting future which is the true solution of all our woes."[136] In the mid-1930s he had believed that Communists were better than Christians, rejecting a god of the greedy. According to Keeble:

> It is ours in England to bring about peacefully a *Christian* Communism— which I think we shall do finally one without tyranny, lack of toleration of others, without irreligion. I am glad to see the Trade-Union Congress speak out so well against fascism. It is really a disguised movement of big business and the middle classes to retain a profitable control of the workers. Hence big business finances it—as Thyssen does in Germany, and his like—multi-millionaires. Hitler depends on such men—hence his failure to reform the economic misery of the German people.[137]

While he agreed with the great struggle against fascism, he was not naive about the cruelties of the Soviet system. In opposition to Hewlett Johnson, he stated even in the war: "As you know I distrust Stalin and cannot take the good Dean's rosy view of him."[138] Keeble was also not totally at ease in the company of Anglicans, no matter how unorthodox politically. Keeble's Nonconformity had been offended earlier by the Anglican Conrad Noel in the Catholic Crusade. As he described Noel: "He is a fine advanced social reformer—but narrow and intolerant religiously, and never does justice to Protestants and Free Churches. He does not understand Puritanism at its best—which claims to be truest to Christ and the New Testament. . . . He is a great colourist too—a thing

---

134. Keeble to Joyce Hinsworth, 18 November 1939, folder 10, 2/20, Keeble Papers.
135. Ibid., 24 July 1932, folder 10, 2/6.
136. Ibid., 11 September 1939, folder 10, 2/19.
137. Ibid., 13 September 1934, folder 10, 2/11.
138. Ibid., 14 April 1940, folder 10, 2/21.

much needed in our dull climate. I am glad he is not a Fascist, as so many of the middle classes are. You had a fine sample of true *Xtian* socialism."[139]

Keeble was clear that his agreement with Marxism was in the area of economics. He never lost sight of his Christian ministry in spite of his association with the extreme Left. His good sense, avoidance of sectarianism, and occasionally quite realistic appraisals of the world of politics and diplomacy would have made him an excellent leader of British Social Christians if he had desired to be a leader.

The Left of Social Christianity was obviously confused and divided in Britain in the 1930s. The proliferation of small and medium-sized organizations, each with its own peculiar and arcane point of view, was unhelpful to the political cause of Social Christianity. The more extreme and less polite Marxism of the English Church Struggle and of the young Reverend Stanley Evans and the so-called Christian Democrats of the early 1940s led to much mischief. In attacking non-Marxists such as V. A. Demant and T. S. Eliot they came close to denouncing as enemies of social progress any who did not entirely agree with them. Evans and other extremists, according to one Anglo-Catholic clergyman, were imposing "the Right-Left fallacy two wings and no bird in the middle—which implies that all those who are not on your side are Fascist reactionaries."[140] The Labour Party also found that Evans and others were undermining their success by supporting Communists.[141]

The division over the question of pacifism was profound. Pacifism had earlier been largely the preserve of the Quakers and other Nonconformists in the Fellowship of Reconciliation. Henry Carter's Methodist Peace Fellowship had also been active in the field.[142] In the mid-1930s the immensely popular radio priest and canon of St. Paul's, the Reverend Dick Sheppard, gained tremendous backing from many clergy of all denominations in his campaign against rearmament. This new pacifism of 1934 was very popular in Social Christian circles. But for many church people Sheppard had disturbing attitudes. Highly critical of the structure of the Church of England, he argued against being "at the beck and call of the merely learned Theologians" while vested interests in church and state dictated. For Sheppard, "the Caesars have largely 'hobbled' the Churches" while determining armament policies and the like. His solution

139. Ibid., 9 August 1939, folder 10, $\frac{2}{17}$.

140. The Reverend J. V. Langmead Casserley to Evans, 30 May 1941, folder $\frac{1}{23}$, "Religion and the People," Papers of the Reverend Canon Stanley G. Evans, Brynmor Jones Library, University of Hull.

141. S. J. Warner, secretary (Plaistow Division) of the Labour Party, to Evans, 14 March 1940, folder $\frac{1}{19}$, "English Church Struggle," Papers of the Reverend Canon Stanley G. Evans.

142. See E. C. Unwin, *Henry Carter, C.B.E.: A Memoir* (London, 1955).

was "a fresh edition of Christianity with the teaching of the Sermon on the Mount."[143]

Joining with fellow Anglicans such as Charles Raven and Nonconformist clergy such as Donald Soper as well as affiliated politicians such as George Lansbury, Social Christians led by Sheppard mingled with the Fellowship of Reconciliation and predominantly secular groups in establishing the Peace Pledge Union. As non-Christian figures such as Bertrand Russell became increasingly powerful within the union, they demanded more of a voice. Gerald Heard, writing to Sheppard about the overabundance of clergy on the executive of the Peace Pledge Union, summarized the situation:

> There will either be a secular or religious advance here—a double advance with overlapping and some misunderstanding, or there will be a single advance combining the secular and the religious in an organization which, without any possibility of misunderstanding on the part of secularists or religious takes the spiritual realities that are present in both efforts and equally discards the particular and exclusive outlook and tradition which are present in both, and combines them into one way of action, a philosophy, an advocacy, a behaviour and a goal. As Aldous [Huxley] has said the Christian will of course go the Christian way, the secularist the psychological way—there need be no conflict here but only the best emulation as to which can best deliver the goods.[144]

A dilemma therefore developed concerning the position of Social Christianity within the framework of the broader movement. The dangers inherent in the mingling of the sacred and the secular were in this case best expressed by William Temple in his advice to Sheppard.

> As far as I can judge, if I were in your position I should continue to officiate as a minister of the C. of E. trying to leaven it from within, and also to influence the world outside. But I think a good deal turns on your answer to the following question:—Do you hold that you are called at this time to put pacifism first, in respect of the question whether those whom you persuade become Christian or not? or do

143. Sheppard to Lawrence Houseman, February 1927, Houseman file, Hugh Richard Lawrie Sheppard Papers (in the possession of the Right Honorable Lady Richardson of Duntisbourne).
144. Heard to Sheppard, 20 June 1936, Heard file, Sheppard Papers.

you put Christianity in its total content first, and urge pacifism chiefly
as a corollary of Christianity?[145]

Sheppard remained a priest until not many months after clashes in the
Church Assembly in 1937; where opposition was rife, he died. Figures such as
V. A. Demant vehemently opposed pacifism. The political impact of Sheppard's
movement was quickly nullified by the Spanish Civil War, the revelations about
the dangers of fascism, and the failure of appeasement. Lansbury fell from
leadership of the Labour Party, most Labourites now being committed to the
defense of social democracy by force if necessary. Charles Raven, Donald
Soper, and a few others remained in the minority among Social Christians in
their continued pacifism once war broke out in September of 1939. By late 1938
efforts to help the German Christian refugees as well as to continue dialogue
with German church authorities in the interests of ecumenism (which was
linked with pacifism in the case of Bishop Bell) ended with the revelations of the
Kristallnacht. By that time, in opposition to Nazism, most Social Christian
figures could also ally themselves with North American figures such as Reinhold Niebuhr, who had also rejected pacifism.

Pacifism in the United States, of course, had been much more divisive for
Social Christianity. The drift toward war had led the influential *Christian
Century,* which saw Roosevelt as responsible for this drift, to withdraw its
support for FDR's New Deal. By the end of the 1930s this journal, which had
been solid in its Social Gospel credentials, could actually support the Republicans as the best way to stay out of war. This then justified the later charge that
the New Deal had exhausted itself and that Roosevelt's bid for a third term was a
move toward fascism.[146] Carter argues that those Social Gospelers of the Left
who tied their socialism firmly to pacifism were less damaged by the general
schism that opened in the mainstream, moderate Social Gospel ranks, though
the active war against fascism after Pearl Harbor would pose further problems
for them. Complications abounded. Kirby Page, for example, though a pacifist,
found that he wanted to strengthen ties with the Soviet Union while distancing
himself from Earl Browder and the American Communist Party.[147] The American Fellowship of Reconciliation, in spite of its strong commitment to the
Socialist Party, also experienced internal divisions from the debate over use of
violence for the sake of the class war as opposed to violence against political

145. Temple to Sheppard, 12 February 1937, Temple file, Sheppard Papers.
146. See Carter, *Decline and Revival of Social Gospel,* 210–12.
147. *Kirby Page, Social Evangelist: The Autobiography of a Twentieth-Century Prophet for Peace,*
ed. Harold E. Fey (New York, 1975), 96–97. For the 1920s, see M. J. Ferrero, "Social Gospelers and
Soviets," *Journal of Church and State* 19, no. 1 (1977): 53–73.

dictatorship. The late influence of Gandhi did not stem the pessimistic attrition out of the movement in the late 1930s and early 1940s, though it did contribute to new approaches to racial justice.[148]

In Canada the great moral prophet in politics, J. S. Woodsworth, did not have the support of the CCF in his opposition to war in 1939.[149] Though anti-imperialist sentiment had risen, so had the fear of fascism. Throughout the 1930s much of the fervor for pacifism within the ranks of early-twentieth-century Protestantism had found expression in the wider religious and secular circles, through the Woodsworth family, and in such organizations as the Canadian Fellowship of Reconciliation.[150] However, realism within the CCF, as in other parties, prevailed in 1939.

The real conduit for Christian Social influence in British politics by the Second World War, as it probably was well before that time, was in fact William Temple and his extended circle of friends and associates. There has been much debate among historians about Temple's actual role in the affairs of the nation in the 1930s and early war years. Laudatory,[151] even idolatrous, accounts have given way in the 1990s to more sharply analytical dissections of his actions. Apart from the Education Act of 1944, there is little evidence of Temple taking a direct hand in tangible political achievements. Likewise, Temple was not actually a member of the Labour Party after the early postwar years. He, then, was not the socialist bishop, the "realized impossibility," of G. B. Shaw's quip. Thus, he did not function as a political leader in any way approaching the manner of J. S. Woodsworth.

Yet Temple did have considerable influence on the course of politics, while not being officially political. He once stated in a BBC radio interview in 1942: "The press lately has given an impression that I am always talking politics. Indeed one paper said whenever I spoke it was about politics. The fact is, five-sixths of my writing and speaking is purely religious, but that doesn't get reported, and when one slips in a solitary political illustration, that is reported by itself as if it were the whole of what one said."[152]

148. See Betty Lynn Barton, "The Fellowship of Reconciliation: Pacificism, Labor, and Social Welfare, 1915–1960" (Ph.D. diss., Florida State University, 1974), 158–59, 170.

149. Mills, *Fool for Christ*, 248.

150. Ibid., 192. The Canadian organization was founded in 1930. For the evolution of Christian influence in the British organization, see G. J. den Boggende, "The Fellowship of Reconciliation, 1914–1945" (Ph.D. thesis, McMaster University, 1986).

151. For example, see Charles W. Lowry, *William Temple: An Archbishop for All Seasons* (Washington, D.C., 1982), or F. A. Iremonger, *William Temple, Archbishop of Canterbury* (London, 1948).

152. Interview with the Reverend Ronald Selby Wright, 1942, appendix 3 in Kenneth M. Wolfe, *The Churches and the B.B.C., 1922–56* (London, 1984).

Temple was indeed a very busy man and wrote and engaged himself in many activities. And Temple was also primarily a religious thinker, regardless of any debate about how good a theologian he was. Adrian Hastings calls him "a theological teacher rather than a theologian, certainly not a theological scholar."[153] Many of his friends in the political realm viewed him as a religious thinker in essence, though R. H. Tawney was quick to add that "he claimed the whole of life as God's kingdom," which implied, of course, moral control of politics and economics by the church.[154] By this view, Temple was, broadly speaking, "political" in blending the sacred and secular. Reinhold Niebuhr, from the American perspective, found him "irenic" and not polemical, even though Niebuhr believed him to be a socialist archbishop: "He could preach his sermon on the meaning of the Eucharist which seemed to make the transformation of the nation into a Christian brotherhood an absolute consequence of this central Christian act of worship. Of course, the sermon was not absolutely convincing to those who saw a greater hiatus between political facts and religious hopes than he did."[155]

This, of course, conveys something of a paradox. Did Temple unknowingly serve as a conduit for new secular political thinking in the twentieth century by pontificating through his high offices in the Established Church? Certainly Bishop Hensley Henson had such suspicions when in 1924 he castigated COPEC as "an expression of the hungry secularism" that was sweeping the nation. Edward Norman has pondered the same question. But similar accusations could be aimed at Social Christian leaders of the Free Churches in the same period. COPEC, organized by Temple, was certainly a pivotal experience for him. Through this gigantic effort he was to emerge as the central Social Christian figure not only for the Church of England (where he attempted to bring his message to the rank-and-file clergy and laity beyond the bishops' bench) but for all the churches of the 1930s and early 1940s. This and other actions prompted the Reverend Vernon Bartlett, a prominent Nonconformist leader, to suggest that he assume "the role of prophet-statesman which the whole complex of movements toward Church unity in thought, feeling, action will call for in the near and further future."[156]

It is conceivable that Temple very deliberately assumed that role by the late 1920s. As Adrian Hastings has said of him, "Chairmanship was certainly one of

153. Adrian Hastings, "William Temple," in *The English Religious Tradition and the Genius of Anglicanism*, ed. G. Rowell (Wantage, Oxford, 1992), 218.

154. Speech to William Temple Society, Cambridge, 5 May 1949, box 20, section 19⁄6, Tawney Papers, British Library of Political and Economic Science.

155. Niebuhr, "Britain," 30.

156. Bartlett to Temple, 15 July 1929, vol. 46, f. 326, William Temple Papers, Lambeth Palace Library.

his fortes."[157] It is ironic that one of the leaders of the Life and Liberty movement to give more autonomy to the Church of England now wished to influence the public life of the nation. But the style belonged to a general prophet role.

As both Adrian Hastings and John Kent have indicated, the ability of this religious teacher to manipulate and bring about specifically desired ends in the actual realm of governance was not impressive, nor were there very concrete results.[158] Jeffrey Cox makes more or less the same point when speaking of Temple's not considering the means by which the social evils (which he preached about) could be ended.[159] No doubt there were contemporaries who shared such opinions. Seebohm Rowntree, who observed Temple's involvement with many public issues from the Coal Stoppage to those of the Second World War found him to be impetuous and shallow. His great critic, Hensley Henson, noted in his own journal that Temple's death exhibited good timing, occurring before "the chill of reaction had chastened enthusiasm" for what he had actually accomplished.[160]

It is clear that his multifaceted activities could not result in detailed work in any one sphere. Concerning politics, COPEC, which surely was his guide in such matters, was quite vague on the specifics of political action. Volume 10 of the commission reports, *Politics and Citizenship,* had spoken in generalities about Christianity and the nature of the state, noting that the inequalities of property demanded "consciousness of a new fellowship," "equalizing of opportunity," and the dawning of a "day of new democracy."[161] For Temple, COPEC was the renewal of the Christian Socialism of Maurice and Westcott. From this point of view, as Edward Norman has pointed out, the social analysis, the solutions recommended, and the wording were "all characteristics of the Labour movement" that recently had formed its first government under Ramsay MacDonald.[162]

There is reason to believe that Temple enjoyed his public political prelacy in spite of suspicions that he spoke only for socialism. Writing to a friend as the recently appointed bishop of Manchester, he could say, "This life is a wild life of

---

157. Hastings, "William Temple," 219.

158. Ibid. and John Kent, *William Temple: Church, State, and Society in Britain, 1880–1950* (Cambridge, 1992). Both authors are also agreed that theology informed his actions throughout his career—Hastings (218), Kent (153–54).

159. Jeffrey Cox, *The English Churches in a Secular Society: Lambeth, 1870–1930* (Oxford, 1982), 264.

160. 27 October 1944, in vol. 3, "Letters 25 April–18 September 1931 and Journal 23 September 1944–13 February 1945," 53, Henson Papers.

161. *Politics and Citizenship,* vol. 10 of *COPEC Commission Report* (London, 1924), 99.

162. Norman, *Church and Society in England, 1770–1970,* 286.

turmoil. But it is jolly to be in a place where so much happens and one is really up against the things that matter."[163] In the course of his later involvement in the real world of political issues his role as public prophet matured.

In the aftermath of the General Strike, he showed a continued concern for labor. But within a decade, according to David Jeremy, he became involved with efforts to draw business leaders into dialogue, consistent with efforts by Joseph H. Oldham to supply guidelines on the application of ethics to industrial society.[164] Always conscious of public opinion, he also saw that business formed the third element in a triumvirate affecting economic issues. As he later wrote: "I believe it is historically correct to believe that those industrial strikes which have been successful in achieving a real advance have not done it by extorting some concession through the pressure of grave inconvenience or economic loss, but through the effect of suffering on the part of the strikers and their families in calling public attention *first* to the sincerity of their belief that they are suffering an injustice and *then* to the reality of the injustice."[165] His actions were predicated on the notion that at root all elements of society were essentially Christian.

He had two advantages in his quest to be the nation's moral guide—the attainment of high ecclesiastical office at a young age and the sense of compre-hension inherited from his Broad Church roots. Being bishop of Manchester in the 1920s, archbishop of York in the 1930s, and finally primate in the early 1940s gave Temple both the power and media attention that a national prophet required. Whatever his difficulties with religious and secular figures, one of his severest critics, Bishop Hensley Henson, credited him with the easy passage of the agenda of a small group of resolute partisans who controlled the Church of England (mostly Anglo-Catholics), which passage he accomplished through his introduction and manipulation of "democratic politics" in such bodies as the Church Assembly.[166] As the highest-profile English clergyman, he related well with the press, granting interviews and becoming a much beloved figure long before his elevation to archbishop of Canterbury. Because of his loose affiliation with Anglican factions, he was able to conceive of a comprehensive National Church, a concept that had been linked to Christian Socialism from the time of Maurice until the time when the Christian Socialist leadership was taken from Broad Churchmen by the less ecumenically inclined Anglo-Catholics. This, in fact, led Temple to value not only the coalition of all factions within the Anglican communion, but also the extension of friendship to the Free

163. Temple to G. F., 10 April 1922, vol. 46, f. 200, Temple Papers.
164. Jeremy, *Capitalists and Christians*, 188.
165. Temple to Irwin, 4 December 1932, vol. 46, f. 329, Temple Papers.
166. 28 October 1944, journal, vol. 3, 55, Henson Papers.

Churches. Such an approach would keep the churches at the center of national life, for he did not envisage the progressive advance of a secular way of life.

His essential approach to keeping Christianity in national life was actually a mixture of approaches stretching well beyond the framework of churches qua churches, with the cutting edge being political in the broadest sense. As he repeatedly stated in speech and print, he saw his duty and that of his church as setting guidelines on roles and goals for the nation as a whole. He did so while maintaining that the state must in no way feel it was less divinely inspired than the church as an institution, in no way subordinate to it. He once made the point that in spite of some admiration for the organic unity of medieval society, the overt subordination of state to church was a weakness of Roman Catholicism.[167]

As part of his approach, Temple not only wrote, lectured, and organized conferences to define the objectives for politicians, labor leaders, and other influential figures, he also engaged in direct dialogue. The vast majority of his acquaintances were to the Left of center. Edward Norman has said that "as a social and political thinker he reflected the view of the moderately left-wing intellectuals but never attained anything like a really professional knowledge of academic social science."[168] This was undoubtedly true, though Temple assiduously sought the advice of intellectuals who could clarify his thoughts in communicating to the nation. It is also worth noting that that he never sought to reach the professional level of any narrow social science speciality.

R. H. Tawney, a disciple of Charles Gore, was a close personal friend and collaborator. Temple was also willing to go outside the circle of practicing Christians for advice. He had a number of exchanges with John Maynard Keynes, who proofread his very popular Penguin book, *Christianity and Social Order*. Though Temple had no profound knowledge of economics, he saw that Keynes was becoming central to government thinking by the early 1940s. William Beveridge, a Liberal and Social Christian, was of course another friend of some vintage and shared a framework of ideas that resulted in the famous Beveridge plan for universal social security. It is not unreasonable to expect that Temple would have been an important overseer or "resource person" to the immediate architects of the postwar welfare state if he had lived beyond 1944. José Harris makes the point that there is "minimal" evidence that Temple played any substantial role in the design of the welfare state.[169] However, he was certainly more involved with this charmed circle of social architects than were

167. William Temple, "Christianity and Politics," *The Pilgrim* 4, no. 3 (1924): 340.

168. Norman, *Church and Society in England, 1770–1970*, 371.

169. José Harris, "Enterprise and Welfare States: A Comparative Perspective," *Transactions of the Royal Historical Society* (London), 5th ser., 40 (1990): 191.

the ICF and other groups of Methodists and Quakers that had things to say about the Beveridge Report only after the fact. His involvement with Tawney in particular is significant, for Harold Perkin has seen in the latter's public lectures, such as *Equality* (1931), and other works "a complete blueprint not only for the welfare state but also for the corporate society."[170] As Tawney himself wrote, the business of the church, in its capacity as "a great teaching organization," should be to "formulate the Christian doctrine as the questions of property, contract, work, luxury, and economic gain." Tawney further argued, "[W]hat is needed for that is spiritual insight, rather than technical knowledge."[171] It is therefore no surprise that upon receipt of *Christianity and the Social Order* Tawney wrote to Temple: "I think it is good and will do good. You have a wonderful gift of packing essentials into a small compass, without giving the impression of excessive comprehension. Nearly everything *I* should desire is here, though, of course, much of it would be expanding, and will be expanded by others."[172]

There is little doubt that Temple favored the Labour Party as the vehicle for the advancement of Christian Socialism, though he was prepared to work with the National Government and Churchill's wartime coalition. Within the Church of England itself Temple preferred to work with the socialist parsons, especially those of the more extreme Left. The Catholic Crusade of Conrad Noel, the "red" vicar of Thaxted, Temple held at arms length, though he retained Noel's friendship until death. Hewlett Johnson was an old acquaintance from the days when they shared a mutual interest in Social Credit.[173] The radical priest-prophets of the Left, such as Noel, Widdrington, and a young Stanley Evans, could temporarily hold the attention of a mixed group of supporters of the Christian Left who otherwise might not have thought of any contact with the Church of England whatsoever. But they remained on the fringe, and Temple kept them there.

An even more difficult group to handle were the pacifists. Adrian Hastings has portrayed pacifism as a main channel of religious rediscovery for Britain during the 1930s.[174] Temple moved gradually toward mainstream support for rearmament by the end of the decade, while retaining the friendship of figures

170. Harold Perkin, *The Rise of Professional Society: England Since 1880* (London, 1989), 335.

171. "Church and Social Order," n.d., pp. 5, 6, 8, box 21, ²⁰⁄₇, "Talks on Christianity and Society," Tawney Papers.

172. Tawney to Temple, 23 March 1943 (dated at Washington, D.C.), vol. 46, f. 383, Temple Papers.

173. This transitional interest in Social Credit came back to haunt Temple when his statements were put to "entirely unscrupulous use" by John Hargrave, who was suspected of Mosleyite Fascism. Temple to Hargrave, 20 March 1943, vol. 41, f. 41, Temple Papers.

174. See Hastings, *History of English Christianity,* chap. 21.

such as the Free Church Oxford classicist Gilbert Murray. He had performed an equally difficult feat a little earlier in keeping the very popular Anglican radio priest, Dick Sheppard, within the Church of England. The assistance of figures such as V. A. Demant against extremism in politics and pacifism was quite useful.

Temple, of course, was not altogether successful in his handling of such a diverse cast of characters. For some the Malvern Conference of 1941 and his Albert Hall speech of 1942 showed an injudicious encouragement of the Left merely to satisfy his desire to give another spark to the social conscience of Anglicans (extreme leftists such as Evans would have thought the opposite). Yet it is significant that Sir Stafford Cripps, speaking on the same platform as Temple at Albert Hall in 1942, could state:

> It is for the Church to provide the moral force and the driving power for social and economic development. The technical details of government and of legislation are for the politicians. But this is not to imply that politicians should be materialists. We require more than ever to-day courageous Christians in our political life. For since this moral driving power is essentially designed to influence political decisions, its creation and its growth must impinge directly upon political thought and action.[175]

These words could easily have been Temple's, and indeed Temple's corrections on this and other "sermonettes" by Cripps indicate the great respect accorded the archbishop by one of the leading members of the Labour Left.[176] That Temple was appreciated by more than Labour can be clearly ascertained. His appointment as primate by Churchill was a recognition of his general stature among all politicians, if not the nation. His death was a blow to the morale of the nation at war.

It seems almost a truism to state that Temple's political influence did not linger much after his death. But such statements can never be verified, even if generally accepted. It is never clear what endures after the death of any individual of charisma. The same could be said of the New Deal Democrats after Roosevelt or of the CCF after Woodsworth. In the later cases political instruments were still in place, but the effectiveness in terms of Social Christianity was in doubt much earlier. Figures as diverse as Seebohm Rowntree and

175. Sir Stafford Cripps, "The Challenge of Christianity," in *The Church Looks Forward: Substance of Archbishop's Albert Hall Meeting, September 26, 1942* (Westminster, ICF, 1942), 26.

176. Letter from Temple attached to Cripps's Albert Hall speech of September 1942, with suggested corrections and Cripps's responses, 30 August 1942, $^{209}/_{171}$b, Sir Stafford Cripps Papers.

Stafford Cripps were convinced that the New Deal had shot its bolt by the late 1930s and was unsuitable for the furtherance of Social Christian objectives in the United States, let alone in Britain. What then would be the vehicle in Britain? The CCF was the voice of a half-secularized Social Gospel in Canada, but it was a minority voice at that. The Second World War and its aftermath focused eyes on newer issues. Pacifism dwindled, and what was left of it tended to drift into the ban-the-bomb movement of the late 1950s and 1960s, with transitional figures such as Lord Soper carrying on. The welfare state in Britain and Canada seemed to meet the criteria of earlier Social Christian ideals, with fewer and fewer Social Christians in prominent government positions, except for places like Saskatchewan. The American postwar anti-Communist crusade and advancing prosperity seemed to move many with the lingering social conscience toward the liberal Democrats, while a few diehards still voted for Norman Thomas for president. Reinhold Niebuhr became chaplain to the liberal establishment. The Civil Rights movement rekindled some of the Social Christian legacy and, of course, now made racial reform, rather than the clash of classes, the central issue. Everywhere the few surviving Christian Marxists, such as the "Red Dean," were treated as cranks or worse (in the case of the McCarthyite period in the United States). That a Social Christian conscience lingered on into the politics of the modern welfare state cannot be doubted, though its form would be peculiar to the particular country in question. In that sense, Sir Stafford Cripps's words at the Albert Hall in 1942 were prophetic.

The political history of Social Christianity contained both success and failure. The failure seemed most visible insofar as Social Christianity as a whole had dropped from public attention as a potent force in politics by the late 1940s. The confused directions of many of its modern prophets had led to political dead ends or to submersion in secular groups. They had also been a prime factor in the dismemberment of the shared ideas and approaches that had characterized Anglo-American Social Christianity. But success was also apparent in the achievement of many of its mainstream social objectives through the agency of government and in the new directions of politics. Many will debate the degree to which Social Christianity actually influenced state policy, particularly in what seemed a natural secular progression toward the welfare state. But these doubts would not have disturbed many Social Christians, whose religious convictions led them to believe that the ideals of the Kingdom would be realized even through the most complicated and compromising world of politics.

# Conclusion

The period from the early 1880s to the Second World War marks the heyday of Social Christianity. During these years influential clergy, assisted by some laity, guided the major Protestant churches of Britain and North America toward the goal of a reconstructed social environment based upon social justice.

These Christians were not alone on their journey, for altruism was abundant among secular social reformers of the day. Though Social Christians did not reject the company of their secular counterparts, they generally kept extreme radicals and revolutionaries at arm's length, though not always in equal measure. This occasionally blurred the line that separated secular reformism from Social Christianity, but this line still existed for the majority of Social Christians, who were linked together by common religious beliefs widely accepted across denominational lines. These beliefs originated well before the 1880s and continued through the early decades of the twentieth century.

Some Social Christians were surely moved toward disbelief by their association with secular movements, but more often they could be suspected of helping to subordinate the social role of churches by cooperating with the secular forces of reform. In some cases this certainly was true. Their early and continuous fixation with the dark side of urban life made them fully conscious of the inadequacy of the tools of the church in dealing with problems of such magnitude. Their gradual shift away from almsgiving through organized philanthropy to sanctioning support for state intervention was driven by the desire to meet these formidable challenges. Social Christians were not afraid to work with and through secular organizations to attain their goal. But the selflessness of their compliance with Christian principles is evident in their willingness ultimately to relinquish social services and their considerable investment in social science in favor of more-expert "professionals" or bureaucrats in order to fulfill the higher mandate of alleviating human misery.

Through the agency of the religious print media and transatlantic travel many leading figures and organizations established firm roots in both Britain and North America. Some, such as W. T. Stead, indeed could be called "Anglo-Americans." As the general religious communication network declined, so did the sense of an Anglo-American Social Christian community. But the parting of friends was more than a mere by-product of changes in the increasingly secularized media. In the first decades of the twentieth century significant elements within Social Christianity were also beginning to depart from earlier theological positions, particularly in North America. Again, this was by no means an inevitable by-product of secularization, and in any case, such trends were resisted by others within the ranks. There was confusion, however. In Britain Anglo-Catholicism began to take center stage for Social Christianity but not necessarily for Christianity in general or for society as a whole. The Anglo-Catholic vision was more coherent theologically, but it was narrow and certainly less significant in a society where religious influence was clearly losing ground. Less transatlantic understanding ensued.

Efforts to provide a unitive means for the redemption of society, through the fusion of church and state, had been frustrated by the early twentieth century. The Social Christian approach to ecumenism had similar aims and experienced some successes in the twentieth century, but fell far short of the socially enveloping visions of a National Church as laid out by F. D. Maurice, W. H. Fremantle, or Richard T. Ely. William Temple practiced a version of national resident prophet that was peculiar to himself and the circumstances of his time and place.

Politics, in various approaches to state interventionism, presented more realistic opportunities to Social Christian ambitions on both sides of the Atlantic from the 1880s to the Great War. But even with seeming success in the period, a clear sense of direction alluded Social Christians, due in part to confusions of definition and action on the part of secular reformers. After 1918 the picture became darker and more complicated, with worries about the misuse of state power, but the future was still full of possibilities. Divergent trends in religious thinking now combined with divergent political conditions in each country, making for the virtual breakup of an integrated transatlantic Social Christian community. This did not mean the imminent collapse of Social Christianity, which always maintained a strong interaction with the surrounding social environment. However, British Social Christianity and North American Social Christianity (if not American and Canadian) would now move to the beat of slightly different drummers. The results varied depending upon the condition of politics, religion, and conflicts among Social Christians in each country. Everywhere there were some who held a growing belief that social justice must finally be achieved, even, for some, at the expense of the oldest Social Christian maxim of social harmony. Yet by the 1940s many Social Christians on both sides of the Atlantic showed some satisfaction regarding the state of society. In that sense the Kingdom of Christ on Earth, the New Jerusalem, had been reached in their last days, though by diverse routes and never to the complete satisfaction of observers then or now.

As with any broad-ranging study such as this one, questions remain that require further consideration. We need even wider geographical coverage, encompassing the Protestant world, as well as wider theological coverage to encompass the parallel emergence of Social Catholicism. Looking from the opposite end of the telescope, it is clear that more regional studies would be helpful. Both kinds of studies will enable us to compare wider conclusions from national and transatlantic studies against the very specific developments in London, the American Midwest, the Canadian West, or the less likely environments such as Northern Ireland. "History too is 'about chaps,' " H.P.R. Finberg once wrote, and "local history brings us nearer to the common run of chaps than any other branch of historical study."[1] Local history always turns up surprises that ultimately affect the wider picture.

Denominational, theological, and organizational peculiarities have been explored here, but more study is welcome. It is particularly important that we learn more about the relationships between prominent Social Christian clergy and their own particular congregations.[2] Such relationships might be worth exploring in the case of lesser clerical figures as well. Significant support or

1. H.P.R. Finberg, *The Local Historian and His Theme*, Department of English Local History Occasional Papers, no. 1, Leicester University (Leicester, 1965), 11.

2. For example, in a letter to George Coe, Alex McConnell of Fleming H. Revell Publishers of Chicago raised doubts about the influence of individual pastors upon the social outlook of their congregations: "I question whether or no the minister is largely responsible for these variations! . . . What would have happened if Frederick W. Robertson had exchanged pulpit permanently with Charles H. Spurgeon? What would happen if all the pulpits in this country could be filled by a Phillips Brooks!" McConnell to Coe, 17 September 1915, box 1, folder 1, George Albert Coe Papers, Yale Divinity School Library.

opposition from the local laity undoubtedly played a role in how Social Christian clergy acted and in what they wrote. At a highest level of church governance, the widespread belief in an alleged Social Christian hegemony, from the upper echelons of the United Church of Canada to "Gore's crowd," as Hensley Henson called them, in the Church of England, might be tested with greater empirical accuracy.

Perceptions of Social Christianity held by secular leaders in government, business, and the professions, both in local communities and nationally, deserve more attention. To what degree did the presence of Social Christians and their interaction with other people influence the developments in these spheres of activity? Here actions of the lay element within the ranks of Social Christianity also deserve special attention.

Then there is the controversial issue of the legacy of Social Christianity. How much does it persist today? What impact does it still have on churches and theological schools? To what degree is the tension between fundamentalists and liberals in North America part of an ongoing debate generated before the 1940s but never ending? Do the current difficulties of Anglo-Catholics in the Church of England, overtly over ecclesiological matters, also relate to wider issues of the Temple era?

On the transatlantic level and beyond there is the question of the special contribution of Social Christians to both the ecumenism and the social and political agenda of the World Council of Churches. Edward Norman, who holds strong views on these matters,[3] should be joined by other scholars who might be able to add more of a historical dimension to the debate.

Within the English-speaking transatlantic world, and slightly beyond the realm of the historian, there is much to consider in the recent resurgence of political conservatism in Britain, the United States, and Canada from the late 1960s to its electoral triumphs of the 1980s. This has closely paralleled and has been related to the growth of Protestant fundamentalism in North America in the same period. Certainly conservative Evangelicalism found greater favor in American governing circles during the 1980s than in earlier decades. The emerging philosophy of recent American political conservatism blended well with the assaults of Thatcherites upon the British welfare state.[4] Thatcherism in turn reinforced the less articulate positions of Reaganites in the United States

---

3. See Edward R. Norman, *Christianity and the World Order: The B.B.C. Reith Lectures, 1978* (Oxford, 1979).

4. For a study of the effects of transatlantic conservatism on the administrative apparatus of the state, see Donald J. Savoie, *Thatcher, Reagan, and Mulroney: In Search of a New Bureaucracy* (Pittsburgh, 1994).

and Conservatives of kindred spirit in Canada. Such crisscrossings formed as much of a transatlantic pattern as did Social Christianity in its heyday. Emphasis upon a return to charity and family values as opposed to state intervention and a developed social policy has been increasingly part of the political baggage of conservatism in Britain and Republicanism in the United States. The belief in a partially realized New Jerusalem, as represented today by the welfare state, must be shaken for many in the much diminished ranks of Social Christianity on both sides of the Atlantic. Their full response is yet to be felt.

# Index